Advance Praise for *Compromised*

"As the mainstream media averts its eyes from the truth, the Government Accountability Institute once again hits the bullseye and reveals the deep corruption at the heart of the FBI and DOJ leadership under the Obama Administration. The vaunted 'independence' of these once respected agencies has turned into unchecked power and unaccountability. By exposing the corruption, the author presents the American people and our elected officials a road map for returning these agencies to their historically respected role in U.S. law enforcement."

—Victoria Toensing, Former Deputy Assistant Attorney General, and Joseph diGenova, Former United States Attorney

"Following the money is an important way to get to the truth. Seamus Bruner has done that precisely in *Compromised*. Anyone concerned about our country should read this book."

—Kenneth Sukhia, Former United States Attorney.

"Our criminal justice system has been horribly corrupted and politicized—especially by the Obama administration. This important book is a must read as it peels back the layers and exposes the truth."

—Sidney Powell, former Assistant US Attorney, Appellate Section Chief, and Author of #1 Bestseller *Licensed to Lie: Exposing Corruption in the Department of Justice.*

COMPROMISED

HOW MONEY AND POLITICS DRIVE FBI CORRUPTION

SEAMUS BRUNER

GOVERNMENT ACCOUNTABILITY INSTITUTE

BOMBARDIER
BOOKS

A BOMBARDIER BOOKS BOOK
An Imprint of Post Hill Press
ISBN: 978-1-64293-075-7
ISBN (eBook): 978-1-64293-076-4

Compromised:
How Money and Politics Drive FBI Corruption
© 2018 by Seamus Bruner
All Rights Reserved

BOMBARDIER
B O O K S

Post Hill Press, LLC
New York • Nashville
posthillpress.com

Published in the United States of America

This book is dedicated to the federal agents and officials who remain uncompromised. To the countless men and women who perform their duties faithfully and free from politics and bias. To all who personify the motto "Fidelity, Bravery, Integrity." Thank you.

CONTENTS

FOREWORD

The Federal Bureau of Investigation (FBI) occupies a trusted position in our society. It infiltrates the mob. It busts drug rings. It vigorously pursues the modern slavery of human trafficking. The FBI is the long arm of the law, protecting America against foreign and domestic terrorists and criminals.

Americans respect the FBI for the bravery of its agents and their fidelity to the mission. Both in real life and in popular culture, the FBI is often the good guy in the blue suit. FBI special agents are known not only for their crime-solving skills in the field but for the professional expertise they bring to cracking the case—in many cases they are lawyers or trained accountants. Special agents in field offices across America even enjoy the admiration of the local police forces whose toes they must sometimes step on.

That is not to say there are not bad apples among the rank-and-file. Of course, those will be found in any large organization, especially one as hierarchical as the FBI. Indeed, the bureau's reputation remains intact despite the well-known abuses of its longtime director J. Edgar Hoover during the civil rights era. As we have seen in the current investigations surrounding the allegations of Russian interference in the presidential election, FBI personnel are human beings too.

In addition to its work against criminals, the FBI also investigates possible corruption by our elected officials. And it is here that the potential for the bureau to be influenced by powerful outsiders is most dangerous. The FBI, as part of the Department of Justice (DOJ), is often tasked with conducting surveillance, undercover work, and sting operations to catch corrupt government officials who are enriching themselves through their public positions, taking bribes, or are unduly influenced by foreign powers. It was the FBI that busted federal employees spying for the Soviet Union, China, and other foreign powers. The FBI obtained the evidence of legislators taking bribes for pushing legislation or pressing regulators to look the other way for their powerful benefactors.

The character and the integrity of the bureau's leadership is critical. The FBI and DOJ must be led by public servants who put aside their political ambitions and personal wealth to serve the public trust. *Compromised* describes what happens when they do not.

As an investigative journalist for thirty years, I have learned how easy and tempting it is for leaders in government service to falter in that trust—to rationalize their pursuit of personal gain and political advantage. Our government is full of ambitious politicians who do this routinely, gaining more power by serving dominant commercial interests. By exploiting vague ethics laws, these bad actors find ways to return favors—sometimes years later and one or two steps removed from the action. But their fingerprints remain.

I co-founded the nonpartisan Government Accountability Institute (GAI) in 2012 to find those fingerprints. We are a nonprofit group of investigative journalists and data analysts. We do our own research and publish our findings in reports, or as raw material shared with media organizations to further pursue, or as books such as *Compromised: How Money and Politics Drive FBI Corruption*. I am proud to say that Seamus Bruner volunteered for me in 2011 and was one of the first people to join our organization. His work on our previous projects has been exceptional.

With the support of our generous donors, GAI has found a niche doing the kind of enterprise journalism that reporters and editors at the major TV networks and the largest newspapers used to do, but no longer have the resources or the time to do themselves.

Previous GAI investigations exposed corruption in Congress, in the bureaucracy, and by politicians who enrich themselves and their relatives through sweetheart deals and complex forms of bribery. My most recent book, *Secret Empires*, became a number one bestseller on *The New York Times* list, revealing the many ways that members of Congress and even a president have enriched their children and closest friends—legally—by taking advantage of loopholes in financial disclosure laws that govern how they can earn money, but place no restrictions at all on their family members.

Released in 2015, *Clinton Cash: The Untold Story of How and Why Foreign Governments and Businesses Helped Make Bill and Hillary Rich*, revealed how Hillary Clinton and her husband leveraged their nonprofit foundation empire for personal gain, and how they engaged in numerous schemes to enrich their friends and donors. That book was also a *New York Times* bestseller, and was quoted and cited extensively during the 2016 presidential campaign. The team at GAI spent almost two years researching the book, and we are proud of its success.

My 2013 book, *Extortion*, showed how the Obama administration targeted industries for criminal investigation but chose not to pursue key political donors. It showed how lawmakers used campaign slush funds to bankroll their own lifestyles. *Throw Them All Out* (2011) documented how legislators enhanced their own stock portfolios based on confidential information they learned in supposedly closed hearings. This led to passage of the STOCK (Stop Trading on Congressional Knowledge) Act, outlawing the practice.

I can tell you that the most common theme of government corruption stories is the famous "revolving door" between public service and big contractors, the white-shoe law firms and lobbying shops. As the door spins, those entering bring special expertise that modern government needs, while those exiting are full of fresh connections and a panoply of favors they did in government service. We ask them to go through that spinning door committed to serve honestly, to use their powers for good. It is up to citizens to hold them to that standard.

We expect certain necessary overlap in positions involving defense, energy, trade, and other commercial areas. However, *justice* is so basic, so essential to American government that we properly demand—without exception—complete integrity among those entrusted with law enforcement. There is absolutely no room for self-dealers and favor-traders in the FBI or DOJ. There is no room for any such compromise. The men and women of the FBI deserve leaders who view this responsibility as the noble calling it truly is.

This is not only because Americans expect justice to be impartial, but because in the post-9/11 world, Americans have granted the FBI and other law enforcement officers vast new powers to conduct surveillance on citizens, to monitor online communications, behavior, and financial movements. We have entrusted immense power in law enforcement and in special courts to weigh the privacy we all enjoy with the possibility there may be terrorists exploiting these same freedoms to do us harm. It is deadly serious work, and no place for corruption of any sort.

In these pages, Seamus will show you there has been such favor-trading among the leadership of the FBI and in the DOJ. His research reveals that some relationships go back decades and that the "revolving door" is more of a perpetual turnstile. The relationships do not stop while the door spins. The players keep in contact both inside and outside public service, never missing a beat.

There is much here that will be new, and Seamus gives you the historical background to understand and not be overwhelmed or frustrated. We believe in providing you with the relevant facts so you can be a well-informed citizen. Seamus offers some recommendations at the end of this book, but those are meant as a starting point. His greatest service is shining the light of truth on what happened at the FBI and DOJ in recent years. We hope this book will be an invaluable tool for fixing it.

—Peter Schweizer
Government Accountability Institute
July 4, 2018

INTRODUCTION

On April 9, 2018, a team of FBI agents stormed the office, home, and hotel room of President Trump's personal attorney, Michael Cohen. The early-morning raid was executed based on a referral from former FBI Director Robert Mueller's special counsel investigation. The FBI agents spent hours collecting documents and records purportedly related to payments made to adult film actress Stormy Daniels. (Daniels allegedly had an affair with Trump and has inexplicably become a central figure in the special counsel's investigation into Russian efforts to influence the 2016 election.)[1] The agents seized privileged communications between Trump and his personal attorney.[2] On May 8, 2018, Daniels's attorney revealed information apparently obtained from some of Cohen's confidential banking records. The Treasury Department inspector general opened an investigation the following day seeking to determine if the records had been leaked.[3]

This escalation in the battle between Trump and Mueller means one of two things: Either Mueller is getting close to snaring Trump or, as Trump alleges, the investigation is "disgraceful" and "a witch hunt." Either way, the raid demonstrates that Mueller has near-unlimited investigative powers to compel Trump and his associates to cooperate.[4] Reporting of the incident has been divided along partisan lines. Trump's media critics celebrated the raid. "The Law Is Coming, Mr. Trump," read a *New York Times* opinion editorial.[5] The audience of Stephen Colbert's late-night talk show literally cheered.[6] The right-wing media was alarmed at the apparent abuse of power. FOX News's Sean Hannity called the raid a declaration of war and said, "Robert Mueller has now officially gone rogue."[7] One of the more striking details to emerge is that Trump's Deputy Attorney General, Rod Rosenstein, personally approved the raid.[8]

Mueller and Rosenstein's raid on Trump's personal attorney raises a number of questions. First, is Rosenstein a neutral party? Second, is Mueller getting close to bringing charges against Trump and/or his attorney? Or is the special counsel investigation a witch hunt, as Trump suggests? Is attorney-client privilege "dead?" Finally, what role does Trump's FBI play in this Shakespearean epic, in which a former FBI director is apparently seeking to oust a sitting U.S. president? These questions and many more will be answered as we seek to uncover answers to the most crucial question of all: Has the FBI been compromised?

Brief History of the FBI

The Federal Bureau of Investigation (FBI) is America's premier law enforcement agency. Tracing its roots to 1908, the bureau has a long, proud history of investigating serious crimes, catching criminals, and helping federal prosecutors lock them up. Federal prosecutors (also known as U.S. attorneys) are, like the FBI itself, part of the Department of Justice (DOJ).[9] Together, they ensure proper investigation and prosecution of federal crimes. Simply put, they are the long arm of the law.

Even in its earliest years, the FBI also functioned as an intelligence and security service, conducting counterintelligence and counterterrorism operations to protect Americans from the wiles of foreign and domestic enemies.[10] Most of the FBI's 35,000 employees are honest, hardworking, selfless men and women who strive to uphold the values of the bureau and personify its motto: Fidelity, Bravery, Integrity.[11] These men and women are agents, analysts, or support professionals, deployed across fifty-six field offices throughout the country.[12]

The FBI has had its fair share of bad press over the years, some of it deserved and some not. For the most part, misdeeds and overreaches of the FBI have been isolated incidents. These misdeeds include the Japanese internment programs in the 1940s, and spying on civil rights activists, environmental groups, and other nonviolent organizations.

The largest blemishes on the FBI's reputation generally have occurred at the hands of its leadership, operating out of the J. Edgar Hoover Building in Washington, D.C. Many of these abuses occurred during the tenure of the building's namesake, Director J. Edgar Hoover. They often involved his Counterintelligence Program (COINTELPRO), which he ran from 1956 until 1971. Hoover's FBI even spied on Reverend Martin Luther King Jr. and blackmailed him, threatening to reveal his "immoral behavior" in what became known as the "suicide letter" (Comey allegedly kept a copy of the historic wiretap request on his desk).[13] Over time, these unfortunate episodes have been forgiven or largely forgotten.

In 2016, the FBI and its parent, the DOJ, began a new episode in the abuse of power. Individuals operating out of Washington—at FBI headquarters (HQ) and the DOJ's Main Justice building—engaged in questionable behavior. This behavior appears isolated to the highest levels of leadership: the FBI director, his deputy and staffers, and the attorney general and her deputies. Their actions have been the subject of much speculation and intrigue. Allegations are swirling, like that of obstruction on the part of former FBI Director James Comey; of classified intelligence leaks by him, his deputy, Andrew McCabe, and others; of political bias and conflicts of interest throughout their offices.[14] These men and many others have since been fired or demoted, or have resigned under pressure.

Plenty of ink has been spilled seeking to figure out exactly *what happened* inside the FBI during the 2016 election and beyond. What's happening now? These are important questions and in due time will be answered. But Americans must also ask themselves and their elected officials *why* the bureau's leadership engaged in dubious behavior during such a consequential election. Was the bureau, the DOJ, or its leadership politicized? If so, how and why? Most important, was 2016 an isolated incident, or is the bureau compromised?

This is a complex story with many moving parts. The names, the dates, and the allegiances blur together and much is unclear. The effort to disentangle the details behind the FBI's and DOJ's 2016 actions (and inactions) starts at the beginning. This story of corruption (like so many others) begins with Hillary Clinton.

Clinton Crash

In early 2015, Hillary Clinton was primed and ready to begin her march to the White House. This was her time, she believed, the time to shatter the glass ceiling once and for all. Her poll numbers peaked after she left the State Department in 2013 with 67 percent popular support.[15] The 67 percent dipped after the infamous Benghazi saga.[16] But Hillary—like her husband, former President Bill Clinton—was a "comeback kid." Many liken them both to Teflon, because the scandals don't stick. Things looked good for her as she neared an April 2015 campaign announcement. She was still riding high on approval ratings. She had near-universal name recognition, a crucial variable in the quest for the U.S. presidency. What could go wrong?

First, on March 2, 2015, *The New York Times* revealed that Hillary Clinton had used a private email address while she served as U.S. secretary of state between 2009 and 2013.[17] The revelation was a bombshell, and the media erupted with questions: What was this all about? Was there a secret server? Was she conducting State Department business on the undisclosed email address, or was it only personal? Was she sending classified material? Was this legal? Clinton claimed it was all a big misunderstanding. She used a personal email account, just as some of her predecessors had, including Colin Powell. She was only talking about her daughter, Chelsea, and yoga.[18] "*Relax*," her supporters urged; Clinton was allowed to have a personal life and a corresponding email account. On March 12, Gallup published a poll and a parallel article under the headline, "Clinton Favorability, Familiarity Bests 2016 Contenders." She had significantly higher favorable (50 percent) than unfavorable (39 percent) ratings than any other contenders.[19] "Ignore the Noise—Clinton Will Win in 2016," read a headline on the website *The Hill*.[20]

But Clinton's troubles were only beginning.

The media focused intensely and repeatedly inquired, *what on earth happened with this private email server?* They were asking the wrong questions, and ultimately, Clinton's secret email server use was forgiven by the FBI leadership; Clinton was fully exonerated by Director James Comey in July 2016.

While everyone was focusing on the *what*, the Government Accountability Institute (GAI), led by *New York*

Times bestselling author Peter Schweizer, answered the *why*. Why had Clinton chosen to use a secret email server?

The answer came in *Clinton Cash: The Untold Story of How and Why Foreign Governments and Businesses Helped Make Bill and Hillary Rich*. The bombshell book dominated press coverage of Clinton for months, and even to this day still dogs "Clinton Inc." The answer was simple; she used a private server because she had business to conduct. The findings in *Clinton Cash* made headlines repeatedly and were confirmed in numerous front-page exposés and deep-dive investigations by the top newspapers in the country: *The New York Times, The Washington Post,* and *The Wall Street Journal,* among others.[21]

To date, none of the major findings in *Clinton Cash* have been debunked, in fact the opposite: It is all true. The Clintons *had* earned over $150 million in speaking fees.[22] Their foundation *had* received nearly $2 billion in donations.[23] Worst of all, Hillary Clinton *had* met with benefactors while she served as secretary of state. As many confirmed, these benefactors appeared to receive favorable treatment, if not outright favors.[24]

The most lethal front-page exposé that *Clinton Cash* generated was the April 2015 *New York Times* story titled "Cash Flowed to Clinton Foundation Amid Russian Uranium Deal" by Pulitzer Prize-winning journalist Jo Becker.[25] The Russian uranium deal in question involved a company called Uranium One. There was instant outrage due to the numerous national security implications involved. In fact, the Uranium One story (along with the other apparent quid pro quos described in the book) led to five separate FBI investigations in field offices across the country. FBI special agents used *Clinton Cash* as a "roadmap" and most readers could not understand how such blatant corruption had been permitted.[26] FBI investigations of the Clintons remain ongoing and will be discussed throughout this book.[27]

Clinton's poll numbers took a hit and never really recovered, despite constant media predictions of her inevitable victory. Damage control efforts led to a struggle between the honest and patriotic FBI field agents and Clinton's allies in the J. Edgar Hoover Building in D.C. The agents were being stonewalled by the FBI leadership.[28] FBI Deputy Director Andrew McCabe essentially told the agents there wasn't a "there, there." FBI Director James Comey issued his unprecedented exoneration of candidate Clinton's email practices in July 2016.[29]

Many of the GOP candidates bemoaned the self-serving actions of the Clintons and campaigned on *Clinton Cash* revelations (of their own volition). Notably, Clinton's Democratic competitors, like Bernie Sanders, were her biggest apologists. They tried to distract from the quid pro quo allegations by conflating them with her email practices. "The American people are sick and tired of hearing about Secretary Clinton's damn emails," croaked Bernie Sanders on October 13, 2015.[30] GOP candidate Donald Trump seized on the *Clinton Cash* revelations with vigor and wouldn't let them go. He tweeted about "Crooked Hillary" constantly. The book was on his desk in a televised *Wall Street Journal* interview with Monica Langley.[31] His campaign staff literally read from the book page by page to a massive audience at one of his rallies.[32] Clinton was done. But her allies didn't know it yet. Even in their overconfidence, some would hedge their bets. Thus began certain FBI agents' plans for an "insurance policy" against Trump.

As Trump's poll numbers continued to climb, the Clinton campaign (along with everyone else) began to take him seriously. Clinton and her campaign hired an opposition research outfit called Fusion GPS in April 2016 to dig up dirt on

Trump.[33] They needed some bombshells of their own. Fusion GPS, as we will see, is at the heart of the burgeoning FBI scandal, and many are wondering, what the heck happened?

Then, on November 2, 2016, just days before the election, *Clinton Cash* (having grown legs of its own) reared its head once more. A *Wall Street Journal* front-page exposé blared, "Secret Recordings Fueled FBI Feud in Clinton Probe," delivering a major blow to Clinton's aspirations.

The *Journal* confirmed not only that Schweizer and his team's findings were being investigated by FBI field offices across the country, but also that the FBI leadership was trying to cover up for Clinton. This was yet another bombshell. The FBI agents were conducting *criminal* probes into the Clintons, their foundation, and the donors who had received favors. Additionally, the agents had obtained secret recordings that, they believed, proved that bribes had been made. They were ready to call in the prosecutors. But again, they were being stonewalled.[34]

This book picks up where that story left off. Many are asking, what happened with this FBI feud? What happened to the investigations? What did FBI Director James Comey, deputy Andrew McCabe, and their lieutenants do? Was President Obama involved in any FBI misdeeds? Who exactly has been compromised by Clinton?

This book seeks to disentangle and explain these complex, decades-old relationships. The FBI investigations remain ongoing as of this writing. There is also the question of Russian interference in the 2016 election and whom it benefitted. A special counsel team led by former FBI Director Robert Mueller was named to answer just that. The same names keep popping up: James Comey, Robert Mueller, Andrew McCabe, and Rod Rosenstein, among others. Here is their story.

Chapter 1: The Insurance Policy

- There's a burgeoning scandal involving the FBI, the DOJ, and the rest of the intelligence community. Various abuses of power during the 2016 election exposed previously undisclosed allegiances. Obama's FBI and DOJ leaderships are central to the election abuses.

- Republicans are every bit as much to blame as Democrats. This is a bipartisan issue.

- FBI bosses used "salacious and unverified" rumors as probable cause to believe Trump's campaign was infiltrated by foreign agents—the FBI used rumors to obtain secret warrants, issued by a secret court typically reserved for terrorists and spies.

- The FBI leadership and staff coordinated with known Clinton operatives to achieve this and referred to their operation as an "insurance policy" against "douche" Trump.

- FBI Director James Comey and top-level FBI lieutenants targeted a candidate during a presidential election with tactics not seen (publicly) since Watergate.

- The Clinton operatives, primarily Fusion GPS, paid Russian operatives and other foreign agents to compile their dossier. They paid media outlets to report on it.

- The dossier was prima facie garbage. Nonetheless, the FBI sought to legitimize it.

- Comey, McCabe, Mueller, Rosenstein, and others have become household names. This may not end well for them.

- Fusion GPS's Glenn Simpson and Mary Jacoby were married in Little Rock, Arkansas. Jacoby, who has deep Clinton ties, visited Barack Obama's residence in April 2016, and publicly credited Fusion with starting the Trump-Russia collusion narrative (and subsequent investigations).

- Mueller appointed a team of registered Democrats and Clinton associates.
- This operation went all the way to the top: President Barack Obama.
- But why would people with so much to lose risk it all? The question answers itself.

Chapter 2: The FBI's Burial of Uranium Scandals

- Still, many are wondering: what happened? It's an important question. A better question is, why? The answer is that the FBI had much to hide.
- The FBI and DOJ could have stopped the sale of Uranium One to Russia. They didn't.
- Worse, the FBI simultaneously knew about Russian nuclear bribery, racketeering, kickbacks, and money laundering schemes directly implicating the Russian nuclear agency (Rosatom) at least one year before the Uranium One takeover.
- When FBI Director Robert Mueller tried to expose a Russian spy ring in June 2010, he was initially rebuffed by the Obama White House. They wanted to preserve their Russian deals under the "reset."
- The Russian spy ring, called the "illegals program," targeted Clinton—successfully.
- Clinton has borne much of the blame for allowing the Russian uranium deal to go through. Rightly so, as the Clinton Foundation received $145 million from Uranium One investors.
- There were more undisclosed Clinton donations, more Russian agents with ties to the Clintons,

and a Rosatom inside man in Hillary Clinton's State Department.

- Clinton's defenders argued that she did not approve the sale by herself. That's true, but is it better? They thought that excuse would exonerate her. In fact, it damned Obama's closest advisors.

- The Committee on Foreign Investment in the United States (CFIUS) deal was compromised from the start.

Chapter 3: The FBI's and DOJ's Foreign Agents Problem (FARA)

- The FBI and DOJ are responsible for investigating and enforcing laws that guard against foreign influence. Objectively, they have failed.

- One safeguard specifically governs the actions of foreign agents. It is called the Foreign Agents Registration Act (FARA), and the DOJ has only eight employees assigned to investigate violations.

- Fusion GPS hinted that Paul Manafort was violating FARA in 2008. Why did it take nine years to indict him? Is it just a coincidence that Fusion GPS's dossier centered around his decade-old Ukrainian schemes?

- A GAI-exclusive, translated recording reveals an imprisoned Kazakh nuclear official who has confirmed Clinton-juiced uranium deals. He identified a $300 million slush fund that he calls "the Democrats' purse."

- Five corporations and foreign governments closely tied to Uranium One hired two D.C. lobbying firms to grease the skids. They were successful.

- Russians did meddle in the 2016 election. Russian foreign agents targeted both campaigns. Among

Mueller's team's first indictments were Paul Manafort and some low-level internet "trolls."

- Fusion GPS coordinated with foreign agents, the media, the State Department, and a U.S. senator to promote Clinton's interests.

- Those in the Clinton campaign wrestled with FARA-linked donations during the 2016 election. Initially they decided against taking the foreign agents' money. In the end, Clinton attorney Marc Elias flipped 180 degrees and the Clinton campaign concluded, "Take the money!"

Chapter 4: The United Surveillance States of America (USSA)

- Former FBI directors James Comey and Robert Mueller have a long history of investigative failures.

- Comey and Mueller have worked together, like a pitcher and catcher, promoting the interests of the surveillance state.

- Comey's net worth skyrocketed over 4,000 percent after he changed the rules of surveillance. Shortly after making the rule change, Comey joined Lockheed Martin, which received billion-dollar surveillance contracts from Robert Mueller's FBI. In one year alone, Comey received $6.1 million from Lockheed Martin.

- Mueller advised surveillance contractors including Edward Snowden's Booz Allen. Mueller received $3.5 million working at a white-shoe firm, and he directly represented surveillance interests such as Booz Allen, Facebook, Apple Inc., and Intel Corp.

Facebook has been cooperating with a special counsel investigation.[35]

Chapter 5: Foreign Intelligence and Surveillance Abuse

- Many believe that George W. Bush and the PATRIOT Act were the culprits behind mass warrantless domestic surveillance and the implied trampling of constitutional rights under the Fourth Amendment. That's not the full story.

- The 2016 election abuses bear many resemblances to Nixon's Watergate affair, but comparatively, Watergate was child's play.

- One law, exacted in response to Watergate, is at the center of the 2016 election abuses: the Foreign Intelligence Surveillance Act (FISA).

- FISA has been widely abused since before the Bush administration. FISA abuse entails widespread spying on innocent American citizens.

- The FBI and DOJ receive secret warrants from a secret court in secret proceedings. The proceedings are nonadversarial, and the accused targets never face their accusers.

- FISA warrants, once approved, are not simply for a wiretap. They allow a retroactive search and analysis of the entire history of a surveillance target's communications, such as phone calls, text messages, emails, financials, and internet history—even private social media accounts are all subject to indefinite collection, search, and analysis.

- The FBI and other intelligence agencies receive rubber-stamp approval from the secret FISA court.

According to an analysis spanning 33 years, more than 1,000 FISA applications on average are submitted each year. All of them are approved (or amended), with only one denial issued every third year (a 99.97 percent approval rate).

All this and much more will be discussed. The FBI and its parent agency, the DOJ, are supposed to investigate crimes and administer justice, not commit crimes and abort justice. How on earth was this allowed to happen? The simplest answers are power and money. The longer answer is the history of power and money and the effect those two things have on people over time. Rome wasn't built in a day, and likewise the so-called "deep state," including the leadership of the FBI, DOJ, NSA, CIA, and other intelligence agencies, has been constructed over many years. This is not a Republican-versus-Democrat issue. This is a liberty-versus-tyranny issue. Both sides are to blame, and both sides must come together to fix it.

In June 2018, we contacted the major players mentioned throughout this book: James Comey, Andrew McCabe, Rod Rosenstein, Robert Mueller, Sally Yates, Andrew Weissmann, Aaron Zebley, Jeannie Rhee, Bruce and Nellie Ohr, Fusion GPS, Glenn Simpson, Mary Jacoby, Marc Elias and Perkins Coie, Daniel Poneman, the Scowcroft Group, Tom Donilon, Theodore Kassinger, Jose Fernandez, Adam Waldman and The Endeavor Group, BGR Group, and Lockheed Martin. We asked if they would like to shed any light on the allegations contained herein. As of this writing, the above parties either denied or ignored our inquiries.

Nonetheless, the story of how the FBI may be compromised is moving quickly. Let's get started.

CHAPTER 1

THE INSURANCE POLICY

- The FBI and DOJ used a politicized dossier as probable cause to obtain a secret surveillance warrant targeting a presidential campaign.
- Republicans James Comey, Andrew McCabe, Rod Rosenstein, and Robert Mueller have continued to rely on the "salacious and unverified" dossier despite its nefarious origins.
- The discredited dossier was paid for by Clinton and the DNC and relied on shady sources, including foreign intelligence services and anonymous Russian officials.
- The Clintons' Whitewater scandal seems like ancient history and yet it ties players like Rosenstein, Comey, and even Fusion GPS to the Clintons over two decades ago.

What Happened?

If you ask Hillary Clinton and her allies how she lost the 2016 election, the answers will vary. The primary culprits in their minds seem to be Vladimir Putin and the Russians' collusion with the Trump campaign, along with then-FBI Director James Comey.[1] As we will see, the "Russian collusion" narrative was an operation spearheaded by the Clinton campaign and coordinated with the highest levels of the U.S. intelligence community (IC), primarily the Department of Justice (DOJ) and the Federal Bureau of Investigation (FBI).[2] Ironically, the FBI and its ex-director James Comey are also at fault, according to Clinton's book *What Happened*. The mainstream media (MSM) follows Putin and Comey on the long list of entities to blame, and even Barack Obama makes an appearance.[3] The facts, however, suggest that her blame is misplaced.

It is important to clarify exactly what happened in order to set the record straight. Beginning in April 2016, the Democratic National Committee (DNC) and the Clinton campaign paid for opposition research on her Republican opponent in the 2016 election. The Clinton camp then promoted that research to allies in Congress, the FBI, and the media. The research became known as "the dossier," and it alleged that the Trump campaign had been compromised by Putin and was colluding with Russian actors to win the 2016 election.[4]

The dossier's claims were "salacious and unverified," according to Comey.[5] To date, investigators have produced no evidence that the Trump campaign colluded with Russia, but not for lack of trying.[6] Multiple inquiries were spawned from the dossier, including a special counsel investigation. Deputy Attorney General Rod Rosenstein appointed former FBI Director Robert Mueller to lead that investigation on

May 17, 2017.[7] Rosenstein has worked with Mueller since 1990. Mueller was Rosenstein's boss when the latter worked in the public integrity section of the DOJ's criminal division.[8] Former FBI Director Comey and Rosenstein were each involved in investigations involving alleged Clinton corruption—Rosenstein in the Whitewater investigation during the Clinton presidency and Comey, of course, in the email scandal and earlier in the Whitewater-related Vince Foster suicide investigation.[9] The team Mueller handpicked to investigate Russian election interference has been marred by alleged conflicts of interest and bias.[10]

Investigators such as Robert Mueller and his former FBI colleagues continue to hunt for Trump's elusive "Russian connection." Meanwhile, it has become increasingly apparent that Mueller's investigation was compromised from the start by some of the same pro-Clinton players involved in the 2016 election debacle. Top-level FBI personnel not only favored the Clinton campaign but also actively sought to undermine her opponent.[11]

These once unknown, shadowy bureaucrats are rapidly becoming household names: former FBI Director James Comey, FBI Deputy Director Andrew McCabe, DOJ deputy Bruce Ohr, and FBI agent Peter Strzok, among many others.[12] We now know that the FBI received information from, and the DOJ's Ohr coordinated closely with, an opposition research team known as Fusion GPS.[13] We now know that Fusion GPS compiled a now-infamous "dossier" with funding from the Democratic National Committee and the Clinton campaign.[14] We now know that the dossier's shady beginnings should easily discredit the claims it contains.[15] There have been specious claims of offers of multi-billion-dollar bribes and the existence of Kremlin blackmail videos involving Trump engaged with Russian prostitutes. The dossier implicates Trump, a self-described germaphobe, in some strange "golden shower" fetish.[16] Overall, the dossier was a research failure. Nonetheless, it facilitated the successful execution of an FBI surveillance operation against a political target.

This was only the beginning. America's top law enforcement officials—the FBI director and the attorney general—played significant roles in the tainted 2016 election operation.[17] FBI Director James Comey directly signed off on surveillance warrants. According to FBI agents working the cases, Attorney General Loretta Lynch sought to downplay the Clinton email investigation while her deputy Sally Yates co-signed the surveillance warrants to spy on Trump associates.[18] Even President Obama appears to have played a role and wanted "to know everything [they were] doing."[19]

The connections can be dizzying. Many citizens and journalists alike want to know what really happened at the FBI. What happened to the Clinton email and pay-to-play investigations? What did former attorney general Loretta Lynch and James Comey actually do, and for whom? What is "the dossier," and what did Trump and the Russians allegedly collude about? What is happening at the FBI and the DOJ now? These are important questions that deserve answers.

The more important question, however, is why?

Why did Comey and his FBI colleagues expend so many resources (funded by taxpayers) on the Trump–Russia investigation despite no direct evidence of collusion?[20] Why did Lynch ask Comey to call the Clinton investigation a "matter" rather than an "investigation" *after* Lynch met privately with Bill Clinton on the tarmac in June 2016?[21] Why did Comey break FBI protocol and give a mid-election press conference in which he effectively excused Clinton's email use before an investigation had been completed?[22] Why did FBI agents working in Deputy Director Andrew McCabe's office discuss an "insurance policy" against a potential Trump presidency?[23]

Ultimately, why did the secret surveillance court, called FISC, allow the FBI to spy on the Trump team given the politicized origins of the unverified dossier?[24] Why did Comey, McCabe, and the other FISA warrant signatories allegedly mislead the court about their evidence (or lack thereof)?[25]

In short, why would people with so much to lose risk everything?

The answer is simple: They had much to hide.

The 2016 election and the machinations of the FBI and DOJ did not occur in a vacuum. Much like the Watergate scandal in the 1970s, the cover-up ultimately has proven to be worse than the crime.[26] The misdeeds committed during the 2016 election must be fully explored. There are criminal allegations of lying under oath, obstruction, leaking classified material, coordination with foreign powers, and coordination with the media, but that is not the whole story. It began as a complex smokescreen apparently orchestrated by the Clinton team to undermine opponent Trump and obfuscate allegiances.[27]

So, who are the players and what are their misdeeds?

At the top is former President Barack Obama. Loretta Lynch was Obama's attorney general, and James Comey was Obama's FBI director. Working under Lynch on the DOJ side were Sally Yates, Leslie Caldwell, Rod Rosenstein, and Bruce Ohr. These players all worked at the DOJ headquarters, or Main Justice building, in Washington, D.C. Specifically, the DOJ's National Security Division (NSD) is a major base of operations implicated in the misdeeds.

Under Director Comey's supervision was his deputy director, Andrew McCabe, and McCabe staffers Peter Strzok and Lisa Page. These FBI players were primarily acting out of the deputy director's office with help from the FBI's Counterintelligence Division at FBI headquarters in D.C. The FBI's New York Field Office (NYFO) also played an important part as the hub of the FBI's surveillance apparatus.[28] McCabe's right-hand man was Peter Strzok. Strzok and his mistress/colleague, Lisa Page, demonstrated clear anti-Trump bias according to their 2016 and 2017 text messages, later subpoenaed by Congress.[29] Page and Strzok's text messages referred to themselves and their associates as "the Secret Society" (which some have suggested was "made in jest").[30] Comments about an "insurance policy" may explain a motive for their anti-Trump activities.[31] Their cloak-and-dagger lingo is indeed comedic, albeit tragic and unsettling. Still, Strzok and Page were instrumental in both the Clinton and Trump FBI investigations and the subsequent special counsel investigation into collusion between Russia and the Trump campaign.[32]

Former FBI Director Robert Mueller was appointed special counsel by Deputy Attorney General Rod Rosenstein. Rosenstein has been a close associate of Mueller's for many years, beginning in 1990 when Rosenstein joined the DOJ's public integrity section.[33] Mueller's special counsel investigation was initiated to ascertain whether collusion took place between the Trump campaign and Russia. The mandate reads: "to ensure a full and thorough investigation of the Russian government's efforts to interfere in the 2016 presidential election…"[34] Mueller's investigation has seemingly focused on Russian interference perceived to benefit Trump and ignored the Russian connections to Team Clinton, according to media reports and evidenced by the charges issued.[35]

Although he is a registered Republican, Mueller assembled a team that was stacked exclusively with non-Republicans and even Clinton supporters, such as Peter Strzok and Lisa Page.[36] These individuals demonstrated anti-Trump sentiments and privately referred to him as an "idiot," a "menace," a "loathsome human," and a "douche."[37] Other Mueller team members have donated heavily to Democrats, and not a single Mueller pick donated to Trump. James Quarles, for example, donated almost $33,000 to Democrats, including to Clinton and former President Barack Obama.[38] Several of the attorneys on Mueller's squad had previously represented or defended Clinton associates in court. Mueller chose Jeannie Rhee, who had represented the Clinton Foundation directly. He also chose Aaron Zebley, who represented the Clinton staffer under investigation for creating the secret email server.[39]

Mueller's team critically does not include experts with electioneering and espionage experience—the kind who could substantiate claims of Russian meddling and collusion. Instead, Mueller picked a team full of criminal prosecutors, many of whom are Clinton loyalists and Democrat donors who seem hostile towards Trump.[40] The conflicts of interest and unethical behavior have led to widespread criticism and there have been multiple departures—notably Peter Strzok, who was removed, and Lisa Page, who left the Mueller team in 2017 and resigned outright in May 2018.[41] Two high-ranking FBI associates of Strzok and Page, Mike Kortan and David Laufman, resigned from the FBI in February 2018.[42]

After the nuances of DOJ and FBI collaboration with Team Clinton are disentangled, a troubling picture emerges. The FBI and DOJ personnel listed above not only ensured that Hillary Clinton was exonerated for her secret email server *and* the pay-to-play allegations, but they also knowingly publicized salacious, unverified rumors against Clinton's opponent, Donald Trump, in an apparent attempt to influence the 2016 electoral outcome or delegitimize the results should that effort be ineffective.[43] Strzok's and Page's uncovered text messages suggested leaks to the media, and their boss, Andrew McCabe, was referred by the DOJ inspector general for criminal prosecution, for lacking candor involving his contacts with media.[44] As mentioned, we sent McCabe's attorney a list of questions and offered to include his comments or rebuttal. Someone who "handles PR for Mr. McCabe" pointed to a previously released statement addressing the IG allegations against McCabe and added "we have nothing further for you."

A July 2017 Senate Report confirmed an "avalanche of leaks" (*felony* leaks in cases concerning classified material) occurred in the first few months of the Trump presidency.[45] President Trump has accused those involved of "treason."[46] That is for judges to decide.

These players and their roles in the 2016 surveillance of Trump associates are the subject of numerous investigations by citizens, journalists, Congress, and even the DOJ Office of the Inspector General (OIG). On June 14, 2018, the DOJ OIG released a long-awaited report on the FBI's handling of the Clinton email investigation and noted that a report on the FISA abuses would be released at a later date. The June report was over 550 pages and filled with confirmations of DOJ and FBI staffers' anti-Trump bias.[47] Despite the direct evidence that agents like Strzok had a "biased state of mind," the IG concluded there was no *documentary* evidence that such bias affected decisions. Some of the most important bombshells in the report were:

- FBI personnel at the highest level prejudged the outcome of the Clinton email investigation before it was completed—even before Clinton had been interviewed. Agents even referred to Clinton as "President Clinton" as the bureau handed out "Queen for a Day" immunity agreements to her associates.
- On May 5, 2015 (the same day that *Clinton Cash* was released), McCabe pleaded with the Washington

Field Office to "[p]lease do not open a case" on Hillary Clinton and the Clinton Foundation.

- One FBI agent acknowledged that one of Clinton's IT aides "[l]ied his ass off" and concluded "aint noone gonna [sic] do shit."
- Another exchange between FBI agents ominously discussed their disdain for "the republic." "I mean, I never really liked the Republic anyway," said one of the agents. "…I have initiated the destruction of the republic…" the other replied.
- FBI personnel improperly received benefits from journalists, which included tickets to sporting events, meals and drinks, and invitations to private social events.
- The report confirmed that President Obama had used a pseudonym to email Clinton on her unsecured private server and even communicated with her *while she was in a hostile territory* (contradicting his claims of ignorance and risking interception).[48]
- James Comey and others within the FBI used private email accounts to communicate about official bureau investigations—as Clinton had in the State Department (hence the investigation). Notably, Hillary Clinton blatantly tweeted a sarcastic comment referring to this revelation as if it exonerated her own email practices.[49]
- Perhaps the most damning messages of all were sent by colleague/lovers Strzok and Page:
  - o Page: "[Trump's] not ever going to become president, right? Right?!"
  - o Strzok: "No. No he won't. We'll stop it."

The report has been both widely criticized and celebrated. James Comey (whom the report described as "insubordinate") penned an op-ed in *The New York Times* that was released shortly after the IG report's release. Comey actually (and perhaps tellingly) praised the OIG and the report (which he called "important" no fewer than four times) for concluding that there was "no evidence that bias" was found to have affected the FBI's investigation. Comey further extolled the virtues of the IG report for concluding, as he had, "that there was [likely] no prosecutable case against Mrs. Clinton." Conveniently, Comey left out the word "likely" when describing the IG's conclusions. Of course, Comey had reason to celebrate: the IG report essentially concluded that the instances of bias were isolated incidents. Strangely, Comey insinuated that he had initiated and "urged the [IG] investigation in the first place."[50]

In a press conference, FBI Director Christopher Wray echoed Comey's sentiment stating, "[t]his report did not find any evidence of political bias or improper considerations actually impacting the investigation under review." Others saw things differently. Legislators from both parties slammed Comey and others named in the report for "an alarming and destructive level of animus."[51] Some called the report "half-baked," while others went a step further and called it "a whitewash of the deep state by the deep state itself."[52] President Trump tweeted that "[t]he IG Report totally destroys James Comey and all of his minions" but equivocated on the conclusions, which he called "ridiculous" and ultimately concluded, "the IG blew it at the end."[53]

It is worth noting that there are numerous IG investigations still underway, including the abuse of FISA during the 2016 election and the number of leaks coming from the agencies. IG Michael Horowitz confirmed that investigations were ongoing as he was grilled by the House Oversight Committee on the more pressing issue: FISA abuse.[54] The

June report of the Clinton email investigation left many questions unanswered, indicating that its findings and recommendations are not the conclusion, rather, they are only the beginning.

Many are still wondering, were crimes committed?

Readers can be sure that the criminal investigators and legislators are investigating several U.S. criminal statutes outlined under 18 U.S.C. and 26 U.S.C. Expect charges related to obstruction, lying under oath, mishandling classified material, and unauthorized disclosure (leaking), as evidenced by the numerous criminal referrals already under investigation.[55]

Beyond the obvious conflicts of interest, such as alleged payments made to FBI players from suspects under investigation, there are larger concerns. Is it illegal to abuse the surveillance tools of the U.S. intelligence community? Is the FBI's surveillance process a rubber-stamped one? Could such things happen to an average citizen?

As we will find throughout this book, the answer to those questions is almost certainly yes. The question Americans should ask is *why* was Comey's FBI able to spy on a presidential campaign in the middle of an election? And why would factions within the FBI and the DOJ compromise themselves, and the entire intelligence community, by seeking to influence a presidential election? The answers will be explored in great detail but suffice it to say they had much to hide. A Trump presidency posed a significant exposure threat to James Comey, Andrew McCabe, and their lieutenants because it would jeopardize their long-developed powers. As a result, an anti-Trump "insurance policy" was devised.[56]

The Origin of the Dossier and the Little Rock Connection

In any complex story, keeping track of the names is difficult. It helps to start at the beginning. When Donald Trump was one of more than a dozen GOP candidates seeking the nomination, Team Clinton did not take him seriously. A leaked DNC memo from August 2015 reveals their primary strategy: Democrats and their allies in the media were to "elevate" Trump.[57] An early Clinton campaign meeting agenda indicated they wanted to "maximize Trump."[58] Clinton's campaign, the DNC, and allies in the media sought to treat Trump as a "pied piper" candidate, so as to pull moderate candidates such as Jeb(!) Bush further to the "extreme" right.[59]

Just after the first GOP debate on August 6, 2015, the Democrats surely realized their "pied piper" strategy had failed as Trump's poll numbers surged.[60] Soon it was clear that the DNC's plan had backfired spectacularly. A January 2016 CNN poll showed record-high numbers for Trump as he "dominated the GOP field."[61] Rather than marginalize the moderate candidates by moving them to the right, they discovered that Trump's popularity was indicative of voters who believed his ideas were not all that extreme.

Clinton needed a Plan B. So began the dossier insurance policy.

In April 2016, the DNC and the Clinton campaign retained Fusion GPS, an opposition research firm used by Democrats in the past.[62] Fusion GPS had been hired in 2012 to dig up dirt on Obama's opponent, Mitt Romney. Fusion GPS has also been hired by Planned Parenthood, and even Russian oligarchs seeking dirt on various political targets.[63] Fusion GPS co-founders Peter Fritsch and Glenn Simpson previously worked for *The Wall Street Journal* and both have significant Clinton connections. Fritsch donated a combined $1,000 to Clinton's 2016 campaign and super PAC called the Hillary Victory Fund.[64]

Simpson's ties are more interesting. His wife, Mary Jacoby, comes from a powerful family in Little Rock. Her father, Jon Jacoby, was a close friend of Arkansas Democratic power broker Jackson Stephens and was his right-hand man in the family business, Stephens Inc.[65] Not only did Jacoby land Stephens Inc. a massive deal with a data company called Systematics, but his daughter, Mary, also worked as a file clerk at Stephens's attorney's Rose Law Firm.[66] It is unclear when exactly Mary Jacoby worked at the firm but we know Clinton worked there for almost fifteen years—from 1977 to 1992. Clinton even worked directly on Systematics matters. Given the extremely close relationships between Clinton and Stephens, Stephens and Rose Law, Jon Jacoby and Stephens's Systematics, Mary Jacoby and Rose Law, and Clinton and Systematics, it is highly unlikely that Clinton and Jacoby didn't know each other at the time.[67] In 1995, Mary Jacoby was asked to comment on the Clintons' bourgeoning Whitewater scandal which involved Rose Law. "I think I have some conflict of interest here. I'm from Little Rock, happen to know some of these people personally, and I don't cover Whitewater," Jacoby stammered.[68]

It is important to realize that in the wake of 9/11, a company close to Systematics called Acxiom collaborated with the FBI to upgrade their surveillance systems.[69] Systematics and Acxiom, both longtime Rose Law clients, pioneered data technology in Arkansas, shared numerous board members, and were backed by Little Rock's shadowy Stephens Inc.—one of the largest investment banks off Wall Street.[70] Stephens Inc. is also a major political player and has bankrolled Bill Clinton's campaigns dating back decades to Clinton's days in Arkansas. Stephens Inc. turned small-town Arkansas businesses like Walmart, Tyson Foods, Alltel, and others into multinational corporate behemoths. The incestuous Little Rock relationships have been lucrative despite the admitted potentials for abuse and conflicts.[71]

As noted previously, Rose Law Firm is significant for obvious reasons: Hillary Clinton worked there, and her dealings with Rose clients led to the Whitewater special counsel investigation during the 1990s. The Whitewater saga is ancient Clinton history but the deceptions are familiar—particularly the destruction of records. That Clinton and her partners from Rose Law destroyed records had the "appearance of criminality." Long before private email servers and BlackBerrys existed, they did it the old-fashioned way: documents were physically shredded.[72]

Three of Hillary Clinton's partners at Rose Law Firm followed the Clintons to Washington in 1992, taking jobs with the DOJ. President Clinton appointed one to the third-highest position at the DOJ: assistant attorney general (AAG). The other two went to the White House as legal counsel. These three men's political careers came to unfortunate ends early in the scandal-filled Clinton presidency. The AAG, Webster Hubbell, was indicted for tax evasion and fraud. William Kennedy III was fired amid the "Travelgate" scandal involving Clinton's apparent politicization of the bureau.[73] The most famous of the three was former Rose partner Vince Foster, who is said to have committed suicide in the first six months of the Clinton presidency. Clinton and her fellow former Rose partners shredded boxes full of files, including Vince Foster's, when they joined the White House, leading to widespread criticism and allegations of criminality.[74]

For her role, Hillary Clinton was cleared by federal investigators, including none other than Rod Rosenstein and a young James Comey. In a recent interview with ABC's George Stephanopoulos, Comey admitted his primary role in the Whitewater investigation centered around Vince Foster's missing files.[75] Rosenstein's wife, attorney Lisa Barsoomian, directly represented defendant Bill Clinton in a separate lawsuit filed on June 11, 1998—just months after Hillary Clinton was interviewed by Rosenstein and Special Counsel Kenneth Starr for her role in the Travelgate fiasco. Rosenstein and Starr interviewed Clinton relating to the Travelgate on January 14, 1998, which would seem to contradict a document Rosenstein submitted to Congress suggesting his independent counsel work ended in 1997.[76]

Understanding Mary Jacoby's longstanding ties to Little Rock sheds light on Fusion GPS's history. It is more Clinton-connected than simple work for hire. Jacoby visited Obama's White House *residence* with a small group of six visitors on April 19, 2016.[77] Could it have had something to do with the fact that her husband had just been hired by the DNC to create the infamous Trump dossier?

Clinton, the DNC, and even Obama's super PAC Obama for America (OFA) made a series of payments to the law firm that paid Fusion GPS—Perkins Coie. The total compensation that Perkins Coie and Fusion GPS received is unknown due to confidentiality privileges enjoyed by attorneys and their clients.[78] If payments to the law firm were meant to then be paid to Fusion, could this be a campaign finance violation or even a form of money laundering? Why wouldn't Clinton's campaign, the DNC, and Obama's OFA pay Fusion GPS directly? The Federal Election Commission (FEC) received a complaint related to DNC funding of the dossier and a separate Democrat campaign finance scandal involving $84 million in laundered funds. The DOJ OIG is currently investigating the dossier connections and a lawsuit is pending regarding the $84 million.[79]

No one knows exactly how much Fusion GPS received to create the dossier, though many have settled on somewhere near $12 million—paid by various Democrats. So what did the company do with that $12 million? Some of it went to Christopher Steele, the retired MI5 agent who assembled much of the dossier. Some of it went to Nellie Ohr, the wife of a top DOJ official. Some of it went to journalists who promoted the salacious findings. And some of it allegedly even went to the dossier's sources, which included Russian officials.[80] Simpson was grilled on the dossier operation, and when asked if Steele paid any of his sources for dirt on Trump, Simpson said, "I don't know." However, former Acting-CIA Director Michael Morell (a Clinton-ally) said, "I subsequently learned that he paid them. That the intermediaries paid the sources and the intermediaries got the money from Chris. And that kind of worries me a little bit because if you're paying somebody, particularly former FSB officers, they are going to tell you truth and innuendo and rumor, and they're going to call you up and say, 'hey, let's have another meeting, I have more information for you,' because they want to get paid some more."[81]

Lest there be any doubt, Glenn Simpson and Mary Jacoby are at the heart of the discredited Trump dossier and subsequent Mueller investigation. In a now-deleted Facebook post from June 24, 2017, Jacoby wrote the following: "It's come to my attention that some people still don't realize what Glenn's role was in exposing Putin's control of Donald Trump. Let's be clear. Glenn conducted the investigation. Glenn hired Chris Steele. Chris Steele worked for Glenn."[82]

To recap, the Clinton-connected Fusion GPS created the Trump dossier. Also, Clinton's campaign and the DNC paid Fusion GPS via an intermediary beginning in April 2016. Fusion's Jacoby visited the White House residence that same month. Fusion GPS colluded with, and possibly even paid, Russian interests for unverified Trump dirt. Obama's super

PAC paid the Fusion GPS intermediary $972,000 between April 2016 and August 2017.[83]

By itself, the dossier's origin is unsettling. But that is only the beginning. The real scandal is what Obama's DOJ did *for* and *with* the dossier.

Mary Jacoby was not the only link between Fusion GPS and Team Obama/Clinton. Fusion GPS and Christopher Steele have a long history working with the FBI and the DOJ. Since at least 2006, Steele has worked with Bruce Ohr on various matters where their interests and abilities intersected.[84] Steele knows the FBI's New York Field Office well, as he advised their Eurasian Joint Organized Crime Squad in the past.[85] In 2010, Steele worked with the FBI (and DOJ's Ohr) investigation of Russian bribes to the international soccer federation (FIFA).[86] Steele even had contacts within the State Department to help legitimize his findings and forward them up the chain, eventually making their way to the DOJ and the FBI with the imprimatur of Victoria Nuland, one of Obama's top national security advisors.[87] While the DOJ's own Bruce Ohr was working the inside track, his wife, Nellie, worked directly for Fusion GPS. FOX News confirmed this apparent conflict of interest with the House Permanent Select Committee on Intelligence (HPSCI).[88] Ohr, like Andrew McCabe, failed to recuse himself when it mattered most. McCabe was later fired, and Ohr has since been demoted twice by Trump.[89]

The Insurance Policy

The dossier was just one part of the story, and what the DOJ and the FBI did with the dossier is even more unsettling. It all started in the office of James Comey's top lieutenant: Andrew McCabe.

In summer 2015, multiple FBI offices began investigating the Clintons' various misdeeds.[90] At that time, McCabe's wife, Jill, was running for a Virginia state senate seat. McCabe received approximately $675,288, more than one-third of her total campaign contributions, from entities controlled by Virginia Governor Terry McAuliffe, a close Clinton confidant.[91] According to documents released under the Freedom of Information Act (FOIA), Andrew and Jill McCabe met with Governor McAuliffe *privately* in March 2015. At that time, McAuliffe himself was reportedly under FBI investigation involving foreign contributions to his 2013 gubernatorial campaign from a Chinese donor tied to the Clintons.[92] McAuliffe's lawyer in that matter was Marc Elias of Perkins Coie, the same firm used by the DNC and Clinton.[93]

McCabe consulted with the FBI's ethics office numerous times about his relationship with his wife's campaign, beginning in March 2015. On April 29, 2015, McCabe was advised to recuse himself in matters involving the state of Virginia. The Clinton email investigation began in July 2015, while McCabe was in charge of the Washington Field Office. He provided "personnel resources" for that investigation, although a set of internal FBI talking points say McCabe "was not told what the investigation was about." The FBI talking points confirm McCabe was promoted to FBI deputy director in February 2016 and began overseeing the Clinton email investigation at that time. That investigation continued for months without recusal from McCabe. The investigation ended in July 2016 with Director Comey's infamous public exoneration. McCabe only recused himself from the *re-opened* Clinton email investigation on November 1, 2016—long after the FBI first cleared Clinton of her controversial email use.[94] Media reporting of McCabe's recusal from the Clinton email investigation suggests that he followed protocols and, since his wife's election campaign had ended in November 2015, he wasn't even required to recuse himself from the Clinton investigation.[95] A few simple questions arise: If McCabe wasn't required to recuse himself, why did he and why so late? And what about the McAuliffe investigation? Did McCabe fail to recuse himself from that investigation while he was in charge of the Washington Field Office? The FBI does not say but, according to the June 2018 IG report, McCabe "did not fully comply with his recusal," specifically relating to the Clinton Foundation investigation. The IG additionally found "potential significant implications" of the donations to Jill McCabe's campaign.[96]

In addition to the prescribed recusals, McCabe was also told not to campaign on his wife's behalf. Nonetheless, he reportedly attended events, was photographed wearing a "Jill McCabe for Senate" shirt, and publicly promoted her candidacy on social media. These may seem like innocuous and harmless decisions, but the bureau takes perceived political bias very seriously. It was the photos that prompted an FBI complaint and an internal investigation of Deputy Director McCabe for violations of the Hatch Act.[97]

McCabe's wife lost the election but was permitted to spend any remaining donations for personal use per a loophole in Virginia campaign laws. Of the $1.67 million total raised, $1.2 million has been publicly accounted for. The remaining $438,000 is listed as in-kind expenditures, which are not dated nor itemized publicly.[98] On April 2, 2018, Jill McCabe published an op-ed in *The Washington Post* denying allegations that the contributions she received from McAuliffe had anything to do with her husband's FBI decisions. She explains that the photo referenced in the FBI complaint was a "family picture." She does not address how campaign funds were spent.[99]

Andrew McCabe started his FBI career in 1996 at the NYFO as an agent. There he worked on a "variety of organized crime matters," earning a promotion to the leadership role of supervisory special agent on the Eurasian Organized Crime Task Force (OCTF) in 2003. In 2006, McCabe was promoted under Robert Mueller and moved from New York to the FBI headquarters in Washington, D.C. First, he was a unit chief in charge of terrorism and extraterritorial investigations, and then he became a deputy assistant director in the FBI's Counterterrorism Division. After Mueller left the FBI in 2013, James Comey took over once he was confirmed in September of that year. Comey immediately appointed McCabe to the position of executive assistant director of the National Security Branch in October 2013. McCabe was promoted to head the Washington Field Office in September 2014.[100]

McCabe's meteoric rise is troubling given the bias that he and his staffers have demonstrated. McCabe and his subordinates, Bill Priestap and Peter Strzok, played crucial roles in the exoneration of Clinton's email practices, as well as the subsequent Trump investigations regarding the Fusion dossier.[101] Priestap is the head of the FBI's Counterintelligence Division and was reportedly Strzok's immediate supervisor.[102]

Priestap's importance was confirmed by Comey in his March 2017 congressional testimony. Comey claims that Priestap was the one who advised that Congress should be kept in the dark about the Russian hacking and Trump collusion investigations.[103] This almost certainly allowed the Russian meddling to continue longer than if it had been made public.

Priestap may have had financial conflicts, though not as apparent as McCabe's. His wife, Sabina, who works on K Street for an international private intelligence firm, contributed a combined $3,000 to Hillary Clinton's 2016 campaign and allied super PAC.[104] She got her start working for the shadowy private intelligence pioneer, Kroll Inc., and later served as special advisor to the FBI on post-9/11 intelligence collection efforts.[105] Her father and uncle are "zillionaire" Goldman Sachs veterans who contribute heavily to Democrat causes.[106]

In the months leading up to the 2016 election, Strzok and his DOJ mistress Lisa Page's own text messages seem to confirm McCabe and Priestap's involvement.[107]

On August 15, 2016, Strzok texted to Page: "I want to believe the path you threw out for consideration in [FBI deputy director Andrew McCabe's] office—that there's no way [Trump] gets elected—but I'm afraid we can't take that risk." He added: "*It's like an insurance policy...* [emphasis added]."[108]

McCabe's financial conflict(s), his failures to recuse himself, and the media leaks coming from his office contributed, no doubt, to mounting pressure for his resignation in early 2018.[109] The FBI's Office of Professional Responsibility (OPR) investigation of McCabe led to his early termination just days before he was set to retire with benefits.[110] A subsequent DOJ OIG report found serious issues with McCabe's conduct. According to a statement by Attorney General Jeff Sessions, "both the OIG and FBI OPR reports concluded that Mr. McCabe had made an unauthorized disclosure to the news [media] and lacked candor—including under oath— on multiple occasions."[111] This sounds like Washington legalese for "lying" and "leaking." On April 19, 2018, CNN reported the DOJ OIG had referred McCabe for criminal prosecution, likely for charges related to lying to the FBI and unauthorized disclosures to reporters centering around the FBI's stonewalling of Clinton Foundation investigations.[112] While McCabe and other top FBI officials close to Priestap have resigned or been fired, Priestap currently remains at his post. Some believe the lack of reporting about Priestap's role may indicate that he is cooperating with investigators.[113]

On the DOJ side, a significant financial conflict possibly implicates Bruce Ohr, former associate deputy attorney general. Ohr was also head of the DOJ's Organized Crime Drug Enforcement Task Force (OCDETF). So, he was able to work on dossier-related matters from the inside of the DOJ—even meeting directly with Glenn Simpson and Christopher Steele—while his wife, Nellie, worked on the dossier outside—directly for Fusion GPS.[114]

One month after Fusion GPS started working for the DNC and the Clinton campaign, Nellie Ohr applied for an amateur (ham) radio license on May 23, 2016. Correspondence via radio frequency would have allowed communication not subject to subpoena or FISA.[115] According to Simpson, he met Bruce Ohr "through organized crime conferences." A June 2010 report from a DOJ working group lists Simpson and the Ohrs on a short list of attendees.[116] Nellie Ohr previously worked on a CIA project called Open Source Works and is fluent in Russian.[117] Her experience in dealing with foreign intelligence, her Russian contacts, and especially her husband's top DOJ clearance would have been major value additions and potential reasons for her hire.

Nellie Ohr received payments directly from the Clinton-financed firm, Fusion GPS, while her husband at the DOJ sought to legitimize their work by passing her findings to the FBI. Bruce Ohr met numerous times with Steele before and after the FBI considered Steele's dossier a source for FISA warrants. Steele allegedly told Ohr he was "desperate that Donald Trump not get elected and was passionate about him not being president." According to a memo released by congressional investigators, this clear evidence of Steele's personal bias was not reflected in the October 2016 FISA warrant application targeting Trump-associate Carter Page.[118] Sometime after the election, around Thanksgiving 2016, Bruce Ohr met with his wife's boss, Glenn Simpson, at a coffee shop, as the surveillance operation was already under-way.[119] Bruce Ohr reportedly concealed these numerous meetings from his DOJ superiors, which led to his removal from a top DOJ post. Furthermore, he failed to disclose the payments from Fusion GPS to his wife on ethics forms—a potential crime.[120]

Andrew McCabe, Peter Strzok, Bruce Ohr, James Comey, Robert Mueller, and others all spent a significant amount of time in the same offices in New York and D.C. over several decades. They have worked together, off and on, for a long time. Some of these conflicted players, such as McCabe, Strzok, and Ohr, have specifically investigated Russian crime and influence for over a decade.[121] Ironically, with all their combined experience, they were unable to prevent the alleged Russian election schemes in 2016. Furthermore, they and their subordinates failed to properly vet or investigate the controversial dossier before obtaining a FISA warrant to spy on Trump's associates.

At Main Justice, the National Security Division (NSD) is integral to reviews by the Committee on Foreign Investment in the United States (CFIUS) (like the 2010 review of Uranium One), as well as to the FISA surveillance process.[122] It was through the NSD and its administration of FISA warrant applications that surveillance of the Trump campaign was made possible using primarily unsubstantiated gossip collected and disseminated by partisan parties and Fusion GPS.[123] The DOJ, according to a July 2015 memo addressed to then-deputy AG Sally Yates, held the opinion that certain DOJ proceedings are not subject to oversight—specifically relating to wiretap programs. The DOJ inspector general (IG) strongly disagreed with that opinion and argued it undermined the IG's independence, as the IG would essentially need to "obtain permission" from DOJ officials to get important documents.[124] According to DOJ Inspector

General Michael Horowitz, this was not an issue under previous administrations. "Prior to 2010, neither the Justice Department nor the FBI questioned our legal authority to access all documents in its possession," Horowitz said.[125] In December 2015, Congress threatened to withhold DOJ's funding if the department failed to restore IG access. The move appeared effective when the DOJ updated the opinion in early 2016. In May 2016, Yates claimed that responding to IG requests was of the "highest priority."[126] Nonetheless, Trump fired Yates in his second week as president for obstructing his agenda and counseling DOJ colleagues to do likewise (Special Counsel Mueller's lieutenant Andrew Weissmann praised and thanked Yates for resisting Trump saying "I am so proud").[127]

Despite the apparent doublespeak, DOJ and FBI transparency issues remain unresolved. Rosenstein, Yates's successor, has been accused of "stonewalling" Congress by not providing documents they have requested.[128]

In March 2017, FBI Director Comey claimed the FBI had "no information" regarding Trump wiretaps.[129] Several months later, the DOJ confirmed in court filings they had "no records related to wiretaps," contradicting Trump's accusations.[130] The media cited these assertions ad nauseam as evidence that Trump and his associates were not under surveillance.[131] We now know that the assertions were dishonest at best.[132] It remains to be seen whether the DOJ and FBI will cooperate with the inspector general or Congress and produce documents relating to the Trump wiretaps.

Clinton Cash Allegations Fuel FBI Feud

The February 2018 DOJ inspector general report (released April 13, 2018) concerning Andrew McCabe revealed details of a growing rift between FBI leadership and the agents working in field offices. The report discusses in detail McCabe and his associates' unauthorized disclosures to the media. These disclosures, or "leaks," were less about McCabe's role in the Trump investigation. Instead, they concerned the Clinton investigations.[133]

Before top-level FBI officials like Andrew McCabe and his associates were working on the 2016 "insurance policy" against Trump, they were involved in multiple investigations regarding the Clintons. There was the private email server handling classified information and a separate investigation into pay-to-play at the Clinton Foundation. The Clinton email investigation was managed in large part by McCabe's deputy Peter Strzok, as evidenced by his text messages and his role performing interviews.[134] That investigation was wrapped up by July 2016, when James Comey controversially recommended exonerating Clinton for her email practices.[135]

The Clinton Foundation investigation began in summer 2015 and had not yet concluded as of early 2018. According to FBI agents investigating the Clinton Foundation, McCabe and others were actively impeding the investigation ahead of the 2016 election. The Clinton Foundation investigation had stemmed from April 2015 revelations in the book *Clinton Cash.* Shortly after the book was released, FBI agents began looking into the Clinton Foundation and pay-to-play allegations detailed in the book. By early 2016, FBI field offices across the country had opened criminal investigations. Initially, the FBI offices investigating were in New York, Los Angeles, Little Rock, and Washington, D.C.[136] When news of the investigations became public in late 2016, a top DOJ official reportedly was "very pissed off" and called Andrew McCabe to demand why agents were pursuing the matter. McCabe asked if he should shut the investigation down to which the DOJ official allegedly said "of course not." FBI agents dispute this and claim they were told to "stand down."

A fifth investigation by the Miami field office was underway by late 2016.[137] The FBI ordinarily does not comment on open investigations and the status is unclear, however, they appear to be active and led by the FBI's Little Rock office.[138]

The field office investigations were the source of internal conflict at the FBI and field agents were met with constant resistance from FBI leadership, primarily Andrew McCabe. The internal struggle publicly erupted days before the November 2016 election when *The Wall Street Journal* published a front-page article titled "Secret Recordings Fueled FBI Feud in Clinton Probe." The article revealed that agents within the FBI were frustrated as they sought to pursue the pay-to-play allegations. They felt they were being stonewalled.[139]

FBI agents seemed reluctant to allow the Clinton Foundation investigation to be swept under the rug like the email investigation. The revelations in *Clinton Cash* (particularly the sale of Uranium One to Russia) involving donations to the Clinton Foundation were potential national security concerns.[140] Officials from multiple agencies confirmed that the FBI agents working on the Clinton Foundation investigation had recorded evidence of a pay-to-play scheme, possibly relating to the Russian uranium deal.[141] The agents were right; their bosses at the FBI and the DOJ were stonewalling, possibly with nefarious rationale. The Uranium One scandal was *not only* a Clinton State Department scandal, *but also* an Obama DOJ scandal. Many of the same individuals at the top of the DOJ who were impeding these investigations were also involved in another investigation that began back in 2009. That investigation involved Russian bribery, kickbacks, and racketeering in the U.S. nuclear industry, and it is inextricably linked to the sale of Uranium One.[142]

FBI agents learned from *Clinton Cash* about Hillary Clinton's myriad conflicts of interest while she was secretary of state. During her tenure, 2009 to 2013, she, her husband, and their foundation received tens of millions of dollars from individuals, corporations, and foreign governments alike. The windfalls came in the form of speaking fees and huge donations to the Clinton Foundation. Many of these international entities had financial matters that the U.S. State Department could positively or negatively affect. Ordinarily, this could pose a conflict of interest. Furthermore, Secretary Clinton reportedly met or talked on the phone with at least 85 individuals who were donors to the foundation.[143] Now, it is clear that this is a major problem, and may even be illegal. The growing number of FBI field offices that were investigating possible crimes across the U.S. confirmed this information.[144]

The law is (and was) clear at the time of Clinton's confirmation hearing in 2009, so what happened? One answer, it seems, is that she implicated Team Obama in her pay-to-play scheme. Clinton and her team negotiated a significant conflict of interest waiver called the memorandum of understanding (MOU). Cheryl Mills, one of Clinton's closest aides, drafted the blanket immunity document that allowed the Clintons to continue their pattern of self-enrichment while Clinton ran the State Department. Team Obama signed off on this unprecedented "get out of jail free" card.

The U.S. has bribery and conflict statutes forbidding payments to elected officials. The MOU allowed Clinton's foundation to continue receiving six-figure checks from foreign interests while serving as America's top diplomat—as long as they were all disclosed (they were not).[145] Without the MOU, each and every payment to the Clintons by parties with matters before the State Department would and should be fully investigated. But the MOU was not what thwarted the FBI agents and their investigation; it was the DOJ's top brass. "Senior officials in the Justice Department and the FBI didn't think much of the evidence, while [FBI] investigators believed they had promising leads their bosses wouldn't let them pursue," *The Wall Street Journal* reported.[146]

Did the DOJ and FBI leaderships simply favor Clinton's chances? Did the anti-Trump FBI lieutenants find Trump so "loathsome" that it led them to devise an "insurance policy," as their leaked text messages indicate?[147] Or was there some other motivation?

What Did They Do with the Dossier, and Why Does It Matter?

The dossier was not meant to be a publicized indictment of Trump. Little, if anything, within it was verified. It was easily discredited. Why pay all this money for dirt that was false?

The dossier was a *private* tool. A chess piece.

Congressional investigators revealed that Fusion GPS paid at least three journalists between June 2016 and February 2017, according to a court filing. Furthermore, the filing specifically confirms that the journalists Fusion paid reported on matters relating to the dossier, indicating journalists were possibly involved in a pay-to-*print* scheme.[148] Legislators further acknowledge that Fusion's dossier was the primary basis for the FBI's Russia investigation, which eventually became the 2017 Mueller investigation.[149]

The goal of the dossier seems to have been to convince the intelligence community that Trump was working with the Russians. Another goal may have been FISA warrants. Initially, if so, it succeeded. FISA was granted, and the Trump team intercepts began to flow. But what dirt came from wiretapping Trump? Surely, we would have heard of it by now, right? Pro-Clinton insiders and Robert Mueller's Clinton-connected investigators have a strong track record of leaking damning Trump revelations as soon as they're discovered.[150] No "smoking gun" has yet been leaked.

The relationship between Fusion GPS and the DOJ presents major questions of financial and ethical conflicts of interest. Fusion GPS and its political operators were paid to undermine Trump. It appears that they may have had ulterior motives for working with the FBI and the DOJ. They may even have had *personal* motivations for helping the Clintons, as was the case with Mary Jacoby—who, as previously noted, hails from Little Rock and has deep ties to the Clintons.

Formal reliance on Fusion GPS's research by the DOJ and FBI in the Trump investigation seems unthinkable, considering the questionable nature of the research and that it was paid for by political operators. The fact that Jacoby *actually worked* at Clinton's Rose Law Firm is newsworthy on its own. Rose Law Firm's post-9/11 ties to the nascent surveillance industry are deeply intertwined with this story.

The recent wave of resignations and firings at the DOJ and the FBI are unprecedented. Many of these career "public servants" have left their careers in government and have retained personal lawyers. Their behavior during the 2016 election and beyond will have profound consequences.

For example, as mentioned previously, James Comey was fired; Andrew McCabe resigned in disgrace and is currently under investigation; and Peter Strzok and Lisa Page were fired from the Mueller investigation. David Laufman was in charge of the DOJ's NSD section on foreign investment (CFIUS) as the FBI investigated pay-to-play at the Clinton Foundation in 2016. He resigned in February 2018, as had his boss, Mary McCord, the previous April. Comey advisers Page and James Baker, FBI general counsel, resigned in May 2018.[151]

The Golden Age of Surveillance

Trump has long been aware that the FBI was listening to Trump Tower. The bureau intercepted Trump Tower conversations prior to telephones becoming digital and the subsequent mass collection of call data. Even if he was colluding with the Russians (thus far, there is no evidence of this), Trump knew that it was in his best interest not to communicate via channels under surveillance. It has long been publicly known that domestic communications are intercepted *en masse*.[152]

Perhaps most alarming of all these facts is the plotting to interfere in a major U.S. presidential election by President Obama's own Department of Justice.

Indeed, as the 2016 election was just getting started, the Clintons were under investigation for scandals involving some of these same investigators. As it turns out, the FBI's top officials overseeing the investigations were well aware of the Clintons' pattern of self-enrichment. Furthermore, the FBI top brass was seemingly aware of Hillary Clinton's role in facilitating the sale of U.S. uranium to Russia. The FBI had multiple informants and whistleblowers informing them of Russian bribes, destined *specifically* for Clinton, long before the 2016 election. The DOJ certainly knew about the Russian uranium deal and even signed a gag order prohibiting one of the FBI's informants from going public. More important, the DOJ was a party to Obama's nine-member panel that, along with Clinton's State Department, approved the uranium deal.

CHAPTER 2

THE FBI'S BURIAL OF URANIUM SCANDALS

- The Russians were permitted to acquire nuclear assets throughout America by the Obama administration in 2010.
- The FBI and DOJ had intimate knowledge of ongoing Russian espionage and bribery schemes, and still failed to block the deal.
- Obama's cabinet officials were required to review the deal, but many of these officials had significant ties to the parties who benefitted.
- A well-known example is the $145 million the Clinton Foundation received from shareholders in Uranium One and others tied to the deal.
- Secretary Clinton wasn't the only Obama official with apparent conflicts.

- A Clinton State Department Advisor Simultaneously Worked for the Russians on the Uranium One Takeover.

The FBI-Uranium One Story

The FBI's role in the 2016 election may take months, or even years, to untangle. The alleged wrongdoing within the FBI and its parent agency, the Justice Department, permeated the upper echelons of both. Allegations include conflict of interest, obstruction, lying under oath, mishandling of classified materials, unmasking of U.S. citizens, and felony leaks to the media. The alleged acts were not the work of junior, no-name staffers, but rather top-level operatives.[1]

Names less familiar than Comey and McCabe surface in this swirling investigation of investigators. Top White House officials, including Obama's CIA Director John Brennan, Director of National Intelligence James Clapper, Attorney General Loretta Lynch, and National Security Advisor Susan Rice, among others.[2] All allegations warrant further investigation.

Why would such successful individuals risk their careers, their reputations, and possibly even their freedom, to stop Donald Trump from reaching the White House? After all, serious criminal investigations are underway. GOP lawmakers allege that the FBI's involvement in the Clinton campaign's dossier operation implicates the participants in numerous crimes, and accordingly referred Clinton, Comey, Lynch, Yates, Strzok and Page for criminal investigation.[3] At least one lawmaker has alleged treason.[4] President Trump has also alleged treason.[5]

The truth is simple: They were protecting their own interests.

The FBI and DOJ players in the 2016 election have complex financial interests. General schedule U.S. government employee salaries are capped around $136,000.[6] Senior Executive Service (SES) employees earn a maximum $189,600.[7] Most U.S. government employees earn less than half of SES, with an average salary of $82,000.[8] FBI and DOJ employees often take their experience and contacts to the private sector to advise large corporations. Top officials are worth millions to major corporations, as evidenced by the seven-figure salaries of former attorney general Eric Holder and former FBI directors Mueller and Comey. They have earned massive sums advising some of the largest banks and corporations in the world.[9]

The financial interests of the world's largest corporations and the financial services industry often overlap significantly.[10] The Justice Department has been criticized for favoring big banks and major corporate interests in the aftermath of the 2007–2008 financial crisis.[11] The Clintons' billion-dollar foundation has received vast amounts of support from heavily regulated corporations such as energy giant Exxon, financial titan Goldman Sachs, and defense contractors including Lockheed Martin (among other foundation donors who also lobbied Clinton's State Department).[12] Silicon Valley billionaires from Facebook, Google, Amazon, and Microsoft donated heavily to Hillary Clinton's political campaigns, and in some cases to the Clinton Foundation.[13] Goldman Sachs paid Clinton $675,000 for just three speeches.[14] This became a campaign issue when Clinton refused to release the Goldman Sachs transcripts.[15] In 2009, Secretary Clinton delivered the Dean Acheson Lecture for the U.S. Institute of Peace. Earlier that year, Lockheed Martin had donated $1 million to sponsor that speech for five years.[16] Combined, the Clintons have been paid over $153 million since 2001 for their orations.[17]

The FBI and DOJ characters in this story are top white-collar criminal prosecutors. Key figures such as Comey, Lynch, Mueller, and Mueller's team have repeatedly taken beneficial exits through the D.C. revolving door. Often, their private sector interests are closely aligned with Clinton interests. Some of these key figures have directly worked for the Clintons or their donors. Some have even donated to the Clintons themselves. The revolving door is not a new phenomenon, but when the top law enforcement officials in the country weave back and forth like the above individuals, justice appears conflicted. Perhaps even compromised.

In May 2017, Mueller left a lucrative job at WilmerHale, a white-shoe firm with close ties to Clinton, to become special counsel in the Justice Department's Russian collusion investigation. Mueller then tapped three of his colleagues, WilmerHale attorneys James Quarles, Jeannie Rhee, and Aaron Zebley, to join the special counsel team. During the 2016 election cycle, WilmerHale employees donated more to Hillary Clinton ($326,798) than all GOP candidates combined ($226,926).[18] Quarles and Rhee maxed out their contributions to Clinton's 2016 presidential campaign. Rhee even legally represented both the Clinton Foundation and Clinton personally in court.[19]

Mueller's former chief of staff at the FBI, Zebley, was the personal attorney for Clinton's IT aide, Justin Cooper. Cooper was investigated by the FBI and Senate for his role in setting up the Clinton email server and destroying her BlackBerry smartphones "with a hammer" (Zebley was accused of "stonewalling" Senate investigators). Zebley is described as Mueller's "right hand man" and earned $10,000 writing Mueller's private speeches.[20] As of this writing, both Rhee and Zebley remain on Mueller's team, despite the obvious conflicts. The FBI agent who questioned Clinton's aides, including Justin Cooper, was none other than Peter Strzok.

As noted, Strzok and his mistress/colleague Page were ousted from Mueller's team only after their pro-Clinton/anti-Trump texts surfaced.

As previously discussed, the FBI and subsequent Mueller investigation relied on the work of Clinton contractor Glenn Simpson. Simpson's wife, Mary Jacoby, credits her husband and his company, Fusion GPS, with creating the dossier operation and the resulting FBI investigation.[21] Jacoby has deep ties to Little Rock and many mutual friends with the Clintons. Jacoby allegedly worked as a file clerk at the Rose Law Firm where Hillary Clinton worked from 1977 until 1992.[22] It seems Jacoby and Simpson met while working at *Roll Call* (A U.S.-based *Economist* publication) and were married in 1994 in Little Rock. The pair later reported for *The Wall Street Journal*, among other publications.[23]

James Comey, another key player with complex Clinton connections, worked for defense contractor Lockheed Martin between 2005 and 2010.[24] Comey was the chairman of the U.S. Chamber of Commerce National Chamber Litigation Center during the same time frame. As general counsel and senior vice president at Lockheed, Comey earned undisclosed millions in compensation—more than $6 million in combined salary and stock options in 2009 alone.[25] Mueller's FBI granted numerous contracts to Lockheed Martin during Comey's tenure. Despite the 2008 downturn, Lockheed Martin's stock value nearly doubled in the Comey years, and has continued to grow since. Comey left Lockheed in September 2010, but his enrichment from the company continued.[26] In October 2010, the American Chamber of Commerce in Egypt paid Bill Clinton $250,000 for a speech.[27] Lockheed Martin, a member of that organization and a Clinton donor, was suspected by some of helping arrange that speech. Just three days prior to the speech, Clinton's State Department approved two contracts for Lockheed Martin. In 2010, the

State Department signed off on seventeen contracts with Lockheed Martin. Lockheed Martin has significant involvement in the U.S. nuclear industry and paid Comey lavish sums to advise the company on the legality of its operations.[28] It seems Lockheed, Comey, and the Clintons have been good for one another's businesses.

Comey, McCabe, and their colleagues at the FBI are implicated in allegations by the Clinton and Trump campaigns regarding meddling in the 2016 election. So are former attorney general Loretta Lynch, former deputy AG Sally Yates, former DOJ deputy Bruce Ohr, and others at the DOJ. Coincidentally, a number of these individuals also have a long history of overseeing Clinton matters. Deputy AG Rod Rosenstein, special counsel Robert Mueller, and associates (such as special counsel investigator Andrew Weissmann, who attended Clinton's star-studded post-election party in New York) have also been involved with investigations into Team Clinton shenanigans—even the various Russian uranium scandals.[29] Many of the FBI's pro-Clinton associates have worked together for decades at the same offices in New York and Washington, D.C. Their connections are tangled and blurred—often a hallmark of Clinton activities.

Whether selling access or favors to corporate donors, transferring missile technology to Chinese communists amid illegal donations, or facilitating the sale of U.S. uranium assets to Russian aggressors, the Clintons have shown a willingness to negotiate for just about anything.[30]

Not long after the spring 2015 release of *Clinton Cash*, public news reports widely confirmed Schweizer's findings relating to the apparent quid pro quos.[31] By summer 2015, as the 2016 campaigns were just beginning, multiple FBI field offices opened investigations into the Clinton's shady dealings and apparent foreign influence peddling.[32] According to Schweizer, the FBI repeatedly sought his counsel. The

Clintons *had* taken money from individuals whom Clinton met with at the State Department. Clinton had granted them favors, perhaps even government contracts.[33] For FBI agents working the case, this was a major problem, and may have been illegal.

As it turns out, the FBI and DOJ officials at Main Justice in D.C. that were overseeing the investigations were well aware that Hillary Clinton was the target of the Russian influence operation.[34] The DOJ has a lead role on the Committee on Foreign Investment in the United States (CFIUS), which reviewed the Uranium One transaction. Top DOJ and FBI officials bore some of the blame for failing to block the transaction in 2010.[35] This crucial fact could explain why top DOJ personnel were stonewalling the field office investigations involving Clinton's Uranium One conflicts.

The DOJ's role in the 2010 CFIUS review is troubling. The DOJ reviewed the uranium sale, along with Clinton's State Department and other top Obama cabinet officials— yet none of them raised any objections. More troubling is the fact that the DOJ allowed the deal to proceed, despite an ongoing FBI investigation into Russian espionage and racketeering schemes targeting the U.S. uranium industry and alleged evidence of bribes specifically implicating Clinton.[36]

With hard evidence of these schemes, the FBI, the DOJ, and other Obama agencies nevertheless allowed the Russian takeover of 20 percent of U.S. uranium production capacity. There have been numerous convictions of Russian players, but they did not occur until *after* Obama's top officials cleared the Russian nuclear deal.[37] The DOJ's failure to raise public objections to the Uranium One purchase, despite its knowledge of ongoing bribery and espionage schemes, raises a major red flag. The fact that Clinton's State Department was not the only party in the CFIUS review with conflicting motives must be fully investigated. Clinton's defenders seem to think that this exonerates Clinton, when in fact it implicates Obama.

Revelations in 2016 highlight Obama administration failures to prevent Russian interference in matters critical to U.S. national security. Beginning in 2009, Mueller's FBI directly investigated Russian espionage rings and bribery schemes. Andrew McCabe and Rod Rosenstein appear to have played a central role.[38] These men also failed to prevent Russian meddling in the 2016 election. Russian infiltration efforts are not new. In fact, many of the Russian nuclear scandals linked to the Clintons began almost twenty-five years ago with a deal called Megatons to Megawatts. This deal is directly tied to more recent Russian influence operations in which the FBI was a central player.[39]

The Megatons to Megawatts (HEU-LEU) Scheme

In January 1994, Bill Clinton's administration signed a deal under the guise of nuclear disarmament with the fledgling post-Soviet regime in Moscow. In a valiant effort to turn "swords to ploughshares," Team Clinton and its Russian counterparts agreed to ship Russian nuclear warhead materials, namely highly enriched uranium (HEU), to the U.S. to be converted into fuel for U.S. nuclear reactors. The $12 billion deal was seen as a win-win: The U.S. claimed a post-Cold War victory while securing essential energy resources, and Russia unloaded 500 tons of HEU on favorable terms, thanks to Clinton's Commerce Department changing certain trade regulations—primarily the suspension of economic anti-dumping laws.[40]

The specifics of the deal were negotiated by Vice President Al Gore on the U.S. side and Viktor Chernomyrdin on the Russian side, and the group became known as the Gore–Chernomyrdin Commission.[41] This commission hammered out the details, and a company called the U.S. Enrichment Corp. (USEC) was given the lucrative task of "down-blending" the highly enriched uranium from Russian warheads to create low enriched uranium (LEU) for U.S. reactor fuel. The Department of Energy (DOE) was the lead agency for administering the terms of the agreement.[42]

Gore's lieutenant and national security advisor, Leon Fuerth, was intimately involved with the HEU-LEU negotiations *and* became the target of an illegal Russian spy ring between 2006 and 2010.[43] According to an archive of a Russian spy's website, Fuerth was an advisor (though Fuerth denies this). Fuerth's bio, according to the spy website, stated he was a "senior administration official responsible for the operation of bi-national commissions with Russia, Ukraine, Kazakhstan, Egypt and South Africa."[44] Most of those countries play a significant role in the global uranium trade and several even have direct links to the Clinton Uranium One scandal.[45]

Gore, Fuerth, and Clinton's deputy energy secretary, Daniel Poneman, were key in the negotiation of the HEU-LEU deal. While at Clinton's DOE in the 1990s, Poneman directly oversaw the negotiation and implementation of the HEU-LEU deal.[46] Between 1993 and 1996, he was the special assistant to the president and senior director for nonproliferation and export controls at the National Security Council. According to Poneman's bio, he left the DOE to join Covington & Burling, and later became a partner at Hogan & Hartson (now Hogan Lovells), both major law firms serving major corporations, including those with nuclear interests.[47] These firms also employed former federal prosecutors, including attorneys general Eric Holder and Loretta Lynch. In 2001, Poneman joined the Scowcroft Group, a defense industry consulting and lobbying powerhouse with close White House connections. Poneman terminated his employment with the Scowcroft Group in May 2009 when he returned to government service.[48]

With the return of the White House to Democratic control in 2009, Poneman was appointed deputy energy secretary by Obama. At the time, Poneman had an interest in the Hogan & Hartson Partners Investment Fund which had undisclosed investments in companies the DOE could influence. On May 21, 2009, Poneman received a conflict of interest waiver, meaning he was allowed to remain invested despite his apparent ability to profit from DOE decisions.[49] Poneman received a second ethics waiver in March 2011 regarding his relationship with the Scowcroft Group and Scowcroft client General Electric. Absent such a waiver, Poneman was "prohibited...from participating in any particular matter" involving the former client. In January 2010, DOE announced the group's president and founder, Brent Scowcroft, would lead a presidential commission on America's nuclear future.[50] Deputy secretary Poneman undoubtedly played a role in selecting his former employer to head a panel that would "provide recommendations" regarding America's nuclear future.[51] According to the 2011 ethics waiver, Poneman stated he had "no relationship" with the Scowcroft Group since he left in 2009. The Commission was immediately criticized by a nuclear watchdog organization for lacking credibility and at least eighty-eight environmental organizations urged DOE to reject the recommendations.[52]

Poneman was an integral player overseeing Russian nuclear deals like the Megatons to Megawatts program in the mid-nineties. From his post then at the National Security Council, Poneman moved to the private sector for Hogan and Scowcroft for thirteen years before his 2009–2014 DOE run. He went back through the revolving door, leaving the DOE and landing a $1.7 million annual salary as CEO of USEC, rebranded as Centrus Energy. This departure is significant because of USEC's long history with the Russians and the favorable contracts, loans, and other "creative" assistance (which some auditors deemed illegal) that Poneman's DOE had granted USEC.[53]

The close relationship between Uranium One, USEC, the Russian nuclear agency and its subsidiaries, and decision-makers in Washington is alarming. The fact that Poneman cashed in on his experience at the very corporation his agency helped enrich was an outrage, and the media reported it as such.[54] The Project on Government Oversight (POGO) investigated the complex history between DOE and USEC, DOE's role in oversight, and Poneman's exit from DOE to lead USEC. Once these developments came to light, the POGO raised objections.[55] The POGO neglected to mention Poneman's longstanding role advancing USEC's dealings with Russian interests.[56]

In March 2015, the website *Politico* published a blistering report titled "Ex-energy official's $1.7 million gig draws fire." The report questioned Poneman's becoming CEO of a company with a long history of "relying on favors from Washington." Likewise, lawmakers were "concerned [Poneman] may have violated post-employment laws for federal personnel" and wrote a letter to DOE Secretary Ernest Moniz requesting documents relating to Poneman's relationship with USEC. The letter, dated March 30, 2015, was signed by the chairman of the House Oversight Committee and contained a long list of requirements for complying with the request. According to *Politico*, "DOE ethics rules will prohibit Poneman from having any contact with his old agency for two years after his departure." However, the watchdog group Public Citizen acknowledged Poneman's situation is unique and not addressed by "the boilerplate 'cooling off' period."[57]

Poneman is still running Centrus Energy (USEC), and the company continues to make nuclear deals with the Russians, specifically with a Russian nuclear company called JSC Techsnabexport ("Tenex"), even after the company was implicated in nuclear bribery and racketeering schemes.[58] Interestingly, Tenex has a long history with Hogan & Hartson having retained the firm throughout the nineties, even before the Soviet Union fell. Hogan & Hartson sued the U.S. government on behalf of Tenex in 1992.[59]

The Megatons to Megawatts deal, or HEU-LEU, opened the door to direct Russian involvement in America's nuclear sector.[60] A diplomatic cable leaked by Wikileaks reveals Rosatom had plans in 2009 to exploit their relationship with USEC and build an alliance with General Electric (Poneman's former client at Scowcroft Group) in order to strengthen Russia's position in European and Ukrainian energy markets. The cable with was sent to Clinton's State Department and Poneman's Energy Department among other recipients and was titled "Russia Flexes Muscle on Ukraine Nuclear Fuel Supply."[61]

Russia's relationship with USEC, which they then sought to exploit to the detriment of European energy interests, is a direct result of the Clinton-era HEU-LEU deal. The HEU-LEU deal was not only a questionable undertaking, but also a national security risk. Notably, two of the Russian parties involved in the HEU-LEU deal have been sentenced to prison for their roles in bribery, racketeering, extortion, and money laundering schemes. One of them, Russian national Vadim Mikerin, formerly an executive at Tenex, later pleaded guilty to lesser charges, courtesy of a DOJ plea agreement. Moreover, the DOJ and FBI knew about Mikerin and his co-conspirators as early as 2009, well before they finally brought charges against him. It took nearly five years for any indictments to materialize. While Russian state-actors were compromising U.S. national security, the Obama administration made multiple decisions benefitting Russian nuclear interests.[62]

Tenex Bribery

Vadim Mikerin is the son of Evgeny Mikerin, who was a key Russian nuclear official throughout the 1980s and 1990s. Both Evgeny and Vadim Mikerin were instrumental in negotiating the Megatons to Megawatts deal.[63] In May 2010, Vadim Mikerin managed the affairs of Tenex as its Pan American director, and by October 2010, he became the president of a new Tenex subsidiary, Tenam, based in the U.S. The DOE Office of the Inspector General and the FBI opened the investigation into Tenex's crimes no later than 2009. The bribery went on for a decade, between 2004 and 2014, meaning both FBI directors Mueller and Comey played some role in the investigation.[64]

By 2014, Vadim Mikerin emerged as the FBI's primary suspect for receiving kickbacks in exchange for contracts to a transportation company moving uranium across American highways. Executives running the American trucking company Transport Logistics International (TLI) were also charged with serious crimes. According to the October 2014 DOJ indictment, TLI had been paying bribes and kickbacks to Mikerin and Tenex dating back to 2006. The charges were serious and carried a penalty of up to twenty years in prison.[65]

Instead of twenty years, the Obama administration quietly and inexplicably gave Mikerin a relative slap on the wrist. Mikerin pleaded guilty to one count of "conspiracy to commit money laundering," which carries a weaker penalty. He was sentenced to just forty-eight months in prison in late 2015.[66] Not only was Mikerin's sentence weak, but the FBI and DOJ kept silent about the Russian nuclear bribes for years; the indictments were finally issued on August 31, 2015, and the sentencing occurred on December 15, 2015. FBI's Andrew McCabe was involved in the investigation and announced charges against Mikerin et al.[67] The primary DOJ attorneys handling the indictments and plea agreement were Rod Rosenstein and Andrew Weissmann.[68]

The Tenex nuclear bribery scheme implicating Mikerin and others started as early as 1996 and continued unimpeded for fifteen years. The DOJ–DOE investigation began more than a decade later in 2009 and charges were not brought until late 2014, well after the Russians successfully acquired Uranium One, an American uranium asset-holder. As a member of CFIUS, then-attorney general Eric Holder was one of the people responsible for reviewing the 2010 Uranium One sale. The DOJ had evidence that the Uranium One deal was closely connected to the Tenex bribery schemes. Rosatom, the state-owned nuclear agency, now owns both companies.[69] Why didn't the FBI and DOJ act sooner? Why didn't Obama's DOJ raise objections to the Rosatom nuclear takeover?

One explanation may be that McCabe, Rosenstein, and Weissmann primarily handled the federal bribery and racketeering case against Tenex. Suffice it to say, the FBI and the DOJ should have known that the 2010 Uranium One deal should not have been approved because of multiple major red flags. Furthermore, the same FBI and DOJ players who handled the bribery case would show up again, years later, to assist Clinton and to target Trump during the 2016 election. McCabe, Mueller, Rosenstein, Weissmann, and possibly even Comey, played significant roles in Russian influence investigations long before Trump was a political player. Many might contend that those investigations were botched.

The Russian Nuclear Espionage Conspiracy

In July 2010, the Obama administration expelled a ring of nearly a dozen Russian spies from the U.S. These spies, including the notorious Anna Chapman, were charged with acting as unregistered foreign agents, a much more lenient charge than espionage.[70] The spies were deported by the DOJ at the same time that the FBI was also investigating the Tenex bribery scheme.

Between 2006 (or perhaps sooner) and 2010, the FBI tracked the Russian spy ring, while Russian agents were targeting high-level American officials. Some of the spies arrived in the U.S. as early as 1999. By 2010, the Russian spy ring had infiltrated Hillary Clinton's inner circle.[71] This is another major Obama and FBI failure that very few seem to know about.

After a delay that favored Russian dealmakers, Obama allowed Mueller's FBI to bust the spy ring on June 27, 2010. Two days later, on June 29, Bill Clinton was in Moscow taking money from powerful Russians.[72] Putin thanked Clinton for the visit, which included a speech for which he was paid $500,000 by a Kremlin-controlled bank tied to Uranium One. The State Department quickly reviewed and cleared Clinton's speech payment of any conflicts just two days after receiving the request. The speech was arranged in March 2010—shortly after Hillary Clinton returned from Moscow where she had met with Putin. Clinton's half-million-dollar payday in Moscow is further significant as the former president sought approval to meet directly with Rosatom supervisory board member, Arkady Dvorkovich.[73]

On July 1, 2010, *The Economist* reported on Clinton's meeting with Putin, during which the Russian leader reportedly joked and tried to downplay the Kremlin's illegal spy ring that had just been exposed. He seemingly mocked the entire incident at the expense of the U.S. law enforcement community:

> In a conversation with Bill Clinton [Putin] almost managed to turn the whole thing into a joke: "You've chosen the right time to come to Moscow. I hear your police have got carried away and put people in jail...but that's their job after all; really, they are all just doing their job..."[74]

Why would the U.S. give Russia its spies back so easily? President Obama demanded it, for one thing. Obama knew about the spies and authorized their release less than two weeks after their capture. Furthermore, Obama was angry that the FBI had even brought the matter to his attention. According to Obama's then defense secretary, Robert Gates, the spy ring threatened Barack Obama and Hillary Clinton's "reset" of Russian relations. Reporter Eli Lake writes:

> The president seemed as angry at Mueller for wanting to arrest the illegals and at Panetta [the CIA director] for wanting to exfiltrate the source from Moscow as he was at the Russians," Gates wrote. [Gates] quoted Obama as saying: "Just as we're getting on track with the Russians, this? This is a throwback to the Cold War.... We put START, Iran, the whole relationship with Russia at risk for this kind of thing?" Gates recounts that the vice president wanted to ignore the entire issue because it threatened to disrupt an upcoming visit from Russia's president at the time, Dmitry Medvedev.[75]

The book *Russian Roulette* by Michael Isikoff and David Corn provides another clue:

> At a meeting in the White House Situation Room, FBI director Robert Mueller informed Obama's aides the Bureau intended to roll up the Russians. But deputy national security adviser Tom Donilon raised an objection. Medvedev had just arrived in Washington for more talks with Obama. To bust a Russian spy ring could blow up the reset, he argued.
>
> The discussion got intense—until Leon Panetta, the CIA director, weighed in. He said that Donilon needed to think long and hard about a potential Washington Post headline that would read, "The U.S. failed to arrest a group of Russian spies." At that point, Panetta later noted, "I saw the lights go off in his head." Soon after the meeting, according to Panetta, Donilon okayed the arrest, but he asked the FBI to wait until Medvedev was out of American airspace.[76]

As Obama's deputy national security advisor, Tom Donilon clearly had a lot of sway. Why would he protect a Russian spy ring against the advice of the FBI and CIA directors? As noted in *Russian Roulette*, Obama and Clinton's deals with the Russians were clearly a priority for Donilon. Furthermore, he tried to keep the Russian espionage ring a secret. The FBI knew that the spy ring had infiltrated Clinton's inner circle and had even compromised a former official with a long history of involvement in Clinton's nuclear deals. Donilon's only concern with the Russian spy ring seemed to be the risk of its becoming publicized.

Before joining the Obama administration, Donilon had earned $3.9 million in one year as a partner at the firm O'Melveny and Myers (OMM). Donilon earned this sizable sum by directly representing OMM clients such as Goldman Sachs and Obama's future commerce secretary, Penny Pritzker.[77]

Donilon's firm had significant ties to the Russian company purchasing Uranium One. A close colleague of Donilon's at OMM, Theodore Kassinger, is considered an expert on CFIUS matters. Between 2010 and 2013, Kassinger advised Russian interests on U.S. nuclear regulatory matters. Specifically, Kassinger was the lead counsel for ARMZ Uranium Holding Co. (ARMZ), a Russian mining company and Rosatom subsidiary, during the completion of the Uranium One takeover (which was reviewed by CFIUS in 2010 and completed in 2013).[78] Shockingly, Kassinger was simultaneously the chairman of the State Department's Advisory Committee on International Economic Policy (ACIEP) during that time. In late 2009, Kassinger and others on the ACIEP made significant policy recommendations to Clinton's State Department—specifically relating to foreign investment from state-owned enterprises like Rosatom.[79]

One of Clinton's deputies, Jose W. Fernandez, who was assistant secretary of state for economic, energy, and business affairs from 2009 to 2013, has taken responsibility for the State Department's role in the CFIUS approval of Uranium One.[80] Fernandez met with Kassinger repeatedly throughout 2010 while ARMZ inched closer to the uranium takeover.[81]

An unreported bombshell is that Secretary Clinton met with Kassinger and Fernandez during an ACIEP meeting on April 15, 2010, just six months before Fernandez (on behalf of Clinton's State Department) reviewed the sale on CFIUS. Kassinger met again with Fernandez during another ACIEP meeting on August 12, 2010, just 19 days before

Uranium One's shareholders approved the sale to ARMZ and shortly before CFIUS approved the transaction.[82] When *Clinton Cash* revealed the Uranium One deal in April 2015, Fernandez immediately jumped in front of the bus. Leaked emails between Fernandez and Clinton's fixer, John Podesta, may shed light on Fernandez's decision to do so. Podesta had landed Fernandez a spot on the Center for American Progress Board of Trustees the month previous. Fernandez found his position "extremely rewarding."[83]

This amounts to a Russian nuclear agent—Kassinger—working *within* the State Department alongside that department's principal CFIUS representative—Fernandez—who approved the Russian takeover of American uranium assets. Furthermore, Fernandez appears to have been rewarded for taking the heat for the deal via a quid pro quo with Podesta.

Figure 1: State Department Adviser Ted Kassinger meets with Clinton and Jose Fernandez months before Uranium One review. Kassinger helped Russians complete nuclear takeover.[84]

For his part, Tom Donilon returned to OMM in May 2014, seven months after ARMZ took full control of Uranium One.[85] At OMM, Donilon and his close colleague Kassinger work together on trade deals involving national security, and they are specifically praised for their CFIUS expertise.[86] In addition, Donilon's past client, Goldman Sachs, played a major role as the financial advisor to the Russians during the 2010 Uranium One transaction, which Obama's CFIUS reviewed.[87]

Who was Donilon *really* working for? Why did he try to cover up the Russian spy ring while the Russians were seeking CFIUS approval, an area in which he was an expert? Did Obama know about Donilon's commercial ties to the deal?

President Obama certainly knew of the Russian spy ring. As noted above, Obama, Donilon, and Vice President Joe Biden seemed agitated that exposing the spy ring would disrupt their ongoing deals with Russia.[88] Obama also knew that there was no internal oversight in Clinton's State Department because he had allowed the department to operate without an inspector general (IG) for five years. This vacancy lasted over Clinton's entire tenure (2009–2013) and was an unprecedented duration for the agency to operate without an IG. In fact, by failing to appoint an IG, Obama effectively *ensured* there were no checks in place at the Clinton State Department.[89]

The Uranium One Deal

As previously discussed, the Uranium One deal involves a company closely tied to the Clintons with significant access to U.S. domestic nuclear production. The purchase by Rosatom gave Vladimir Putin a strategic nuclear foothold in the U.S. Because it had significant national and energy security implications, the transaction required a full review by Obama's top cabinet secretaries.

Clinton Cash revealed that the State Department had been compromised at the highest levels. The secretary of state had provided her closest advisors, Huma Abedin and Cheryl Mills, with Special Government Employee (SGE) status.[90] SGE "waivers" allowed Clinton's staff to simultaneously hold positions within the State Department and the Clinton Foundation, while the latter received over $145 million from no fewer than nine investors linked to Uranium One.[91]

Furthermore, the Clinton Foundation concealed payments totaling $2.35 million from Ian Telfer, the chairman of Uranium One.[92] This concealment of payments was a major violation of the Clinton–Obama MOU. A strict condition for Clinton's confirmation as secretary of state was prompt disclosure of such payments, per the MOU. After *Clinton Cash* revealed the concealed payments, the Clintons quickly apologized and retroactively disclosed 21 secret donors, many linked to the Uranium One deal. This seems like an admission of guilt. Yet the Clintons neglected to reveal more than 1,100 additional secret donors, citing privacy rights. Those donations have still not been disclosed, in flagrant violation of the MOU.[93]

As the deal proceeded throughout 2010, lawmakers on both sides of the aisle were outraged and demanded explanations. In particular, representatives Ileana Ros-Lehtinen (R-FL), Spencer Bachus (R-AL), Peter King (R-NY), and Buck McKeon (R-CA) warned CFIUS chairman and treasury secretary Timothy Geithner that "signing over control of this U.S. uranium processing facility to the Russian government unnecessarily jeopardizes U.S. security interests."[94] By the time their letter to CFIUS was made public in October 2010, it was too late. The State Department and the other CFIUS members, including the DOJ, had raised no objections. Ultimately, the Uranium One deal came and went with little media scrutiny and the congressional inquiries apparently went unanswered.

It took more than four years for the story to be told. In April 2015, *The New York Times* vetted and confirmed Peter Schweizer's findings with a blistering front-page exposé titled "Cash Flowed to Clinton Foundation Amid Russian Uranium Deal."[95] Pushback on the story from the Clinton camp was immediate and centered around two major claims: first, that Schweizer did not have any evidence of a quid pro quo (a claim Schweizer didn't make); second, that CFIUS is made up of multiple agencies, and Hillary Clinton's alleged conflicts played no part in the acquiescence of others.[96]

On April 26, 2015, ABC chose George Stephanopoulos to grill Schweizer repeatedly using these very talking points. As Stephanopoulos put it, "There's no smoking gun, no evidence that she changed the policy based on donations to the foundation."[97] He was soon excoriated for his biased interview with Schweizer.[98] Stephanopoulos, who had served as communications director in Bill Clinton's presidential campaign and in his administration as a senior aide from 1993 to 1996, was forced to recuse himself from hosting any 2016 political debates after it was revealed that he was a major Clinton Foundation donor and had failed to disclose this information.[99] The Clintons and their defenders seem to overlook the fact that *Clinton Cash* presents 180-plus pages of *solid evidence* backed by over 600 endnotes and sources. This makes their other excuse, the CFIUS defense, particularly interesting.

Are Clinton defenders implying that the other agencies who make up CFIUS are also somehow conflicted? Why else would they, or anyone, have signed off on the Russian takeover of U.S. nuclear assets?

CFIUS is a nine-member composition of the president's top cabinet officials.[100] Clinton's State Department was not the only Obama agency to give the Russians the green light. The FBI and the DOJ had knowledge of Russian espionage and bribery schemes *before* the Russian takeover of Uranium One. As the DOJ was a party to CFIUS, this amounts to either a massive failure or a major conflict for it.[101]

CFIUS Compromised

Clinton defenders used the unanimity of the CFIUS panel's decision to ameliorate her responsibility. So, nine of Obama's most critical agencies raised no objections and unanimously approved the Russian takeover of nuclear assets based in the U.S.[102] Is it better that nine agencies supported this travesty rather than just one? We do not know the motivations of the other eight agencies, but we do know Hillary Clinton accepted cash and granted favors—actions that have been widely reported and confirmed.[103] Her aides' emails prove it, and a full investigation is long overdue.[104] But what about those other eight agencies that were also CFIUS members?

According to the Treasury Department, the CFIUS parties are:

1. Department of the Treasury (Chair)
2. Department of Justice
3. Department of Homeland Security
4. Department of Commerce
5. Department of Defense
6. Department of State
7. Department of Energy
8. Office of the U.S. Trade Representative
9. Office of Science & Technology Policy[105]

The secretaries of these agencies at the time of the 2010 transaction were, in order, as follows: Timothy Geithner, Eric Holder, Janet Napolitano, Gary Locke, Robert Gates, Hillary Clinton, Steven Chu, Ron Kirk, and John Holdren.[106]

Most of those agency heads are multi-millionaires with hundreds of complex investments in a wide range of stocks and hedge funds.[107] It is important to note that Uranium One, like many commodity deals, was every bit a stock market play as it was a physical resource play.[108] Obama's CFIUS players had close links to investment funds who were heavily involved in Uranium One.[109] A full accounting of each of the CFIUS parties' various financial interests is outside the scope of this book. However, at first glance, they all have potential ties to Russian nuclear deals.

The "CFIUS Nine" and Their Relevant Connections

Two of the nine agencies on CFIUS have documented conflicts related to the Uranium One deal. The Russians attempted to bribe State Department secretary Hillary Clinton. They may have been successful. Eric Holder's DOJ and Robert Mueller's FBI seemingly covered up the Russian lies, the Russian spies, and the Russian bribes *during* the CFIUS review.

The Department of Treasury heads CFIUS. Then secretary Timothy Geithner has long been cited as a friend of Goldman Sachs.[110] Goldman Sachs represented the Russians in the uranium transaction. They claimed that the deal was unprecedented (likely due to CFIUS approval).[111] Geithner denies having any formal ties to Goldman Sachs, yet his chief of staff, Mark Patterson, was a top lobbyist for the company. Other Department of Treasury staff were also linked to Goldman as well.[112]

Department of Homeland Security (DHS) secretary Janet Napolitano had long been working to ban mining on certain federal lands, and this benefitted the Russians as domestic uranium supplies dwindled.[113] Commerce Secretary Gary Locke has longstanding ties to the American nuclear industry. As governor of Washington state, Locke oversaw the contaminated and decommissioned Hanford nuclear site in the southeastern part of the state and advocated for increased funding for nuclear contractors such as Lockheed Martin, Fluor Daniel, Bechtel Northwest Corp., and CH2M Hill.[114] Locke, the first Chinese American governor, has been caught up in numerous campaign finance scandals, including the Clinton's 1996 Chinagate fundraising scandal.[115]

In the mid-1990s, convicted DNC staffer John Huang arranged six fundraisers for Locke's 1996 gubernatorial bid. Suspicious funds were raised and linked to Clinton's Chinese associates—Charlie Trie and Ng Lap Seng—and Locke reluctantly returned a portion of the donations and was cleared of any intentional wrongdoing.[116] Locke's ties to Uranium One are not through China though; they are through a Seattle-based firm called Davis Wright Tremaine (DWT). From 2004 and 2009, Locke was a high-ranking partner and co-chair at DWT before joining the Obama administration.[117]

In 2007, Uranium One, then based in Toronto, began buying American uranium assets. A large cluster of nuclear assets came from an American company called Energy Metals Corp.[118] DWT represented Energy Metals Corp. in the United States for the $1.6 billion sale to the Canadian company.[119] The deal apparently required CFIUS approval according to a filing that mentions DWT.[120] CFIUS approved the sale in July 2007 and the deal was completed on August 10, 2007.[121] This deal was a significant acquisition for Uranium One and paved the way for the Russian takeover in 2010. Locke left DWT in 2009 to lead Obama's

Commerce Department. Locke was in charge of Commerce during the Uranium One CFIUS decision before serving as the U.S. ambassador to China from 2011 to 2014. In 2015, Locke returned to DWT to advise international clients on trade, regulatory, and investment matters. That same year, DWT announced they had successfully advised on another foreign acquisition of U.S. uranium assets, which required national security (CFIUS) review.[122]

Defense Secretary Robert Gates was close to Hillary Clinton and supported her version of the "Russian reset." She initially gave pushback on Obama's idea, declaring, "I'm not giving up anything for nothing," but later called it "a brilliant stroke."[123] Gates, keeping with the reset, even switched positions on a missile defense program in Poland—a program he had previously advocated.[124] Obama's decision (advised and executed by Gates) was praised by Putin who expected more concessions to come (reportedly without offering any compromise from Russia). In the U.S. press, the decision was widely ridiculed for demonstrating weakness, particularly as Russia had just recently invaded the neighboring country of Georgia.[125] One Russian official reportedly mocked the reversal plans calling them "birthday presents for President Medvedev and Prime Minister Putin."[126]

Before becoming secretary of defense in 2006, Gates was the chairman of the independent trustees of the Fidelity funds and held $1.1 million in Fidelity investments.[127] Fidelity also happened to be the single largest, western-based shareholder in Uranium One at the time Russia completed its acquisition in late 2010.[128] Perhaps coincidentally, Fidelity also held 8.32 percent of the U.S. enrichment company (USEC) as the Uranium One deal was underway in 2010, making it the single largest shareholder in that Russian nuclear affiliate (via HEU-LEU) as well.[129] Robert Gates and Fidelity have a long history together, and Gates was even named as a defendant in a 2010 class action securities lawsuit against Fidelity. Gates was identified as the Chairman of Fidelity's Independent Trustees for the Fair Value Oversight Committee, according to court filings. The suit settled for $7.5 million.[130] In 2010, Gates was invested in 19 separate Fidelity funds. His combined Fidelity holdings were worth between approximately $1.5 million and $3.5 million.[131]

The DOE's Steven Chu allowed his deputy, Daniel Poneman, to handle CFIUS matters.[132] Poneman, as discussed, negotiated the Russian nuclear deals in the 1990s, making him unquestionably aware of their tactics. Furthermore, he remained closely connected to a law firm that had represented Rosatom interests and still represents major nuclear clients.[133] Poneman now earns seven figures running Centrus Energy Corp., formerly USEC, the largest beneficiary of Russian uranium deals.[134]

The Office of the U.S. Trade Representative's (USTR's) Ron Kirk was a lobbyist for Energy Future Holdings before he joined the Obama administration. In 2014, after Kirk left the Obama administration, he joined the Clean and Safe Energy (CASEnergy) Coalition as a lobbyist, where he spent much of his time "championing nuclear energy."[135]

In October 2010, John Holdren was given a service award at a gala partly sponsored by General Atomics, one of the largest nuclear companies in the world.[136] Steven Chu, Daniel Poneman, and Holdren were seen chatting and drinking with a private group on the margins of the event.[137]

When one member of a committee has a conflict of interest, a recusal is expected or perhaps forgiven. But what happens when the entire committee has intersecting conflicts? We may never know the full involvement of Obama administration officials until Congress or the DOJ subpoenas the bank records of everyone responsible for the Uranium One–CFIUS decision.

President Obama allowed Clinton's financial conflicts to fester during her tenure as Secretary of State, despite criticism. Perhaps Obama's complicity in Hillary Clinton's ethical dilemmas is what compromised CFIUS. How could Clinton have compromised Obama? How Obama permitted her State Department to operate is telling.

Hillary Clinton's closest aides—Huma Abedin, Cheryl Mills, and Justin Cooper—had multiple Clinton-backed revenue streams.[138] Clinton and her State Department aides frequently blurred ethical lines by communicating with, and granting State Department access to, Clinton Foundation donors.[139] Also, these individuals arranged and approved speaking engagements for Bill Clinton—a duty clearly not in typical State Department job descriptions.[140]

Obama Compromised by Clinton

To appreciate Hillary Clinton's role on CFIUS, one must understand the nature of the Clinton pay-to-play model. The Clintons accepted payments in the form of speaking honoraria to Bill Clinton and donations to the Clinton legacy project—the group of charitable initiatives known as the Clinton Foundation. Many of those payments came from foreign corporations, governments, and individuals potentially seeking access and favors from Hillary Clinton's State Department.[141] All told, the Clintons earned just under $105 million between 2001 and 2013, when she stepped down as Secretary of State. After amassing this large sum of money, Hillary Clinton famously declared that they were "dead broke" when they left the White House in 2001.[142] The Clinton Foundation would eventually amass more than $2.5 billion in total commitments.[143]

Less than a month after Obama was elected in November 2008, Hillary Clinton was tapped as his choice for Secretary of

State and signed the aforementioned MOU with the Obama presidential transition team (PTT). It sought to resolve what would be Clinton's ethical quagmire. The December 2008 memo began:

> WHEREAS, in considering Senator Clinton's potential service as Secretary of State, the Parties seek to ensure that the Foundation may continue its important philanthropic activities around the world, which do valuable and critical work...[144]

The memo went on to detail a "set of protocols" to mitigate and indeed absolve Clinton of any conflicts, or even the appearance of conflicts. However, the MOU was simply a formality—a means to an end. Over time, Clinton repeatedly violated the spirit and terms of the agreement, primarily by concealing payments.[145]

The Clinton–Obama MOU should have been invalidated from the start. Two parties cannot agree to disregard laws like the conflict of interest and bribery statutes delineated in Title 18 of the U.S. criminal code. Signing such a document is unseemly at best and a political liability at worst.[146] Furthermore, an MOU may not even be legally binding nor enforceable. This means that the Clinton–Obama MOU was basically a "gentleman's" agreement—largely toothless.[147]

That may be the reason why President Obama never signed the document. Rather, Obama's top advisor, Valerie Jarrett, signed the document in her capacity as co-chair of the transition team—a *private*, tax-exempt entity, or 501(c)(4).[148] Another co-chair of the transition team was none other than Clinton-fixer John Podesta.[149] Inexplicably, the MOU not only continues to protect Clinton from conflict of interest and bribery allegations to this day, but it has also allowed the Clintons to collect untold billions of dollars in speech payments and donations to their foundation. The MOU is at the heart of the Uranium One scandal, as it was repeatedly violated due to the concealment of foreign donors like Uranium One's chairman Ian Telfer and others implicated in the deal. The fact that concealed Clinton donations were only disclosed years later (and only after they were discovered independently) demonstrates the MOU was essentially toothless. This is especially true given the fact there are over 1,000 undisclosed Clinton-affiliated donors.[150]

A Review of Shady Russian Nuclear Deals and the 2016 Election Implications

Russian involvement in the U.S. nuclear industry began in 1993 with the Megatons to Megawatts deal and continued through the Uranium One sale in 2010. The Clinton officials who approved these deals remained involved until the Russians took complete control of the company by buying all remaining shares in 2013.[151]

The Clintons and their allies were targeted by a Russian spy ring and a Russian bribery scheme—both involving nuclear concerns. The FBI knew about these schemes for years and only busted the Russian conspirators after they had apparently infiltrated the Secretary of State's inner circle. Obama should have been outraged. Yet he and his top officials seemed more concerned that the publicity would threaten the thawed relationship with Russia under "the reset." Obama's most vocal advocate for keeping the Russian spy ring under wraps, Tom Donilon, happened to be a CFIUS legal expert in the private sector at a firm that would eventually represent Russian nuclear company.[152] Donilon was apparently a revolving door expert as well, making $3.4 million the year *before* he joined the Obama White House. His colleague at that firm, Ted Kassinger, simultaneously advised Clinton's State Department and the Russian nuclear company linked to the nuclear bribery schemes. A Kassinger associate within the State Department was Jose Fernandez. Fernandez claimed responsibility for the State Department's 2010 CFIUS review and Kassinger helped complete the Russian nuclear takeover. Yet the State Department isn't the only seemingly compromised agency.

Both FBI investigations, the Russian spy ring and the nuclear bribery, should have been raised as national security concerns during the 2010 CFIUS review of Rosatom's takeover of Uranium One.[153] Yet the FBI (and thus the DOJ) apparently failed to raise these concerns.[154] The FBI is supposed to be an independent agency, and yet FBI Director Robert Mueller allowed the White House National Security Advisor to dictate the terms for the spy ring bust. Who in the Obama White House (besides Clinton, Donilon, and Poneman) had commercial ties to Russian nuclear deals? Why did the FBI remain silent about Russian conspiracies until after it was too late to prevent the Russian takeover of American nuclear assets?

These are important questions, given the players and their agencies roles in CFIUS review. The DOJ's Rod Rosenstein, the DOE's John Hartman, and the FBI's Andrew McCabe issued the first Tenex charges.[155] Rosenstein and the DOJ's Andrew Weissmann signed the subsequent plea agreement in the case in August 2015.[156] By late April 2017, Rosenstein had ascended to deputy attorney general and appointed Robert Mueller as special counsel three weeks later to investigate Russian attempts to interfere with the 2016 election. This move was curious considering the special counsel investigation was initiated after Comey's dismissal—a move Rosenstein strongly recommended.[157] Weissmann, described as Mueller's "pit bull," was handpicked for Mueller's current investigation.[158] McCabe, as you well know by now, was the FBI's deputy director under Comey, and both men were fired.[159]

The fact that all these men play or played a major role in the ongoing 2016 election investigation *and* played a role in the Russian bribery schemes that festered for nearly a decade may be a coincidence; a growing body of evidence suggests otherwise. The DOJ played a unique role in the Russian uranium saga and warrants closer examination. The DOE and Treasury do as well. In fact, all nine of the CFIUS agencies that reviewed the Russian purchase of Uranium One bear further investigation, as an increasing number of them appear to have been compromised or otherwise conflicted.

Hillary Clinton's "Russian reset" is one of the largest failures of the Obama administration. President Obama himself failed to see Russia's motives. During the 2012 election cycle, Obama mocked his Republican opponent, Mitt Romney, for being wary of Russia. Obama taunted Romney about his concerns, saying in a debate: "The 1980s are now calling to ask for their foreign policy back because, you know, the Cold War's been over for twenty years."[160] At the same time, Obama was caught on a "hot microphone" reassuring Putin's prime minister, Dmitry Medvedev, that the U.S. would have "more flexibility" to make deals "after my election."[161]

America's most sensitive infrastructure—energy, defense, and even the election process—was targeted by Russia following Hillary Clinton's infamous red "reset" button.[162] There are more systemic concerns. For example, the FBI and the DOJ have repeatedly failed to prevent (or even mitigate) Russian interference in crucial institutions. The DOJ and the committee in charge of safeguarding American assets, CFIUS, failed to prevent the Russian takeover of major U.S. uranium production assets. The State Department failed to prevent Hillary Clinton's conflicts from influencing her decisions. The national security implications of these blunders cannot be overstated. Most of the media failed to cover this aggressively.

Beyond the obvious national security implications, there were health, safety, and environmental concerns with the nuclear schemes of the aforementioned players. The Russian nuclear deals made over the past 30 years involved one company, USEC, that operates two enrichment facilities.

These American industrial plants in Piketon, Ohio, and Paducah, Kentucky, have both been shut down due to contamination and the poisoning of American workers.[163]

The Megatons to Megawatts program was lauded at the time as "the deal of the century."[164] While that may be true for the insiders who got wealthy from the deal, nothing could be further from the truth for nuclear workers in Piketon and Paducah. The arrangement between Tenex and USEC led to increased enrichment operations at the Piketon plant. As a result of years of enrichment without observation of proper safeguards, the Piketon plant is an ecological disaster. Workers from the Piketon plant have filed toxic-exposure claims that have been denied (more often than not) by the U.S. Department of Labor.[165] The Paducah plant was shut down in 2013 and a massive decontamination and deconstruction operation is now underway.[166]

Jeff Walburn was one of the security guards at the Piketon plant that processed the Russian uranium. He sued the site's operator, Lockheed Martin, numerous times beginning in 1996 and in the early 2000s over the radiation he and other workers were exposed to at the plant.[167] Walburn accused Lockheed of making false claims concerning the radiation exposure indicators (dosage readings) at the Piketon plant. Walburn's court actions went nowhere but he has continued to seek remedies for the past twenty years. At the same time that Walburn was pressing for justice against Lockheed, the company appointed a little-known deputy attorney general named James Comey as its general counsel.[168] Walburn's actions against Lockheed continued throughout Comey's tenure at Lockheed and were delayed and eventually dismissed. According to a forty-one-page internal Lockheed report uncovered in discovery, Walburn's complaint had merit, but the courts sided with Lockheed.[169]

Walburn is not alone in his beliefs. Thousands of nuclear workers from Ohio and Kentucky were injured, and many corroborate his accusations.[170] Over the years, Lockheed has settled multiple suits similar to Walburn's over its uranium operations. The lawsuits began well before Comey became Lockheed's general counsel and extended long after he left in 2010.[171] Comey's name does not show up on any court documents, but one can safely assume that multiple million-dollar lawsuit would have caught the attention of the general counsel's office. Walburn claims to have evidence that the DOE report was a sham.[172] A full investigation into the Russian nuclear deals and the potential fallout is long past due.

Lockheed's involvement in the nuclear sector and Comey's possible involvement may be a coincidence. What is clear today is that Comey earned millions by helping to ensure that Lockheed's operations remained lawful. Lockheed paid Comey more than $6 million in a single year to serve as Lockheed's general counsel and senior vice president.[173] Was Comey involved in Lockheed's nuclear legal troubles? Why else hire a deputy attorney general for such an enormous sum during that time frame?

We will examine Comey's role in the intersecting scandals involving Russian espionage and bribery schemes, his longstanding relationship with Robert Mueller, and how these topics are linked to Lockheed and its construction of a massive surveillance infrastructure. Lockheed's history in the nuclear and surveillance industries is enduring, but also disconcerting. It is not only the single largest government contractor in the history of the U.S., but it also consistently relies on those contracts for 95 percent of its revenue. It received government contracts totaling $485.5 billion—nearly half a trillion dollars—since it hired Comey in 2005. Overall, Lockheed typically receives more taxpayer dollars each year than the year before.[174]

The deal, celebrated by Russia after its approval, relied on bribery, racketeering, kickbacks, money-laundering, and other Russian subversions. Worse, many of the same people responsible for peddling the Russian–Trump collusion narrative since the 2016 election have been accommodating to the Russians for over twenty years. The Clintons, Poneman, Gore, and Fuerth, among others, capitulated to Russian demands long before Trump decided to run for president. All the while, the Clintons and their associates have gotten rich by taking money directly from Russian entities and their counterparts.[175]

Beyond its handling of earlier Russian bribery and spy schemes, the FBI's surveillance of candidate Donald Trump testifies to the terrifying capabilities of the ever-growing surveillance state. There are two laws, both administered and enforced by the FBI and its parent agency, the DOJ, that demonstrate the tenuous relationship between foreign influence and domestic surveillance. These laws, the Foreign Agents Registration Act (FARA) and the Foreign Intelligence Surveillance Act (FISA), played a significant part in the FBI's 2016 operations.

CHAPTER 3

THE FBI'S AND DOJ'S FOREIGN AGENTS PROBLEM (FARA)

- Foreign agents have influenced American decision-makers for a very long time.
- The FBI and DOJ have failed to prevent, or in many cases failed to detect, foreign agents operating at the highest levels in Washington.
- Paul Manafort was indicted in 2017 for violating the Foreign Agents Registration Act (FARA), even though Fusion GPS founders investigated and reported Manafort's pro-Kremlin ties in 2008.
- Russian agents coordinated with Fusion GPS, the media, the State Department, and even a U.S. Senator to promote Clinton's interests.
- The Clinton campaign debated internally about taking campaign donations from registered foreign agents. Ultimately the conclusion was "Take the Money!"

Russian Agents and the FBI

The ethical and financial conflicts surrounding the Uranium One deal reflect a dangerous drift: The FBI has failed to detect or prevent foreign influence at the highest levels of U.S. government. Unchecked Russian espionage and influence, the national security implications of uranium racketeering schemes, *and* the involvement of D.C. insiders in abetting these things shock even the most jaded observer. Worst of all is the apparent complicity of two FBI directors, Robert Mueller and James Comey; two attorneys general, Eric Holder and Loretta Lynch; and even a sitting president, Barack Obama.

The FBI's and the DOJ's failures to mitigate or adequately punish multiple interrelated Russian nuclear scandals, combined with their controversial roles in the 2016 election surveillance, demand full investigation. All FBI personnel ultimately answer to the FBI director, who in turn answers to the Attorney General (AG).[1] That means that Mueller, Comey, and their respective AGs should be held accountable for their staffers' misdeeds and mishandled investigations.[2] This is especially so given their apparent awareness (and even complicity) in politicized investigations. The buck must stop with them (and ultimately with President Obama).

The pattern of abuse of spying tactics by U.S. intelligence agencies points to a more disturbing trend: a rapidly growing and seemingly unaccountable surveillance state.[3] The U.S. surveillance state has been accused of violating the constitutional rights of virtually every American, including vast numbers of innocent citizens and even journalists, sitting lawmakers, and allied heads of state. In 2016, the Foreign Intelligence Surveillance Act (FISA) was used to permit spying on a presidential candidate. This law is central to the FBI's 2016 surveillance operation of candidate Trump.[4]

During the 2016 campaign, both campaigns were warned (and repeatedly claimed) that they were targets of espionage.[5] Clinton said that the Russians had spied on her. She and her supporters allege, without conclusive evidence, that the email accounts of the DNC and her campaign chairman, John Podesta, were "hacked" by Russian government operatives who publicly leaked stolen emails through a website called WikiLeaks.[6] Trump's campaign *was* spied on, but apparently not by Russia. Instead, it was President Obama's FBI and the intelligence community who sought (and received) permission from a secret surveillance court to monitor communications of Trump's associates.[7] Obama's closest aides have confirmed this and, in September 2017, CNN corrected its yearlong reporting to the contrary.[8] Clinton's allegations, like Trump's, involve FISA.

Law enforcement could have mitigated (or even prevented) the alleged Russian espionage operation targeting Team Clinton's emails with more careful use of FISA. After all, there were numerous warning signs. Starting in 2013, reports surfaced of a Romanian hacker calling himself "Guccifer" who had stolen Clinton's emails by hacking into the account of her close confidant, Sidney Blumenthal.[9] Guccifer's Internet Protocol (IP) address was traced to Russia in 2013.[10] A separate hacker named "Guccifer 2.0" also claimed that he was a Romanian citizen (and denied being a Russian spy). He mysteriously took credit for the notable summer 2016 DNC breach, and also a less-consequential hack in 2015.[11] Guccifer 2.0 has yet to be identified, although a March 2018 report from *The Daily Beast* claims that he is a confirmed operative from Russia's military intelligence directorate (also known as GRU), again without conclusive evidence.[12]

In the case of Trump, the election spy mechanism *was* FISA. Beginning in October 2016, FBI Director James Comey, Deputy Director Andrew McCabe, Deputy Attorney

General Rod Rosenstein, and others signed and/or submitted multiple FISA warrant applications and renewals seeking permission to spy on the Trump team. Among the targets were Paul Manafort and Carter Page, two of Trump's close advisors.[13] Through the "two-hop" protocols of FISA surveillance that are detailed in Chapter 5, the FBI would have access to anyone that Manafort and Page talked with *and* anyone that their associates talked with. (Using a conservative average of 100 direct contacts per person, the number of individuals subject to a single FISA warrant quickly balloons to over 10,000.)[14]

If the Russians did spy on Clinton's campaign, FISA surely would have been law enforcement's tool to counter the operation. So far, there is no direct evidence that Russia provided campaign-related emails to WikiLeaks. In January 2017, Obama's top intelligence agencies published a report alleging that the DNC emails were hacked by Russia at the direction of Vladimir Putin. However, once again, this intelligence community assessment not only lacked any conclusive evidence, but also was based only on the analysis of CrowdStrike, a DNC contractor.[15]

Armed only with this dubious report, Team Clinton maintains that the Russians spied on its campaign and colluded with the Trump campaign to win the election.[16] Since his May 17, 2017, appointment, Mueller and his special counsel team have been hunting for Russian interference for over a year.[17] Mueller has recommended over 100 charges (none directly proving Russian collusion) against 2016 actors, including former Trump campaign chairman Manafort, former national security advisor Mike Flynn, and thirteen members of a low-level Russian internet operation.[18]

Mueller charged the Russian internet operators, called "trolls," with identity theft and fraud. Flynn was charged with making false statements to the FBI. Manafort and advisor

Rick Gates were both charged with violating FARA, among other charges.[19] FISA and FARA are deeply intertwined, linked by the concept of a "foreign agent."

FARA is a disclosure law that requires individuals to register with the DOJ when acting as an agent or lobbyist for a foreign government.[20] Manafort and Gates's FARA indictments concerned activities they performed on behalf of a Ukrainian political party between 2006 and 2016.[21] Clinton's accusations of email espionage and Russian hacking were not mentioned in the Manafort and Gates indictments. No specific link between Manafort's Ukrainian operation and the 2016 U.S. election was identified in the indictment by Mueller.[22] Nonetheless, the charges are revealing because they shed light on the shadowy world of foreign influence operations and the DOJ's failure to prevent or even detect them. Influence operations covered under FARA are central to both campaigns' accusations against each other.

Donald Trump, Hillary Clinton, and their respective campaigns have significant international interests that present opportunities for foreign agents of influence. Trump has his international real estate empire with properties all over the world. Clinton has her foundation, which takes multi-million-dollar checks from foreign corporations and governments directly. These international interests fueled fiery campaign rhetoric on both sides. Both campaigns further accused each other of colluding with foreign agents. Clinton and most Democrats allege that the Trump team colluded with the Russians. Trump and many Republicans allege that the Clinton team colluded with multiple foreign powers through Fusion GPS.

Congressional investigations have confirmed that Fusion GPS retained a former British spy who hired Russian operators and distributed Fusion's findings to European,

Ukrainian, and Australian officials. While "collusion" is a vague term without any statutory definitions and is not a crime, Trump and Clinton's accusations implicate the perpetrators in a common violation: FARA.

The FBI is the investigator, and its parent agency, the DOJ, is the enforcer of FARA. According to the POGO, the 2016 election cycle demonstrates that the investigation and enforcement of FARA has been an abysmal failure. In September 2016, the DOJ's inspector general confirmed that FARA enforcement had been lacking (to put it mildly).[23]

A Brief History of FARA

The threat of influence from foreign interests upon America has been constant since our founding. President George Washington warned in his famed 1796 Farewell Address:

> Against the insidious wiles of foreign influence (I conjure you to believe me, fellow-citizens) the jealousy of a free people ought to be constantly awake, since history and experience prove that foreign influence is one of the most baneful foes of republican government. But that jealousy to be useful must be impartial; else it becomes the instrument of the very influence to be avoided, instead of a defense against it.[24]

Today, Washington's prescient words are truer than ever. Foreign influence-peddling by lobbyists is a highly lucrative business, particularly for former legislators and other D.C. insiders.[25]

Countries with radical sociopolitical and/or religious beliefs, such as Saudi Arabia, China, and Russia, have sought favorable treatment from the U.S. government by showering D.C. with cash, contributing to the Washington "boomtown" effect seen in the past two decades. It was the late-1930s threat of Nazi propagandists that led to the passage of FARA in 1938, requiring foreign government agents to register with the DOJ and comply with strict disclosure requirements.[26] According to the Sunlight Foundation:

> Congress believed that if you were a foreign actor in the U.S., your disclosure should be deeper and broader; this was not just a lobbying disclosure act, but a counter-espionage provision of the law meant to provide transparency to areas of potential foreign influence.... FARA requires that someone register with the Department of Justice within 10 days of agreeing to be an agent. Then that individual must file reports every six months detailing their activities.

Basically, FARA supplements the routine disclosures that every lobbyist must file, provided that the client is either a foreign government or is closely aligned with a foreign government.[27] In 1993, the Clinton administration imposed FARA registration fees. The rules regarding FARA disclosures changed with the passage of, and Clinton's signature on, the Lobbying Disclosure Act (LDA) of 1995. This carved out a significant exemption to FARA and since then, the number of disclosures, cases, and prosecutions have plummeted, while foreign influence seems as pervasive as ever. On that, at least, Republicans and Democrats seem to agree.[28]

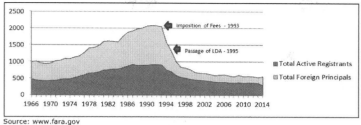

Source: www.fara.gov

Figure 2: FARA registrations plummeted after the Clinton administration made changes to the filing requirements and created an exemption.

The Relationship Between FISA and FARA

Both FARA and FISA are major legislative protections that are supposed to prevent subversion by foreign powers. FISA is covered extensively in Chapter 4, but its relationship with FARA will be discussed in this chapter, as both laws address the concept of a foreign agent. Under FARA, professional lobbyists who have foreign state-linked clients must register as "agents" of those governments. Lobbyist agents are supposed to be subject to FARA penalties if they fail to disclose these associations.

FISA authorizes law enforcement agencies to conduct comprehensive surveillance on any individual in the U.S., once law enforcement demonstrates to a FISA court that it has probable cause to suspect that this individual is acting as a foreign agent. This includes listening to phone calls; searching property and financial records; and surveilling past, present, and future digital communication and usage, and so forth. Whereas FARA requires simple disclosure of foreign associations, FISA is used to investigate anyone that the government believes may be engaged in foreign influence operations (such as espionage or even terrorist activities within the U.S.). With such a broad reach, FISA is often criticized as potentially violating the U.S. Constitution's Fourth Amendment prohibition of unreasonable searches.[29]

Putting the relationship simply: If an individual fails to register as a foreign agent under FARA, he or she may be subject to surveillance under FISA—perhaps years later, as in the case of Manafort.[30]

FISA was enacted in 1978 in response to Nixon's domestic surveillance activities during the Watergate scandal. The act defines a foreign agent broadly as:

> Any person who acts as an agent, representative, employee, or servant, or any person who acts in any other capacity at the order, request, or under the direction or control, of a foreign [government] or of a person any of whose activities are directly or indirectly supervised, directed, controlled, financed, or subsidized in whole or in major part by a foreign principal, and who directly or through any other person engages within the United States in political activities for or in the interests of such foreign principal...

Basically, FISA surveillance is warranted as long as the surveillance target is a suspected "foreign agent" acting on behalf of a foreign government (as approved by the surveillance court). The Justice Department's National Security Division administers both FISA and FARA.[31]

In 2003, FBI Director Mueller created a FISA division within the bureau. This move centralized and streamlined foreign intelligence and surveillance operations within the FBI, thus making it easier and faster to prepare the applications needed to obtain surveillance warrants. According to Mueller's announcement:

> We created a FISA Unit responsible for ensuring that FISA applications move expeditiously through the FISA process. This unit is developing and implementing an automated FISA management system, and it oversees the expeditious distribution of FISA Court orders and warrants to the appropriate field offices, telecommunications carriers, Internet service [providers], and other specified persons. With the FISA management system on line, we will have the ability—for the first time—to transfer FISA applications between the field offices, FBI headquarters, and the Office of Intelligence Policy and Review in a secure electronic format and to monitor the progress of each application to prevent the processing delays that have, at times, been a source of frustration for our investigators.[32]

FARA and FISA were used extensively throughout the 2016 election. Beginning in 2016, the FBI applied for FISA surveillance warrants to monitor the Trump campaign. As mentioned earlier, Mueller's special counsel team indicted multiple Trump campaign associates in 2017 with charges relating to FARA. The intersection of these two laws vis-à-vis the 2016 election is crucial to understanding the accusations made by the Trump and Clinton campaigns.

History of the FBI's and DOJ's FARA Failures

The September 2016 internal audit of FARA enforcement conducted by the DOJ's IG found that compliance rates were "unacceptable." At the time, 62 percent of new registrations were filed late, 50 percent were incomplete, and 15 percent of active registrants "had ceased filing altogether or were over six months delinquent." The audit provides no analysis of *undisclosed* foreign agents, and states that "it is difficult for NSD to ensure the timely registration of a foreign agent when it has no easy independent way to know of the foreign agent's obligation to register." The audit confirms that the DOJ lacks an effective process to identify violations and clear authority to enforce them Instead, the department relies primarily on "voluntary compliance."[33]

The DOJ audit demonstrates the claim above that FARA enforcement plummeted when Bill Clinton signed the LDA of 1995, creating a loophole for avoidance of FARA disclosure. That loophole has been widely criticized for allowing undisclosed foreign lobbying activity. In addition to the registration failures, the IG audit found the FARA division within the DOJ to be severely lacking in resources. In a federal department employing over one hundred thousand, the eight-employee FARA division is "poorly funded and lacks power to compel possible violators to produce information, relying instead on voluntary disclosure."[34]

According to the prominent D.C. law firm Baker Mackenzie, three high-profile examples of potential FARA violations highlight the NSD's enforcement failures: former Trump campaign chairman Paul Manafort, Virginia governor Terry McAuliffe, and more than one hundred legislators who have left office since 1990.[35] In August 2016, the Associated Press (AP) reported that Manafort "helped a pro-Russian governing party in Ukraine secretly route at least $2.2 million in payments to two prominent Washington lobbying firms in 2012." Despite denials from the accused, the DOJ and the FBI are nevertheless investigating both firms.[36]

Manafort is a central figure in the 2016 election debacle and subsequent investigations. Oddly, Manafort's foreign influence operation has been an open secret in Washington for over a decade. Manafort's role in the pro-Russian lobbying efforts is intriguing, given that the FARA charges materialized only after he became involved with Trump and that they neglect to mention Clinton-connected firms also involved in the pro-Russian effort.[37]

Virginia governor McAuliffe was placed under FBI investigation for payments he received from a Chinese billionaire. Reports have cited a $120,000 contribution to McAuliffe's 2013 gubernatorial campaign made by businessman and Chinese national, Wang Wenliang. Wenliang, a former delegate to China's National People's Congress, also donated millions of dollars to the Clinton Foundation.[38] McAuliffe invited Wenliang to attend a 2013 fundraiser at Hillary Clinton's personal Washington, D.C., home.[39]

The investigation is also reportedly focused on McAuliffe's previous role on the Clinton Global Initiative's board of directors.[40] McAuliffe later came under fire for donations made to Jill McCabe, the wife of FBI deputy Andrew McCabe, during her 2015 state senate campaign. Jill McCabe denies that the McAuliffe donations affected her husband's FBI duties.[41]

In October 2016, *Politico* reported that 114 former U.S. lawmakers, or 11 percent, who have left office since 1990, are registered foreign agents. Foreign agents' contracts with foreign principals typically range in the millions of dollars. Per FARA, "foreign principals" can include foreign governments, foreign-owned companies, and think tanks. While many of these *disclosed* relationships are troubling, even more alarming are the apparent loopholes, lax enforcement, and unknown violation rates already discussed.[42]

The Manafort–FARA connection is integral to Clinton and other Democrats' accusations of a Trump–Russian collusion.[43] The connections and intersecting interests are complex and worthy of a full examination. As discussed previously, in April 2016, prior to the DNC email breach, the DNC and the Clinton campaign had retained opposition research firm Fusion GPS to create a dossier on Trump's Russian connections.[44] The collusion accusations first materialized shortly after.[45] That dossier (along with a *Yahoo!* news article) was used as a basis for FBI surveillance warrants, and Paul Manafort was a target, along with Carter Page.[46] The Steele dossier operation is the key to understanding both FARA and FISA abuses. Fusion GPS's investigation of Manafort (which seemingly led to his FARA indictments) began much earlier than most people realize.

Paul Manafort, FARA, and the Fusion GPS Connection

In early 2016, the Trump campaign was undergoing a leadership crisis that resulted in the ouster of Trump's original campaign chairman, Corey Lewandowski, on June 20.[47] GOP lobbyist Manafort replaced Lewandowski. Manafort had repeatedly sought to play a role in the Trump campaign and offered his services *gratis*. Trump and Manafort's mutual friend, Tom Barrack, advocated for Manafort's hire through Trump's son-in-law, Jared Kushner.[48]

Barrack, like Manafort, has some shady dealings in his past. Barrack runs Colony Capital, one of the largest private equity companies in world, and it has been criticized for business dealings with disgraced Hollywood mogul Harvey Weinstein.[49] Barrack has been involved in questionable deals in Haiti, Qatar, Italy, and elsewhere.[50]

On October 27, 2017, Robert Mueller first charged Manafort with multiple serious crimes, ranging from failure to disclose foreign lobbying arrangements to considerable money laundering and tax evasion. These charges under

FARA stemmed from Manafort's work on behalf of the government of Ukraine between 2006 and 2015—his ties to a pro-Russian political group called the European Centre for a Modern Ukraine (ECFMU, or the Centre) are specifically cited.[51] The relationship was initiated a decade before 2016, thus the work itself has nothing to do with the 2016 election. Manafort's relationship with the Centre also brought to light his relationship with Russian oligarch and close Putin confidant, Oleg Deripaska, whose name will re-emerge throughout our discussion of the 2016 campaign. The ECFMU was a political operation aimed at electing Ukrainian presidential candidate Viktor Yanukovych, a pro-Russian figure whom Manafort advised beginning in 2004. The Centre not only hired Manafort for his consulting, but also retained the Podesta Group and another lobbying firm called Mercury.[52]

Manafort's work for the ECFMU was central to the claims of the Fusion GPS dossier, believed to be the work of former British spy-turned-opposition-researcher Christopher Steele. Manafort was fired by the Trump campaign in August 2016, before the dossier allegations were made public.[53] In the dossier, first reported on by David Corn of *Mother Jones* and Michael Isikoff of *Yahoo! News*, Steele and/or Fusion GPS alleges that Manafort received kickback payments from Yanukovych, who relayed the information to Vladimir Putin:

> Ex-Ukrainian President YANUKOVYCH confides directly to PUTIN that he authorised kick-back payments to MANAFORT, as alleged in western media. [Yanukovych] Assures Russian President however there is no documentary evidence/trail.

It was this exact allegation that landed Manafort in trouble with Mueller's investigation and eventually resulted in the FARA charges against him and business partner Rick Gates. The charges are curious for several reasons. First, why wasn't Manafort investigated for crimes committed between 2006 and 2016 *before* he became Trump's campaign chairman? If the Podesta Group received $1 million from the Centre, why were they not indicted under FARA as well? Why was Podesta Group permitted to register under FARA retroactively?[54] Finally, who was Fusion GPS's source for the kickbacks assertion?

The answer to the third question may provide insight. Fusion GPS's source for the claim of Yanukovych's kickbacks to Manafort appears to be Fusion GPS itself. The claim actually dates back to a 2007 *Wall Street Journal* article titled "How Lobbyists Help Ex-Soviets Woo Washington." The article details complex lobbying arrangements and directly names Manafort, noting his relationship with Yanukovych and Deripaska (the latter through his work with Bob Dole). "Mr. Manafort, who isn't registered as a consultant to the Ukrainian leader, didn't respond to requests for comment." None other than Fusion GPS's own Glenn Simpson and his wife, Mary Jacoby, wrote the article.[55]

Let's take a step back to process what this means. Nearly a decade before the 2016 election, Simpson and Jacoby were investigating Manafort for the very crimes that Mueller charged him with (FARA). The Podesta Group, which also performed undisclosed lobbying for the Centre, is never mentioned by Simpson despite the Podesta Group's 2017 admission demonstrated by retroactive filings.[56] Crucially, Manafort's hire as Trump campaign chairman happened contemporaneously with the Clinton campaign's contracting Fusion GPS and Christopher Steele.[57]

It is a strange coincidence, but not necessarily damning. What it tells us is that the FBI surveillance warrants used to spy on the Trump campaign, specifically on Manafort, were based on FARA violations that had been public knowledge for many years.[58]

This fact pattern sets the stage for another incident that occurred around the same time: the DNC email breach.

The DNC Email Breach Kicks Off the Trump-Russian Collusion Narrative

On June 12, 2016, WikiLeaks founder Julian Assange announced that he had obtained emails that were potentially damning to the Clinton campaign.[59] Two days later, on June 14, *The Washington Post* reported that the DNC had been hacked by Russia, citing anonymous sources.[60] The very next day, June 15, the DNC IT firm CrowdStrike confirmed *The Washington Post's* report, citing analysis that attributed the breach to known Russian hackers.[61] Notably, hack attribution is notoriously hard to prove, as internet addresses and identities can easily be mimicked or spoofed.[62]

CrowdStrike's compensation from the DNC and the Clinton campaign was paid through the law firm Perkins Coie, which was also paying Fusion GPS to compile the dossier. The CrowdStrike analysis was the basis for a subsequent January 2017 assessment by Obama's intelligence agencies.[63] The assessment, though inconclusive, was immediately seized upon as proof of Russian hacking of Clinton and her allies.[64] Criticism of the assessment has been bipartisan.

On August 9, 2017, the progressive magazine *The Nation* issued a critique:

> [Our] journalistic mission led The Nation to be troubled by the paucity of serious public scrutiny of the January 2017 intelligence-community assessment (ICA) on purported Russian interference in our 2016

presidential election, which reflects the judgment of the CIA, the FBI, and the NSA. That report concluded that Russian President Vladimir Putin personally ordered the hacking of the DNC and the dissemination of e-mails from key staffers via WikiLeaks, in order to damage Hillary Clinton's candidacy. This official intelligence assessment has since led to what some call "Russiagate," with charges and investigations of alleged collusion with the Kremlin, and, in turn, to what is now a major American domestic political crisis and an increasingly perilous state of US-Russia relations. To this day, however, the intelligence agencies that released this assessment have failed to provide the American people with any actual evidence substantiating their claims about how the DNC material was obtained or by whom. Astonishingly and often overlooked, the authors of the declassified ICA themselves admit that their "judgments are not intended to imply that we have proof that shows something to be a fact." [65]

The Clinton team's accusations of Trump's Russiagate were based on its own analysis and were not independently verified. Assange denies Russia's involvement and "a self-described 'close associate'" asserted that the DNC emails were obtained from an insider.[66] Assange suggested that a DNC insider *leaked*—rather than hacked—the emails and has even hinted that the insider was a DNC IT staffer. Assange and others even named the staffer as Seth Rich.[67] Rich, a twenty-seven-year-old DNC staffer, was murdered on July 10, 2016. The case remains unsolved. The official story concerning

Rich was that he was murdered in a "botched robbery" (but his phone, wallet, watch, and a gold chain were reportedly left on his person, the bullet casings were retrieved, and the crime scene appeared "almost sanitized"). Alternative views posit a "hired killer or serial murderer."[68] In August 2016, within a month of the incident, WikiLeaks offered a $20,000 "reward for information leading to conviction for the murder of DNC staffer Seth Rich."[69] As perhaps the only person who could know *definitively* who WikiLeaks's source was, Assange's interest in the Rich murder is either legitimate or a very dark political stunt.

Former DNC chairwoman Donna Brazile knew Rich personally and dedicated her November 2017 tell-all book, *Hacks: The Inside Story of the Break-ins and Breakdowns that Put Donald Trump in the White House*, to "patriot, Seth Rich."[70] In the book, Brazile claims that the Rich murder haunted her, made her fear for her life, and caused her to install security cameras.[71] In a November 2017 interview with ABC's George Stephanopoulos regarding the book's release, the host cited Brazile's Democratic critics, who questioned her loyalty to the party and felt betrayed by her somber description of the Clinton campaign. Brazile was defiant in her responses and at one point even appeared to link the DNC email breach and the Rich murder by saying, "They don't know what it was like to [preside] over the DNC during this hacking. They don't know what it's like to bury a child. I did: Seth Rich."[72]

The book was a clear shot across the bow at the Clinton campaign, as Brazile accused the Clinton campaign of treating her like "Patsey the slave." Brazile equivocated on the possible suspects, both of the breach and of the murder, ultimately accusing unnamed Russians as the likely culprits. Brazile is the first (and apparently only) high-level DNC insider to insinuate a connection between the murder of Seth Rich and the DNC server breach.[73] She mentions the incident repeatedly throughout her book, including one passage in which she describes allegedly reminding Clinton of the incident on a telephone call after the 2016 election. "'Don't forget the murder of Seth Rich, I told her. Did she want to contribute to Seth's reward fund? We still hadn't found the person responsible for the tragic murder of this bright young DNC staffer,' she wrote. Clinton apparently responded, 'You're right…. We're going to get to that.'" Was Brazile hinting at something? Why give fodder to the conspiracy theorists?[74]

In fairness to Brazile, the controversy her book caused over Rich's murder may have simply been a marketing tactic, or her way of distancing herself from the failed Clinton campaign. It is a disturbing choice either way.

Nonetheless, subsequent forensic data analysis performed by multiple independent parties suggests that the DNC breach was more likely a leak performed by an insider than a hack by outside parties. Specifically, the DNC email files were apparently transferred at a speed that rules out long-distance hacking and implies that the files were obtained locally, from a machine on the DNC's own network.[75] Clinton campaign chief, John Podesta, and DNC ex-chair, Debbie Wasserman Schultz, both blamed the FBI for not preventing the alleged hacking incident from happening. Wasserman Schultz further accused DHS Secretary Jeh Johnson of being "wrong in every respect" and "utterly misinformed" when he said before the House Intelligence Committee in June 2017 that the DNC refused DHS's help.[76] Yet the DNC refused to turn over its computer servers for FBI analysis in January 2017.[77] The FBI instead relied on the *private* analysis of the DNC contractor CrowdStrike.[78] The Clinton campaign, the DNC, and even President Obama's super PAC have used Perkins Coie for various, possibly nefarious, off-book operations. Something again is fishy about the DNC story.

Hillary Clinton, her campaign, the DNC, and their allies repeatedly accused Donald Trump of having been compromised by Russia. They cite the DNC email breach and their own inconclusive findings linking the breach to Russian hackers. The truth is that Clinton and her benefactors have far more connections to Russia than the ones they allege regarding Trump. In an ironic twist, not only does Clinton have concrete financial ties to Putin and the Russians, but it also appears that her entire campaign was compromised by FARA-linked contributions.

The Clinton Campaign on the Issue of FARA: "Take the Money!"

Trump campaign chairman Paul Manafort may be the most prominent example of a recent FARA indictment; however, FARA indictments are *very rare*. Before Manafort's FARA indictment, widespread reporting suggested that the Clintons are the most glaring example of widespread foreign influence peddling. The enormous contributions received by the Clinton Foundation—directly from foreign governments—should qualify the foundation as an off-the-books FARA lobbying outfit. Hillary Clinton's own campaign staffers confirmed this and even cited the foundation as justification to take FARA-linked campaign donations.

On April 13, 2015, Clinton staffer Dennis Cheng emailed the newly formed Clinton campaign team about accepting campaign donations from foreign agents. Cheng was previously a director of development at the Clinton Foundation. At the time of the email, Cheng was serving as the national finance director of Hillary for America (the 2016 campaign). His subject line reads: "Foreign registered agents." The email chain from Cheng begins: "We really need [to] make a policy decision on [FARA] soon—whether we are allowing those lobbying on behalf of foreign governments to raise $ for the campaign. Or case by case."[79]

The Clinton team, including campaign manager Robby Mook, aide Huma Abedin, campaign chair and fixer John Podesta, and general counsel Marc Elias (a Perkins Coie partner using an @hillaryclinton.com private email address/server), considered whether or not it should accept campaign cash bundles from foreign agents. The view behind the curtain is telling. A campaign staffer on the email chain raised the issue of multiple Clinton donors representing questionable foreign regimes. The staffer identified at least twenty-seven bundlers who represented foreign interests, and specifically named the Podesta Group as a troubling source of donations. According to that staffer:

> If we were looking at these folks below on a case by case basis, I'd want to specifically raise: Tony Podesta (Iraq, Azerbaijan, Egypt), Ben Barnes (Libya), John Merrigan (UAE), Wyeth Weidman (Libya), and Mike Driver (UAE connections).

Cheng pushed back and pressed multiple times for a Clinton team legal decision, as he argued for accepting the money linked to foreign interests. "I feel like we are leaving a good amount of money on the table," Cheng wrote, "and how do we explain to people that...the Foundation takes $ from foreign govts [sic] but we now won't."[80]

Initially, it appears that the Clinton legal team decided not to take the foreign-linked money. But then, on April 16, Perkins Coie attorney Marc Elias prompted the Clinton campaign to make a "complete U-turn" and counseled that banning FARA money does not "really get you anything."

In a decisive final message almost four hours later, Clinton campaign spokesperson Jennifer Palmieri exclaimed, "Take the money!!"[81]

This email exchange demonstrates several things. First, that the Clinton campaign lawyers (and even Clinton herself) knew the risks of taking foreign-linked cash. Second, they were aware that the Clinton Foundation was taking money from foreign governments and knew the FARA implications of that. Third, despite the risks, they were willing to "Take the money!!"[82]

Uranium One Unregistered Agents

A stunning FARA development is the Clinton campaign's admission that Tony Podesta is a FARA risk who lobbies for controversial foreign principals like Iraq, Azerbaijan, and Egypt. At the time of the FARA email discussions, the Podesta Group represented another foreign interest, this one fully controlled by the Russian government: Uranium One.[83]

According to lobbying disclosures the Podesta Group filed with the Senate, Uranium One paid the Podesta Group $140,000 between 2014 and 2015. Inexplicably, the Podesta Group never filed with the DOJ. Uranium One is unquestionably an agent of a foreign principal—the Russian government. In January 2013, the Russian state-owned nuclear corporation ARMZ, a Rosatom subsidiary, agreed to buy all the remaining shares of Uranium One and to take the company private prior to the full purchase in October 2013.[84] The English translation of the ARMZ website describes the nature of the Russian state-owned interests in Uranium One:

> In 2013, taking into consideration the situation on the world natural uranium market, ARMZ Uranium Holding Co. completed

a transaction to acquire a 100% stake in Uranium One Inc. Under the terms of the agreement, all of Uranium One Inc. common shares, which JSC Atomredmetzoloto and its affiliates did not own at that moment, were purchased. In accordance with the decision made by ROSATOM State Atomic Energy Corporation, management of uranium assets located abroad was entrusted to Uranium One Holding N.V. Since December 2013, JSC Atomredmetzoloto has been in charge of the Russian uranium mining assets.[85]

It is clear that Uranium One was then fully controlled by the government of Russia. That is why Obama's committee on foreign investment (CFIUS) had to review the deal in the first place. Russia purchased a company that controlled 20 percent of American domestic production capacity and allowing Putin to control domestic nuclear supplies presented numerous national security risks. Multiple legislators raised objections to the deal (which is even now the subject of numerous inquiries). Thus far, the FBI and congressional investigations of Clinton's questionable dealings have provided more questions than answers. On May 21, 2018, twelve House Republicans introduced a resolution calling for the appointment of a new special counsel to examine the FBI's alleged misconduct. The resolution specifically identifies the Obama DOJ's failure to adequately investigate Uranium One and the high-level decision to kill the Clinton Foundation investigation.[86]

The questions that remain unanswered: Why are Clinton-linked entities seemingly exempt from DOJ investigations under FARA? What role did Clinton-connected lobbyists play in the Obama administration's CFIUS approval?

And why have the FBI and DOJ failed to monitor foreign influence at the highest levels of government? This seems, at best, a major ethical lapse and, at worst, a constitutional breach of duties in furtherance of widespread cronyism and self-enrichment.

The Podesta Group has represented Uranium One dating back to 2012. The specific Podesta Group lobbyist for Uranium One is a man named Stephen Rademaker.[87] Before Uranium One became a Podesta Group client, Rademaker represented it at another Clinton-linked lobbying firm: the Barbour Griffiths Rogers (BGR) Group (traditionally a GOP-allied firm).[88] BGR was one of the few who responded to our inquiries as of this writing. We sent BGR a simple question regarding their lobbying efforts on behalf of Uranium One and Uranium One's affiliates. A representative pointed to BGR's public filings and ultimately confirmed Stephen Rademaker was their only lobbyist for Uranium One and when Rademaker left BGR for the Podesta Group, he "took the client with him." Their full response is included in the endnotes.[89]

Notably, the BGR Group was actually mentioned in the 2007 *Wall Street Journal* article by Glenn Simpson and Mary Jacoby that reported Manafort's FARA violations. With regard to BGR, Fusion GPS co-founder Simpson left out some crucial details.[90]

What Is "the Democrats' Purse?"

The BGR Group's connections to the Uranium One sale extended far beyond the company itself. Including Uranium One, the BGR Group represented five major parties involved in the deal:

- Uranium One: Paid BGR Group $160,000 in 2010 and 2011. Seventy-five percent of BGR's haul from Uranium One ($120,000) came in 2010—the year the Russian takeover was approved by CFIUS.[91]
- Alfa Bank: One of the largest private Russian banks run by oligarchs with significant financial ties to Rosatom, ARMZ, Tenex, and Uranium One. Alfa Bank paid the BGR Group nearly $6 million between 2004 and 2015.[92]
- The government of Kazakhstan: As revealed in the book *Clinton Cash*, Kazakh dictator Nursultan Nazarbayev's nuclear agency, Kazatomprom, provided Uranium One founder, Frank Giustra, with valuable nuclear assets after Bill Clinton met with them in 2005. Kazakhstan had major interests in Russian–American uranium dealings and paid the BGR Group $2 million between 2010 and 2013.[93]
- Kazatomprom: This state-owned atomic company paid BGR $90,000 in 2010.[94]
- The United States Enrichment Corp. (USEC): Prime beneficiary of Russian uranium deals dating back to the mid-1990s (as described in Chapter 2). USEC paid the BGR Group $880,000 between 2008 and 2012.[95]

Ultimately, each of these clients is either a foreign principal or possible foreign agent (except USEC). Alfa Bank finances Kremlin nuclear projects, and even facilitated Iran's controversial nuclear operations, such as the Bushehr reactor. And, while paying American lobbyists for years, the Russian Alfa Bank has never appeared in FARA filings.[96]

The Government Accountability Institute obtained an exclusive English translation of a 2009 video interview with the head of Kazatomprom, a man named Mukhtar

Dzhakishev (pronounced "jahk-ee-shev"). Dzhakishev was arrested and imprisoned in 2009 for a fourteen-year term on charges of corruption and embezzlement specifically involving Giustra's 2005 uranium deal. It is widely believed that the arrest was politically motivated and that Nazarbayev was involved.[97] Dzhakishev has a long history with the Clintons and their friend, Frank Giustra.

In 2005, Dzhakishev presided over Kazatomprom when, in September, Bill Clinton and Giustra flew to Kazakhstan to meet with Nazarbayev. According to *The New York Times*, Giustra received valuable uranium mining concessions forty-eight hours after the visit. These Kazakh mining concessions were rolled into Giustra's company UrAsia Energy Ltd., which was acquired for $3.1 billion in February 2007 by Uranium One. That same month, Dzhakishev met with Giustra and Clinton at the Clinton *residence* in Chappaqua, NY. Both Clinton and Giustra initially denied meeting with the Kazakh nuclear official, but *The New York Times* caught them in the lie. Giustra blamed a faulty memory. Giustra made a hefty sum off the 2007 sale—over $7 per share for stocks valued at ten cents per share just two years previous. In the 2009 video interview, Dzhakishev specifically accuses then-Senator Hillary Clinton and her associates of pressuring him to facilitate transfer of the uranium rights to Giustra's company. The transfer was concluded on November 7, 2005. Dzhakishev claims that kickback payments were made to an unnamed lobbying outfit he calls "the Democrats' purse."[98]

Was Dzhakishev referring to the BGR Group? Was BGR's Stephen Rademaker involved, and does that further implicate the Podesta Group? Or could the Clinton Foundation (which received $145 million in contributions from Frank Giustra, Uranium One chairman Ian Telfer, and other associated investors) be the Democrats' purse? Dzhakishev does not say. What is clear is that those involved in the Uranium

One deal needed to grease the skids in Washington for it to be approved, and the BGR Group, the Podesta Group, and the Clinton Foundation seemed well poised to help.

Clinton Inc.'s Other Russian Agents

Before Kazatomprom retained BGR, it used yet another lobbying firm tied to the Clintons: APCO Worldwide (APCO). Kazatomprom paid APCO $220,000 in 2007, but that is hardly APCO's most interesting connection to the Clintons and the Uranium One deal. APCO represented another Russian nuclear client: Tenex. Tenex is the company, well known to the FBI, that engaged in bribery, racketeering, and kickback schemes in the U.S. for years. In October 2017, multiple outlets reported that Tenex paid APCO $3 million in 2010 and 2011.[99] In fact, the figure seems to be closer to $4 million according to lobbying disclosures that specifically identify the pursuit of Rosatom interests. Tenex is a Rosatom subsidiary and, thus, the Russian-owned sister company of Uranium One (as of the 2010 CFIUS review). Tenex was named by an FBI informant as a central player in the Russian nuclear schemes, implicating the Clintons and their foundation in 2010. The FBI's informant, William Douglas Campbell, testified in writing to three congressional committees that Russian officials told him:

> ...at various times that they expected APCO to apply a portion of the $3 million annual lobbying fee it was receiving from the Russians to provide in-kind support for the Clintons' Global Initiative. The contract called for four payments of $750,000 over twelve months. APCO was expected to give assistance free of charge to the Clinton

Global Initiative as part of their effort to create a favorable environment to ensure the Obama administration made affirmative decisions on everything from Uranium One to the U.S.-Russia Civilian Nuclear Cooperation agreement.[100]

Reporting by John Solomon of Capitol Hill news website *The Hill* first revealed Campbell's testimony, in which he described providing documents to congressional committees that his FBI handlers were aware of in 2010. These documents show that Russian and American executives specifically asked Campbell to try to help get the Uranium One deal approved by the Obama administration. Further, there is the assertion that the Clinton Foundation was specifically involved in the Tenex bribery scheme. These allegations were denied by both APCO and the foundation. APCO told *The Hill* in a statement, "APCO Worldwide's activities involving client work on behalf of Tenex and The Clinton Global Initiative were totally separate and unconnected in any way." A spokesman for Clinton, Nick Merrill, said that the allegations are being used to distract from the investigations into President Trump and Russian election meddling."[101]

Coincidentally, APCO is connected to the Fusion GPS dossier through a lobbyist and FARA-registered foreign agent that worked for APCO between 2008 and 2013—Jonathan Winer. Before and after working for APCO, he was also a State Department official. A former aide to John Kerry, Winer later helped share the dossier findings, beginning in September 2016 after he met directly with Christopher Steele. In fact, he circulated over one hundred Steele reports within the State Department. He admits to meeting with Steele prior to the election and his role in promoting the dossier to Obama advisor Victoria Nuland, but denies that anything nefarious took place.[102] Winer worked at APCO while APCO was lobbying for Tenex and was simultaneously providing in-kind contributions to the Clinton Foundation. Before APCO, Winer worked at Alston & Bird and Oleg Deripaska was reportedly his client.[103] With his history as a foreign agent and later a State Department official, his involvement in promoting the Trump–Russia dossier is significant and disturbing at the same time.

That's not all. *Yet another* Clinton-affiliated lobbyist was working for the Russians (including Deripaska) while simultaneously promoting the Fusion GPS dossier. Adam Waldman, a foreign agent and founder of the Endeavor Group, contacted Senator Mark Warner (D-VA) in February 2017 to set up meetings between the senator and Steele. Senator Warner sought to keep the discussions secret and expressed his desire not to leave a "paper trail." Waldman is apparently friends with Steele, which calls into question Steele's pattern of close connections to known Russian agents.[104]

Since at least 2009, Waldman has represented Deripaska and even Putin's chief diplomat, Sergei Lavrov, according to the FARA database. In 2006, the Bush administration barred Deripaska from entry into the U.S. because of concerns about possible ties to organized crime. Deripaska wanted to visit the U.S., at least in part, to save his "debt-burdened" aluminum business and to meet with General Motors, so he hired Waldman when Obama's team (including Clinton) took over in 2009. Likewise, Lavrov wanted better relations with the U.S. In 2009, Waldman was successful in both matters: Deripaska was allowed to visit the U.S. and Lavrov was presented with the infamous Russian "reset" button by Clinton herself.[105] At the time, Waldman's Endeavor Group was on a monthly retainer of $40,000 from the Russians to lobby on Deripaska's behalf and had received $2.36 million by 2014.[106] The contracts continued.

Waldman and his firm, Endeavor Group, have a long history with the Clintons. He is also closely tied to Senator Dianne Feinstein (D-CA), employing her husband, Richard Blum. In his texts to Warner, Waldman reveals that one of Feinstein's staffers, Daniel Jones, was working for Fusion GPS and promoted the dossier through other avenues in D.C.[107]

In early 2001, Waldman was a DOJ official during the administration of Bill Clinton, where he had worked on an antitrust case against Microsoft. Later in 2001, Waldman began the Endeavor Group and helped Microsoft's founder, Bill Gates, along with Bono and George Soros, set up a charitable foundation focused on HIV in 2001, according to Endeavor Group's website.[108] Waldman also worked with celebrity philanthropists, including Brad Pitt and Angelina Jolie, and Cher, as a form of public relations, tax avoidance, and whatever altruistic motivations they had.[109]

According to FARA registration documents filed in 2017, Waldman was still lobbying on behalf of Deripaska and possibly other Russian interests and received $562,802 from the Russian oligarch in 2017 alone. By December 2017, Waldman's Endeavor Group had received nearly $5 million from Deripaska-controlled entities.[110] His contacts with senators such as Warner are supposed to be documented under FARA rules, but Waldman discloses no such discussions in the FARA database.[111]

At the time of his correspondence with Waldman, Senator Warner was the new vice chairman and ranking member of the Senate intelligence committee, which was investigating Trump. Warner had publicly and vehemently opposed the nomination and confirmation of Attorney General Jeff Sessions. On February 8, 2017, Warner repeatedly questioned Sessions' independence in a prepared speech on the Senate floor. Just one month later, Sessions acquiesced to Democrats' demands for recusal from the Russia probe.

Sessions' recusal meant that DOJ deputy AG Rod Rosenstein was able to appoint Robert Mueller as special counsel. Warner grilled AG Sessions regarding the AG's alleged ties to Russia in a June 2017 hearing, and essentially demanded a guarantee that Sessions would not interfere with the Mueller probe citing Sessions' recusal.[112] Was Warner's confidence in the Trump team's ties to Russia based on discussions with Waldman, a Russian foreign agent? Can Russian advocates like Waldman be trusted, given Russian agents' long history of spreading misinformation to sow discord? Why was Adam Waldman, a Clinton ally and Russian agent, promoting the Fusion GPS dossier to Democratic lawmakers? Perhaps the last question answers itself.

FARA Failures Are FBI and DOJ Failures

As previously noted, according to the DOJ's own inspector general, the Foreign Agents Registration Act (FARA) has been ignored flagrantly and the DOJ's enforcement is lacking (to put it mildly). The most prominent examples of (confirmed) FARA violators are Paul Manafort and Rick Gates, who were indicted by Robert Mueller's special counsel team. The problem with Mueller's indictment is that Manafort and Gates were known FARA violators as early as 2007. In fact, Mueller's indictment seems based entirely on Fusion GPS opposition research. The Fusion GPS dossier recycles Glenn Simpson's decade-old reporting to implicate the Trump campaign in a 2016 Russian conspiracy. In 2008, the DOJ and FBI had every opportunity to investigate and charge Manafort with FARA violations. So why wait nine years to do so?

Furthermore, the decision to indict Manafort and Gates for a Ukrainian lobbying scheme that directly involved the Clinton-connected and unindicted Podesta Group reeks of politics. No doubt, Manafort *and* those in the Clinton orbit represent the clearest patterns of repeat FARA violations, yet Clinton Inc. seems immune to FARA regulation. The relationships documented heavily in *Clinton Cash* clearly show that the Clintons appropriated vast amounts of money from both foreign agents and foreign principals since leaving the White House "dead broke" in 2001.

Furthermore, the Clintons are closely tied to numerous Russian foreign agents who both lobbied extensively on behalf of Uranium One *and* advanced the Fusion GPS dossier. The connections are complex and can be confusing. In the case of the BGR Group, though, the connections are clear: No fewer than five players directly tied to Russian nuclear deals (Alfa Bank, Kazakhstan, Kazatomprom, Uranium One, USEC) paid the group a total of $8.51 million from 2004 to 2014. While BGR is typically a GOP-allied firm, the firm's contributions to Democrats peaked the year their client (Uranium One) sought Obama's CFIUS approval. The amount BGR contributed to Democrats in 2010 was more than double the amount contributed in 2008.[113]

Ironically, Fusion GPS's Glenn Simpson and Mary Jacoby accused BGR in 2007 of being a foreign agent that helped "Ex-Soviets Woo Washington."[114] Furthermore, the Clintons took in-kind contributions from APCO Worldwide while the firm represented Russian Tenex—a company later implicated in bribery schemes. The FBI and DOJ acted *after* the Russians got what they wanted (Uranium One). In 2016, Jonathan Winer, a former APCO lobbyist during the Tenex–Clinton operations, worked at the State Department where he disseminated the Fusion GPS findings. Another Russian agent, Adam Waldman, promoted the dossier from the outside and tried to set up meetings between lawmakers and Christopher Steele in 2017. The Warner-Waldman exchange began before Attorney General Jeff Sessions' recusal. Warner, one of Sessions' most vocal critics, wanted dirt on Team Trump and ironically seemed unconcerned about colluding with a Russian oligarch's agent. This may explain why Warner did not want to leave a paper trail. Given the associations, it's hard to imagine Warner and Waldman had any objective other than further delegitimizing the results of the 2016 election—ultimately, the primary objective of Trump's critics seems to be impeachment.

The connections between Deripaska, Waldman, Steele, and U.S. lawmakers like Warner have been confirmed and are in the public record. Why are they not being actively investigated?

Mueller's special counsel mandate (drafted by Rosenstein) does not differentiate between Russian interference with the Trump campaign and Russian interference with the Clinton campaign.[115] The absence of any charges implicating the Clinton-connected Russian agents above should prove once and for all that the Mueller investigation is a political cover-up.

As the premier law enforcement and investigative agencies for gathering domestic intelligence (surveillance) and preventing foreign agent influence (lobbying and espionage), the FBI and the DOJ have immediate oversight of FARA and FISA. Therefore, both bear responsibility for any and all failures.

CHAPTER 4

THE UNITED SURVEILLANCE STATES OF AMERICA (USSA)

- James Comey and Robert Mueller have advocated mass domestic surveillance for many years.
- These men have worked like a tag team promoting the interests of surveillance contractors under the guise of protecting America.
- A top-level FBI whistleblower revealed the surveillance programs that Comey and Mueller have steadily expanded are largely ineffective and a huge waste of money.
- In the private sector, both Comey and Mueller have cashed in, advising the very surveillance contractors that the FBI and other intelligence agencies pay billions to.
- In 2008, Mueller's FBI gave a controversial surveillance contract to Comey's private sector employer, Lockheed Martin, valued at $1 billion. Plagued by

delays and cost overruns, the program has been called a massive "boondoggle."

Background on Domestic Surveillance

To quickly recap, the Foreign Agents Registration Act (FARA) has been violated repeatedly, according to the DOJ's own inspector general. Foreign agents and related foreign influence operations were a central theme in the 2016 election. Since Paul Manafort was indicted on FARA violations (among other serious crimes) in 2017, FARA registrations have skyrocketed. The 2016 election was a major wake-up call for DOJ and FBI enforcers of FARA. FARA is closely linked to another law called the Foreign Intelligence Surveillance Act (FISA). FISA allows FBI surveillance of anyone that the FBI or the DOJ suspects of being a "foreign agent."[1] The oversight seems incredibly lax, and this allowed then-FBI director Comey and others to spy on the Trump campaign. This aided the anti-Trump operation spearheaded by the Clinton campaign and its contractor Fusion GPS.

In addition to the FBI, the White House, the CIA, the NSA, and other intelligence agencies were possibly involved in the anti-Trump spying effort as well.[2] Even Barack Obama is implicated.[3] Obama's involvement with the scandal dates back to April 2016, when the operation had just begun. On April 19, 2016, Fusion GPS's Jacoby visited the White House residence.[4] Throughout 2016 and into 2017, Obama's super PAC poured money into the same conduit that Hillary Clinton and the DNC had used to pay Fusion GPS.[5] In Obama's final weeks as president, his administration loosened the restrictions on sharing NSA-captured raw signal intelligence (private citizen phone calls, emails, social media, and the like). This effort began on December 15, *after* Trump had won the November election.[6]

These changes allowed the NSA to share highly classified information with sixteen different agencies, including the FBI and the CIA.[7] The shared intel would include the private communications of Trump's team—all of whom were U.S. citizens. This intel-sharing ability took effect in the weeks *before* Trump was sworn in as president. These new rules enhanced cooperation and collaboration among the very intelligence agencies, staffed with Obama appointees, investigating the salacious dossier claims as Trump took office in January 2017—the operation that led to Robert Mueller's special counsel investigation in May 2017.[8]

The credibility of Mueller's team was compromised from the start by allegations of partisanship, bias, and ethical lapses. Not a single member of Mueller's team is a registered Republican (Mueller is the sole exception). Instead, Mueller picked a team composed almost entirely of Democrat donors and known Clinton lawyers or operators, including Jeannie Rhee, Andrew Weissmann, and Aaron Zebley.[9]

Mueller's team seemingly has one mission—to take down Trump. Two of Mueller's appointees, Peter Strzok and Lisa Page, were virulently anti-Trump. As noted, they departed the investigation after demonstrating their unethical bias, as evidenced by their leaked text messages.

Subsequent subpoenaed texts demonstrate that Strzok had a close personal relationship with FISA court (FISC) judge, Rudolph Contreras. Contreras also presided over former Trump advisor Michael Flynn's criminal case. Contreras inexplicably recused himself from the case days after Flynn pleaded guilty to lying to the FBI. Strzok participated in the FBI's questioning of Flynn in late January 2017, prior to joining Mueller's team. Six months earlier on July 25, 2016, Page texted Strzok the following: "Rudy is on the [FISC]!... Did you know that? Just appointed two months ago." Strzok replied, "I did…I need to get together with him." The two even discussed planning a dinner party as a social cover for an apparent effort to talk politics with the FISC judge, and it is not known whether or not this event took place.[10]

When Mueller fired Strzok (following Page's departure) in 2017, it was likely not because Mueller had just found out that they were politically compromised. They left the Mueller team after the DOJ IG discovered their partisan views in a series of texts. Given Mueller's history of failures outlined in this book and elsewhere, he too appears to be compromised.[11]

Strzok and Page joked about their anti-Trump bias. For example, in an August 2015 text, Page mentioned seeing "my first Bernie Sanders bumper sticker. Made me want to key the car." Strzok responded, "He's an idiot like Trump... Figure they cancel each other out." In March 2016, Strzok said, "God, Hillary should win 100,000,000 - 0."[12]

Their actions may have been known, and even condoned, at the highest levels of the Obama administration. Strzok and Page's "Secret Society" and "insurance policy" references may have been a private joke, but these FBI staffers were united in a secret mission to use surveillance tools against President Trump and his team. Secretary Clinton had her own secret society on the seventh floor of the State Department (according to email investigation documents since removed from the FBI's website). It was called "The Shadow Government." One member of the Clinton inner circle, Under Secretary of State Patrick Kennedy, "pressured the FBI to unclassify certain emails from Clinton's private server that were previously deemed classified."[13] This nonpartisan alliance of top-level bureaucrats (both career and revolving door) is sometimes referred to as the "deep state." It seems the players in Clinton's State Department and Comey's FBI fancied themselves just that (based on their own words and pattern of secretive and elitist bias).

The institutional collaboration against Trump is hardly the full story. The 2016 election story is not only about FBI failures and corruption, but also about the incredible surveillance power of the U.S. intelligence community. According to credible top-level FBI whistleblowers, these capabilities are out of control. Worse yet, according to a decorated FBI communication analysis unit chief, surveillance protocols are not even effective at stopping terrorism, which is their primary purpose. (The FBI had ample warning about individuals involved in multiple recent mass shootings or terror acts and failed to prevent them.)[14]

The FBI is the central player in U.S. domestic surveillance operations. The bureau has had just two directors between 2001 and 2017: Robert Mueller and James Comey, who, upon close examination of their track record, epitomize the so-called deep state. Along with their associates, Mueller and Comey have used their political and technical powers to target millions of innocent American citizens in mass surveillance operations. This intel has been used against citizens, journalists, and the occasional politician.[15] Meanwhile, it is apparent that insiders like the Clintons are given special treatment. It is only natural to ask why.

The simple answer is money. Former FBI directors Mueller and Comey have earned massive sums helping to construct the modern U.S. surveillance state, which was weaponized in 2016 against a political outsider presidential candidate. And when they are not working for the government, they are making millions working for private surveillance contractors. (In 2003, Comey was worth just $206,000. By 2009, Comey earned $6.1 million from one source in a single year.) Combined, their 2018 net worth that ranges between $9 and $29 million, using conservative estimates. It could be over $30 million, but disclosures for Comey are vague.[16]

The FBI and the DOJ have long been lucrative stops in the revolving door between the public and private sectors in D.C. This intersection of money and politics at the top of the FBI and the DOJ is concerning. Personnel from government agencies, such as the Departments of Defense, Energy, and the Interior, also have a history of drifting between the public and private sectors.[17]

The FBI and the DOJ are the top law enforcement agencies in the country and are supposed to remain neutral.[18] This particular revolving door creates substantial conflicts of interest and erodes the credibility of justice. When the individuals in charge of justice are financially conflicted, justice itself becomes co-opted. The financial interests of Mueller and Comey are telling. Have the leaderships of the FBI and the DOJ been compromised? The record of failures and pattern of abuse indicate they have.

Mueller's and Comey's biggest paydays have come in the form of legal counsel compensation from two of the largest surveillance contractors in the world: Lockheed Martin and Booz Allen Hamilton.[19] Comey worked for Lockheed between 2005 and 2010 and, as mentioned, earned more than $6 million in one year alone. Several years before Mueller joined the FBI in 2001, he earned $400,000 a year in private practice—arguably a reasonable sum. Mueller's compensation after he left the FBI skyrocketed. He made over $3.4 million from the beginning of 2016 through May 2017—a significant raise, even by Washington's standards.[20]

Mueller and Comey have also worked as a tag team for twenty years, drifting between FBI and DOJ leadership positions before cashing in on their valuable intel and experience. Mueller officially joined the FBI as director just one week before the 9/11 terror attacks. Before that, he served as deputy attorney general, a position that Comey would later hold. In 2013, Comey replaced Mueller after the latter left the FBI for a lucrative job at a major D.C. law firm and lobbying powerhouse called WilmerHale.[21] While there, Mueller represented and advised clients such as Apple, Booz Allen Hamilton, Facebook, and Intel. As it turns out, these clients work intimately with the FBI and NSA on surveillance tools. Shockingly, one of Mueller's more influential clients at the time, Facebook, is now cooperating with a special counsel probe, according to CEO Mark Zuckerberg. In Zuckerberg's April 10, 2018, testimony to Congress, he first claimed that Facebook had received a subpoena to cooperate with Mueller's investigation. He immediately clarified that he was unaware of any subpoenas.[22]

While Mueller helped build the post-9/11 intelligence-gathering apparatus, Comey advised three large private-sector clients: Lockheed, Bridgewater Associates, and HSBC Bank.[23]

Decisions made by both men while in the public sector helped facilitate the impressive growth of the modern surveillance state. Thus, Mueller and Comey have fertilized this growth, while blurring the lines between the public and private sectors.

Not surprisingly, Mueller and Comey's private sector employers have recurring themes: major IT surveillance companies, major defense industry contractors, and major hedge funds. When clients such as Lockheed, Bridgewater, HSBC, and Booz Allen were implicated in scandals, Comey and Mueller readily stepped in as the consummate "fixers." The Project on Government Oversight tracks contractor abuses and, according to its database, Booz Allen and Lockheed have over ninety violations against them related to U.S. contractor waste, fraud, and abuse that have led to numerous lawsuits.[24]

A public records search of the Pacer court filings database shows that there were more than 5,400 civil lawsuits filed against Lockheed between 2005 and 2010—the time when Comey served as general counsel. This is the maximum number of results that Pacer can display at one time, indicating that the total number of times Lockheed is listed as a defendant is even higher than that. As general counsel, Comey advised Lockheed on its numerous legal proceedings, and was granted power of attorney for every Lockheed executive. As such, Comey signed off on the company's annual reports. In 2009, the year Comey received $6.1 million in compensation, he signed off on a report that highlighted the numerous legal actions against Lockheed. The report said: "We are a party to or have property subject to litigation and other proceedings, including matters arising under provisions relating to the protection of the environment. We believe the *probability is remote* that the outcome of *these matters will have a material adverse effect* on the Corporation as a whole [emphasis added]."[25] The report proceeded to list no fewer than seven major, international lawsuits, including one relating to Lockheed's nuclear operations. Again, Comey directly signed off on this disclosure on behalf of Lockheed's fifteen top executives and directors.[26]

In the 2009 report signed by Comey, Lockheed acknowledges an existing lawsuit against the company involving its disposal of nuclear waste from a plant in Kentucky. According to that report, it "dispute[s] the allegations and [is] defending against them."

Nonetheless, in February 2016, Lockheed settled the suit for $5 million—small change for a contractor receiving $50 billion a year in taxpayer-funded contracts. The suit alleged that Lockheed was illegally dumping hazardous nuclear waste from a plant in Paducah, Kentucky.[27] Lockheed's nuclear operations in Paducah and in Piketon, Ohio, were part of the Uranium One story and the Russian bribery scandals.

The overlap between Lockheed, USEC, and the Russian nuclear agencies caught up in bribery schemes is unsettling. The worst part is Lockheed's apparent complicity in nuclear contaminations and subsequent cover-ups.[28]

Comey's other benefactors, Bridgewater and HSBC, are two of the largest financial companies in the world. Bridgewater manages over $160 billion in assets, thus making it the single largest hedge fund. HSBC has trillions in assets and is one of the world's largest financial institutions. On January 30, 2013, HSBC announced that Comey would join the advisory board (several months before he was named FBI director).[29] This announcement came amid a scandal implicating HSBC in drug cartel money laundering, where the previous month it was ordered to pay a $1.9 billion penalty by the DOJ.[30] Perhaps just the small cost of doing business.[31] He promised to recuse himself from HSBC matters during his FBI confirmation hearing, but there is no way of knowing what role he may have played in future investigations. Despite the large settlement, not a single HSBC executive was charged with a crime. Many believe that the FBI and the DOJ treated HSBC favorably.[32]

Overall, the relationship between Comey and HSBC's money-laundering settlement warrants further examination. He was a paid board member and served on a committee tasked with sorting through the company's legal woes. However, the amount that Comey earned while working for HSBC pales in comparison to the enormous sums he earned working for Lockheed. Why did Lockheed pay him so much? And why did Booz Allen pay Mueller? The answer to both of these questions is the same: Comey and Mueller helped Lockheed and Booz Allen build and maintain the modern surveillance state (preserving legitimacy amid negative press).

History of the Modern Surveillance State

The American public has been left with the impression that President George W. Bush and his administration built the NSA surveillance state. While this is partially true, surveillance (spying and eavesdropping) has been around as long as communication itself. In the aftermath of 9/11, George W. Bush and his advisors certainly popularized the concepts of "warrantless" and "mass" domestic surveillance. However, the U.S. government has been spying on citizens since long before George W. Bush was born, and, in some cases, even without warrants. The fact is that surveillance has grown *alongside* modern technology since the advent of the telegraph.

Electronic surveillance dates back to Abraham Lincoln's use of telegraph technology during the Civil War in 1862. Lincoln's crafty secretary of war, Edwin Stanton, established the military's first telegraph branch and, by executive order, took "military possession of all the telegraph lines in the United States." According to the Public Radio Institute, "Intercepted telegrams routinely landed on Abraham Lincoln's desk during the Civil War."[33]

Since their early days of operation, private companies like Western Union and the American Telephone and Telegraph Company (AT&T) capitulated to the state's surveillance access demands. This cozy relationship dates back to the post-World War I days of the 1920s, and into the World War II era of the 1940s. For example, Operation Shamrock was a mass surveillance program that began in 1945. The early NSA administered Operation Shamrock and worked with the Western Union telegraph company to collect and photograph every telegram sent and received.[34] The intercepts were passed on to the FBI, the CIA, and others, much like is done today. Abuses in the Shamrock and other sister operations, such as one called Project Minaret, were uncovered in the Watergate investigations in the 1970s. During that era, President Richard Nixon used surveillance technology to spy on political opponents, leading to a standoff with his FBI Director, J. Edgar Hoover.[35]

COINTELPRO to Watergate

The use of surveillance technologies has been a hallmark of the FBI, particularly under its longest-serving director, J. Edgar Hoover. Hoover joined the Bureau of Investigation in 1924 and before that worked for the DOJ during the "Red Scare," where he rounded up and deported suspected communists in the 1910s. Between 1956 and 1971, Hoover pushed FBI surveillance to an extreme under the FBI's Counterintelligence Program (COINTELPRO).[36] Hoover's FBI used COINTELPRO to spy on American citizens, mostly political activists, under the guise of "national security." Civil rights and feminist activists, antiwar protesters, and others were labeled radicals or communist sympathizers. COINTELPRO's targets were blackmailed, harassed, and subjected to extortion. Hoover spied on activists across the progressive spectrum, which was then called the New Left.[37]

Targets of intrusive surveillance under COINTELPRO and Minaret included prominent civil rights activists such as Martin Luther King Jr. The FBI's surveillance took a sinister turn when agents actually pressured King to commit suicide. In 1964, the agency intercepted King's conversations with alleged mistresses, and agents were dispatched to threaten and expose him. They drafted a threatening letter that said, "There is but one way out for you. You better take it before your filthy, abnormal fraudulent self is bared to the nation." King's assassination in 1968 abruptly ended the FBI's psychological operation.[38]

Director Hoover used FBI technologies for political warfare, but when President Nixon sought to expand Hoover's surveillance operations to include Nixon's political foes, Hoover drew a line by refusing to authorize that.[39] This led to the first *known* standoff between the FBI director and the president. Nonetheless, Hoover won and Nixon lost.

Without FBI aid, Nixon spied on his political opponents using a group assembled by close White House aides. This group was called the Plumbers and, on June 17, 1972, they were caught red-handed attempting to install recording devices at the Democratic National Committee's headquarters at the Watergate Hotel in Washington, D.C.[40]

The name Watergate became synonymous with "scandal," yet the affair was fairly tame compared with the FBI's actions in 2016. (Interestingly, the author of the 1982 *Atlantic* exposé sourced above, Pulitzer Prize-winning author Seymour Hersh, claimed that Seth Rich placed dozens (or more) emails in an electronic drop box to which WikiLeaks had access.)[41]

The Watergate scandal, and ensuing congressional investigations, led to the demise of COINTELPRO and operations Shamrock and Minaret. The ad hoc operation of the Plumbers ended too, along with Nixon's political career.[42] The end of the Nixon presidency and the FBI's warrantless spying programs brought a new threat to privacy: the Foreign Intelligence Surveillance Act (FISA), which will be examined in detail in Chapter 5.

When telecommunications technology advanced through the 1980s, so did the underlying routing infrastructure, known as "switches." Contractors such as AT&T built and operated the modern switches and data centers with "back doors" under the direction of the intelligence community.[43] AT&T even gave the NSA an *inside* office, called Room 641A, to physically intercept the massive flow of communications.[44] These contractors were generously compensated by the NSA for their cooperation, and still receive billions in surveillance contracts today.[45]

Lockheed Martin, Echelon, and the Clintons

The two biggest contributors to the construction and operation of the modern surveillance state are AT&T and Lockheed Martin. The NSA has used Lockheed as a major contractor dating back to the use of reconnaissance spy planes in the 1950s.[46] Project Groundbreaker was a major contract for Lockheed; it sought to rebuild the NSA's massive telephone and computer systems.[47] That project "encountered serious technical issues, from computers freezing up for hours to telephone lines delivering 'garbled intelligence.'" In the essential book *Prophets of War*, author William Hartung explores Lockheed's deep ties to the surveillance industrial complex:

> In the late 1990s, Lockheed Martin was implicated in a global surveillance scheme known as Echelon, which intercepted phone calls, faxes, and e-mails. A Lockheed Martin employee, Margaret Newsham, blew the whistle on the operation in 1997 when she was working at an NSA listening post in the United Kingdom and heard intercepts of calls being made by conservative U.S. Senator Strom Thurmond (R-SC). The revelation sparked several congressional inquiries, as well as a July 1998 report by the European Parliament that suggested that the information generated by Echelon was being used in

part to transmit information on European
businesses to their U.S. competitors.[48]

The Europeans thus accused Lockheed and the U.S.
intelligence community with large-scale *economic* espionage.
If true, this was an unprecedented abuse of power.

In March 2000, former CIA Director R. James Woolsey
confirmed this embarrassing fact when he admitted, under
his own byline, that the U.S. was spying on its allies for commercial purposes. Woolsey wrote an open letter published in
The Wall Street Journal titled, "Why We Spy on Our Allies."
The article revealed the following bombshell: "Yes, my con-
tinental European friends, we have spied on you. And it's
true that we use computers to sort through data by using
keywords." The U.S. spymaster cited a blunt justification
for using Lockheed's Echelon to spy on our European allies:
"Why, then, have we spied on you?…we have spied on you
because you bribe."[49]

Given Lockheed's involvement with the foreign and
domestic surveillance programs of the U.S. IT security complex, Woolsey's comment is particularly ironic. Lockheed has
a notorious history of making bribes—it has been investigated and convicted of this several times.[50] The U.S. statute
prohibiting foreign bribes is known as the Foreign Corrupt
Practices Act, and some members of the intelligence community believe that it was written specifically for Lockheed.[51]

The United States' use of surveillance technologies has
repeatedly caused diplomatic scandals. After former CIA
Director Woolsey's admission, one would expect the U.S.
intelligence community to be more sensitive to the diplomatic dilemmas posed by mass global surveillance. However,
in 2013, the United States was once again accused of spying on European allies. President Obama authorized the
intelligence community to spy on German Chancellor

Angela Merkel, according to information from files leaked by NSA whistleblower Edward Snowden.[52] Chancellor Merkel phoned Obama and demanded an explanation, and a German publication, *Der Spiegel*, reported that the U.S. spy agency has targeted Merkel's phone since 2002—before and after she was elected chancellor.[53] The 2013 Snowden revelations showed that the NSA has also spied on thirty-four other world leaders.[54]

Total Information Awareness

In the weeks after 9/11, the entire country scrambled to find out how it had happened and who was behind it. Acxiom, the Little Rock-based company with close ties to the Clintons offered the first actionable intelligence on the identity of the 9/11 terrorists. As CNN reported:

> When America was attacked on 9/11, Acxiom was in a unique position to help. Shortly after the FBI released the names of the 19 hijackers on Sept. 14, Acxiom located 11 of them in its databases. "Call the FBI," suggested company director Mack McLarty, former chief of staff in Bill Clinton's White House. By day's end, subpoena in hand, a team of FBI agents had moved into Acxiom's headquarters.[55]

Former president Clinton called his friends at Acxiom a few days after the attack and asked: "Isn't there something you guys can be doing to help?" Apparently, Clinton did not know that then-FBI Director Mueller had already dispatched a team of agents to Little Rock. "We are," said Clinton's friend at Acxiom. Clinton visited the Acxiom headquarters a few weeks later, on October 5, 2001, and once there called

Attorney General John Ashcroft and encouraged him to use Acxiom's extraordinary surveillance technology. The attorney general was impressed.[56]

Retired U.S. Army general Wesley Clark was also captivated. "This is very powerful data—absolutely what the government needs to be aware of," Clark said. Clark, who had declined to join Acxiom's board a year earlier, started working as a consultant and lobbyist for the company. He joined the Acxiom board in December 2001 and was paid $460,000 in fees.[57]

Also, it was Wesley Clark's presidential campaign that employed Mary Jacoby from Fusion GPS fame. Jacoby had close ties to Little Rock-based data companies, mega-investor Stephens Inc., and Rose Law Firm, through her father, Jon Jacoby.[58] The Clintons were also close to those companies and may have helped to introduce them to the D.C. intelligence community. As early as 1977, Hillary Clinton had even represented Acxiom's sister company, Systematics Inc., at Rose Law Firm. The relationship between Clinton, Systematics, and Rose Law was exposed during the Whitewater investigations and was closely linked to Systematics dealings with Bank of Credit and Commerce International (also known as the BCCI terrorist money laundering scandal).[59] Vince Foster was allegedly a liaison between Systematics and the NSA.[60]

Acxiom stockpiles every type of consumer data publicly available and builds profiles on tens of millions of Americans. Phone and credit card numbers, addresses, internet and shopping habits...Acxiom gathers, bundles, and analyzes information to sell as "consumer data" to advertisers. Whereas Acxiom focuses on personal data, Systematics focuses on financial data. Stephens Inc. bankrolled both Acxiom and Systematics, along with other major Clinton benefactors such as Walmart and Tyson Foods.[61]

Shortly after Mueller and the FBI joined forces with Acxiom in late 2001, Congress passed the PATRIOT Act, which was signed into law by President George W. Bush on October 26, 2001.[62] The PATRIOT Act vastly expanded the surveillance potential of the FBI, the CIA, and the NSA, among other intelligence agencies. Over the next few years, the U.S. government contracted with Acxiom, Lockheed, Booz Allen Hamilton, and many others to build new mass surveillance programs. One program was called Total Information Awareness (TIA), which was an operation where the FBI and other agencies would build profiles, like Acxiom's, on millions of law-abiding Americans.[63]

The program was conceived by retired Admiral John Poindexter, who formally proposed it to the Defense Advanced Research Projects Agency (DARPA) shortly after 9/11. Poindexter, Reagan's National Security Advisor, had previously been charged and convicted on five felony counts during the Iran-Contra scandal, but was later exonerated due to an immunity agreement. He worked in the private sector at a contractor, Syntek, which was chosen to be among the TIA contractors. In fact, Syntek received nine DARPA/TIA-related contracts since 1997—well before the 9/11 attacks. A Center for Public Integrity investigation revealed that DARPA awarded $88 million to surveillance contractors between 1997 and 2002. Of that $88 million, Lockheed Martin and Booz Allen Hamilton were the top awardees, earning at least $50 million (or 57 percent). In January 14, 2002, Poindexter returned to government service through the revolving door and began the implementation of mass surveillance programs that would benefit his previous employer.[64]

A May 2002 email written by Lieutenant Colonel Doug Dyer to Poindexter confirms Acxiom's nascent role in TIA. According to the email, obtained under the Freedom of Information Act, Acxiom was an ideal contractor to help create and implement TIA and, thus, the modern surveillance state. The email demonstrated not only Acxiom's willingness to share its databases with intelligence agencies, but also that Acxiom maintained more than 80 percent data "coverage" of the entire U.S. population and the same percentage in the United Kingdom.[65]

The email listed four ways "we can win with Acxiom." The first two items described how Acxiom would help to build the databases. Item number three on the list described a way to mitigate public outcry: "Acxiom's Jennifer Barrett is a lawyer and chief privacy officer. She's testified before Congress and offered to provide help," the email states. According to Ms. Barrett, "people will object to Big Brother, wide-coverage databases," but not to "relevant data for specific purposes." Item three concluded: "we should start with the goal, tracking terrorists to avoid attacks, and then identify the data needed (…models of terrorists are good places to start). Already, this guidance has shaped my thinking." Less than a year later, the author of the email and a "key technologist for the project," Lt. Col. Dyer, expressed Barrett's sentiment more precisely. "Three thousand people died on 9/11. When you consider the potential effect of a terrorist attack against the privacy of an entire population, there has to be some trade-off," Dyer said at a 2003 IBM-sponsored conference.[66] The privacy of American citizens has taken a back seat ever since.

What this means is that the intelligence agencies behind TIA worked with Acxiom, Lockheed, Booz Allen, and others to devise a strategy for using their technologies for warrantless mass surveillance. The intelligence agencies likely believed that the public would "object to Big Brother," so the masterminds behind TIA thought that using the threat of terrorism would be an effective way to convince the public that massive worldwide databases were necessary. Item four in the email confirmed the true motives behind TIA: "Ultimately, the US may need huge databases of commercial transactions that cover the world.... Acxiom could build this mega-scale database."[67]

Acxiom's business model of selling consumer data to corporate advertisers is no doubt lucrative, but pales in comparison to the swelling—estimated to be $180 billion by 2010—yearly government-contracted surveillance industry.[68] Acxiom's Chief Privacy Officer explicitly mentioned the public's aversion to "Big Brother" databases, yet that's exactly what the company builds. Was Acxiom more concerned with stopping actual terrorists or receiving the inevitable billion-dollar contracts to build the surveillance state?

Figure 3: TIA's umbrella agency logo: The Information Awareness Office[69]

Plans for Total Information Awareness predated 9/11 and Poindexter's formal proposal. Before he joined DARPA in 2002, he worked on numerous private surveillance programs. The Center for Public Integrity reported, "One month after [Poindexter] joined the board of directors of Saffron Technology in September 2000, the company announced it had received funding from DARPA for Genoa, which is now part of the TIA program...Many of the components of TIA, such as Genoa, have been ongoing projects since the Clinton administration." Furthermore, a 1999 DARPA purchase order specifically identified "Project Genoa and Total Information Awareness" indicating TIA (and its components) definitively pre-dated the September 11, 2001, terrorist attacks.[70]

TIA's funding almost tripled between 2001 and 2003 before it came under fire due to apparent illegalities, including violations of privacy and due process under the Fourth Amendment. (Some reporters cite the "creepy illuminati" logo specifically as the reason TIA was shut down.) But as one official commented, "when TIA got taken apart, it didn't get thrown away." The FBI's infamous "national security letters" jumped from 8,500 in 2000 to 47,000 in 2005. But instead of offering more transparency, the new programs were even more intrusive and the budgets were often concealed—further growths of the domestic mass surveillance state.[71]

Agencies like the FBI, NSA, and CIA contracted with Lockheed, Acxiom, Booz Allen Hamilton, and others to replace and expand TIA capabilities. In July 2002, Acxiom lobbyist Wesley Clarke and Acxiom chief Charles Morgan met with Vice President Cheney to pitch a program to screen airline passengers based on Acxiom's ability to "collect and sort" data on "virtually every American." *The Washington Post* reported, "Seven months later, Acxiom won a Department of Homeland Security subcontract to help create CAPPS II, a passenger-screening database considered one of the largest surveillance programs ever devised." Acxiom's partner on the project, Lockheed, was tasked to "develop, integrate, deploy and operate" the CAPPS II system.[72]

A Department of Defense (DOD) program called Counterintelligence Field Activity (CIFA) created in 2002 was also managed by Lockheed. CIFA was highly classified and had a "black budget," which means that even its costs are classified. The intelligence collected by CIFA was compiled into a database (also managed by Lockheed) called

Threat and Local Observation Notice (TALON). CIFA and TALON were used to spy on individuals suspected of ties to terrorism, narcotics, or espionage against the United States.[73] Remarkably, there was insufficient oversight. In a 2005 *Washington Post* article, military and intelligence expert William Arkin explains that "some military gumshoe or over-zealous commander just has to decide someone is a 'threat to the military.'"[74]

James Comey left the DOJ and joined Lockheed as general counsel in 2005. As noted, he earned over $6 million in 2009 (the only year fully disclosed) making sure that Lockheed's operations were legal. Likewise, Robert Mueller left the FBI in 2013 and headed to a white-shoe law firm to advise (for $3.4 million per year) surveillance data analysts and providers, including Booz Allen Hamilton and Facebook.[75] It makes sense that surveillance interests would pay former FBI directors to legitimize their operations, but don't American citizens deserve to know what these parties are doing with their data? In 2013, Edward Snowden shocked the world with his answer to that question.

Edward Snowden Reveals the Modern Surveillance State

In June 2013, an employee of one of the biggest NSA contractors shocked the world by exposing many of the mass domestic surveillance programs in detail. Edward Snowden, who worked for breach-prone Booz Allen Hamilton, publicized the surveillance state's operations in *The Guardian* and *The Washington Post*.[76] His leaks confirmed that the surveillance state had existed long before 9/11. Snowden also revealed that surveillance operations were broadened after 9/11, and that the modern surveillance state was not looking for specific actors but was rather aiming to capture anything and everything.[77]

Snowden also exposed mass surveillance programs, such as Lockheed's Echelon program, and revealed the existence of a new program called PRISM, which captures and analyzes practically every method of communication for virtually every American citizen. In addition to all phone call data, the NSA, FBI, and others have access to data from Facebook, Google, Twitter, and every other major platform for every citizen.[78]

Another Snowden groundbreaking revelation was the existence of the XKEYSCORE tool, which is a search engine, like Google, for private data collected on citizens and foreigners alike. According to Snowden, "I, sitting at my desk [could] wiretap anyone, from you or your accountant, to a federal judge or even the president, if I had a personal email."[79]

The surveillance tools exposed by the former Booz Allen Hamilton employee analyze Facebook, Twitter, and other social networks.[80] Contractors such as Booz Allen Hamilton and Lockheed make it possible for the FBI and other intelligence agencies to access citizens' cell phones, laptops, and even television microphones and cameras in real time. Not only can they watch and listen to everything Americans do, but they have also built malware to "hack and destroy."[81] Within days of his revelations, Snowden was charged with espionage against the U.S. He is currently living as a fugitive in Russia.[82]

Agencies like the FBI, the NSA, and the CIA are aggressive in their use of these technologies, with scant regard for the Fourth Amendment. A *Washington Post* report in July 2014 confirmed Snowden's revelations, and found that approximately 90 percent of individuals under surveillance, many average American citizens, are not foreign spies or targets. Innocent Americans were "caught in a net the agency had cast for somebody else" and much of the gathered information retained was personal and offered little to no intelligence value.[83]

Like George W. Bush, Obama not only authorized, but also reauthorized these programs. Obama even expanded their capabilities, despite running for president on a pro-privacy platform. "That means no more illegal wiretapping of American citizens. No more national security letters to spy on citizens who are not suspected of a crime…No more ignoring the law when it is inconvenient," promised candidate Obama in August 2007.[84]

The Surveillance State "Tag Team": Comey, Mueller, and their Conflicts

Throughout the early 2000s, James Comey repeatedly advocated for expanded surveillance capabilities. In his 2003 Senate confirmation hearing, Comey endorsed the PATRIOT Act and the surveillance tools Congress had authorized. Comey also praised the PATRIOT Act for lowering the "so-called wall between intelligence and criminal responses to terrorism." "The tools of the PATRIOT Act have been very, very important to the FBI agents and the prosecutors in the field," said Comey. "So we are very grateful to Congress for those tools."[85]

Also revealed in his 2003 Senate confirmation hearing was Comey's meager net worth. Comey was worth just $206,000 at the time, according to documents filed with Congress.[86] In 2005, Comey left the DOJ to join Lockheed as general counsel and senior vice president and moved to Bridgewater Associates in 2010. When Obama appointed him FBI director in 2013, Comey had amassed well over $10 million in compensation from just two sources: Lockheed and Bridgewater Associates. As it turns out, Lockheed is the single largest defense (and surveillance) contractor in the world, and Bridgewater is the single largest hedge fund in the world.[87]

James Comey's Nixonian Showdown

On May 15, 2007, James Comey, as a private citizen, testified before the Senate Judiciary Committee about a "dramatic" encounter he had with the Bush White House in March 2004. In that hearing, Comey provided the first public account of an incident involving him, FBI Director Mueller, Attorney General Ashcroft, and other Bush White House legal advisors.[88]

On March 4, 2004, Attorney General Ashcroft fell deathly ill with a sudden case of gallstone pancreatitis.[89] On March 10, Comey learned that President Bush, Vice President Cheney, and their legal counselors were going to compel Ashcroft to reauthorize the controversial terrorist surveillance program. Days earlier, Comey, as deputy attorney general, had explained his concerns to those in the Bush White House and was alarmed that they were planning to proceed anyway.[90]

An article by the Brookings Institution titled "James Comey's Damning Testimony" sets the scene for that fateful night:

> [It] was the stuff of Hollywood movies: a frantic race between White House and Justice Department officials to the hospital room of John Ashcroft; a dramatic showdown at the gravely ill man's bedside, in which the White House tried to get him to overrule Comey's

decision not to reauthorize the National Security Agency's (NSA) domestic surveillance program.[91]

At the time, Comey was the number-two man at the DOJ under Ashcroft, and Mueller was leading the FBI. According to Comey's testimony and the media's portrayal of the story, Comey disagreed with aspects of the Bush administration's post-9/11 warrantless surveillance.[92] So, when it came time for Attorney General Ashcroft to reauthorize the program's use, Comey staged a coup. He convinced Mueller and others within the FBI and the DOJ to threaten to resign if their demands were not met.[93]

Such resignations would be akin to Nixon's "Saturday Night Massacre," when Nixon's attorney general and deputy both resigned after Nixon fired the special prosecutor. Based on the similarity between the two events about three decades apart, it appears that FBI directors use the threat of resignation at pivotal moments, but it is hard to imagine that constitutional principles are the true motivation behind these actions. Hoover did it with Nixon, and Mueller used the threat of resignations multiple times to get his way.[94] As it turns out, the resignation of the DOJ and FBI's leadership would have been devastating to Bush's 2004 re-election effort, even though he managed to retain the presidency.[95]

At the time, Christopher Wray was one of Comey's and Mueller's cohorts and said, "Look, I don't know what's going on, but before you guys all pull the rip cords, please give me a heads-up so I can jump with you." To date, FBI Director Wray has not denied reports that he, again, threatened to resign after Trump asked him to fire top FBI officials, including Andrew McCabe.[96]

But back in March 2004, FBI director Mueller was Comey's backup in the showdown at AG Ashcroft's sickbed.

Mueller brought with him a team of FBI agents to barricade Comey in the room with Ashcroft to demand the program's demise. Mueller even authorized the FBI agents' use of force against the Secret Service if they attempted to intervene in Comey's dramatic act—an unprecedented and unthinkable situation.[97]

According to Comey's 2007 testimony of the encounter, Ashcroft seemed "pretty bad off" and needed to "get oriented." Comey was not sure that effort succeeded. He was shocked when Ashcroft, seemingly on the verge of death, agreed with his and Mueller's opinion that the program needed to end. Comey testified that Ashcroft "lifted his head off the pillow and in very strong terms expressed his view of the matter…But that doesn't matter," Ashcroft reportedly said, "because I'm not the attorney general. There is the attorney general." Ashcroft pointed to Comey, according to the 2007 testimony.[98]

Comey was now in charge. Regardless, the Bush White House reauthorized the program without Comey's signature, just as Nixon had done without J. Edgar Hoover's signature. Comey later met with Bush and convinced him that changes must be made—but these have never been disclosed and may have been "legalized" under FISA, the rubber stamp secret surveillance court at the heart of the FBI's 2016 campaign to spy on candidate Trump.[99]

Did Comey really have a moral conviction favoring Americans' privacy, as the media reporting suggests? Throughout the reporting of the 2004 incident, reporters cast Comey, Mueller, and their associates in a positive light, even heroically.[100] Comey, ever the "Boy Scout," was overcome with conviction and simply could not support the FBI and NSA's mass collection of domestic data.[101]

A decade later, a 2014 DOJ memo spelled out the state of modern intel collection and confirmed Comey's contemporary pro-surveillance leanings:

> In many ways, we live in an age of enlightenment that touches more people than any other great period of knowledge advancement in history.... The Director of the FBI Jim Comey has eloquently expressed concern about the increasing blackout of information from law enforcement and has said "We need our private sector partners to take a step back, to pause to consider, I hope, a change of course."[102]

The 2013 Snowden revelations show that mass domestic surveillance never went away. If anything, the surveillance became more pernicious and shadowy. The FBI's "private sector partners," such as AT&T, Facebook, Google, Lockheed, and Booz Allen Hamilton, have a habit of paying intelligence community directors, such as Comey and Mueller, huge sums to "advise" them while profits soar.[103] Comey went to Lockheed, and Mueller went to advise Booz Allen Hamilton and Silicon Valley data providers.

Intelligence officer James Clapper also advised Booz Allen Hamilton, between 1997 and 1998, and returned to government service during George W. Bush's administration shortly after 9/11. He briefly left that position in October 2006 and returned in April 2007. He remained in service through the end of Bush's tenure and was appointed Obama's director of national intelligence (DNI) in June 2010. [104] He was confirmed two months later and served through the 2016 election. (Clapper is now "part of the CNN family" as a paid contributor.)[105] The DNI coordinates the intel-sharing between agencies, such as the FBI, CIA, NSA, and others. Clapper, like Comey, played a major role in the Obama administration's 2016 election abuses, and has been accused of lying about those abuses to Congress.[106] Clapper had reportedly lied under oath to Congress in the past.[107] And both Clapper and Comey are deeply tied to the military industrial complex of the surveillance state.

James Comey's Conflicts

According to Comey's Office of Government Ethics (OGE) financial disclosure form, filed June 2013, Bridgewater Associates paid Comey a $6,632,616 in salary and an additional $521,104 for "unused vacation." He received a combined $63,542 from HSBC and Columbia University in directors' fees and salary, respectively. All told, Comey's net worth as of June 2013 was anywhere between $8,961,746 and $16,191,654, using conservative estimates.[108] Only Comey knows.

This is an astronomical increase since Comey's 2003 net worth of just $206,000—at least 40 times that (or approximately 4,250 percent) using the lower range and nearly 80 times greater using the upper range—all in about a decade. That is more than Eric Holder, Robert Mueller, Loretta Lynch, or any other comparable DOJ executive has earned through the revolving door (according to public financial disclosures available through Open Secrets Revolving Door).[109] Of course, there are extreme outliers, such as the Clintons, who left the White House "dead broke" only to gross more than $230 million over the next fifteen years.[110]

Also, it must be noted that these figures may not include Comey's continuing income from stock dividends, which are believed to be in the hundreds of thousands of dollars. Finally, Comey's $3 million Connecticut home, a real estate asset purchased in 2010, is not reported in Comey's OGE disclosure. The inclusion of these assets and incomes would further increase Comey's 2013 conservative net worth.[111]

Notably, these calculations do not account for the prolific Lockheed Martin stock options which Comey was awarded (and is entitled to exercise through 2020). It is difficult to calculate exactly how much Comey could have netted from these lucrative options, and it is further unclear if and when he ever exercised them. As an example, Lockheed Martin granted Comey 40,400 shares at a favorable share price of $74.89.[112] If Comey decided to exercise those options at a peak, they could've been sold for $361.00 per share and his net gain from 2010 stock options would be over $11.5 million.[113] These options do not expire until January 31, 2020, meaning as Lockheed's stock price climbs, Comey's options are worth more—options he ostensibly would not have to exercise until after leaving public service (when public reporting requirements cease). Comey was awarded 206,600 Lockheed Martin stock options over the course of his employment there and most of them had not yet expired by the time he was fired from the FBI.[114] Given that the FBI is in a position to grant Lockheed Martin billion-dollar contracts, is it possible Comey had a conflict of interest?

From 2005 to 2010, while Mueller's FBI was operating under precedents set by Comey and the DOJ, Comey and the Lockheed legal team ensured that programs were implemented legally.[115] During Comey's time at Lockheed, Mueller's FBI granted Lockheed contracts exceeding $1 billion for various IT and surveillance programs. These vast FBI contracts with Lockheed paid for tools ranging from facial recognition and biometric surveillance systems to the rebuilding of the entire FBI computer network and file system. As general counsel and senior vice president of the company, Comey counseled Lockheed on the legality of its operations and was a signatory of behalf of the entire executive team, as mentioned. He physically signed off on Lockheed's operations.

So, as Comey was earning seven figures per year advising Lockheed on the legalities of its various operations, Mueller was granting the company nine- and ten-figure surveillance contracts. First up was a sizable contract for a $305 million IT program called Sentinel. In an announcement of the contract award, director Robert Mueller praised Lockheed's endeavor saying, "Sentinel will strengthen the FBI's capabilities by replacing its primarily paper-based reporting system with an electronic system designed for information sharing." However, it was soon clear the program was plagued by delays and cost overruns. These delays and cost overruns brought Lockheed's total haul closer to $450 million.[116] FBI staff complained about Sentinel's search and indexing functions—critical to performing their duties. The DOJ Inspector General audited the program repeatedly and produced no fewer than ten reports criticizing Sentinel program specifically for its expensive delays and lack of critical features.[117]

Despite the apparent failures with Sentinel, Mueller's FBI awarded Lockheed yet another giant contract—this one valued at $1 billion. The program, called the Next Generation Identification (NGI) system, was tasked to Lockheed to build national biometric surveillance systems. Lockheed had previously helped the FBI build a national fingerprint system (known as "AFIS"), and the NGI contract sought to identify individuals using facial recognition. IBM protested Lockheed's billion-dollar award with the Government Accountability Office (GAO). The NGI program also suffered from delays and was criticized as a "boondoggle."[118] Why did IBM formally protest the FBI's NGI award to Lockheed? Perhaps there was something suspicious about Lockheed's bid, or maybe it was the fact that IBM knew of the FBI director's chummy relationship with Lockheed's general counsel and senior vice president. IBM refused to comment on their complaint against the NGI contract but a billion-dollar boondoggle raises serious questions about Comey and Mueller's pitcher-catcher-esque relationship.

Robert Mueller's Conflicts

Mueller has profited from his trips back and forth through the revolving door between the white-collar criminal defense world and the DOJ, dating back to the 1970s.[119] During the 1990s, Mueller earned substantial sums at a law firm to which he would later return. In 1993, Mueller became senior partner at Hale and Dorr, a prestigious Boston-based law firm now called WilmerHale. While there, he earned $400,000 per year as a partner. In 1995, Mueller called Eric Holder and requested to lead the homicide division of the FBI's D.C. field office—a strange move considering that Mueller was earning close to half a million dollars annually at the Boston firm.[120]

On August 23, 1996, the Associated Press reported that DOJ deputy AG Eric Holder was "shocked" when Mueller called him asking to return to public service. As reported by the AP, "Mueller, who headed the Justice Department's criminal division from 1991 to 1993, traded spacious and plush quarters at a prestigious corporate law firm for a spartan 15-by-25-foot office in the U.S. attorney's office near the District of Columbia police headquarters." Predictably, Mueller's private sector colleagues regarded this move as "a most unusual job switch."[121]

On July 23, 1998, Clinton rewarded Mueller's service as head of the D.C. homicide office by appointing him to the U.S. Attorney's Office in San Francisco, California. Among other duties, this office polices high-tech crime in Silicon Valley, where Mueller served for three years as interim U.S.

Attorney and fixer. While there, Mueller did what Mueller does best: cleaned up the messes and image after the office received bad press for, among other things, leaking case details to the press.[122] When deputy attorney general Holder left, along with the rest of the Clinton administration, Mueller was his interim replacement. A few months later, Mueller was appointed FBI director, and served a full ten-year term. Obama apparently approved of Mueller's performance and sought a rare term extension, which was granted.[123]

Following his twelve-year tenure leading the FBI—the longest since J. Edgar Hoover's forty-eight-year run—Mueller returned to WilmerHale, the large firm with offices in Boston, New York, and D.C. WilmerHale represents major corporations including Bank of America, Apple, Deutsche Bank, and HSBC. HSBC had recently and coincidentally employed James Comey to help clean up its money-laundering woes. Jared Kushner and Ivanka Trump are WilmerHale clients and were thus cited as a possible ethical conflict for Mueller's special counsel investigation. WilmerHale specializes in cyber-security for multinational corporations and compliance with the PATRIOT Act, FISA, and CFIUS matters among other focuses.[124]

One of Mueller's main clients at WilmerHale was none other than Booz Allen, the breach-prone surveillance contractor.[125] As mentioned earlier, Edward Snowden, the man who exposed mass domestic surveillance in the U.S., worked for Booz Allen Hamilton, giving him access to highly classified programs.

Interestingly, it was announced that Mueller would be stepping down as FBI director just before the Snowden leaks became public. Just after, he declared that the FBI would hold Snowden accountable for the leaks.[126] Potentially much to the relief of future client Booz Allen Hamilton. He rejoined WilmerHale in March 2014 and has directly advised client

Booz Allen Hamilton, according to a 2016 disclosure. The disclosure also lists Intel, Apple, and Facebook as Mueller's direct clients. All three plus Booz Allen Hamilton represent significant surveillance interests working with the FBI. On April 10, 2018, Facebook's CEO confirmed the company was helping Mueller's special counsel team investigate Trump. Absent a subpoena, this appears to be a massive conflict of interest, given Facebook's history with Mueller and his firm WilmerHale.[127]

As *Politico* reported, "Mueller was also on the paid-speaking circuit in recent years, addressing businesses like Goldman Sachs, charities and lecture series, as well as industry groups like the Nuclear Energy Institute." The Nuclear Energy Institute (NEI) is associated with Uranium One players, including USEC, Tenex, and NEI board-member Daniel Poneman. In 2016 and 2017, Mueller was paid $241,600 to deliver seven speeches. Special counsel investigator Aaron Zebley (the lawyer for Clinton's IT staffer) earned $10,000 in 2016 helping Mueller with his speech business. Mueller's going rate averaged just under $35,000 per speech.[128] In sum, Mueller received nearly $3.5 million per year from WilmerHale advising clients such as Booz Allen, Intel, and Facebook, and sometimes as much as $52,000 for a single speech.[129]

Booz Allen Hamilton is notorious for its failure to safeguard highly sensitive classified material. In October 2016, Booz Allen Hamilton announced their largest security breach since the Snowden leaks from June 2013.[130] Millions of classified documents were among the fifty terabytes of stolen data—the equivalent of approximately fifty million books. The trove even contained top secret intrusion (hacker) tools and malware (viruses). According to *The New York Times*:

That volume dwarfs the hundreds of thousands of N.S.A. documents taken by Edward J. Snowden in 2013 and exceeds even the more voluminous Panama Papers, leaked records of offshore companies obtained by a German newspaper in 2015, which totaled 2.6 terabytes.[131]

On October 27, 2016, just twelve days before the 2016 election, Booz Allen Hamilton announced that it had hired Mueller "to conduct an external review of the firm's security, personnel, and management processes and practices." Booz Allen receives 97 percent of its revenue from the U.S. government and 25 percent from intelligence agencies like the NSA. The firm declared "if our relationships with such agencies are harmed, our future revenue and operating profits would decline."[132]

The Pattern of Failure

The surveillance systems that contractors such as Lockheed and Booz Allen Hamilton build, maintain, or facilitate are vast and powerful. Their legality under the U.S. Constitution has long been a subject of debate. Former FBI directors James Comey and Robert Mueller claim to have strong scruples about the use of these tools against American citizens. Not once have they substantively spoken out about the abuse of surveillance tools, and in fact have praised these tools repeatedly while attacking critics. When certain spy tools were revealed by Snowden, Mueller excoriated the former Booz Allen Hamilton employee, saying they caused the U.S. "significant harm."[133] In 2016, Comey and his FBI lieutenants took surveillance abuse to a level not seen since Watergate.

Furthermore, the two men have become notably wealthy (even by D.C. standards, where the revolving door never stops) while working for the very contractors whose operations are legally, or at least morally, suspect. As pointed out earlier, and using the most conservative estimates, Comey's net worth skyrocketed and Mueller made millions representing contractors (including one with a habit of losing national security secrets). Yet there is something even worse than the surveillance and the self-enrichment in these cases: the pattern of investigative failures.

Beginning in 2001, Comey worked with Mueller on multiple cases that were later overturned or otherwise deemed failures. Mueller and Comey, the consummate "fixers," have consistently emerged and re-emerged as prominent investigative figures in highly controversial matters. And yet, most of the big fish seem to get away and are seldom held accountable for their crimes. As the older of the two, Mueller has had a longer history of overseeing investigations widely criticized for abusive tactics.

One of the first instances of Mueller's prosecutorial abuse dates back to the mid-1980s (long before Comey was in public service). Mueller, who was the acting U.S. Attorney in Boston at the time, sought to entrap the defense counsel in a perjured evidence scheme. The attorney on the defense side, Harvey Silverglate, claimed that Mueller sent a false witness wearing a wiretap who solicited false testimonies. Mueller apparently hoped that Silverglate would take the bait and later, "half-apologetically," claimed it was his "duty" to follow a lead.[134]

Years later, in December 1990, Silverglate would encounter Mueller again. Silverglate alleges his client, a former Princeton classmate of Silverglate and Mueller's and Green Beret named Jeffrey MacDonald, had been framed for a 1979 murder by military personnel and FBI agents.

Silverglate claims Mueller, who was running the DOJ's criminal division, dismissed the exculpatory evidence presented. Silverglate says, "Mueller walked into the room, went to the head of the table, and opened the meeting with this admonition, reconstructed from my vivid and chilling memory: 'Gentlemen: Criticism of the Bureau is a non-starter.'" MacDonald appealed the courts' findings of guilt repeatedly, but MacDonald remains in prison. Numerous reports indicate MacDonald may, in fact, be innocent.[135]

In the early 1990s, Mueller investigated the Bank of Credit and Commerce International (BCCI) in a terrorist money-laundering case. The case concerned the bank's complicity in laundering money for known terrorists.[136] Benefactors of Bill Clinton and George H.W. Bush both were wrapped up in the scheme, including Marc Rich, the fugitive billionaire who traded oil with Iran during the hostage crisis.[137] In 1990, the bank was found guilty of the terrorist money-laundering charges. Mysteriously, Mueller's investigation resulted in only five convictions by plea bargain, and a relatively minor $14 million fine for the bank. Other criticisms of the investigation were limits on future investigations forced by the plea bargains and that Mueller "passed the buck," and stonewalled prosecutors.[138]

Rich was later pardoned by President Clinton during his final hours as president in January 2001. The scandal became known as Pardon-gate. Rich's wife, Denise Rich, had donated hundreds of thousands to Clinton's library project and appealed to the White House in person on behalf of her husband.[139] A young James Comey investigated the pardon (among numerous Clinton scandals) and has never recommended charges.[140] The Pardon-gate scandal, and subsequent investigation, were widely condemned. *The New York Times* called it "indefensible" and a "shocking abuse of presidential power."[141]

Mueller's and Comey's patterns of failure and prosecutorial abuse continued. Shortly after Mueller began the investigation into the 9/11 attacks, he and Comey reportedly tried to frame an innocent man during the anthrax scare of 2001. In this case, the two men worked together to frame U.S. Army scientist Steven Hatfill, despite there being no evidence of Hatfill's involvement. According to Bush's deputy secretary of defense, Paul Wolfowitz, Comey and Mueller pressed hard to indict Hatfill. Comey was "absolutely certain" it was Hatfill, Wolfowitz said.[142]

Other reports confirmed that Mueller and Comey had overstepped their bounds. The FBI was accused of harassing Hatfill through an aggressive surveillance tactic known as "bumper locking," where Hatfill was followed so closely that a surveillance van ran over his foot—for which Hatfill was fined five dollars for "walking to create a hazard." Furthermore, Mueller's FBI was accused of leaking details to the press in an apparent smear campaign. On August 26, 2003, exonerated of any wrongdoing, Hatfill filed a lawsuit alleging that his constitutional rights had been violated. Once again, American taxpayers footed the bill for the misconduct through a settlement that totaled nearly $6 million (not including the costs of the abusive surveillance investigation).[143]

Around the same time as the botched Hatfill and Pardon-gate investigations, Mueller's tendency to cover up apparent FBI abuses was again demonstrated. This time in a case involving Boston drug kingpin Whitey Bulger dating back to the 1970s. To help build his own criminal enterprise, Bulger had become an FBI informant around 1975. Bulger apparently saw this risky partnership as a way to eradicate his Italian mob rivals. Bulger provided false testimony to the FBI, which led to the arrest of four men for a murder. The men were tried, convicted, and given the death penalty, which was later reduced to life imprisonment. Two of the men (including a decorated World War II veteran) were incarcerated for decades and eventually died in prison. The only problem is that the men were innocent.[144]

In 2002, FBI director Mueller reportedly directed FBI personnel to oppose their exoneration, despite the revelation of potentially exculpatory evidence (which the Mueller's subordinates termed "fodder for the cross examination"). Throughout the 1980s, Mueller (as an assistant US attorney and later as Boston's acting US attorney), opposed clemency for the innocent men in letters written to the parole and pardons board. After spending nearly thirty years in jail, the other two men were found innocent and set free in 2001. The FBI had apparently known the men were innocent the whole time, and their innocence only became public during an investigation of corruption at the FBI's Boston field office. The FBI's blunder ended up costing American taxpayers over $100 million for the false charges.[145]

The media has offered scant coverage of Mueller's and Comey's prosecutorial abuses and failures. In fact, it often praises the men for what little prosecutorial successes they do have. In particular, the 2004 Martha Stewart conviction is cited among Mueller's and Comey's *top* accomplishments.[146] The Stewart case is hardly a profile in courage. While she was charged with insider trading—earning less than $45,000 in shorted stock sales—Comey and Mueller failed to prove those accusations. The insider trading and securities fraud charges were dropped. Still, the men aggressively pursued Stewart for lying to the FBI. She pleaded guilty and spent a meager five months in jail. *The New York Times* called Comey's and Mueller's actions vindictive. *The Daily Beast* concurred, adding that the conviction was "petty and vindictive."[147] Meanwhile, *serious* insider trading on Wall Street remains rampant and routine.

On the Wall Street front, it is not clear what the FBI investigated regarding the 2007–2008 financial crisis, but the media coverage indicates that there were widespread failures.[148] In the aftermath, remarkably only a single banker was ever convicted of a crime.[149] The attorney general and longtime colleague of Mueller's and Comey's, Eric Holder, was accused of a conflict of interest because he represented many of the perpetrators in private practice at Covington & Burling.[150] Holder's and Mueller's track records seem to indicate that they were more likely to overlook the crimes of their banker and Silicon Valley clients than they were to have properly investigated them.

The Russian bribery and espionage operations discussed in Chapter 2 represent a significant failure on Mueller's part because of his inability to prevent them and for allowing them to continue for years. This failure contributed to the successful sale of domestic U.S. uranium assets to Russia.[151] Inexplicably, Mueller was not only aware of the Russian uranium schemes but was also directly involved in a separate Russian uranium episode of his own.[152]

On September 21, 2009, Hillary Clinton's State Department dispatched Mueller to return stolen, highly enriched uranium samples to Vladimir Putin. The HEU had been stolen from a Russian facility and smuggled out through the country of Georgia for sale on the black market. American spies intercepted the material before it was possible to use it in a "dirty bomb" nuclear attack. The United States was under no obligation to return the nuclear materials to Putin, but Mueller was handpicked by the State Department to carry out the transfer.[153] Why did that happen? *HuffPost* doubted the significance of the cable, stating, "The claim, if true, would be a hugely damaging revelation that would throw the whole investigation into chaos."[154] There has never been any explanation for Mueller's alleged trip to Moscow. This must be fully investigated.

Overall, there is no telling how many high-level investigations Mueller botched or mishandled in his twelve years as FBI director. To be certain, each one is worthy of a full investigation. Between 2001 and 2017, only two men led the FBI: James Comey and Robert Mueller. And when Comey took over the FBI in 2013, he simply continued Mueller's legacy of investigative fiascos. As of the writing of this book, Comey's failures and abuses, particularly during the 2016 election, are still being investigated.

In his 2013 FBI director confirmation hearing, Comey promised to recuse himself in matters relating to past benefactors such as Lockheed Martin, but there is no evidence that he ever did.[155] In fact, the evidence indicates that he and Mueller worked as a tag team, building the surveillance apparatus that made it possible to spy on the Trump team. And what did it cost taxpayers for this gigantic undertaking? The answer is tens of billions of dollars and, more important, the end of privacy for American citizens.

The FBI's surveillance capabilities allow the agency's leadership to spy on every single American citizen, with or without a warrant. This modern-day surveillance state has been weaponized against innocent citizens, members of the press, and even members of Congress. And this has all been done under the guise of laws such as FISA and the PATRIOT Act, significantly broadening the FBI's spying abilities in the wake of 9/11.

Even before 9/11, as discussed, the U.S. government spied on private citizens without a warrant using a variety of surveillance tools. But in 2016, surveillance laws, such as FISA, and tools, such as the ones created by Comey and

Mueller's employers and clients, were used against a presidential candidate. The sheer scope of the FBI's 2016 FISA operation is unprecedented in American history.

CHAPTER 5

FOREIGN INTELLIGENCE AND SURVEILLANCE ABUSE

- Domestic surveillance has been a feature of American intelligence agencies for decades.
- Nixon's Watergate affair led to the passage of the Foreign Intelligence Surveillance Act in 1978. Since then, the FBI and other agencies have used the law to conduct secret surveillance warrants with minimal oversight.
- FISA has been called a "rubber stamp" due to the tiny fraction of warrant applications that are denied.
- The vast majority of FISA warrants are approved and, through secret protocols, a single application can be used to spy on hundreds or even thousands of largely innocent individuals. Citizens, journalists, and even Members of Congress have been victims of FISA abuse.

- In 2016, FISA was pushed to new limits when the FBI used the secretive law to spy on a presidential campaign..

Background on Foreign Surveillance

The conflict between liberty and security is not new. Law enforcement has always struggled to protect citizens while preserving their rights to privacy and freedom. The Fourth Amendment protects American citizens from unwarranted searches or surveillance and upholds the freedom of privacy. Despite Fourth Amendment protections, American communication networks have been subject to arbitrary, warrantless surveillance for many years, beginning with the U.S. Cipher Bureau, also known as the Black Chamber.[1] The FBI has been the focal point of the state's struggle to maintain both liberty and security since its creation in the early twentieth century. The bureau's first director, J. Edgar Hoover, became notorious for abusing the FBI's surveillance tools and compromising the liberties enshrined in the Fourth Amendment.[2]

We have seen that former FBI directors Mueller and Comey and their lieutenants have continued Hoover's legacy of unnecessary surveillance. Since 2001, both Mueller and Comey have overseen the construction of mass surveillance programs at the expense of American citizens' constitutional rights to privacy.[3] During the 2016 election, the FBI and the DOJ coordinated with political operatives hired by Hillary Clinton's campaign in a controversial surveillance operation against presidential candidate Donald Trump.

Further, the FBI's leadership used this opposition research produced by Clinton operatives as the basis for its investigation. Comey testified that the research was unproven. Nonetheless, the unverified rumors compiled in the infamous Steele dossier were inexplicably used as "probable cause" to justify secret surveillance warrants. This was an abuse of power that has led to an ongoing purge of the various FBI and DOJ personnel involved in the surveillance operation. To date, more than twenty-five senior FBI and DOJ employees have been fired, demoted, or have resigned since the operation was made public.[4] The purge included Comey, who became only the second FBI director in the history of the bureau to be dismissed (Director William Sessions was dismissed by President Bill Clinton in 1993).[5]

A week after Comey's dismissal in May 2017, Deputy Attorney General Rod Rosenstein continued the DOJ's political operation against Trump by appointing former FBI director Mueller to lead a special counsel investigation based, at least in part, on the dossier's claims. However, Mueller's investigation looks like a smokescreen, and his team of Clinton loyalists and Democrat donors still has not found evidence of collusion between the Trump campaign and Russia, despite its insistence on continuing the investigation.[6] In spite of Mueller's broad mandate to investigate "Russian interference," his team has focused primarily on the Trump team. Meanwhile, a growing pile of evidence suggests that Russian interference may have benefited the Clinton team.[7]

At the heart of this multifaceted and bourgeoning scandal is the FISA surveillance law enacted after President Nixon used surveillance tools to spy on his political opponents.

As Watergate unfolded, Congress sought resolutions to investigate the surveillance questions and subsequent cover-up. "On February 5, 1973, Senator Ted Kennedy (D-MA) offered Senate Resolution 60 to establish a Select Committee on Presidential Campaign Activities." The committee was tasked with investigating Nixon's criminal behavior and "all other illegal, improper, or unethical conduct occurring during the presidential campaign of 1972, including political espionage and campaign finance practices." This select committee issued its final report and recommendations on June 27, 1974. Following the report, "the House Judiciary Committee adopted three articles of impeachment. Before the full House could vote, Nixon resigned on August 9, 1974."[8] The Watergate affair left such an imprint on the national ethos that the suffix "-gate" became commonly added to future political and social scandals.

Three years later, Senator Kennedy sponsored FISA, and President Jimmy Carter signed it into law on October 25, 1978.[9] The law itself was crafted by legislators behind closed doors, largely with the help of the DOJ.[10] Since its adoption, FISA tools and operations have been shrouded in secrecy and classified under "national security." While its name and origins imply that the law concerns the U.S. government's surveillance of foreign individuals, it applies equally to American citizens.[11]

The previous chapter exposed the powerful surveillance capabilities built by corporations such as Lockheed Martin and Booz Allen Hamilton. Such tools have been a mainstay of U.S. intelligence-gathering for years, as leaders have become better at monitoring citizens. Modern communication technology has expanded the government's capabilities. Today, virtually every type of communication is intercepted, collected, stored, and potentially subjected to search.[12]

In 1970, before FISA, the Nixon administration hatched a plan to remove restrictions on domestic intelligence-gathering. At the time, Nixon and veteran FBI Director Hoover were both concerned with "revolutionary terrorism" and "Red Fascism." Nixon allowed the FBI and other intelligence agencies to have unprecedented power to spy on virtually every form of domestic communication used by American citizens. The plan authorized operations to wiretap and record phone calls, to intercept and read mail, and even to break in and search physical domains, such as homes and offices, all without the benefit of a warrant.[13]

Nixon justified these unauthorized searches and seizures by claiming that he was fighting "terrorism" committed by "those who are determined to destroy our society."[14] Nixon carried out his operations despite Hoover's objections. When the FBI director refused to authorize the program, Nixon did so himself, *verbally*, without leaving an authorization trail. According to Hoover's deputy, Hoover "went through the roof."[15] As journalists have noted, Hoover's main concerns were less with the constitutionality of the program than with being left "holding the bag"—a bag containing lock picks and wiretaps.[16]

As previously mentioned, this standoff between Nixon and Hoover proved to be Nixon's downfall. After Hoover's refusal to sign off on Nixon's surveillance program, Nixon enlisted his "Plumbers," who spied on political opponents by breaking in and planting listening devices in their private offices. And, once the Plumbers were caught, the Watergate scandal began to unfold. Notably, the Nixon White House was suffering from damaging internal leaks to the press (and Nixon's Democrat opponents), and one of the primary goals of Nixon's Plumbers was to plug the leaks—hence the name "plumbers." Many forget this important fact.[17]

Fresh out of Yale Law School, a young Hillary Rodham began her political career as an impeachment inquiry staffer on the House Judiciary Committee per the recommendation of her Yale law professor Burke Marshall (who was also the Kennedy family lawyer representing Senator Ted Kennedy in the infamous Chappaquiddick scandal). Coincidentally, and perhaps ironically, Hillary Rodham and this select committee reviewed past presidential indiscretions and developed the modern precedents for presidential impeachment.[18] As mentioned in this chapter, the select committee's findings and recommendations led to impeachment proceedings against Nixon and the regulation of domestic spying activities under FISA.

FISA remains more relevant than ever. Nixon's Watergate operation now seems to pale in comparison to the scandals surrounding the Obama administration, especially those involving the FBI and the DOJ. Overall, the 2016 surveillance campaign of the Obama administration clearly eclipses the small-scale surveillance operations of Nixon's Plumbers. Simply put, Obama's "Spygate" is much worse than Nixon's Watergate.

As previously demonstrated, Obama's looming scandal involves known collusion between Hillary Clinton's presidential campaign and allies within Obama's intelligence agencies—primarily the FBI. Clinton's nongovernmental operatives, including Fusion GPS, originated the accusations that Trump was compromised by Russia. Obama and Clinton's media allies quickly tagged it Russiagate.[19] And, while the House Intelligence Committee and Senate Judiciary Committee have closed their investigations of possible Russian collusion with the Trump campaign, Mueller's special counsel investigation remains active. The Russiagate sand castle is built entirely on the strength of a Clinton-funded dossier and improper FISA surveillance. Therefore, it is crucial to determine what abuses occurred, how they occurred, and how they can be prevented in the future.

History of FISA

In 1970, after FBI Director Hoover defied President Nixon's request to deploy domestic surveillance tools, Nixon began spying without the FBI.[20] Hoover's objection to Nixon's plan does not mean that the former was innocent. By then, Hoover had already authorized the domestic surveillance of political groups, such as Vietnam War protesters and civil rights activists. These two men's repeated surveillance abuses were the direct catalysts for the 1978 law called FISA.[21] So, what is FISA really all about?

FISA defines the rules for U.S. federal surveillance techniques. The law centers on the FBI's and DOJ's procedures for intelligence-gathering. FISA established a special federal court, known as FISC, that would consider requests for warrants to search and monitor communications involving foreign targets. The U.S. government has long had the legal authority to intercept foreign communications. But foreign communications intersect with domestic communications more often than not in the modern, connected world. A closer look at the Foreign Intelligence Surveillance Act reveals its ironic misnomer: FISA seems to have less to do with *foreign* surveillance and more to do with *domestic* surveillance.

Moreover, FISA in practice creates many questions, such as:

- Is it lawful to eavesdrop on a foreign spy if the person is talking to a U.S. citizen?
- Does the interception of a U.S. citizen's phone call to a foreign entity require a warrant?
- How many people can be included in a single FISA warrant?
- Do amorphous definitions of "national security" override the constitutional protections of the Fourth Amendment?

These are among the questions that FISA sought to clarify. Ultimately, FISA simplified these issues by essentially making it *technically* legal to intercept and collect *all* calls, both foreign and domestic.[22]

Prior to FISA's enactment, the Fourth Amendment was the law of the land and unwarranted searches and seizures were explicitly forbidden. Though short, the amendment is powerful:

> The right of the people to be secure in their persons, houses, papers, and effects, against unreasonable searches and seizures, shall not be violated, and no warrants shall issue, but upon probable cause, supported by oath or affirmation, and particularly describing the place to be searched, and the persons or things to be seized.[23]

The United States of America's founders deemed this amendment vital to maintaining a free society. In 1791, when the Bill of Rights was ratified, the founding fathers knew that the "tyrant King George III" and his British army had detained, arrested, and tried their fellow countrymen, arbitrarily using a catch-all search warrant called a "writ of assistance."[24]

Abuse of this writ of assistance search warrant was one of the major offenses by the British, leading directly to the American Revolution and Declaration of Independence. According to future President John Adams, the abuses of King George III caused the early patriots "to take arms against Writs of Assistance. Then and there was the first scene of the first act of opposition to the arbitrary claims of Great Britain. Then and there the child Independence was born. In fifteen years, that is in 1776, he grew up to manhood, and declared himself free."[25] In other words, freedom from arbitrary searches and seizures (that is, privacy) was a cornerstone in the foundation of the United States of America.

To this day, warrantless searches and seizures are anathema to American constitutional rights. The Fourth and Fifth Amendments guarantee American citizens the right to due process. This means that the federal government may not arbitrarily detain, imprison, or even spy on American citizens without justification (also known as "probable cause"). According to the Fifth Amendment, "No person shall...be deprived of life, liberty, or property, without due process of law."[26]

Numerous Supreme Court decisions ruled that these amendments also apply equally to state governments under the Fourteenth Amendment's "due process clause." Section one of the Fourteenth Amendment says: "nor shall any state deprive any person of life, liberty, or property, without due process of law."[27]

These are essential rights of every American citizen.

The Fourth Amendment, and other amendments addressing due process, are enforced through what is known legally as the "exclusionary rule," which states that any evidence gathered by violating an individual's right to privacy and any evidence gathered as a result of an illegal search is inadmissible in court—it is considered the "fruit of the poisonous tree."[28]

Of course, the Fourth Amendment notably provides an essential exception to a citizen's right to freedom from searches and seizures: "probable cause," which is law enforcement's only *constitutional* authority to search an American citizen's property. Probable cause is narrowly defined and must be "supported by oath or affirmation, and particularly describing the place to be searched, and the persons or things to be seized." Furthermore, a criminal act must either be imminent or have already been committed.[29]

In 1978, FISA redefined "probable cause."[30] Under FISA, an imminent criminal act was no longer required to demonstrate probable cause. Following the September 11, 2001, terrorist attacks, the subsequent PATRIOT Act further diluted the term, with regard to mass collection of domestic communications. Today, FBI and other federal agents need only demonstrate probable cause in *suspecting* that a "target of the surveillance is a foreign power or agent of a foreign power." Furthermore, "agents do not need to demonstrate that commission of a crime is imminent."[31]

FISA and the PATRIOT Act use the words "probable cause," but instead of requiring a target to be involved in criminal behavior, agents need only demonstrate suspicion. This is tricky wordplay, but the result is that every American citizen who communicates with someone in a foreign country is a potential suspect of foreign influence. Amendments to both broadened the criteria to include any foreign communication whatsoever, so that even an American communicating with another American on vacation in England, for example, was caught in the dragnet. A 2017 report from the director of national intelligence found that the NSA collected 151 million phone records in 2016, despite having FISA warrants for only forty-two suspects.[32]

Ultimately, FISA and the PATRIOT Act provide agencies such as the FBI with "probable cause" to believe that nearly everyone is a potential foreign agent. The bottom line: Everyone is a suspect.

Civil rights organizations such as the American Civil Liberties Union (ACLU), the Electronic Frontier Foundation (EFF), and the Electronic Privacy Information Center (EPIC) have challenged the government repeatedly over FISA, its amendments, and the PATRIOT Act. A FOIA lawsuit filed by EPIC in 2000 sought details on an FBI domestic surveillance program called Carnivore. Notably, Deputy Attorney General Rosenstein's wife, Lisa Barsoomian, was the attorney of record representing the FBI and its use of this *pre-9/11* email surveillance program.[33] In 2006, the ACLU sued the DOJ over mass surveillance conducted by the NSA. The case was initially dismissed and appealed until the United States Supreme Court ruled that the ACLU "did not have standing" and could not prove that it had been targeted by surveillance.[34] In 2013, the ACLU sued the DOJ again for information regarding FISA, after its Freedom of Information Act (FOIA) requests were stonewalled by the DOJ. Eventually, the Supreme Court ruled against the ACLU once again and found that the ACLU lacked standing.[35]

FISA warrant applications are seldom refused.[36] The courts, including the Supreme Court, have ruled repeatedly in favor of mass domestic surveillance under FISA. Apparently, the FISA warrant application process satisfies "due process." Nonetheless, civil rights organizations strongly object and assert that FISA and the PATRIOT Act are unconstitutional, or more specifically, *illegal.*[37]

Foreign and Domestic Surveillance vs. Warrantless Surveillance

It is important to distinguish between the various definitions of "surveillance" used generally and during the 2016 election cycle. First, there is legitimate foreign surveillance, which is legal and *does not* require a warrant. Second, there is domestic surveillance, which *does* require a warrant based on "probable cause." Third, there is the legal gray area of "mass surveillance" or "warrantless domestic surveillance." FISA and the PATRIOT Act concern all three.

Foreign Surveillance

The FBI, NSA, CIA, and other agencies are legally authorized to perform surveillance on overseas communications.

This is "foreign surveillance." Generally, foreign surveillance is not a matter of dispute among American legal analysts.

Domestic Surveillance (With a Warrant)

Before 1928, the Fourth Amendment was the guiding principle governing domestic surveillance warrants with a strict legal test: 1. Sworn oath by law enforcement officer to a magistrate judge; 2. backed by probable cause; 3. evidence of a crime; and 4. location and duration clearly defined. In the landmark 1928 Supreme Court case Olmstead v. U.S., the court ruled that if the target's home was not entered, then electronic eavesdropping was not a violation of the Fourth Amendment. This precedent was overturned by the court in the 1967 Katz v. U.S. ruling. In that case, the court held that wiretapping constitutes a search and, regardless of location, citizens' Fourth Amendment rights protect their communications, wherever they have a "reasonable expectation of privacy."[38] But as communication technology developed and spread, new questions arose, such as:

- Do citizens have a reasonable expectation to privacy if their communications are anonymized (also known as "masked")?
- If masked communications are collected in bulk, can they be unmasked without a search warrant?
- What if a U.S. citizen communicates with a foreign agent or power?
- What if a foreign agent communicates with a non-U.S. citizen residing in the United States?

The Foreign Intelligence Surveillance Act (FISA) was supposed to answer these questions. As technology has advanced, so has the sophistication of legal analysis and, thus, authorized surveillance. The act created a highly secretive court (FISC) to authorize surveillance requests known as FISA warrants. FISC is composed of eleven judges, plus the chief justice of the Supreme Court, who appoints them. This ought to give Democrats cause for concern, as all eleven justices were appointed by Republican John Roberts. FISC is a secret court with secret proceedings, and the proceedings are classified.[39]

The only persons who appear in front of the FISC are DOJ attorneys seeking approval for spy warrants. The FISC proceedings are *ex parte* and nonadversarial, meaning no one represents or speaks on behalf of the DOJ's potential targets. This mocks American respect for fairness, such as being able to face one's accusers. FISC proceedings are also highly classified and generally sealed, which also implies minimal public or press oversight.[40]

In recent years, the FISC process has become known as a rubber stamp. In 2013, *The Wall Street Journal* reported aggregated FISA statistics in an article titled "Secret Court's Oversight Gets Scrutiny." *WSJ* found that, "From 1979 through 2012, the court overseeing the Foreign Intelligence Surveillance Act has rejected only 11 of the more than 33,900 surveillance applications by the government." The DOJ reported these astounding numbers directly to Congress.[41] This represents a 99.97 percent approval rate. In other words, the FISA court averaged more than 1,000 requests per year, every year, for thirty-three years. Of those requests, all of them were approved year after year except for, on average, one denial issued every three years. This appears to be a rubber stamp, though former NSA and DOJ officials dispute the allegation.[42] In any case, denials are beyond rare—about one denial for every 3,000 approvals. It is therefore fair to say that FISC proceedings are a mere formality and surveillance warrants are issued whenever the DOJ wants them. In

2016, the FISA court denied in-full only nine of the 1,752 applications it received that year, according to a formal letter to the House Judiciary Committee.[43] That is essentially a 99.5 percent approval rate, which is still, effectively, a rubber stamp. The fundamental reason for these bloated numbers is that FISA allows the perverse definition of "probable cause" mentioned earlier in this chapter.[44] This interpretation of the term has been challenged in court repeatedly, but with minimal success.

In practice, the DOJ and other requesting agencies can simply state that a proposed target poses "national security risks." Citing vague threats to national security, the DOJ then argues that surveillance is needed to determine the actual threat level. The agency does that, without demonstrating probable cause that any crime has been or will be imminently committed. Overall, FISA, its amendments, and the PATRIOT Act were all crafted under this guise of "national security"—shorthand for "Don't ask questions."[45]

Mass Surveillance (Warrantless)

The twenty-first century brought about a new kind of warrantless surveillance: mass surveillance. By definition, mass surveillance is "warrantless" because it involves the bulk collection of communications and the underlying information, also known as "metadata," on everyone, foreign and domestic. Much like King George III's writs of assistance, mass surveillance flouts the principles of the Fourth Amendment's prohibitions against warrantless surveillance and other guarantees of "due process."[46]

Currently, mass surveillance is the most universally intrusive area of the U.S. intelligence community's collection efforts, made possible by new technologies that centralized communications among the telecom giants, such as AT&T, Verizon, and BellSouth.

Essentially, there are just two kinds of surveillance in the U.S.:

- Surveillance *with* a warrant, and
- Surveillance *without* a warrant, also known as "warrantless."

Over time, FISA, the PATRIOT Act, and their subsequent amendments have altered the legalities of both warranted and warrantless surveillance activities. These laws now allow the bulk data collection of everything—phone calls, text messages, the underlying phone metadata (such as time stamps), Global Positioning System (GPS) locations, and internet-based communications such as email, social media activity, and internet browsing history. "Collection" means all of these data points are stored indefinitely and available for retroactive search.

So not only has the justification for surveillance of communications become easier in this new era of mass surveillance, but the ease with which that information can be stored and retained indefinitely also has changed significantly.

History of FISA Abuse

During the 2016 election, the broad definitions of "probable cause" under FISA were pushed to new limits. As previously mentioned, the FBI used a salacious and unverified dossier full of rumors and political opposition research as justification to spy on Trump's advisors. And in October 2016, just weeks before Election Day, FBI Director Comey, Deputy Director McCabe, DOJ Deputy AG Yates, and Deputy AG Rosenstein and their staffers submitted, under oath, unsubstantiated claims from the Steele dossier as *evidence* before a FISC judge. Worse than that, Comey's team bolstered the dossier's claims with a September 2016 *Yahoo! News* article written by Michael Isikoff, who was in direct communication with the Clinton contractor who drafted the Steele dossier. In other words, Comey's team circuitously corroborated unverified rumors with media reports based on the same exact source of the original allegations.[47]

Comey and McCabe signed the FISA applications and failed to disclose the origins of their so-called evidence. These two men neglected to mention that the *Yahoo! News* article was based on the same source as the dossier. Because FISA protocols allow agencies such as the FBI and the NSA to spy not only on the immediate target of the FISA warrant, but also on everyone the target communicates with, Comey, McCabe, and their agents were able to spy on the entire Trump team using the same rules intended for spying on suspected terrorists.[48]

Operation Code-Named "Crossfire Hurricane"

A shocking development in the FBI's Trump–Russia investigation saga (code-named "Crossfire Hurricane") is the fact the machinations began much sooner than the FBI has let on. On May 16, 2018, *The New York Times* reported fresh details of the FBI's targeting of the Trump campaign. The 4,000-word exposé provides insight into the distinction between the FISA surveillance of Carter Page et al. and the larger investigation into Trump's Russia ties generally. Crossfire Hurricane allegedly began in "summer 2016" and a specific date of July 31, 2016, is identified as when the FBI opened their investigation—predating the FISA warrants by several months. Furthermore, the FISA surveillance (which began in October 2016) concerned the analysis of signals intelligence

(SIGINT), but Operation Crossfire Hurricane stemmed from human intelligence (HUMINT). There was at least one FBI informant who was paid to lure members of the Trump campaign into his confidence—beginning around the time the DNC contracted with Fusion GPS to create the Steele dossier.[49] The *Times* did not identify this informant, but his name, Stefan Halper, was revealed in previous reporting in March 2018, and has since been confirmed. Halper has a long, strange history with spy agencies and political operations. He was accused of running a similar political espionage operation targeting the Carter administration in 1980 (ex-CIA Director George H.W. Bush was reportedly Halper's "handler"). CIA operative Halper is a "highly sketchy" individual in more ways than one, having been arrested for possession of "crack cocaine" in 1994.[50]

The espionage Halper conducted for the FBI under the code name Crossfire Hurricane appears to be the crucial link between Fusion GPS and the FBI's subsequent FISA surveillance (collectively referred to as "Spygate" by Trump and others). *The Washington Post* revealed a mutual friend of Halper and Steele: Sir Richard Dearlove, former head of MI6 (Steele's ex-boss and a close friend of Halper since 2004). Dearlove connects numerous antagonists in the Spygate saga to the Trump aides who were the apparent targets (namely Carter Page and the lesser known George Papadopoulos).[51]

The connections revolve around British intelligence agencies like MI6 and GCHQ, and organizations based in London, such as the private intelligence firm named Hakluyt. Individuals caught up in the US-UK spy scheme include ex-MI6 spooks Christopher Steele and his business partner Christopher Burrows, ex-Soviet spy Rinat Akhmetshin (an attendee of the infamous Trump Tower meeting with Russian lawyer Natalia Veselnitskaya—both connected to Glenn Simpson and Fusion GPS), Australian diplomat Richard

Downer (a Clinton benefactor who met repeatedly with Papadopoulos *and* FBI personnel no later than May 2016), London-based professor Josef Mifsud (a Steele associate who met with Page and Papadopoulos in early 2016), Sir Andrew Wood (a friend of Steele who met with Senator John McCain about the Steele dossier), Russian national Sergei Millian (who met with Papadopoulos and is believed to be Steele's dossier "source D"), and many others.[52]

The FBI's Crossfire Hurricane intersection with Clinton interests is undeniable. Alexander Downer once arranged a $25 million grant to the Clinton Foundation and his signature appears on the same documents as Clinton's.[53] Shortly before the 2016 election, Halper (who had allegedly sought an advisory position with Trump) endorsed Clinton over Trump on November 3, as posted in the Russian propaganda outlet called Sputnik.[54] Perhaps the most bizarre twist is that the Obama administration paid Halper over $1 million through a highly secretive office within the Defense Department that has a history of contracting with the "best friend" of Chelsea Clinton (some accounts say Halper's compensation was closer to $2 million).[55]

The connections are no doubt dizzying, but as they become clearer, a sinister picture begins to emerge: Spygate involved foreign and domestic intelligence agencies working alongside private contractors whose apparent mission was to prove Trump was connected to Russia.

The DOJ and FBI claimed to have opened their Crossfire Hurricane operation July 31, 2016, but the contacts between Halper, his British associates, and Trump's campaign associates began months earlier—by March 2016 at the latest. By August 2016, FBI leadership had dispatched agent Peter Strzok to London as Crossfire Hurricane was allegedly just heating up—right around the time Strzok and Page discussed the "insurance policy." Earlier Strzok-Page texts cryptically reference approval of "OCONUS [outside the contiguous U.S.] lures," which may indicate that the operation began as early as December 2015—more than six months before the FBI claims they started the Trump–Russia investigation.[56]

Based on the evidence, Trump's closest advisors were definitively spied on from October 2016—perhaps much earlier—until well past the election, as proved by numerous FISA renewals in 2017. Even after President Trump was inaugurated in January 2017, the surveillance continued. This means that the FBI used FISA to target advisors to a *sitting* U.S. president, which may be an unprecedented abuse of power by the bureau. (Hoover may have spied on President JFK and others, but this has not been confirmed.)[57]

Although FBI surveillance may have never been used against a U.S. president prior to 2017, the tool has been abused repeatedly since its inception. As noted in Chapter 4, most people assume that mass surveillance was a product of the Bush administration, but the FBI, CIA, and NSA engaged in mass surveillance without warrants throughout the twentieth century. Operation Shamrock began in 1945 and involved the FBI's mass collection of telegrams entering and exiting the United States. In addition, Project Minaret was a sister program of Shamrock, and continued the practices under the aegis of the NSA through 1975.[58]

The book *Prophets of War* details Lockheed's role in creating the surveillance state, especially Lockheed's work for the Echelon program that "intercepted phone calls, faxes, and e-mails." As mentioned in Chapter 4, the existence of this program was kept secret until Lockheed employee Margaret Newsham first blew the whistle in 1988. Newsham appeared on *60 Minutes* in 2000 and reaffirmed that Echelon had been used against a sitting U.S. senator. According to Newsham, she was listening to a phone call when she heard the distinctive voice of Republican Senator Strom Thurmond. Her revelations sparked several U.S. congressional and European parliamentary inquiries, but those investigations appear to have stalled.[59] Newsham worked in the United Kingdom at a secret NSA-GCHQ outpost called Menwith Hill (GCHQ is the U.K.'s version of the NSA). Lockheed has operated Menwith Hill for decades under the aegis of the Echelon program, and in 2012 the site underwent a massive expansion. Notably, GCHQ was instrumental in the Trump–Russian surveillance operation and may have even originated it. Furthermore, Lockheed Martin provided tools ("Cyber Kill Chain") for collaboration between the FBI and the Department of Homeland Security in March 2016 to evaluate Russia's cyber attempts to compromise "U.S. critical infrastructure," which now includes "election systems" as designated by the U.S. intelligence community.[60] The relationship between the FBI, Lockheed, the NSA, and GCHQ bears further investigation—specifically their involvement in the surveillance of the Trump campaign.

Senator Thurmond is not the only U.S. senator whose privacy was violated by the FBI, the CIA, and the NSA. On March 11, 2014, Democratic Senator Dianne Feinstein accused the CIA of hacking the Senate computer system and spying on her and her staff. (Notably, former FBI agent Daniel Jones was then a Feinstein staffer working on a CIA torture report. Jones would later work for Fusion GPS, where he promoted the Steele dossier, as revealed by Russian foreign agent Adam Waldman in texts to Senator Mark Warner.) According to Senator Feinstein, "I have asked for an apology and a recognition that this CIA search of computers used by its oversight committee was inappropriate. I have received neither." Republican Senator Lindsey Graham weighed in: "Heads should roll, people should go to jail.... If [true], the legislative branch should declare war on the CIA."[61] Eventually, the CIA admitted that the allegations were true, but ironically Senators Feinstein and Graham, longtime vocal proponents of FISA and domestic surveillance of civilians, voted yet again to reauthorize controversial spy programs in 2018.[62]

The DEA's Parallel Construction

On August 5, 2013, Reuters broke the news that the mass surveillance tools of the FBI and the NSA had regularly been used to build cases against ordinary citizens suspected of drug crimes. "U.S. directs agents to cover up program used to investigate Americans," the headline read. Exclusive documents provided to Reuters revealed a sinister scheme: Through a multi-agency Drug Enforcement Agency (DEA) task force, the FBI and the NSA passed sensitive information to DEA agents.

The documents were highly classified, but revealed a pattern of taking intercepted surveillance data, obtained without a warrant, then re-creating a criminal case using legitimate means. Since the DEA had not discovered the criminal lead using legitimate tactics, the agency needed to document building its own case from scratch to mask the source of the original information. Reuters confirmed with multiple senior DEA officials a process called "parallel construction."[63]

In other words, to get around the problem of the "fruit of the poisonous tree," the DEA chopped down the tree and grew one of its own in the same spot.

FBI and NSA surveillance tools used to track terrorists are also being used in minor drug-related cases against average citizens, which appears to be a clear violation of the Fourth Amendment. Nancy Gertner, a Harvard Law School professor who served as a federal judge until 2011, was shocked to learn that such a program existed: "I have never heard of anything like this at all," she told Reuters. Finn Selander, a former DEA agent, said: "It's just like laundering money—you work it backwards to make it clean."[64]

"Parallel construction" has received sharp rebukes from everyone, ranging from citizens and journalists to civil rights organizations. Members of both parties in Congress criticized the tactic and demanded answers from the DOJ Office of the Inspector General (OIG). Outrage seems universal, except for the agencies involved. High-ranking officials from those agencies have stubbornly defended the practice as routine. "Parallel construction is a law enforcement technique we use every day," one DEA official said. "It's decades old, a bedrock concept."[65]

On August 5, 2013, White House spokesman Jay Carney confirmed that the DOJ IG had opened an investigation into the DEA's "shielding of sources" and its use of other parallel construction tactics.[66] Five years later, the OIG investigation remains "ongoing"—as does the use of the tactic.[67] The Steele dossier that formed the basis of the FBI's FISA warrants seems like an extreme form of information laundering or perhaps a new surveillance slime: political parallel construction.

The Abuse of Civilian Privacy (Not Even Nudes Are Sacred)

Agencies such as the FBI, the NSA, and their contractors regularly eavesdrop on innocent civilians, according to NSA whistleblower Edward Snowden. In 2013, as noted previously, Snowden revealed that it was common for his colleagues at Booz Allen Hamilton to share extremely private details that the corporation had collected. In an exclusive interview with *The Guardian*, Snowden stated:

> During the course of their daily work [military personnel] stumble across something

that is completely unrelated to their work…
for example an intimate nude photo of someone in a sexually compromising situation, but
they're extremely attractive. So what do they
do? They turn around in their chair and they
show their co-worker—and their co-worker
says "hey, that's great. Send it to Bill down
the way."[68]

So innocent civilians not suspected of any crime are
caught in the mass surveillance dragnet. Worse than that,
their most compromising vulnerabilities are casually shared
by young men (in fairness, likely women too) such as
Snowden's colleagues. According to Snowden, many of the
personnel reviewing the data for agencies such as the FBI and
the NSA are between the ages of eighteen and twenty-two.
The privacy rights of American citizens are violated monthly
at Booz Allen Hamilton and are "seen as the fringe benefits of
surveillance positions," said Snowden. These incidents were
never even reported, let alone investigated.[69]

In 2014, the chief of the FBI's Communication Analysis
Unit, Bassem Youssef, specifically warned FBI Director
Comey that surveillance programs were open to abuse.
Youssef said, "I believe that the program, as it was, was ripe
for potential abuses. I think that every law-abiding citizen
should feel comfortable and secure in their home in terms of
their privacy, and that was not the case."[70]

Youssef is a decorated FBI special agent and a previous
whistleblower who was retaliated against by Mueller's FBI.
He supervised the FBI's surveillance program on a daily basis
from 2005 to 2014. However, Comey ignored the unit chief's
pleas for reform. In 2012, Youssef had also warned FBI deputy McCabe, who not only ignored the warnings, but also
actively tried to silence him. Over the years, Youssef repeat-

edly warned top FBI brass that the surveillance programs were a considerable waste of time and resources, and they had disrupted only one terrorist plot in more than twelve years, according to an analysis performed by Youssef's team.[71]

Journalists Spied On, Subpoenaed, and Intimidated

Perhaps more disturbing than the casual sharing of civilian nude photos by surveillance contractors is the targeted surveillance of members of the press. Several major cases of journalists under surveillance have been publicized by civil liberties groups since Obama took office. The first major case of modern surveillance of journalists began under the Bush administration and its surveillance of CIA critic and *New York Times* reporter James Risen. Risen won the Pulitzer Prize in 2006 for his reporting on NSA warrantless surveillance, specifically revealing details about Lockheed Martin's Stellar Wind operation. Risen dodged a 2008 subpoena to testify against his CIA source.[72] He escaped the wrath of Bush's DOJ only to be again subpoenaed by Obama's DOJ in 2010. His source, Jeffrey Sterling, was charged with and convicted of espionage.[73] Risen again refused to testify against his source and, in 2013, a U.S. Court of Appeals ruled that he must testify or face jail time. So, the Obama administration's abuse against journalists began in his first year as president.

The abuse continued with the surveillance of the Associated Press in 2012. According to the AP's bombshell report:

> The Justice Department secretly obtained two months of telephone records of reporters and editors for the Associated Press in what the news cooperative's top executive called a "massive and unprecedented intrusion" into how news organizations gather the news.

The records obtained by the Justice Department listed incoming and outgoing calls, and the duration of each call, for the work and personal phone numbers of individual reporters....

In all, the government seized those records for more than 20 separate telephone lines assigned to AP and its journalists in April and May of 2012.[74]

In the AP spying case, it appears that *only* the phone call metadata (incoming, outgoing, duration) was obtained and the content of calls and emails was not subjected to search.[75] But in 2013 it was revealed that the Obama administration accused FOX News reporter James Rosen of publishing classified materials relating to North Korea in 2009. In 2010, the Obama administration authorized the surveillance of Rosen's personal Gmail account in an attempt to prove that he was publishing classified materials and charge him with espionage, according to an FBI affidavit. This was a step beyond the usual perusal of phone call metadata evidenced in a later scandal involving the Associated Press. This was surveillance of the contents of Rosen's personal email account.[76] In order to widen the net, the Justice Department targeted Rosen's parents, along with more than thirty FOX News telephone lines.[77]

Sharyl Attkisson, a former CBS News reporter, was the subject of another high-profile case of the Obama administration's spying on reporters. On August 7, 2013, CBS News confirmed that Attkisson was a surveillance target after she began reporting on the DOJ's ill-fated Operation Fast and Furious gun-running scheme.[78] According to CBS News, "Attkisson's computer was accessed by an unauthorized, external, unknown party on multiple occasions late in 2012.…This party also used sophisticated methods to remove all possible indications of unauthorized activity, and alter system times to cause further confusion."[79]

The AP, James Rosen, and Sharyl Attkisson were spied on only from afar. In 2014, the Department of Homeland Security paid $50,000 to settle charges that it had *physically* broken into the home of award-winning journalist Audrey Hudson. Hudson's employer, *The Washington Times*, also received $25,000 as compensation for its legal fees.[80]

From day one, the Obama administration became notorious for targeting journalists and "cracking down on whistleblowers."[81] Jake Tapper (at ABC at the time) emailed then-Obama aide John Podesta in May 2009 and said "What's the plan? To try to intimidate reporters who ever report on anything the White House disapproves of? Disgusting."[82] Many reporters, like James Risen, were in fear of facing retaliation and even jail time. Sources would no longer talk to journalists. Eventually, Attorney General Eric Holder relented in 2014 by changing prosecutorial guidelines and declared, "no reporter's going to jail as long as I'm attorney general." However, *The New York Times'* editorial board criticized Holder's updated guidelines for their vague wording, which created a "potential loophole," allowing for prosecution relating to reports on "classified information."[83] As *The Guardian* noted, even the most Obama-friendly publications criticized "Obama's war on whistleblowers." A longtime Watergate-era attorney for *The New York Times* said, "President Obama will surely pass President Richard Nixon as the worst president ever on issues of national security and press freedom."[84] In total, Obama's administration prosecuted more whistleblowers than all the other administrations in U.S. history, *combined*.[85]

FBI Agents Use Spy Tech to Get Rich

The mass surveillance tools developed over the past twenty years are "omniscient" and "automatic." In addition, the safeguards are "incredibly weak."[86] The personnel entrusted with safeguarding America's most personal secrets routinely abuse their access and casually share compromising material with one another. Furthermore, these programs are largely ineffective in their primary mission: stopping terrorists.[87] To top it all off, some personnel within the FBI have supplemented their taxpayer-funded salaries by *selling* inside information, as illustrated by the following examples.

In 1996, FBI agent Earl Edwin Pitts was arrested in Virginia and charged with espionage. Pitts worked in the FBI's New York field office, where he had intimate access to the FBI's surveillance sources and methods. He sold secrets to Russian spies covering "a wide range of sensitive and highly classified operations," including the FBI's "internal policies, documents, and procedures concerning surveillance of Russian intelligence officers."[88] According to the FBI, Pitts received over $244,000 in income from KGB and SVR sources. In February 1997, Pitts pleaded guilty to spying for the Kremlin both before and after the Soviet Union's downfall. [89]

On February 18, 2001, FBI agent Robert Hanssen was arrested and charged with espionage. Hanssen had been selling top-secret information to the Russians for twenty-two years and was paid more than $1.4 million in cash and diamonds. Hanssen gave Russian adversaries extensive information about American counterintelligence operations, which compromised numerous projects, including a tunnel the FBI and NSA were constructing beneath the Russian embassy. Hanssen's treachery cost American taxpayers untold sums as the agencies were forced to abandon the billion-dollar tunnel project. He also revealed U.S. Measurement and Signature Intelligence (MASINT) capabilities. MASINT is an umbrella term covering various clandestine surveillance collection, such as spy satellites, radar intelligence, nuclear and biological intelligence, as well as other signal and chemical intercepts. Hanssen also sold the Russians top-secret human intelligence (HUMINT) which identified U.S. secret agents (and "KGB double-agents"), causing the arrests of dozens of American intelligence assets, and even the execution of several. On February 20, 2001, *The Guardian* reported: "FBI agent 'sent spies to their death' for cash and diamonds."[90] Hanssen narrowly escaped the death penalty and on July 6, 2001, was sentenced to fifteen consecutive life sentences. When Hanssen was arrested, he reportedly asked the FBI agents, "What took you so long?"[91]

Hanssen made a great point: He had been spying for the Soviet Union and Russia for twenty-two years. In the Pitts case, the FBI had placed him under FISA surveillance well before his arrest, and Pitts had specifically named Hanssen as a potential Soviet mole.[92] Still, it took another four years to catch Hanssen. How did the FBI miss him?

There have been more agents from the FBI and other intelligence agencies that have sold surveillance secrets and access to FBI databases. FBI agent Richard Miller peddled the FBI counterintelligence manual and other documents to Russian spies for $65,000 worth of gold and cash (and sexual favors). Miller also routinely sold access to the FBI criminal database for $500 per search until he was caught by the CIA.[93] Aldrich Ames was an infamous American double-agent, who sold secrets to the KGB for $4.6 million. Ames, a CIA officer, had compromised more U.S. agents than any spy in history and was regarded as the most damaging mole until Hanssen was caught a few years later.[94]

Most such cases involved crooked FBI personnel selling secrets to foreign nations, notably Russia. However, between 1996 and 2001, FBI agent Jeffrey Royer engaged in a unique scheme: Royer sold FBI insider secrets to stock traders. A DOJ press release from the Eastern District of New York on October 2, 2006, about Royer had the headline, "Defendant Provided His Co-conspirators with Confidential Law Enforcement Information Used in 'Short Selling' Stock Fraud Scheme." Royer was not the only FBI agent involved. First, he persuaded a young clerk, Christy Sarkey, in the FBI's Oklahoma City office to invest in the scheme. The clerk was Royer's girlfriend at the time and reportedly lost thousands of dollars on the botched manipulation scheme. A separate FBI colleague (and girlfriend) was also arrested in the scheme. Royer had left the FBI in 2001, going to work full time for the trader that had paid him for the stock tips. His ex-wife claimed he was strapped for cash and struggling to pay alimony (Sarkey claims Royer was "totally driven by money"). According to the DOJ announcement, Royer convinced his girlfriend, "another FBI Special Agent, Lynn Wingate, to continue to steal information from the FBI and give it to the scheme's participants."[95]

And the story continues. David Chaves was one of the FBI agents assigned to investigate Royer's insider-trading stock scheme. Chaves was a supervisor in the FBI's Criminal Fraud section. In December 2016, Chaves came under fire for leaking details to *The New York Times* and *The Wall Street Journal* of a high-profile, insider-trading case against pro gambler Billy Walters and involving pro golfer Phil Mickelson. Agent Chaves's leak first came to light in the defendants' motion to dismiss.[96]

Reuters reported that "according to [the defendant's] filings, Chaves and possibly other agents in the FBI's white-collar unit seemed to have made a habit of leaking about investigations to goose witnesses and intimidate targets in other insider trading cases." According to the U.S. government, everyone at the FBI and the U.S. Attorney's Office was "outraged" at Chaves's behavior. He was placed under investigation as the DOJ claimed they could "no longer trust" him. He has since quietly left the bureau.[97] This raises the question, was Chaves trying to help the FBI's case or sabotage it?

Overall, cases of FBI agents' profiting from the sources and methods they are sworn to protect reveal a troubling arrangement. The FBI is trusted with the most powerful surveillance tools on the planet, but safeguards against their abuse continue to fail. The cases of rogue intelligence agents selling access to sensitive surveillance technology for personal profit are symptoms of a deep, systemic problem. As mentioned in Chapter 4, even the intelligence community's leadership has admitted to conducting economic espionage.

One might find it forgivably within America's national interest to spy on global competitors (particularly if they gain advantages through corrupt acts like bribery), but the self-enrichment by spy agency leadership—through the revolving door—is unseemly at best. This practice earned former FBI directors Comey and Mueller millions to advance the interests of Lockheed Martin and Booz Allen Hamilton, respectively—two corporations involved in controversial global espionage operations.

Mueller Investigation: Fruit of the Poisonous Tree?

In this chapter, we have provided some historical context about the evolution of surveillance in the United States. To recap, surveillance methods and techniques were used in some form or another for the better part of the twentieth century. The 1970s investigation into the Watergate scandal revealed a sophisticated level of political espionage for that era. Several years later, FISA was signed into law to presumably address U.S. government surveillance of foreign individuals, but it opened the door still wider to surveillance of American citizens.

The U.S. government is legally authorized to conduct secret surveillance on U.S. citizens under FISA, provided that the government receives a FISA court-approved warrant. This warrant is backed by a sworn oath that there is probable cause to suspect that the surveillance target is working for a foreign government. The "probable cause" standard under FISA differs significantly from its constitutional meaning that a crime has been committed or is imminent. According to the DOJ's understanding of FISA, "agents do not need to demonstrate that commission of a crime is imminent."[98]

The events of 9/11 led to the enactment of the PATRIOT Act, and a new era of surveillance was born, aided by the communications technology boom of electronic devices, and human ingenuity found avenues to spy on those communications in ever more sophisticated ways. As a result, some high-profile individuals (including public officials), have been able to exploit and profit from the modern surveillance system.

This exploitation and profit have occurred under the cover of "national security" and infringe on the privacy rights of unwitting American citizens, including a sitting United States president. That is why this matters.

The evidence to date has revealed that the FBI definitely spied on Trump campaign advisors Carter Page, Paul Manafort, and Mike Flynn during the 2016 election cycle. By extension, anyone who communicates with a FISA target is also subject to surveillance. According to surveillance experts, the entire Trump campaign staff and those with whom they communicated may have also been spied on.[99]

Another whistleblower, former NSA cryptographer William Binney, built the underlying spy agency infrastructure. Binney indicates that the NSA uses a term called "hop" to refer to the degrees of separation from a target's communications. For example, "one hop" includes anyone directly communicating with the target. "Two hops" means anyone in communication with *either* the target or those one hop from the target.[100]

In 2013, NSA officials testified to Congress that the agency could even perform "three-hop queries." This has exponential ramifications. Essentially, once a FISA warrant has been granted, agencies such as the FBI and the NSA have unlimited access to *anyone.* And through a process known as "reverse targeting," the FBI and other agencies are able to use the NSA as a "'backdoor' to gain warrantless access" to the communications of American citizens. Moreover, these agencies may use any communication with a foreign citizen as a pretense to begin a domestic investigation.[101]

This type of spying, according to Binney, creates a rarely matched surveillance state: "It's better than anything that the KGB, the Stasi, or the Gestapo and SS ever had."[102] In 2013, German Chancellor Angela Merkel "confronted Obama" about the intrusive surveillance apparatus of the United States. "This is like the Stasi," she said. A former Stasi officer would have agreed: "the vast scope of NSA's surveillance surprised me." Another quipped, those capabilities would have been "a dream come true" for the communist East German secret police.[103]

Were Fourth Amendment rights violated when the FBI listened in on Flynn, Manafort, Page, and others' phone calls, and intercepted their electronic communications?

First, Fusion GPS built the dossier. Then, the company laundered it through various allies within the State and Justice Departments, Congress, and allies in the media. The end goal was to take down Trump. In order to achieve this goal, these groups used the Steele dossier as the primary basis for a FISA warrant, which permitted them to spy on Trump team members. Furthermore, the warrant had to be approved by FISC (the FISA court). FISC reviewed at least four warrant applications and renewals, with signatories including Comey, McCabe, and Rosenstein. According to congressional investigative documents, Comey and McCabe both misled FISC and withheld crucial information. And, as previously mentioned, Comey and McCabe repeatedly applied for, and were granted, FISA warrants based on the "salacious and unverified" information contained in the dossier.

Former FBI director Mueller knows exactly what happened because he led the bureau for twelve years and had a significant hand in creating the very processes that were abused. To date, Mueller's investigation has not focused on any of these abuses, and it appears that he is engaging in a massive cover-up.

CONCLUSION

On President Obama's last day in office, January 20, 2017, one of his closest advisors on national security, Susan Rice, sent a classified email documenting a meeting that she had attended two weeks earlier. The meeting was between her, President Obama, Vice President Joe Biden, FBI Director James Comey, and Deputy Attorney General Sally Yates. It came after a separate "briefing by IC [intelligence community] leadership on Russian hacking during the 2016 Presidential election," according to the email. In this message, sent minutes after Donald Trump was sworn in as the forty-fifth president, Susan Rice apparently wanted to be sure that she had all her facts straight, so she typed up her recollections of the January 5 meeting with the president, vice president, and FBI and DOJ leadership. She wrote:

> President Obama began the conversation by stressing his continued commitment to ensuring that every aspect of this issue is handled by the Intelligence and law enforcement communities "by the book". The President stressed that he is not asking about, initiating or instructing anything from a law enforce-

ment perspective. He reiterated that our law enforcement team needs to proceed as it normally would by the book.[1]

The email went on to mention discussions from the meeting about whether or not they could, or should, share certain information with the incoming Trump administration, particularly as it related to the Obama administration's Russian investigations.

Whom did Susan Rice send this email to? She sent it to herself.[2]

By the Book or CYA?

Emailing oneself is a strange move for someone seeking to do things "by the book." Why would she reiterate Obama's alleged motives like that? Why document her intent in an eleventh-hour email to herself? The email, after some redactions of classified information, goes on to say, "The President asked Comey to inform him if anything changes in the next few weeks that should affect how we share classified information with the incoming team. *Comey said he would* [emphasis added]."[3]

The reluctance by Obama and his closest advisors to share their alleged intelligence on Russian election interference is telling. If Russia had in fact hacked anyone in an attempt to influence the 2016 election, and there was conclusive evidence demonstrating that, wouldn't that be a matter of national security the incoming administration should know about? Wouldn't they want to be sure that Trump did something about it? And if he didn't, wouldn't they want to show that they had made their best effort to advise him to do so?

The email is further revealing in that it names James Comey as a point of contact for Obama during the transition.

Did Obama intend for then-FBI director Comey to communicate with him after Trump's inauguration? Was Comey supposed to be Obama's mole? Comey would later be fired by Trump in May 2017. Comey has been accused of leaking classified material to damage President Trump and, after he was fired, allegedly leaked further details—perhaps as retaliation for the firing—implicating Trump in obstruction for requesting that he close the Mike Flynn investigation.[4]

Apparently, sometime after Trump fired Comey on May 9, 2017, Comey began leaking written memos of his conversations with the president—implying that Trump may have said untoward things. *The Washington Post* consequently ran the headline, "Why Trump should be very afraid of James Comey's memos." The piece told readers what to think about Comey's alleged memos, which *The Washington Post* said "should strike fear into the White House." Comey's memos are, the article added, "significant enough and will lead to more allegations of Trump obstructing justice."[5]

The Democrats and their allies across the media seized on Comey's alleged memos and immediately began drafting articles of impeachment based on exactly that charge: obstruction of justice.[6] The fiasco directly led to Deputy Attorney General Rod Rosenstein's appointment of former FBI Director Robert Mueller to lead a special counsel investigation. (Attorney General Jeff Sessions had earlier recused himself under pressure from matters relating to the Russia investigation.) The June 2018 IG report indicated that Comey had been insubordinate in his handling of the Clinton email scandal, having "deviated from well-established Department policies in a way intentionally designed to avoid supervision."[7] Senator Grassley quizzed IG Horowitz about Comey's use of private email to conduct bureau business and specifically identified Comey's leaked memos as possible grounds for criminal investigation. Horowitz confirmed that he received a referral from the FBI to investigate Comey further for possible mishandling of classified information (a felony punishable for up to ten years in prison).[8]

To date, Comey has not published these memos, but his tell-all book, titled *A Higher Loyalty: Truth, Lies, and Leadership*, lays out his version of the events contributing to his demise.[9] James Comey has a very peculiar version of truth, lies, and leadership.

For example, Comey admits that the reason he was comfortable announcing the reopening of Clinton's email investigation just one week before the November 2016 election was due to her strong showing in the polls.[10] Clinton and her allies excoriated Comey for the announcement.[11] As much as any factor, Clinton blames that one specific incident on her electoral loss. Comey explains: "It is entirely possible that, because I was making decisions in an environment where Hillary Clinton was sure to be the next president, my concern about making her an illegitimate president by concealing the restarted investigation bore greater weight than it would have if the election appeared closer or if Donald Trump were ahead in all polls."[12] It's a long and confusing sentence, but what Comey basically admits is that because Clinton was heavily favored to win, that may be why he was comfortable announcing that she was still under investigation. Is Comey implying that if Clinton weren't heavily favored, he might have kept the investigation quiet? If the polls had been more accurate and shown that the race was too close to call, would Comey have covered up Clinton's email troubles better? Comey's intimate involvement with the FBI surveillance operation against Trump suggests just that.

Compromised: Truth, Lies, and Leadership Failures

Comey's memoir seeks to justify his and his deputies' actions throughout the 2016 election. Comey's book contains mischaracterizations and petty personal attacks on President Trump (the "slightly orange" Trump "appeared shorter than he seemed").[13] The truth is that Comey, his FBI lieutenants, and their 2016 "insurance policy" against Trump were built on lies and failures of leadership. This book has examined many of those troubling failures.

A quick recap of what we've learned:

Chapter 1: The Insurance Policy

FBI Director James Comey and his deputy, Andrew McCabe, were central to the 2016 election abuses and each may be guilty of a number of the following abuses of power: mishandling classified information, leaking classified information to the press, lying under oath, lying to Congress and, ultimately, politicizing the FBI and DOJ during the 2016 election. Republicans and Democrats work together to maintain a unified front to support a swampy status quo. Republicans are as much to blame as Democrats. After all, James Comey, Andrew McCabe, Robert Mueller, and Rod Rosenstein were all registered Republicans (the FISA court is dominated by Republicans as well).[14] This is a bipartisan issue.

Chapter 2: The FBI's Burial of Uranium Scandals

The FBI and DOJ could have stopped the sale of Uranium One to Russia. They didn't, despite intimate knowledge of Russian nuclear-related bribery, espionage, racketeering, kickbacks, and money-laundering schemes that directly implicated the Russian nuclear agency (Rosatom) at least one year before the Uranium One takeover. Clinton has received the lion's share of criticism for allowing the deal to go through, and rightfully so, since the Clintons received $145 million from Uranium One investors and failed to disclose (read: hid) millions donated to them from the chairman of the company.

We've learned that there were even more undisclosed Clinton donations, more Russian agents with ties to the Clintons, and the closest thing to a smoking gun: The Russian's U.S. attorney who advised on the Uranium One acquisition—Theodore Kassinger—was working within the State Department. Hillary Clinton's defenders argue that she did not approve the sale by herself. That's true, but is it any better? They believe that excuse should exonerate her. In fact, it damns Obama's closest advisors. Ultimately, Obama's entire committee on foreign investment (CFIUS), which approved the deal, may have been compromised from the start.

Chapter 3: The FBI's and DOJ's Foreign Agents Problem (FARA)

The FBI and DOJ are responsible for investigating and enforcing laws that guard against foreign influence. They have objectively failed. Trump opponents claim that Russians and their agents colluded with Trump (or at the very least meddled). Clinton opponents similarly claim that the Clintons got paid handsomely amid numerous Russian dealings. One safeguard specifically governs the lobbying disclosures, and thus the political influence, of foreign agents. It's called FARA, and only eight employees in the DOJ are assigned to investigate any violations of it.

Chapter 4: The United Surveillance States of America (USSA)

Former FBI directors James Comey and Robert Mueller have a long history of investigative failures. Comey and Mueller have worked together, pitcher and catcher, promoting surveillance interests from inside the FBI and out. Comey's net worth skyrocketed over 4,000 percent after he, in essence, changed the rules regarding domestic surveillance and reporting and advocated programs to his benefactors' gain. In one year alone, Comey received $6.1 million from a single source: Lockheed Martin, the single largest U.S. contractor in history and a major surveillance state player.

Chapter 5: Foreign Intelligence and Surveillance Abuse

Surveillance abuses have been legion since before 9/11. Abuses, including widespread spying on innocent American citizens, are "legally" permitted under the Foreign Intelligence Surveillance Act (FISA). The FBI and DOJ obtain secret warrants from a secret court in secret proceedings. The proceedings are nonadversarial, and the accused targets never face their accusers.

These FISA warrants, once approved, do not stop at a simple wiretap. They allow retroactive search and analysis of the entire history of a surveillance target's communications. Phone calls, text messages, email, financials, internet use history, and even private social media activity—are all subject to indefinite collection, search, and analysis.

The FBI and other intelligence agencies get rubber stamp approvals from the secret FISA court. According to an analysis spanning thirty-three years, more than 1,000

FISA applications are submitted each year on average. All of them are approved (or amended) with the exception of one denial issued every third year (a 99.97 percent approval rate). The 2016 election abuses bear many resemblances to Nixon's Watergate affair, but in comparison, Watergate was child's play.

The Schemes of Lawyers

James Comey was with Susan Rice during that January 2017 "by the book" meeting with Obama. According to Rice's email to herself, Comey agreed to pass on information about this. Justice and transparency advocate Tom Fitton of Judicial Watch says of Rice's email:

> *The corrupt Susan Rice CYA email confirms [the] need to question Obama and Biden about Clinton/DNC Dossier. The whole Russia collusion investigation is a scam targeting [President Trump].*[15]

The recollections of both Rice and Comey appear as either weapons or defensive maneuvers. This is a very lawyerly tactic.

Virtually every major player mentioned throughout this book is an attorney. Obama is an attorney. Hillary Clinton is an attorney. Bill Clinton *was* an attorney, until he was disbarred for lying under oath. Most of Clinton's closest aides are attorneys. Former attorneys general Eric Holder and Loretta Lynch are obviously two of the most experienced in the country. Former FBI directors Comey and Mueller are attorneys, along with most of their lieutenants. Almost all of these individuals have worked in the criminal justice system most of their careers. Why is this important? As the nation's top authorities on the law, the president and his cabinet officers—particularly the DOJ—are supposed to determine what constitutes a federal crime. If they appear to be above the law, that is because they *are the law*. For twenty years, they have decided what constitutes criminal activity and, beyond that, what crimes are prosecutable.

Like *Clinton Cash,* the research for this book began with the mantra of every white-collar criminal investigator: "Follow the money." With the Clintons, it was a simple path: Bill was overpaid to give a speech, the Clinton Foundation received a massive donation, and Hillary Clinton's office returned the favor with some beneficial State Department action. *Clinton Cash* provided no fewer than ten concrete examples of such quid pro quos.

Men like Comey and Mueller are more guarded. They fancy themselves "Boy Scouts." Nonetheless, patterns of their own enrichment began to emerge. Through our investigation, we soon realized that Comey, Mueller, and others became rich passing back and forth through the revolving door. We were unable to link their huge compensation to direct official action. This led us to the hypothesis of a more complex (and harder to *prove*) business model: the retainer model.

The Retainer Model

As attorneys, these individuals are obviously familiar with the concept of a retainer. A retainer is the upfront and ongoing compensation paid to attorneys so that when their services are needed, they will be on call. This same model, applied to government employees, might explain the massive sums that individuals such as Clinton, Holder, and Comey received. It is not even illegal.

The rules say that government employees must recuse themselves from matters involving previous employers, but there is no evidence that Clinton, Comey, or any of the rest of them recused themselves on any matter, even those with apparent conflicts. The only relevant recusal came from Comey's deputy, Andrew McCabe. McCabe's recusal from the Clinton email investigation came just a week before the election, after he had been working on the case for more than a year. Hardly a profile in integrity.

It is often difficult to prove a quid pro quo without evidence of intent. Powerful operators, such as the Clintons and Comey, know this. The most frequent defense of this sort of corruption is, "There's no evidence of quid pro quo." It is a convenient defense and often leads to the questions, what did they know, and when did they know it? The investigation becomes very complicated and technical, much like investigating insider trading. To establish intent, the investigator must connect the timing of certain transactions to corresponding favorable actions by public officials in order to identify possible law-breaking.

Yet, the retainer model avoids that possibility. After all, how can you prove a quid pro quo if the payments and favorable actions are separated from each other by months or even years? It is especially difficult when payments are made to a separate entity such as the Clinton Foundation.

The theory goes, if you separate the timing of payments from the actions they are meant to influence, they no longer look like obvious bribes. At worst, they look like a conflict of interest, which typically carries little risk of a penalty and, ultimately, might be excused by promises of future recusal. Such recusals, though, are rare and often applied after the damage is done.

This model fits with the well-known revolving door between public service and private business, where one is paid in advance for what they will do in government service, or rewarded for what they have done…or both.

The FBI's and DOJ's Triple-F Rating

Throughout the book, we discussed FISA and FARA—the two big protections against subversion by foreign powers. Both laws were involved in the FBI's and DOJ's notable failures in 2016. But there is a third law at work too: The Freedom of Information Act (FOIA). Like FISA and FARA, FOIA has been abused and violated.

One group of stakeholders has been noticeably absent from discussions of 2016 abuses: American voters. Voters had their rights violated too—their government has not been transparent. FOIA is specifically designed to ensure transparency by the federal government. The law guarantees citizens the right to request timely production of unclassified or declassified government documents of its proceedings. Unfortunately, FOIA requests go largely unanswered for months and even years (if they are ever answered at all). Foot-dragging by the government, or partial responses to FOIA requests, are common.[16]

Across administrations, DOJ and FBI effectiveness can be judged based on how they administer these three laws: FISA, FARA, and FOIA ("the three Fs"). In grading the FBI's and DOJ's performance, one finds that these three F's are symptomatic of the larger picture. FISA, FARA, and FOIA concern surveillance, foreign influence, and transparency, respectively. Each law played a major role in the 2016 elections. Each law has been abused and improperly enforced for at least twenty years.

When the FBI abuses FISA, civil liberties are trampled. When FARA enforcement is weak, foreign influence runs amok. When FOIA is stifled, crucial transparency becomes opaque. When these laws fail, as demonstrated throughout this book, we need serious investigations and reform.

FARA is administered by the DOJ directly, yet prosecutions under this law are at an all-time low. Since the rules changed under Bill Clinton's administration, FARA filings plummeted. That seems awfully convenient, given that the Clinton Foundation itself operated like an off-the-books foreign lobbying outfit. It is only since Paul Manafort was indicted in 2017 that registrations of lobbyists for foreign interests have grown. Still, this is welcome news, and shows that when the law is properly enforced, lobbyists for foreign powers will comply.

The Freedom of Information Act (FOIA) exists so citizens may know what their government is doing. American taxpayers finance the $4 trillion U.S. annual budget. As the key stakeholders in America, we the people are entitled to review unclassified proceedings and documents. The FBI and DOJ's administration of FOIA is atrocious.[17]

Recommendations

There are numerous ongoing investigations, and at least twenty-five individuals, including James Comey, Andrew McCabe, and several of their associates, have resigned or been fired. All of this is a good start, but not nearly enough. The approval of the sale of Uranium One by CFIUS in late 2010 still needs a full and public accounting. Who on that committee was compromised by conflicting loyalties? When will the questions be answered?

After Manafort's indictment, FARA registrations by lobbyists representing foreign powers suddenly skyrocketed.[18] But for the disingenuous charging of Manafort with very old crimes, this is a great example of how justice under the rule of law is supposed to work. The increase of disclosures is a good start, but continued pressure is the only thing fighting the temptation for these lobbyists to once again "forget" to declare that they are working for a foreign government.

The culture of corruption in Washington, D.C., has earned it a famous nickname: "The Swamp." The self-enrichment and myriad abuses of power are like a fungus infecting America's capital city. The best way to ensure that Trump and his cronies do not continue down the path laid by previous administrations is to conduct full, fair, and open investigations. Sunlight—that is, transparency—is, as always, the best disinfectant. Once the crooks (on all sides) are exposed, those found guilty must be publicly sentenced, and the sentence must be commensurate with their crimes. Only then will justice be restored.

ENDNOTES

Introduction

[1]   Matt Apuzzo, "F.B.I. Raids Office of Trump's Longtime Lawyer Michael Cohen; Trump Calls It 'Disgraceful,'" *The New York Times*, April 9, 2018, https://www.nytimes.com/2018/04/09/us/politics/fbi-raids-office-of-trumps-longtime-lawyer-michael-cohen.html; "Charlie Hurt: Changing Focus from 'Russia Collusion' to Stormy Daniels Like 'Going After Al Capone for Tax Evasion,'" video clip, Fox News, May 3, 2018, http://insider.foxnews.com/2018/05/03/trump-mueller-probe-going-russia-collusion-stormy-daniels-al-capone-and-tax-evasion.

[2]   Ryan Lucas, "Does FBI Raid on Trump Lawyer Cohen Mean Attorney-Client Privilege is 'Dead'?" NPR, April 10, 2018, https://www.npr.org/2018/04/10/601153729/does-fbi-raid-on-trump-lawyer-cohen-mean-attorney-client-privilege-is-dead.

[3]   Luis Sanchez and Sylvan Lane, "Treasury Watchdog Probing How Stormy Daniels Lawyer Got Cohen Bank Records," *The Hill*, May 9, 2018, http://thehill.com/homenews/administration/386931-treasury-watchdog-probing-how-stormy-daniels-lawyer-got-cohens-bank.

[4]   Pat Ralph, "The Michael Cohen Raid Shows that Mueller Doesn't Really Have Any Limits on His Investigation," *Business Insider*, April 10, 2018, http://www.businessinsider.com/cohen-raid-mueller-limits-on-investigation-2018-4.

[5]   "The Law Is Coming, Mr. Trump," *The New York Times*, April 10, 2018, https://www.nytimes.com/2018/04/10/opinion/trump-michael-cohen-raid.html.

[6]   Avery Anapol, "Colbert Audience Cheers News of Cohen Office Raid," *The Hill*, April 10, 2018, http://thehill.com/blogs/in-the-know/382420-colbert-audience-cheers-at-news-of-michael-cohen-office-raid.

7   "Mueller Has Gone 'Rogue': Hannity Says Probe 'Off the Rails' After Cohen Raid," Fox News, April 10, 2018, http://insider.foxnews.com/2018/04/10/hannity-rips-mueller-probe-declared-war-donald-trump-cohen-raid.

8   Kevin Breuninger and Mike Calia, "Rosenstein Personally Approved FBI Raid Against Trump Lawyer Michael Cohen: NYT," CNBC, April 10, 2018, https://www.cnbc.com/2018/04/10/rosenstein-personally-approved-fbi-raid-against-trump-lawyer-michael-cohen-nyt.html.

9   Federal Bureau of Investigation, "A Brief History: The Nation Calls, 1908-1923," accessed April 9, 2018, https://www.fbi.gov/history/brief-history.

10   Ibid.

11   Federal Bureau of Investigation, "Frequently Asked Questions," accessed April 13, 2018, https://www.fbi.gov/about/faqs; Federal Bureau of Investigation, "Seal & Motto," accessed April 13, 2018, https://www.fbi.gov/history/seal-motto.

12   Federal Bureau of Investigation, "Contact Us: Field Offices," accessed April 13, 2018, https://www.fbi.gov/contact-us/field-offices.

13   Federal Bureau of Investigation, "A Brief History: And Justice for All, 1954-1971," accessed April 9, 2018, https://www.fbi.gov/history/brief-history/and-justice-for-all; Beverly Gage, "What an Uncensored Letter to M.L.K. Reveals," *The New York Times*, November 11, 2014, https://www.nytimes.com/2014/11/16/magazine/what-an-uncensored-letter-to-mlk-reveals.html?.

14   U.S. Department of Justice, Office of the Inspector General, "All Reports," accessed April 9, 2018, https://oig.justice.gov/reports/all.htm; Sarah N. Lynch, "Former FBI No. 2 McCabe Fired; Says Trump Administration Targeted Him," Reuters, March 16, 2018, https://www.reuters.com/article/us-usa-trump-mccabe/former-fbi-no-2-mccabe-fired-says-trump-administration-targeted-him-idUSKCN1GT02J; Ian Schwartz, "Turley: Comey May Have Lied to Congress About Not Leaking, McCabe Firing Hurts Case," *Real Clear Politics*, March 18, 2018, https://www.realclearpolitics.com/video/2018/03/18/turley_comey_may_have_lied_to_congress_under_oath_leaking_mccabe_firing_hurts_case.html; United States Senate, "Letter from members of congress to the Honorable Jeff Sessions, Attorney General, the Honorable Christopher Wray, Director, Federal Bureau of Investigation, and the Honorable John Huber, United States Attorney for the District of Utah," April 18, 2018.

15   Jon Cohen and Aaron Blake, "Hillary Clinton Reaches New Heights of Political Popularity," *The Washington Post*, January 23, 2013, https://www.washingtonpost.com/news/the-fix/wp/2013/01/23/record-high-for-hillary-clinton-as-she-faces-little-regarded-congress/?utm_term=.949f6ef91817.

16   C. Eugene Emery Jr., "Hillary Clinton's Approval Ratings as Secretary of State Were High, But They're Not Now," *Politifact*, May 22, 2016, http://

www.politifact.com/truth-o-meter/statements/2016/may/22/hillary-clinton/hillary-clintons-approval-rating-secretary-state-w/.

[17] Michael S. Schmidt, "Hillary Clinton Used Personal Email Account at State Dept., Possibly Breaking Rules," *The New York Times*, March 2, 2015, https://www.nytimes.com/2015/03/03/us/politics/hillary-clintons-use-of-private-email-at-state-department-raises-flags.html.

[18] Z. Byron Wolf, "8 Oddities of Hillary Clinton's Email Presser," CNN, March 17, 2015, https://www.cnn.com/2015/03/10/politics/hillary-clinton-press-conference-will-satisfy-few/index.html.

[19] Jeffrey M. Jones, "Clinton Favorability, Familiarity Bests 2016 Contenders," Gallup, March 12, 2015, http://news.gallup.com/poll/181949/clinton-favorability-familiarity-bests-2016-contenders.aspx.

[20] Fernando Espuelas, "Ignore the Noise—Clinton Will Win in 2016," *The Hill*, March 12, 2015, http://thehill.com/blogs/pundits-blog/presidential-campaign/235507-ignore-the-noise-clinton-will-win-in-2016.

[21] Jo Becker and Mike McIntire, "Cash Flowed to Clinton Foundation Amid Russian Uranium Deal," *The New York Times*, April 23, 2015, https://www.nytimes.com/2015/04/24/us/cash-flowed-to-clinton-foundation-as-russians-pressed-for-control-of-uranium-company.html; Chris Cillizza, "Of Course the Media Should Report on 'Clinton Cash,'" *The Washington Post*, April 20, 2015, https://www.washingtonpost.com/news/the-fix/wp/2015/04/20/of-course-the-media-should-report-on-clinton-cash/?utm_term=.0a9037f70676; James V. Grimaldi, Rebecca Ballhaus, and Peter Nicholas, "Gifts to Hillary Clinton's Family Charity Are Scrutinized in Wake of Book," *The Wall Street Journal*, April 22, 2015, https://www.wsj.com/articles/gifts-to-hillary-clintons-family-charity-are-scrutinized-in-wake-of-book-1429754883.

[22] Robert Yoon, "$153 Million in Bill and Hillary Clinton Speaking Fees, Documented," CNN, February 6, 2016, https://www.cnn.com/2016/02/05/politics/hillary-clinton-bill-clinton-paid-speeches/index.html.

[23] Dan Merica, "Bill Clinton Defends Foundation's Acceptance of Foreign Money," CNN, March 7, 2015,https://www.cnn.com/2015/03/07/politics/bill-clinton-family-foundation/index.html.

[24] Associated Press, "Many Who Met with Clinton as Secretary of State Donated to Foundation," CNBC, August 23, 2016, https://www.cnbc.com/2016/08/23/most-of-those-who-met-with-clinton-as-secretary-of-state-donated-to-foundation.html.

[25] Jo Becker and Mike McIntire, "Cash Flowed to Clinton Foundation Amid Russian Uranium Deal," *The New York Times*, April 23, 2015, https://www.nytimes.com/2015/04/24/us/cash-flowed-to-clinton-foundation-as-russians-pressed-for-control-of-uranium-company.html.

[26] Peter Schweizer, *Clinton Cash* (New York: HarperCollins, 2015); "Rep. Sean Duffy on the Possible Prosecutions of Clinton; Rep. Tim Ryan Speaks Out About Challenging Pelosi," video clip, Fox News, November

22, 2016, http://www.foxnews.com/transcript/2016/11/22/rep-sean-duffy-on-possible-prosecutions-clinton-rep-tim-ryan-speaks-out-about. html; "The Corruption of Hillary Clinton," *FrontPage Magazine*, November 28, 2016, https://www.frontpagemag.com/fpm/264968/corruption-hillary-clinton-frontpagemagcom.

27   Richard Pollock, "Behind the IG Report – How the Obama Justice Department Tried to Shut Down the FBI's Investigation into the Clinton Foundation," *The Daily Caller*, April 15, 2018, http://dailycaller.com/2018/04/15/fbi-clinton-foundation-investigation/.

28   Devlin Barrett and Christopher M. Matthews, "Secret Recordings Fueled FBI Feud in Clinton Probe," *The Wall Street Journal*, November 2, 2016, https://www.wsj.com/articles/secret-recordings-fueled-fbi-feud-in-clinton-probe-1478135518; Michael Doran, "The Real Collusion Story," *National Review*, March 13, 2018, https://www.nationalreview.com/2018/03/russia-collusion-real-story-hillary-clinton-dnc-fbi-media/;   "Clinton: Favorable/Unfavorable," polling data, *Real Clear Politics*, accessed May 23, 2018, https://www.realclearpolitics.com/epolls/other/clinton_favorableunfavorable-1131.html#polls.

29   Max Kutner, "Comey Drafted Statement Ending Clinton Email Investigations Months Before Interviewing Her, FBI Confirms," *Newsweek*, October 16, 2017, http://www.newsweek.com/james-comey-fbi-clinton-emails-drafted-statement-686140.

30   Shoshana Weissmann, "Bernie Rescues Hillary: 'Tired of Hearing About Your Damn Emails,'" *Real Clear Politics*, October 13, 2015, https://www.weeklystandard.com/bernie-rescues-hillary-tired-of-hearing-about-your-damn-emails/article/1045251.

31   "Donald Trump's Tour of His Manhattan Office," YouTube video, posted by "*The Wall Street Journal*," September 14, 2015, https://www.youtube.com/watch?v=BAKYvvM6IpE&feature=youtu.be&t=13.

32   Tim Hains, "Trump Advisor Stephen Miller Reads from 'Clinton Cash' at NM Rally: Nepotism in Haiti Earthquake Relief Money," *Real Clear Politics*, May 24, 2016, https://www.realclearpolitics.com/video/2016/05/24/trump_advisor_stephen_miller_reads_from_clinton_cash_at_new_mexico_rally.html.

33   Adam Entous, Devlin Barrett, and Rosalind S. Helderman, "Clinton Campaign, DNC Paid for Research that Led to Russia Dossier," *The Washington Post*, October 24, 2017, https://www.washingtonpost.com/world/national-security/clinton-campaign-dnc-paid-for-research-that-led-to-russia-dossier/2017/10/24/226fabf0-b8e4-11e7-a908-a3470754bbb9_story.html.

34   Barrett and Matthews, "Secret Recordings Fueled FBI Feud in Clinton Probe."

35   Ibid.

Chapter 1: The Insurance Policy

[1] Anthony Zurcher, "What Happened: The Long List of Who Hillary Clinton Blames," BBC News, September 13, 2017, http://www.bbc.com/news/world-us-canada-41244474.

[2] Entous, Barrett, and Helderman, "Clinton Campaign, DNC Paid for Research That Led to Russia Dossier"; Kyle Cheney and John Bresnahan, "House Republicans Quietly Investigate Perceived Corruption at DOJ, FBI," *Politico*, December 20, 2017, https://www.politico.com/story/2017/12/20/house-republicans-quietly-investigate-doj-fbi-310121.

[3] Zurcher, "What Happened."

[4] Doran, "The Real Collusion Story"; Entous, Barrett, and Helderman, "Clinton Campaign, DNC Paid for Research That Led to Russia Dossier"; The Clinton camp then promoted that research to allies in Congress, the FBI, and the media. The research became known as "the dossier," and it alleged that the Trump campaign had been compromised by Putin and was colluding with Russian actors to win the 2016 election.

[5] "Full Text: James Comey Testimony Transcript on Trump and Russia," *Politico*, June 8, 2017, https://www.politico.com/story/2017/06/08/full-text-james-comey-trump-russia-testimony-239295.

[6] "Full Clapper: 'No Evidence' of Collusion Between Trump and Russia," video clip, NBC News, March 5, 2018, https://www.nbcnews.com/meet-the-press/video/full-clapper-no-evidence-of-collusion-between-trump-and-russia-890509379597; Eric Lichtblau and Steven Lee Myers, "Investigating Donald Trump, F.B.I. Sees No Clear Link to Russia," *The New York Times*, October 31, 2016, https://www.nytimes.com/2016/11/01/us/politics/fbi-russia-election-donald-trump.html.

[7] Office of the Deputy Attorney General, "Appointment of Special Counsel to Investigate Russian Interference with the 2016 Presidential Election and Related Matters," press release, Order No. 3915-2017, https://www.justice.gov/opa/press-release/file/967231/download.

[8] Theresa Seiger, "Who is Rod Rosenstein? Things to Know About the Deputy US Attorney General," WSBTV, April 12, 2018, https://www.wsbtv.com/news/trending-now/who-is-rod-rosenstein-things-to-know-about-the-deputy-us-attorney-general/730266619.

[9] Ruben Castaneda, "Profile of Rod Rosenstein, U.S. Attorney for Maryland," *The Washington Post*, on Internet Archive, October 9, 2011, https://web.archive.org/web/20170303202238/https://www.washingtonpost.com/local/profile-of-rod-rosenstein-us-attorney-for-maryland/2011/09/29/gIQAfOTWYL_story.html (the screenshot was captured March 3, 2017); "Transcript: James Comey's Interview with ABC News Chief Anchor George Stephanopoulos," transcript, ABC News, April 15, 2018, http://abcnews.go.com/Site/transcript-james-comeys-interview-abc-news-chief-anchor/story?id=54488723.

[10]   Shannon Vavra, "The Democratic Leanings of Bob Mueller's Team," *Axios*, June 25, 2017, https://www.axios.com/the-democratic-leanings-of-bob-muellers-team-1513303211-1c289ad8-7276-4bb9-8fca-2bd6f3e16520. html.

[11]   Josh Gerstein, "In Texts, FBI Agents on Russia Probe Called Trump an 'Idiot,'" *Politico*, December 12, 2017, https://www.politico.com/story/2017/12/12/fbi-agents-trump-mueller-texts-294156; Gregg Jarrett, "Robert Mueller and his Politically Biased Team of Prosecutors Need to Go," Fox News, December 8, 2017, http://www.foxnews.com/opinion/2017/12/08/gregg-jarrett-robert-mueller-and-his-politically-biased-team-prosecutors-need-to-go.html; Kyle Cheney, "GOP Escalates Law Enforcement Probes as Russia Inquiry Heats Up," *Politico*, January 23, 2018, https://www.politico.com/story/2018/01/23/congress-fbi-russia-republicans-escalate-probes-364616.

[12]   Laura Jarrett, "How Mueller's Path Was Muddied in Two Weeks," CNN, December 14, 2017, https://www.cnn.com/2017/12/14/politics/muellers-path-was-muddied-in-two-weeks/index.html; Maegan Vazquez, Pamela Brown, and Laura Jarrett, "Trump's Lawyer Wants a Special Counsel to Investigate DOJ Official with Fusion GPS Ties," CNN, December 12, 2017, *https://*www.cnn.com/2017/12/12/politics/bruce-ohr-special-counsel/index.html.

[13]   Kaitlyn Schallhorn, "Fusion GPS's Ties to Clinton Campaign, Russia Investigation: What to Know," Fox News, February 7, 2018, www.foxnews.com/politics/2018/02/07/fusion-gpss-ties-to-clinton-campaign-russia-investigation-what-to-know.html.

[14]   Kenneth P. Vogel, "Clinton Campaign and Democratic Party Helped Pay for Russia Trump Dossier," *The New York Times*, October 24, 2017, https://www.nytimes.com/2017/10/24/us/politics/clinton-dnc-russia-dossier.html.

[15]   Andrew C. McCarthy, "Beating a Hasty Retreat from the Steele Dossier," *National Review*, January 3, 2018, https://www.nationalreview.com/2018/01/fusion-gps-steele-dossier-collusion-narrative-falls-apart/; Paul Roderick Gregory, "The Trump Dossier Is Fake—And Here Are the Reasons Why," *Forbes*, January 13, 2017, https://www.forbes.com/sites/paulroderickgregory/2017/01/13/the-trump-dossier-is-false-news-and-heres-why/#2017dc376867.

[16]   Gregory, "The Trump Dossier Is Fake—And Here Are the Reasons Why"; Jason Le Miere, "Trump and Comey Talked Russian 'Hookers' and 'Golden Shower' Scandal," *Newsweek*, June 7, 2017, http://www.newsweek.com/trump-comey-hookers-golden-showers-622604.

[17]   Sharyl Attkisson, "Was Lynch Coordinating with Comey in the Clinton Investigation?" *The Hill*, January 1, 2018, http://thehill.com/opinion/campaign/370019-was-lynch-coordinating-with-comey-in-the-clinton-investigation.

[18]   Jack Crowe, "Comey, Yates, McCabe, Rosenstein All Signed Off on Misleading FISA Apps," *The Daily Caller*, February 2, 2018, http://dailycaller. com/2018/02/02/comey-yates-mccabe-rosenstein-fisa/; Tal Kopan, "Comey: Lynch Asked for Clinton Investigation to be Called a 'Matter,'" CNN, June 8, 2017, https://www.cnn.com/2017/06/08/politics/james-comey-loretta-lynch/ index.html.

[19]   Adam Edelman and Mike Memoli, "FBI Texts: Obama 'Wants to Know Everything We're Doing,'" NBC News, February 7, 2018, https://www. nbcnews.com/politics/politics-news/fbi-texts-obama-wants-know-every-thing-we-re-doing-n845531; Doran, "The Real Collusion Story."

[20]   Matthew Rosenberg and Matt Apuzzo, "Days Before Firing, Comey Asked for More Resources for Russia Inquiry," *The New York Times*, May 10, 2017, https://www.nytimes.com/2017/05/10/us/politics/comey-russia-in-vestigation-fbi.html; "Full Clapper: 'No Evidence' of Collusion Between Trump and Russia."

[21]   Tal Kopan, "Comey: Lynch Asked for Clinton Investigation to be Called a 'Matter'"; Eli Watkins, "Bill Clinton Meeting Causes Headaches for Hillary," CNN, June 30, 2016, https://www.cnn.com/2016/06/29/ politics/bill-clinton-loretta-lynch.

[22]   Max Kutner, "Comey Drafted Statement Ending Clinton Email Investigation Months Before Interviewing Her, FBI Confirms," *Newsweek*, October 16, 2017, http://www.newsweek.com/james-comey-fbi-clinton-emails-drafted-statement-686140.

[23]   Del Quentin Wilber, "In FBI Agent's Account, 'Insurance Policy' Text Referred to Russia Probe," *The Wall Street Journal*, December 18, 2017, https://www.wsj.com/articles/in-fbi-agents-account-insurance-policy-text-referred-to-russia-probe-1513624580.

[24]   Max Greenwood, "Officials Disclosed Source's Political Funding in FISA Application: Report," *The Hill*, February 3, 2018, http://thehill.com/ policy/national-security/372134-officials-disclosed-sources-political-fund-ing-in-fisa-application.

[25]   "The Nunes FBI Memo, Annotated," *Politico*, February 2, 2018, https:// www.politico.com/interactives/2018/02/01/what-is-in-the-nunes-memo-fbi-released-analysis/.

[26]   Rich Galen, "It's Not the Crime, It's the Cover-up," CNS News, May 20, 2013, https://www.cnsnews.com/blog/rich-galen/its-not-crime-its-cover.

[27]   "Letter from members of congress to the Honorable Jeff Sessions, Attorney General, the Honorable Christopher Wray, Director, Federal Bureau of Investigation, and the Honorable John Huber, United States Attorney for the District of Utah"; Doran, "The Real Collusion Story"; Brooke Singman, "Grassley Says Comey Leaked Classified Information to Professor Pal, Demands Answers," Fox News, January 4, 2018, http://www.foxnews. com/politics/2018/01/04/grassley-says-comey-leaked-classified-informa-tion-to-professor-pal-demands-answers.html.

28   Federal Bureau of Investigation, "FBI New York History," accessed March 26, 2018, https://www.fbi.gov/history/field-office-histories/newyork.

29   Jessica McBride, "Peter Strzok & Lisa Page: 5 Fast Facts You Need to Know," *Heavy*, December 2, 2017, https://heavy.com/news/2017/12/peter-strzok-lisa-page-fbi-trump-texts-affair/.

30   "'Secret Society' Text Between Agents: Was It Meant in Jest?" ABC News, January 24, 2018, http://abcnews.go.com/Politics/full-secret-society-text-fbi-agents-meant-jest/story?id=52592241.

31   Kaitlyn Schallhorn, "Strzok, Page and the FBI Texting Scandal Explained," Fox News, April 27, 2018, http://www.foxnews.com/politics/2018/04/27/strzok-page-and-fbi-texting-scandal-explained.html.

32   Mary Kay Linge, "Lisa Page, FBI Agent Who Bashed Trump in Texts, Resigns," *New York Post*, May 5, 2018, https://nypost.com/2018/05/05/lisa-page-fbi-agent-who-bashed-trump-in-texts-resigns/.

33   Jordan Poll, "U.S. Deputy AG Rod Rosenstein Tells M Law Crowd, 'Nobody Dictates What Cases We Take,'" Michigan Law, November 17, 2017, https://www.law.umich.edu/newsandinfo/features/Pages/rrosenstein_111717.aspx.

34   Office of the Deputy Attorney General, "Rod Rosenstein's Letter Appointing Mueller to Special Counsel," Order No. 3915-2017, *The New York Times*, May 17, 2017, https://www.nytimes.com/interactive/2017/05/17/us/politics/document-Robert-Mueller-Special-Counsel-Russia.html.

35   Paul Roderick Gregory, "No One Mentions that Russian Trial Leads to Democratic Lobbyists," *Forbes*, February 18, 2017, https://www.forbes.com/sites/paulroderickgregory/2017/02/18/no-one-mentions-that-the-russian-trail-leads-to-democratic-lobbyists/#7c461d183991; Deroy Murdock, "Russian Collusion, Clinton $tyle," *National Review*, March 27, 2018, https://www.nationalreview.com/2018/03/clinton-russia-collusion-evidence/; "Jarrett: Mueller Is Still Focused Squarely on Donald Trump," Yahoo Finance, February 16, 2018, https://finance.yahoo.com/video/jarrett-mueller-still-focused-squarely-024644151.html; U.S. Department of Justice, "Special Counsel's Office," accessed April 4, 2018, https://www.justice.gov/sco.

36   Brooke Singman, "Special Counsel Mueller's Team Has Only One Known Republican," Fox News, February 23, 2018, http://www.foxnews.com/politics/2018/02/23/special-counsel-muellers-team-has-only-one-known-republican.html.

37   Gerstein, "In Texts, FBI Agents on Russia Probe Called Trump an 'Idiot'"; Linge, "Lisa Page, FBI Agent Who Bashed Trump in Texts, Resigns."

38   Vavra, "The Democratic Leanings of Bob Mueller's Team," https://www.axios.com/the-democratic-leanings-of-bob-muellers-team-1513303211-1c289ad8-7276-4bb9-8fca-2bd6f3e16520.html.

39   Matt Zapotosky, "Mueller, Several Team Members Gave Up Million-Dollar Jobs to Work on Special Counsel Investigation," *The Washington Post*, August

8, 2017, https://www.washingtonpost.com/world/national-security/mueller-several-team-members-gave-up-million-dollar-jobs-to-work-on-special-counsel-investigation/2017/08/08/e11169da-7b78-11e7-83c7-5bd5460f0d7e_story.html?utm_term=.56cc7cdd6045.

40   Ibid.

41   Max Kutner, "Why Robert Mueller Threw an Agent Off the Trump-Russia Probe," *Newsweek*, December 2, 2017, http://www.newsweek.com/robert-mueller-threw-agent-trump-russia-probe-strzok-729517;   Mike Levine and Pierre Thomas, "Robert Mueller's Russia Investigation Team Loses 2nd FBI Veteran," ABC News, September 28, 2017, https://abc-news.go.com/US/robert-muellers-russia-investigation-team-loses-2nd-fbi/story?id=50166109; Victor Davis Hanson, "Hillary's 'Sure' Victory Explains Most Everything," *National Review*, January 30, 2018, https://www.nationalreview.com/2018/01/expected-clinton-victory-explains-federal-employee-wrongdoing/; Linge, "Lisa Page, FBI Agent Who Bashed Trump in Texts, Resigns."

42   Josh Gerstein, "Two More Officials Cited in FBI Texts Step Down," *Politico*, February 8, 2018, https://www.politico.com/story/2018/02/08/fbi-texts-officials-resign-400533/.

43   Gregg Jarrett, "Did the FBI and the Justice Department, Plot to Clear Hillary Clinton, Bring Down Trump?" Fox News, December 15, 2017, http://www.foxnews.com/opinion/2017/12/15/gregg-jarrett-did-fbi-and-justice-department-plot-to-clear-hillary-clinton-bring-down-trump.html.

44   John Solomon, "FBI Agents' Text Messages Spur Congressional Probe into Possible News Leaks," *The Hill*, January 8, 2018, http://thehill.com/homenews/house/368003-fbi-agents-text-messages-spur-congressional-probe-into-possible-news-leaks; Mollie Hemingway, "Media Fight for Democrats in Washington Leak Wars," *The Federalist*, March 6, 2018, http://thefederalist.com/2018/03/06/media-fight-for-democrats-in-washington-leak-wars/; Karoun Demirjian and Matt Zapotosky, "Inspector General Referred Findings on McCabe to U.S. Attorney for Consideration of Criminal Charges," *The Washington Post*, April 19, 2018, https://www.washingtonpost.com/world/national-security/inspector-general-referred-findings-on-mccabe-to-us-attorney-for-consideration-of-criminal-charges/2018/04/19/a200cabc-43f3-11e8-8569-26fda6b404c7_story.html?utm_term=.d0b262284fe5.

45   Chuck Ross, "Senate Report Shows Staggering Number of Leaks Under Trump Compared to Obama, Bush," *The Daily Caller*, July 6, 2017, http://dailycaller.com/2017/07/06/senate-report-shows-staggering-number-of-leaks-under-trump-compared-to-obama-bush/.

46   Graham Lanktree, "Who Is Peter Strzok, FBI Agent Accused of Treason by Trump?" *Newsweek*, January 12, 2018, http://www.newsweek.com/who-peter-strzok-fbi-agent-accused-treason-trump-779481.

47 Office of the Inspector General, U.S. Department of Justice, "A Review of Various Actions by the Federal Bureau of Investigation and Department of Justice in Advance of the 2016 Election," June 2018, https://www.justice.gov/file/1071991/download.

48 John Kass, "Obama's Silky Lie and FBI Bias in the Clinton Investigation," *Chicago Tribune,* June 15, 2018, http://www.chicagotribune.com/news/columnists/kass/ct-met-james-comey-report-kass-0617-story.html.

49 Hillary Clinton, Twitter post, June 14, 2018, 5:36 p.m., https://twitter.com/HillaryClinton/status/1007376361101582336.

50 Office of the Inspector General, U.S. Department of Justice, "A Review of Various Actions by the Federal Bureau of Investigation and Department of Justice in Advance of the 2016 Election"; James Comey, "This Report Says I Was Wrong. But That's Good for the F.B.I.," *The New York Times,* June 14, 2018, https://www.nytimes.com/2018/06/14/opinion/comey-clinton-inspector-general.html.

51 Andrew O'Reilly, "Lawmakers accuse FBI of 'destructive level of animus' following release of IG report," Fox News, June 14, 2018, http://www.foxnews.com/politics/2018/06/14/lawmakers-accuse-fbi-destructive-level-animus-following-release-ig-report.html.

52 Andrew McCarthy, "The IG's Report May Be Half-Baked," *National Review,* June 15, 2018, https://www.nationalreview.com/2018/06/ig-report-fbi-no-bias-conclusion-may-not-supported/; Jeanine Pirro, "Pirro Blasts DOJ Over IG Report: 'The Deep State Is Alive and Well in Washington,'" Fox News, June 17,2018, http://insider.foxnews.com/2018/06/17/judge-jeanine-pirro-justice-department-inspector-general-report-deep-state-alive-and-well.

53 Donald Trump, Twitter post, June 16, 2018, 11:01, a.m., https://twitter.com/realDonaldTrump/status/1007986538985197568; Terrence Dopp, "Trump Says DOJ Conclusion 'Ridiculous,' Claims 'Total Bias,'" *Bloomberg,* June 15, 2018, https://www.bloomberg.com/news/articles/2018-06-15/trump-says-doj-conclusion-ridiculous-claims-total-bias.

54 "House Hearing on Inspector General Report on Clinton Email Probe," C-SPAN, June 19, 2018, https://www.c-span.org/video/?446817-1/doj-inspector-general-michael-horowitz-testifies-clinton-email-probe-report&start=9171.

55 H.R. Res 907, 115th Cong. (2018), https://zeldin.house.gov/sites/zeldin.house.gov/files/ZELDIN_051_xml%205.21%20v2.pdf; Letter from members of congress to the Honorable Jeff Sessions, Attorney General, the Honorable Christopher Wray, Director, Federal Bureau of Investigation, and the Honorable John Huber, United States Attorney for the District of Utah"; William L. Gensert, "Indictments Are Comey...er, Coming," *American Thinker,* April 30, 2018, https://www.americanthinker.com/articles/2018/04/indictments_are_comeyer_coming.html.

56   Gregg Jarrett, "Did the FBI and the Justice Department, Plot to Clear Hillary Clinton, Bring Down Trump?" Fox News, December 15, 2017, http://www.foxnews.com/opinion/2017/12/15/gregg-jarrett-did-fbi-and-justice-department-plot-to-clear-hillary-clinton-bring-down-trump.html; Brooke Singman, "Republicans Turn Focus to FBI's McCabe over Texts on 'Insurance' Against Trump," Fox News, December 14, 2017, http://www.foxnews.com/politics/2017/12/14/republicans-turn-focus-to-fbis-mccabe-over-texts-on-insurance-against-trump.html; Kimberley A. Strassel, "About That FBI 'Source,'" *The Wall Street Journal*, May 10, 2018, https://www.wsj.com/articles/about-that-fbi-source-1525992611.

57   "Friday Strategy Call at 8:00 AM ET," Wikileaks, April 23, 2015, https://wikileaks.org/podesta-emails/emailid/1120.

58   "Agenda for Weekly Long-Term Message Planning Meeting," WikiLeaks, email sent on July 29, 2015, https://wikileaks.org/podesta-emails/emailid/10348; Gideon Resnick, "Hillary Clinton on Election Night: 'They Were Never Going to Let Me Be President,'" *The Daily Beast*, April 20, 2018, https://www.thedailybeast.com/hillary-clinton-they-were-never-going-to-let-me-be-president.

59   Gabriel Debenedetti, "They Always Wanted Trump," *Politico*, November 7, 2016, https://www.politico.com/magazine/story/2016/11/hillary-clinton-2016-donald-trump-214428.

60   Jennifer Agiesta, "Post-Debate, Trump Pulls Clear of Competition," CNN, August 18, 2015, https://www.cnn.com/2015/08/18/politics/donald-trump-presidential-poll-debate/.

61   Jennifer Agiesta, "CNN/ORC Poll: Donald Trump Dominates GOP Field at 41%," CNN, January 26, 2016, https://www.cnn.com/2016/01/26/politics/donald-trump-ted-cruz-polling/index.html.

62   Entous, Barrett, and Helderman, "Clinton Campaign, DNC Paid for Research That Led to Russia Dossier."

63   Paul Sperry, "Sketchy Firm Behind Trump Dossier Is Stalling Investigators," *New York Post*, June 24, 2017, https://nypost.com/2017/06/24/inside-the-shadowy-intelligence-firm-behind-the-trump-dossier/; U.S. Senate Committee on the Judiciary, "Testimony of William Browder to the Senate Judiciary Committee on FARA Violations Connected to the Anti-Magnitsky Campaign by Russian Government Interests," July 26, 2017, https://www.judiciary.senate.gov/imo/media/doc/07-26-17%20Browder%20Testimony.pdf.

64   Sperry, "Sketchy Firm Behind Trump Dossier Is Stalling Investigators."

65   "The Investment Bankers' Buried Treasure," *Fortune*, February 12, 1990, http://archive.fortune.com/magazines/fortune/fortune_archive/1990/02/12/73061/index.htm; Steve Barnes, "Private Sector; Building a Bridge on the Fairway," *The New York Times*, March 18, 2001, https://www.nytimes.com/2001/03/18/business/private-sector-building-a-bridge-on-the-fairway.html; Company Overview of The Stephens Group, LLC, *Bloomberg*,

accessed April 5, 2018, https://www.bloomberg.com/research/stocks/private/person.asp?personId=329232&privcapId=23119.

66   Company Overview of The Stephens Group, LLC, *Bloomberg*, accessed April 5, 2018, https://www.bloomberg.com/research/stocks/private/person.asp?personId=329232&privcapId=23119; Garance Franke-Ruta, "Fan Friction," *American Prospect*, September 23, 2003, http://prospect.org/article/fan-friction; "BCCI: The Mystery Lingers," *The Wall Street Journal*, September 29, 1998, https://www.wsj.com/articles/SB907022152360146500.

67   "BCCI: The Mystery Lingers"; "Jacoby Enterprises, Inc.," InterCreditReport, accessed May 1, 2018, http://wyoming.intercreditreport.com/company/jacoby-enterprises-inc-1986-000233127; Laura Meckler and Peter Nicholas, "Hillary Clinton's Forgotten Career: Corporate Lawyer," *The Wall Street Journal*, October 28, 2016, https://www.wsj.com/articles/hillary-clintons-forgotten-career-corporate-lawyer-1477674562.

68   CNN & Company, Show aired December 11, 1995, 4:30 am ET.

69   Richard Behar, "Never Heard of Acxiom? Chances Are It's Heard of You. How a Little-Known Rock Company—The World's Largest Processor of Consumer Data—Found Itself at the Center of a Very Big National Security Debate," *Fortune*, February 23, 2004, http://archive.fortune.com/magazines/fortune/fortune_archive/2004/02/23/362182/index.htm; Michael Moss and Ford Fessenden, "America Under Surveillance: Privacy and Security; New Tools for Domestic Spying, and Qualms," *The New York Times*, December 10, 2002, https://www.nytimes.com/2002/12/10/us/america-under-surveillance-privacy-security-new-tools-for-domestic-spying-qualms.

70   "Walter Smiley," Arkansas Academy of Computing, July 12, 2012, http://araoc.org/walter-smiley/; "Jerry Jones," Heifer International, accessed May 23, 2018, https://www.heifer.org/about-heifer/inside-heifer/board-of-directors/members/jerry-jones.html; Alexandra Zendrian, "Briefing Book: Warren Stephens," *Forbes*, September 21, 2009, https://www.forbes.com/2009/09/19/stephens-private-equity-intelligent-investing-ipo.html#39a29b6839b9; Emma N. Hurt, "States Tech Giants Nurtured Burgeoning Startups," *Arkansas Democrat-Gazette*, May 21, 2017, http://www.pressreader.com/usa/arkansas-democrat-gazette/20170521/283261687781040; Steve Rice, "How Little Rock Is Returning to Its Fintech Roots," *Technically*, April 13, 2016, https://technical.ly/2016/04/13/little-rock-returning-fintech-roots/.

71   Alexandra Zendrian, "Briefing Book: Warren Stephens," *Forbes*, September 21, 2009, https://www.forbes.com/2009/09/19/stephens-private-equity-intelligent-investing-ipo.html#39a29b6839b9; Michael J. Goodman and John M. Broder, "Clinton's Rein on Bonds Linked to Contributions: Politics: Finance Authority He Controls Formed a Pool of Moneyed Elite That's Often Tapped for Campaign Funds," *Los Angeles Times*,

June 29, 1992, http://articles.latimes.com/print/1992-06-29/news/mn-895_1_finance-authority.

72 William Safire, "Shredding the Files of Clinton Aide Has Look of Criminality," *Chicago Tribune*, September 1, 1994, http://articles.chicagotribune.com/1994-09-01/news/9409010016_1_clintons-lawyer-whitewater-files-documents-storage.

73 John M. Broder, "Clinton Aide Is Penalized in Tax Dispute: White House Associate Counsel William H. Kennedy III Is Relieved of Some Duties. He Had Failed to Pay Social Security Levies for a Nanny," *Los Angeles Times,* March 24, 1994, http://articles.latimes.com/1994-03-24/news/mn-37899_1_white-house-aide; Ann Devroy and Michael Isikoff, "Clinton Staff Went Past Reno to FBI," *The Washington Post*, May 25, 1993, https://www.washingtonpost.com/archive/politics/1993/05/25/clinton-staff-went-past-reno-to-fbi/3699eeea-ad25-41df-ac21-f1822e382058/?utm_term=.498f5340d0d1; Michael Weisskopf and Susan Schmidt, "Rose Law Firm Has Hard Landing After Auspicious National Takeoff," *The Washington Post*, December 25, 1994, https://www.washingtonpost.com/archive/politics/1994/12/25/rose-law-firm-has-hard-landing-after-auspicious-national-takeoff/97b60675-ea57-4b92-a1a3-01a9592e767d/?utm_term=.c26e5938e478.

74 William Safire, "Shredding the Files of Clinton Aide Has Look of Criminality," *Chicago Tribune*, September 1, 1994, http://articles.chicagotribune.com/1994-09-01/news/9409010016_1_clintons-lawyer-whitewater-files-documents-storage.

75 Ruben Castaneda, "Profile of Rod Rosenstein, U.S. Attorney for Maryland"; "Transcript: James Comey's Interview with ABC News Chief Anchor George Stephanopoulos," ABC News, transcript, April 15, 2018, http://abcnews.go.com/Site/transcript-james-comeys-interview-abc-news-chief-anchor/story?id=54488723.

76 Hamburg v. Clinton, 1:98-cv-01459-TPJ (filed June 11, 1998), https://www.fbcoverup.com/docs/library/2017-05-22-Lisa-Barsoomian-represented-William-J-Clinton-98-cv-01459-TPJ-06-11-1998-PACER-accessed-May-22-2017.pdf; Pete Yost, "Whitewater Prosecutors Question Hillary Clinton," *The Seattle Times*, January 14, 1998, http://community.seattletimes.nwsource.com/archive/?date=19980114&slug=2728707; United States Senate Committee on the Judiciary, "Questionnaire for Non-Judicial Nominees, to Rod Jay Rosenstein," accessed May 1, 2018, https://www.judiciary.senate.gov/imo/media/doc/Rosenstein%20SJQ%20(Public).pdf.

77 White House visitor logs, Mary Jacoby, https://obamawhitehouse.archives.gov/briefing-room/disclosures/visitor-records.

78 Kenneth P. Vogel, "The Trump Dossier: What We Know and Who Paid for It," *The New York Times*, October 25, 2017, https://www.nytimes.com/2017/10/25/us/politics/steele-dossier-trump-expained.html; Julia Glum, "Did the Obama Campaign Fund the Trump-Russia Dossier?

$972,000 in 'Legal Services' Payments Scrutinized," *Newsweek*, October 30, 2017, http://www.newsweek.com/trump-dossier-obama-clinton-funded-golden-shower-tape-696402.

[79] Catherine Herridge, Pamela K. Browne, and Cyd Upson, "House Republicans Expand Dossier Probe, Seek Info from Obama Officials," Fox News, March 9, 2018, http://www.foxnews.com/politics/2018/03/09/house-republicans-expand-dossier-probe-seek-info-from-obama-officials.html; "DOJ to Probe Potential Obama-era Surveillance Abuses," Fox News, transcript, February 19, 2018, http://www.foxnews.com/transcript/2018/02/19/doj-to-probe-potential-obama-era-surveillance-abuses.html; Veronica Stracqualursi, "Who is John Huber, the Utah US Attorney Investigating Claims of FBI Misconduct?" CNN, March 29, 2018, https://www.cnn.com/2018/03/29/politics/who-is-john-huber/index.html; Margot Cleveland, "Bombshell: FEC Records Indicate Hillary Campaign Illegally Laundered $84 Million," *The Federalist*, April 24, 2018, http://thefederalist.com/2018/04/24/bombshell-fec-records-indicate-hillary-campaign-illegally-laundered-84-million/.

[80] Kenneth P. Vogel, "Clinton Campaign and Democratic Party Helped Pay for Russia Trump Dossier," *The New York Times*, October 24, 2017, https://www.nytimes.com/2017/10/24/us/politics/clinton-dnc-russia-dossier.html; Vogel, "The Trump Dossier: What We Know and Who Paid for It"; Leonid Bershidsky, "Commentary: It Appears Kremlin Was Playing Both Sides Against Each Other," *Chicago Tribune*, October 31, 2017, http://www.chicagotribune.com/news/opinion/commentary/ct-perspec-kremlin-steele-dossier-russia-1101-20171031-story.html; Aaron Klein, "Fusion GPS Founder: Not Sure if Steele Paid Sources for Trump Hoax Dossier," *Breitbart*, January 16, 2018, http://www.breitbart.com/jerusalem/2018/01/16/fusion-gps-founder-not-sure-steele-paid-sources-trump-hoax-dossier/; United States Senate Committee on the Judiciary, Interview of Glenn Simpson, August 22, 2017, https://www.feinstein.senate.gov/public/_cache/files/3/9/3974a291-ddbe-4525-9ed1-22bab43c05ae/934A3562824CACA7BB4D915E97709D2F.simpson-transcript-redacted.pdf; Andrew C. McCarthy, "Was the Steele Dossier the FBI's 'Insurance Policy'?", *National Review*, December 23, 2017,https://www.nationalreview.com/2017/12/trump-russia-collusion-fbi-investigation-steele-dossier-hillary-clinton-campaign/.

[81] Ken Dilanian, "Clinton Ally Says Smoke, But No Fire: No Russia-Trump Collusion," NBC News, March 15, 2017, https://www.nbcnews.com/news/us-news/clinton-ally-says-smoke-no-fire-no-russia-trump-collusion-n734176.

[82] Lee Smith, "Did President Obama Read the 'Steele Dossier' in the White House Last August?" *Tablet*, December 20, 2017, http://www.tabletmag.com/jewish-news-and-politics/251897/obama-steele-dossier-russiagate.

83   Glum, "Did the Obama Campaign Fund the Trump-Russia Dossier? $972,000 in 'Legal Services' Payments Scrutinized."

84   James Rosen, "Top DOJ Official Demoted Amid Probe of Contacts with Trump Dossier Firm," Fox News, December 7, 2017, http://www.foxnews.com/politics/2017/12/07/top-doj-official-demoted-amid-probe-contacts-with-trump-dossier-firm.html.

85   Howard Blum, "How Ex-Spy Christopher Steele Compiled His Explosive Trump-Russia Dossier," *Vanity Fair*, March 30, 2017, https://www.vanityfair.com/news/2017/03/how-the-explosive-russian-dossier-was-compiled-christopher-steele.

86   Mark Hosenball, "Former MI6 Spy Known to U.S. Agencies Is Author of Reports on Trump in Russia," Reuters, January 12, 2017, https://www.reuters.com/article/us-usa-trump-steele/former-mi6-spy-known-to-u-s-agencies-is-author-of-reports-on-trump-in-russia-idUSKBN14W0HN.

87   Eric Felten, "The Weird Tales of Jonathan Winer," *The Weekly Standard*, February 10, 2018, http://www.weeklystandard.com/the-weird-tales-of-jonathan-winer/article/2011542.

88   James Rosen and Jake Gibson, "Wife of Demoted DOJ Official Worked for Firm Behind Anti-Trump Dossier," Fox News, December 11, 2017, http://www.foxnews.com/politics/2017/12/11/wife-demoted-doj-official-worked-for-firm-behind-anti-trump-dossier.html.

89   Matt Apuzzo, "Andrew McCabe, Fired F.B.I. Deputy, Is Said to Have Kept Memos on Trump," *The New York Times*, March 17, 2018, https://www.nytimes.com/2018/03/17/us/politics/andrew-mccabe-fbi-memos-trump.html; Jake Gibson, "DOJ Official Who Concealed Meetings with Trump Dossier Figures Loses Another Job Title," Fox News, January 8, 2018, http://www.foxnews.com/politics/2018/01/08/doj-official-who-concealed-meetings-with-trump-dossier-figures-loses-another-job-title.html.

90   Barrett and Matthews, "Secret Recordings Fueled FBI Feud in Clinton Probe"; Michael S. Schmidt and Matt Apuzzo, "Hillary Clinton Emails Said to Contain Classified Data," *The New York Times*, July 24, 2015, https://www.nytimes.com/2015/07/25/us/politics/clinton-clinton-email-classified-information-inspector-general-intelligence-community.html.

91   Barrett, "Clinton Ally Aided Campaign of FBI Official's Wife."

92   "The Face of FBI Politics: Bureau Boss McCabe Under Hatch Act Investigation," *Circa*, June 27, 2017, https://www.circa.com/story/2017/06/27/the-face-of-fbi-politics-bureau-boss-mccabe-under-hatch-act-investigation; Laura Vozzella and Simon Denyer, "Donor to Clinton Foundation, McAuliffe Caught Up in Chinese Cash-for-Votes Scandal," *The Washington Post*, September 16, 2016, https://www.washingtonpost.com/local/virginia-politics/clinton-foundation-mcauliffe-donor-caught-up-in-chinese-cash-for-votes-scandal/2016/09/16/bfb3b8fc-7c13-11e6-ac8e-cf8e0dd91dc7_story.html?noredirect=on&utm_term=.42ba3bbc82fa.

93   Jacquelyn Martin, "Official: Feds Investigating Virginia Gov. Terry McAuliffe," CBS News, May 23, 2016, https://www.cbsnews.com/news/official-feds-investigating-virginia-governor-terry-mcauliffe/; "Marc E. Elias", Perkins Coie profile, accessed May 2, 2018, https://www.perkinscoie.com/en/professionals/marc-e-elias.html.

94   Federal Bureau of Investigation, "Electronic Communication, Protocol Regarding Potential Conflicts of Interest," electronic communication, April 29, 2015, https://vault.fbi.gov/deputy-director-mccabe-ethical-guidance-and-recusal/deputy-director-mccabe-ethical-guidance-and-recusal-part-01-of-01/view; United States Senate Committee on the Judiciary, "Letter from Charles E. Grassley, Chairman, to the Honorable Michael E. Horowitz, Inspector General Horowitz, U.S. Department of Justice," June 29, 2017, https://www.judiciary.senate.gov/imo/media/doc/2017-06-29%20CEG%20to%20DOJ%20IG%20(McCabe%20Conflicts).pdf; Michael S. Schmidt and Matt Apuzzo, "Hillary Clinton Emails Said to Contain Classified Data"; Kutner, "Comey Drafted Statement Ending Clinton Email Investigations Months Before Interviewing Her, FBI Confirms."

95   Julia Manchester, "FBI Ruled McCabe Had No Conflicts of Interest in Clinton Probe: Docs," *The Hill*, January 5, 2018, http://thehill.com/blogs/blog-briefing-room/news/367701-fbi-ruled-mccabe-had-no-conflict-of-interest-in-clinton-probe; Max Kutner, "FBI Deputy Director Andrew McCabe Was Warned About Conflicts of Interest, But Not for Clinton Email Probe," *Newsweek*, January5, 2018, http://www.newsweek.com/andrew-mccabe-hillary-clinton-emails-conflict-interest-fbi-772331.

96   Office of the Inspector General, U.S. Department of Justice, "A Review of Various Actions by the Federal Bureau of Investigation and Department of Justice in Advance of the 2016 Election."

97   "The Face of FBI Politics: Bureau Boss McCabe Under Hatch Act Investigation"; Devlin Barrett, "Clinton Ally Aided Campaign of FBI Official's Wife."

98   "Jill McCabe," finance summary, vpap.org, accessed April 4, 2018, https://www.vpap.org/candidates/257116/finance_summary/.

99   Jill McCabe, "The President Attacked My Reputation. It's Time to Set the Record Straight," *The Washington Post*, April 2, 2018, https://www.washingtonpost.com/opinions/jill-mccabe-the-president-attacked-my-reputation-its-time-to-set-the-record-straight/2018/04/02/e6bbcf66-366b-11e8-8fd2-49fe3c675a89_story.html?utm_term=.2d74b4088f00.

100 Federal Bureau of Investigation, "Andrew McCabe Named Executive Assistant Director of National Security Branch"; Federal Bureau of Investigation, "Andrew McCabe Named Deputy Director of the FBI," press release, January 29, 2016, https://www.fbi.gov/news/pressrel/press-releases/andrew-mccabe-named-deputy-director-of-the-fbi; Federal Bureau of Investigation, "FBI Announces Executive Appointments," press release,

September 4, 2014, https://www.fbi.gov/news/pressrel/press-releases/ fbi-announces-executive-appointments; Federal Bureau of Investigation, "Andrew McCabe Named Executive Assistant Director of National Security Branch," press release, October 23, 2013, https://archives.fbi. gov/archives/news/pressrel/press-releases/andrew-g.-mccabe-named-executive-assistant-director-of-national-security-branch.

[101] United States Senate Committee on Homeland Security and Governmental Affairs, "Chairman Ron Johnson, letter to the Honorable Christopher Way, Director, Federal Bureau of Investigation," December 14, 2017, https:// www.scribd.com/document/367205031/2017-12-14-RHJ-to-FBI-Re-Comey-July-5-Statement.

[102] Federal Bureau of Investigation, "E.W. Priestap Named Assistant Director of the Counterintelligence Division," press release, December 21, 2015, https://www.fbi.gov/news/pressrel/press-releases/e.w.-priestap-named-assistant-director-of-the-counterintelligence-division; Daniel John Sobieski, "McCabe and Mr. Mueller," *American Thinker*, December 19, 2017, https://www.americanthinker.com/articles/2017/12/mccabe_and_mr_ mueller.html.

[103] Jeff Carlson, "Where Is Bill Priestap—FBI's Counter-Intelligence Head," *Markets Work*, December 28, 2017, https://www.themarketswork. com/2017/12/28/where-is-bill-priestap-fbis-counter-intelligence-head/.

[104] Federal Election Commission, individual contributions search, "Sabina Menschel," January 1, 2015–December 31, 2016, https://www.fec.gov/data/ receipts/individual-contributions/?two_year_transaction_period=2016&-contributor_name=sabina+menschel&min_date=01%2F01%2F2015&-max_date=12%2F31%2F2016.

[105] "Executive Leadership: Sabina Menschel," Nardello & Co., accessed May 1, 2018, http://www.nardelloandco.com/executive-leadership-senior-staff/ sabina-menschel/; William Finnegan, "The Secret Keeper," *The New Yorker*, October 19, 2009, https://www.newyorker.com/magazine/2009/10/19/ the-secret-keeper.

[106] Frank Friday, "How Husbands and Wives Figure in the Latest Government Scandal Revelations," *American Thinker*, December 16, 2017, https:// www.americanthinker.com/blog/2017/12/how_husbands_and_wives_fig-ure_in_the_latest_government_scandal_revelations.html.

[107] Charles Lipson, "The Hidden Bombshell in the McCabe Report," *Real Clear Politics*, April 23, 2018, https://www.realclearpolitics. com/articles/2018/04/23/the_hidden_bombshell_in_the_mccabe_ report_136882.html; Chuck Ross, "Strzok-Page Texts Show Concern with 'Security/Monitoring Issues,'" *The Daily Caller*, February 1, 2018, http://dailycaller.com/2018/02/01/strzok-page-texts-show-concern-with-security-monitoring-issues/.

108   Laura Jarrett, "Months-worth of FBI Employees' Texts Dreading Trump Victory Released to Congress," CNN, December 13, 2017, https://www.cnn.com/2017/12/12/politics/peter-strzok-texts-released/index.html.

109   Matt Apuzzo and Adam Goldman, "Andrew McCabe, Ex-Deputy Director of F.B.I., Will Be Faulted for Leaks," *The New York Times*, March 1, 2018, https://www.nytimes.com/2018/03/01/us/politics/justice-deptandrewmccabe.html?mtrref=undefined&gwh=555F8DE20B-C4D62BF648FD5795FF7CCE&gwt=pay.

110   Matt Zapotosky, "Former FBI Deputy Director Andrew McCabe Fired Just Before Full Eligibility for Retirement Benefits," *The Salt Lake Tribune*, March 17, 2018, https://www.sltrib.com/news/nation-world/2018/03/17/former-fbi-deputy-director-andrew-mccabe-fired-just-before-full-eligibility-for-retirement-benefits/; Mike Levine, "FBI Officials Recommend Former Deputy Director McCabe Be Fired, Source Says," ABC News, March 14, 2018, https://abcnews.go.com/US/fbi-officials-recommend-deputy-director-mccabe-fired-source/story?id=53747108.

111   Pat Ralph and Sonam Sheth, "DOJ's Watchdog Refers Andrew McCabe to US Attorney for Criminal Investigation," *Business Insider*, April 19, 2018, http://www.businessinsider.com/andrew-mccabe-criminal-referral-charges-justice-department-report-2018-4.

112   Pamela Brown and Laura Jarrett, "Justice Dept. Watchdog Sends McCabe Findings to Federal Prosecutors for Possible Charges," CNN, April 19, 2018, https://www.cnn.com/2018/04/19/politics/justice-mccabe-criminal-referral/index.html.

113   Thomas Lifson, "FBI-Gate: The Outlines of the Story Are Coming into Focus," *American Thinker*, February 13, 2018, https://www.americanthinker.com/articles/2018/02/fbigate_the_outlines_of_the_story_are_coming_into_focus.html.

114   Sobieski, "McCabe and Mr. Mueller"; Jake Gibson, "DOJ Official Who Concealed Meetings with Trump Dossier Figures Loses Another Job Title."

115   Federal Communications Commission, Universal Licensing Archive System, "Amateur License—KM4UDZ—Ohr, Nellie H," last action May 23, 2016, http://wireless2.fcc.gov/UlsApp/LicArchive/license.jsp?archive=Y&licKey=12382876.

116   John T. Picarelli, "Export Working Group Report on International Organized Crime," National Criminal Justice Reference Service, June 2010, https://www.ncjrs.gov/pdffiles1/nij/230846.pdf.

117   Chuck Ross, "Fusion GPS Confirms Hiring DOJ Official's Wife to Investigate Trump," *The Daily Caller*, December 12, 2017, http://dailycaller.com/2017/12/12/fusion-gps-confirms-hiring-doj-officials-wife-to-investigate-trump/; Vazquez, Brown, and Jarrett, "Trump's Lawyer Wants a Special Counsel to Investigate DOJ Official with Fusion GPS Ties."

118   Matt Zapotosky and Beth Reinhard, "Why the Nunes Memo Takes Aim at a Justice Dept. Official Specializing in Gangs and Drugs," *The Washington Post*, February 2, 2018, https://www.washingtonpost.com/world/national-security/why-the-nunes-memo-takes-aim-at-a-justice-department-official-specializing-in-gangs-and-drugs/2018/02/02/82e836e8-0847-11e8-94e8-e8b8600ade23_story.html?noredirect=on&utm_term=.6d5db6dbd0ff.

119   U.S. House of Representatives, Executive Session, Permanent Select Committee on Intelligence interview of Glenn Simpson, November 14, 2017, http://docs.house.gov/meetings/IG/IG00/20180118/1067 96/HMTG-115-IG00-20180118-SD002.pdf; Andrew Prokop, "Carter Page, the Star of the Nunes Memo, Explained," *Vox,* February 2, 2018, https://www.vox.com/policy-and-politics/2018/2/2/16956014/nunes-memo-carter-page.

120   Victor Davis Hanson, "Colluders on the Loose," *National Review,* April 17, 2018, https://www.nationalreview.com/2018/04/colluders-washington-clinton-obama-loaylists/; Rosen, "Top DOJ Official Demoted Amid Probe of Contacts with Trump Dossier Firm."

121   Federal Bureau of Investigation, "Andrew McCabe Named Assistant Director of Counterterrorism Division"; U.S. Department of Justice, "International Organized Crime," Executive Office for United States Attorney's Office of Legal Education 51, no. 5 (September 2003), https://www.justice.gov/sites/default/files/usao/legacy/2006/02/14/usab5105.pdf; Laura Jarrett and Evan Perez, "FBI Agent Dismissed from Mueller Probe Changed Comey's Description of Clinton to 'Extremely Careless,'" CNN, December 4, 2017, https://www.cnn.com/2017/12/04/politics/peter-strzok-james-comey/index.html.

122   U.S. Department of Justice, Organization, Mission, & Functions Manual: National Security Division, last updated July 8, 2016, https://www.justice.gov/jmd/organization-mission-and-functions-manual-national-security-division.

123   "The Nunes FBI Memo, Annotated."

124   U.S. Department of Justice, Office of Legal Counsel, Office of the Principal Deputy Assistant Attorney General, Memorandum for Sally Quillan Yates Deputy Attorney General, July 20, 2015, https://www.ignet.gov/sites/default/files/files/OLC%20IG%20Act%20Opinion%20-%207-20-15%20.pdf; U.S Department of Justice, Office of the Inspector General, "Statement regarding the Office of Legal Counsel's (OLC) July 23, 2015 Memorandum to the Deputy Attorney General," July 23, 2015, https://oig.justice.gov/press/2015/2015-07-23.pdf.

125   Susan Shelley, "Obama's FBI Withheld Information from Investigator Now Probing Them," *Los Angeles Daily News,* November 30, 2017, https://www.dailynews.com/2018/03/04/obamas-fbi-withheld-information-from-investigator-now-probing-them/.

126 Eric Lichtblau, "Justice Dept. Takes Steps to Restore Watchdogs' Access to Records," *The New York Times*, May 3, 2016, https://www.nytimes.com/2016/05/04/us/justice-dept-restoring-inspectors-access-to-records.html.

127 Michael D. Shear, Mark Landler, Matt Apuzzo, and Eric Lichtblau, "Trump Fires Acting Attorney General Who Defied Him," *The New York Times*, January 30, 2017, https://www.nytimes.com/2017/01/30/us/politics/trump-immigration-ban-memo.html; David Shortell, "Mueller Attorney Praised Yates As DOJ Official, Email Shows," CNN, December 6, 2017, https://www.cnn.com/2017/12/05/politics/mueller-emails-praise-doj-yates/index.html.

128 Aruna Viswanatha and Byron Tau, "Dispute with Congress Adds to Pressure on Rosenstein," *The Wall Street Journal*, April 12, 2018, https://www.wsj.com/articles/dispute-with-congress-adds-to-pressure-on-rosenstein-1523575398.

129 "Essential Washington: Immunity Offer from Michael Flynn Greeted with Skepticism," *The Los Angeles Times*, accessed May 1, 2018, http://www.latimes.com/politics/washington/la-na-essential-washington-updates-comey-fbi-and-justice-department-has-1490022347-htmlstory.html.

130 Dustin Volz, "Justice Department Affirms No Evidence Obama Wiretapped Trump," Reuters, September 2, 2017, https://www.reuters.com/article/us-usa-trump-surveillance/justice-department-affirms-no-evidence-obama-wiretapped-trump-idUSKCN1BD0UO.

131 Nina Burleigh, "Trump's Claim That Obama Wiretapped His Campaign Is False: U.S. Department of Justice," *Newsweek*, September 2, 2017, http://www.newsweek.com/trump-russia-investigation-wiretap-fbi-obama-658888.

132 "White House Spied on Trump and Lied About It, Says CNN – Is This Worse Than Richard Nixon?" *Investor's Business Daily*, September 19, 2017, https://www.investors.com/politics/editorials/white-house-spied-on-trump-and-lied-about-it-says-cnn-is-this-worse-than-richard-nixon/.

133 Office of the Inspector General, "U.S. Department of Justice, Redacted: A Report of Investigation of Certain Allegations Relating to Former FBI Deputy Director Andrew McCabe," February 2018, https://oig.justice.gov/reports/2018/o20180413.pdf; U.S. Department of Justice, Office of the Inspector General, "All Reports."

134 Office of the Inspector General, "U.S. Department of Justice, Redacted: A Report of Investigation of Certain Allegations Relating to Former FBI Deputy Director Andrew McCabe," February 2018, https://oig.justice.gov/reports/2018/o20180413.pdf; Jonathan Easley, "Republicans Demand News Special Counsel Over Lost FBI Text Messages," *The Hill*, January 22, 2018, http://thehill.com/policy/national-security/370097-republicans-demand-new-special-counsel-over-lost-fbi-text-messages; Matt Zapotosky, "FBI Interviewed Top Clinton Aide Huma Abedin After

Saying Investigation of Her Boss Had Concluded," *The Washington Post*, March 2, 2018, https://www.washingtonpost.com/world/national-security/fbi-interviewed-top-clinton-aide-huma-abedin-after-saying-investigation-of-her-boss-had-concluded/2018/03/02/1be1cd04-1be0-11e8-b2d9-08e748f892c0_story.html?utm_term=.d2519cb8a27a.

[135] Attkisson, "Was Lynch Coordinating with Comey in the Clinton Investigation?"

[136] Barrett and Matthews, "Secret Recordings Fueled FBI Feud in Clinton Probe"; Devlin Barrett, "FBI in Internal Feud over Hillary Clinton Probe," *The Wall Street Journal*, October 30, 2016, https://www.wsj.com/articles/laptop-may-include-thousands-of-emails-linked-to-hillary-clintons-private-server-1477854957; John Solomon, "FBI Launches New Clinton Foundation Investigation," *Hill*, January 4, 2018, http://thehill.com/homenews/campaign/367541-fbi-launches-new-clinton-foundation-investigation.

[137] Richard Pollock, "Now Five FBI Field Offices Are Probing Clinton Charity, Adding Fuel to the Fire," *Daily Caller*, October 30, 2016, http://dailycaller.com/2016/10/30/now-five-fbi-field-offices-are-probing-clinton-charity-adding-fuel-to-the-fire/.

[138] Solomon, "FBI Launches New Clinton Foundation Investigation."

[139] Barrett and Matthews, "Secret Recordings Fueled FBI Feud in Clinton Probe."

[140] Louis Nelson, "What You Need to Know About Clinton and the Uranium One Deal," *Politico*, November 14, 2017, https://www.politico.com/story/2017/11/14/hillary-clinton-uranium-one-deal-russia-explainer-244895.

[141] Barrett and Matthews, "Secret Recordings Fueled FBI Feud in Clinton Probe"; John Solomon, "FBI Informant Gathered Years of Evidence on Russian Push for US Nuclear Fuel Deals, Including Uranium One, Memos Show," *The Hill*, November 20, 2017, http://thehill.com/homenews/administration/361276-fbi-informant-gathered-years-of-evidence-on-russian-push-for-us.

[142] Andrew C. McCarthy, "The Obama Administration's Uranium One Scandal," *National Review*, October 21, 2017, https://www.nationalreview.com/2017/10/uranium-one-deal-obama-administration-doj-hillary-clinton-racketeering/.

[143] Stephen Braun and Eileen Sullivan, "Clinton Foundation Donors Got Face Time with Her at State," Associated Press, accessed April 5, 2018, https://elections.ap.org/content/clinton-foundation-donors-got-face-time-her-state; Rosalind S. Helderman and Michelle Ye Hee Lee, "Inside Bill Clinton's Nearly $18 Million Job As 'Honorary Chancellor' of a For-profit College," *The Washington Post*, September 5, 2016, https://www.washingtonpost.com/politics/inside-bill-clintons-nearly-18-million-job-as-honorary-chancellor-of-a-for-profit-college/2016/09/05/8496db42-655b-11e6-be4e-23fc4d4d12b4_story.html?noredirect=on&utm_term=.3fb94cdefb74; Kennedy Elliott et

al., "From 'Dead Broke' to Multimillionaires," *The Washington Post*, May 19, 2015, https://www.washingtonpost.com/graphics/politics/clinton-speeches/.

144   Barrett, "FBI in Internal Feud over Hillary Clinton Probe"; Pollock, "Now Five FBI Field Offices Are Probing Clinton Charity, Adding Fuel to the Fire."

145   Jonathan Swan, "Seven Ways the Clinton Foundation Failed to Meet Its Transparency Promises," *The Hill*, August 27, 2016, http://thehill.com/homenews/campaign/293507-seven-ways-the-clinton-foundation-failed-to-meet-its-transparency-promises; United States Senate Committee on the Judiciary, "Chairman Charles E. Grassley, letter to Attorney General Lynch," August 15 ,2016, https://www.grassley.senate.gov/sites/default/files/constituents/2016-08-15%20CEG%20to%20DOJ%20%28Clinton%20Foundation%29.pdf.

146   Barrett and Matthews, "Secret Recordings Fueled FBI Feud in Clinton Probe."

147   Wilber, "In FBI Agent's Account, 'Insurance Policy' Text Referred to Russia Probe."

148   Author note: Fusion's founder Glenn Simpson seems to confirm this when he described Fusion's work as "journalism for rent" at a 2017 symposium (the panel was called "Investigations with an Agenda").

    Jack Gillum and Shawn Boburg, "'Journalism for Rent': Inside the Secretive Firm Behind the Trump Dossier," *The Washington Post*, December 11, 2017, https://www.washingtonpost.com/investigations/journalism-for-rent-inside-the-secretive-firm-behind-the-trump-dossier/2017/12/11/8d5428d4-bd89-11e7-af84-d3e2ee4b2af1_story.html?utm_term=.da785c19db5d; Todd Shepherd, "Fusion GPS Paid Journalists, Court Papers Confirm," *The Washington Examiner*, November 21, 2017, https://www.washington-examiner.com/fusion-gps-paid-journalists-court-papers-confirm.

149   Alex Pappas, Catherine Herridge, and Brooke Singman, "House Memo States Disputed Dossier Was Key to FBI's FISA Warrant to Surveil Members of Team Trump," Fox News, February 2, 2018, http://www.foxnews.com/politics/2018/02/02/house-memo-states-disputed-dossier-was-key-to-fbi-s-fisa-warrant-to-surveil-members-team-trump.html; Andrew C. McCarthy, "The Schiff Memo Harms Democrats More Than It Helps Them," *National Review*, February 25, 2018, https://www.nationalreview.com/2018/02/schiff-memo-russia-investigation-harms-democrats-more-than-helps-them/.

150   "Robert Mueller's Leak Problem," *New York Post*, November 6, 2017, https://nypost.com/2017/11/06/robert-muellers-leak-problem/.

151   Sharyl Attkisson, "Justice Dept. and FBI Personnel Changes Amid Probes," Sharyl Attkisson's website, February 11, 2018, https://sharylattkisson.com/2018/02/11/justice-dept-and-fbi-personnel-changes-amid-probes/; Tom Porter, "Comey Advisers James Baker and Lisa Page

Resign from FBI," *Newsweek*, May 5, 2018, http://www.newsweek.com/two-former-advisers-james-comey-are-leaving-fbi-911873.

[152] Ewen MacAskill, "Trump's Wiretap Paranoia and the Reality of Modern Surveillance," Guardian, March 6, 2017, https://www.theguardian.com/world/2017/mar/06/trumps-wiretap-paranoia-reality-modern-surveillance.

Chapter 2: The FBI's Burial of Uranium Scandals

[1] Ruth Brown, "Trump: Comey Leaked Classified Information to the Media," *New York Post*, July 10, 2017, https://nypost.com/2017/07/10/trump-comey-leaked-classified-information-to-the-media/; Katie Bo Williams, "Five Things to Know About Fusion GPS," *The Hill*, August 25, 2017, http://thehill.com/policy/national-security/347858-five-things-to-know-about-fusion-gps; "Nunes Talks McCabe IG Report, Efforts to Get Comey Memos," Fox News, transcript, April 13, 2018, http://www.foxnews.com/transcript/2018/04/13/nunes-talks-mccabe-ig-report-efforts-to-get-comey-memos.html; United States Senate, "Letter from multiple parties, Senate, to the Honorable Jeff Sessions, Attorney General, the Honorable Christopher Wray, Director, Federal Bureau of Investigation, and the honorable John Huber, U.S. Attorney for the District of Utah"; Manu Raju, "Exclusive: Rice Told House Investigators Why She Unmasked Senior Trump Officials," CNN, September 18, 2017, https://www.cnn.com/2017/09/13/politics/susan-rice-house-investigators-unmasked-trump-officials/index.html.

[2] House Permanent Select Committee on Intelligence, "Report on Russian Active Measures," March 22, 2018, https://docs.house.gov/meetings/IG/IG00/20180322/108023/HRPT-115-1_1-p1-U3.pdf; Jack Crowe, "Clapper May Have Lied to Congress About Steele Dossier Leak," *National Review*, April 27, 2018, https://www.nationalreview.com/news/james-clapper-steele-dossier-testimony-false/; Byron Tau and Shane Harris, "House Intelligence Panel Issues Seven Subpoenas As Russia Probe Ramps Up," *The Wall Street Journal*, June 1, 2017, https://www.wsj.com/articles/house-intelligence-committee-said-to-have-issued-seven-subpoenas-in-russia-probe-1496261435; Lee Smith, "Did President Obama Read the 'Steele Dossier' in the White House Last August?" *Tablet*, December 20, 2017, http://www.tabletmag.com/jewish-news-and-politics/251897/obama-steele-dossier-russiagate.

[3] United States Senate, "Letter from multiple parties, Senate, to the Honorable Jeff Sessions, Attorney General, the Honorable Christopher Wray, Director, Federal Bureau of Investigation, and the honorable John Huber, U.S. Attorney for the District of Utah."

[4] Cristiano Lima, "GOP Lawmaker Calls for FBI, DOJ Officials to Face 'Treason' Charges," *Politico*, February 2, 2018, https://www.politico.com/story/2018/02/02/nunes-memo-treason-paul-gosar-386089.

5   Sonam Sheth, "Trump Alleges That the FBI Agent Mueller Ousted Committed 'Treason' by Sending Anti-Trump Texts," *Business Insider*, January 11, 2018, http://www.businessinsider.com/trump-peter-strzok-page-texts-treason-mueller-russia-2018-1.

6   Salary tables 2018, OPM.gov, accessed April 5, 2018, https://www.opm.gov/policy-data-oversight/pay-leave/salaries-wages/salary-tables/pdf/2018/saltbl.pdf.

7   Salary table no. 2018-ES, OPM.gov, effective January 2018, https://www.opm.gov/policy-data-oversight/pay-leave/salaries-wages/salary-tables/pdf/2018/ES.pdf.

8   Average salary for U.S. Government Employees, Payscale, accessed April 5, 2018, https://www.payscale.com/research/US/Employer=U.S._Government/Salary.

9   David Corn, "Why Eric Holder Represents What's Wrong with Washington," *Mother Jones*, January 14, 2009, https://www.motherjones.com/politics/2009/01/why-eric-holder-represents-whats-wrong-washington/; Josh Gerstein and Darren Samuelsohn, "Special Counsel Robert Mueller's Finances Go Public," *Politico*, August 9, 2017, https://www.politico.com/story/2017/08/08/robert-mueller-counsel-financial-records-241414; Opensecrets.org, "Comey, James B.," employment history, accessed May 2, 2018, https://www.opensecrets.org/revolving/rev_summary.php?id=70344.

10   Bruce Upbin, "The 147 Companies That Control Everything," *Forbes*, October 22, 2011, https://www.forbes.com/sites/bruceupbin/2011/10/22/the-147-companies-that-control-everything/.

11   Patrick Radden Keefe, "Why Corrupt Bankers Avoid Jail," *The New Yorker*, July 31, 2017, https://www.newyorker.com/magazine/2017/07/31/why-corrupt-bankers-avoid-jail; Terry Gross, "Is the Justice Department Shying Away from Prosecuting Corporations?" NPR Books, transcript, July 11, 2017, https://www.npr.org/2017/07/11/536642560/is-the-justice-department-shying-away-from-to-prosecuting-corporations.

12   Jonathan Allen, "181 Clinton Foundation Donors Who Lobbied Hillary's State Department," *Vox*, April 28, 2015, https://www.vox.com/2015/4/28/8501643/Clinton-foundation-donors-State.

13   Joanna Pearlstein, "Techies Donate to Clinton in Droves. To Trump? Not so Much," *Wired*, August 31, 2016, https://www.wired.com/2016/08/techies-donate-clinton-droves-trump-not-much/; Li Zhou "Senate Intel Deadline for Tech Giants," *Politico*, January 8, 2018, https://www.politico.com/newsletters/morning-tech/2018/01/08/senate-intel-deadline-for-tech-giants-067601.

14   Chris Cillizza, "The New York Times Just Perfectly Explained Hillary Clinton's Goldman Sachs Speech Problem," *The Washington Post*, February 26, 2016, https://www.washingtonpost.com/news/the-fix/wp/2016/02/26/the-new-york-times-just-perfectly-explained-why-hil-

lary-clintons-answers-on-her-paid-speeches-dont-work/?utm_term=. c5828ff2e11f.

15 Miles Mogulescu, "Clintons's $200,000 an Hour Pay from Goldman Sachs is Nothing to Laugh At," *HuffPost*, December 6, 2017, https:// www.huffingtonpost.com/miles-mogulescu/clintonss-200000-an-hour_b_9069720.html; Lee Fang, Zaid Jilani, Alex Emmons, and Naomi LeChance, "Excerpts of Hillary Clinton's Paid Speeches to Goldman Sachs Finally Leaked," Intercept, October 7, 2016, https://theintercept. com/2016/10/07/excerpts-of-hillary-clintons-paid-speeches-to-goldman-sachs-finally-leaked/.

16 U.S. Department of State, Secretary of State Hillary Rodham Clinton, Remarks at the United States Institute of Peace, October 21, 2009, https://2009-2017.state.gov/secretary/20092013clinton/ rm/2009a/10/130806.htm; United States Institute of Peace, "Lockheed Martin Contributes $1 Million to Endowment of the United States Institute of Peace," press release, April 22, 2009, https://2009-2017. state.gov/secretary/20092013clinton/rm/2009a/10/130806.htm.

17 Robert Yoon, "$153 Million in Bill and Hillary Clinton Speaking Fees, Documented," CNN, February 6, 2016, https://www.cnn. com/2016/02/05/politics/hillary-clinton-bill-clinton-paid-speeches/index. html.

18 Josh Gerstein, "Mueller's Law Firm's Clients Could Cause 'Wrinkle' in Appointment," *Politico*, May 17, 2017, https://www.politico.com/ story/2017/05/17/mueller-clients-special-prosecutor-238532; Opensecrets. org, "WilmerHale Llp: Recipients," 2016 cycle, https://www.opensecrets. org/orgs/toprecips.php?id=D000022322&cycle=2016; Matt Zapotosky, "Mueller, Several Team Members Gave Up Million-Dollar Jobs to Work on Special Counsel Investigation," *The Washington Post*, August 8, 2017, https://www.washingtonpost.com/world/national-security/mueller-several-team-members-gave-up-million-dollar-jobs-to-work-on-special-counsel-investigation/2017/08/08/e11169da-7b78-11e7-83c7-5bd5460f0d7e_story. html?utm_term=.331070d45647.

19 Marshall Cohen, "Special Counsel Team Members Donated to Dems, FEC Records Show," CNN, June 13, 2017, https://www.cnn. com/2017/06/12/politics/robert-mueller-donations-democrats-fec/ index.html; Brooke Singman, "Top Mueller Investigator's Democratic Ties Raise New Bias Questions," Fox News, December 7, 2017, http:// www.foxnews.com/politics/2017/12/07/another-mueller-investigators-democratic-ties-raise-new-bias-questions.html.

20 Debra Heine, "Mueller's 'Right-Hand Man' on Russia Probe Represented Clinton IT Aide Who Set Up Unsecure Server," PJ Media, December 8, 2017, https://pjmedia.com/trending/muellers-right-hand-man-russia-probe-represented-clinton-aide-set-unsecure-server/; Nick Gass, "The 12 Juiciest Bits from the FBI's Clinton Report," *Politico*, September

2, 2016, https://www.politico.com/story/2016/09/best-of-clinton-fbi-report-227692; Gerstein and Samuelsohn, "Special Counsel Robert Mueller's Finances Go Public."

[21] Smith, "Did President Obama Read the 'Steele Dossier' in the White House Last August?"

[22] Garance Franke-Ruta, "Fan Friction," *American Prospect*, September 23, 2003, http://prospect.org/article/fan-friction; Meckler and Nicholas, "Hillary Clinton's Forgotten Career: Corporate Lawyer."

[23] Matt Flegenheimer, "Fusion GPS Founder Hauled from the Shadows for the Russia Election Investigation," *The New York Times*, January 8, 2018, https://www.nytimes.com/2018/01/08/us/politics/fusion-gps-glenn-simpson.html; Laura McGann, "Main Justice Founder on the Rise of Niche News, When to Turn Down Cash, and Focusing on Your Focus," *NiemanLab*, May 14, 2010, http://www.niemanlab.org/2010/05/main-justice-founder-on-the-rise-of-niche-news-when-to-turn-down-cash-and-focusing-on-your-focus/; "Our History," The Economist Group, accessed May 23, 2018, https://economistgroupcareers.com/our-history/; Lois Romano, "The Reliable Source," *The Washington Post*, September 30, 1994, https://www.washingtonpost.com/archive/lifestyle/1994/09/30/the-reliable-source/61ce6d7b-21e4-44b7-87f3-caf1cf741136/?utm_term=.4ff614a47812; Glenn R. Simpson and Mary Jacoby, "How Lobbyists Help Ex-Soviets Woo Washington," *The Wall Street Journal*, April 17, 2007, https://www.wsj.com/articles/SB117674837248471543.

[24] "James Comey Fast Facts," CNN, April 17, 2018, https://www.cnn.com/2017/05/03/us/james-comey-fast-facts/index.html.

[25] Opensecrets.org, "Employment History," accessed May 24, 2018, https://www.opensecrets.org/revolving/rev_summary.php?id=70344id=70344.

[26] According to Lockheed Martin's SEC filings, James Comey's compensation didn't stop when he left the company. His compensation was structured in such a way that stock incentives remained attractive long after he left the company.

In 2009, James Comey was awarded 27,000 shares in Lockheed Martin common stock (NYSE:LMT). Between when he was awarded these shares and when he left the company in 2010, the SEC has recorded only one sale: 6,202 shares in June 2010. Comey was also awarded 65,200 option-to-buy shares in 2009. Those options don't expire until 2019.

As of February 2010, James Comey beneficially owned 162,482 shares in Lockheed according to the Definitive 14A Proxy Statement filed with the SEC. At that time the stock was valued around $75 per share meaning James Comey beneficially owned approximately $12,186,150 in LMT stock. Today, those same shares would be worth $50,266,045.

In 2010, Comey was awarded 40,400 option-to-buy shares in Lockheed at highly favorable prices. The options weren't exercisable until 2011, *after* Comey left Lockheed. It is unclear if he exercised those options between the time he left the company and when he joined the FBI in 2013. Furthermore, the options were priced just over $74.89 per share and they don't expire until 2020. On April 23, 2018 LMT share price hit $358.60 per share. If Comey purchased all 40,400 shares he was awarded at the favorable price ($74.89 x 40.4k = $3,025,556 cost) and sold them on April 23, 2018 ($358.60 x 40.4k = $14,487,440) he would have made a *profit* of $11,461,884.

Comey may or may not have exercised these options (or the other tens of thousands he had received in previous years). The SEC tracks insider trades but after Comey left Lockheed he was no longer required to file these insider trade reports.

Finally, in 2015 Comey received a lump pension payout from Lockheed when he turned 55. He "expected" this was only worth $400,000 according to his 2013 confirmation hearing testimony in 2013. According to his 2017 personal financial disclosure (the last year he was at the FBI), the deferred benefit plan (also known as "pension") was worth between $500,000 and $1 million. This means Comey had financial incentive to see Lockheed succeed during the time he was FBI director, a potential conflict of interest.

Federal Bureau of Investigation, "FBI Announces Award of Sentinel Contract," press release, March 16, 2006, https://www.fbi.gov/news/pressrel/press-releases/fbi-announces-award-of-sentinel-contract; David Hubler, "Lockheed Team Rolls Out Next Gen ID System for FBI," *Washington Technology*, April 12, 2011, https://washingtontechnology.com/articles/2011/04/12/lockheed-team-next-gen-id-system-for-fbi.aspx; U.S. Securities and Exchange Commission, "Comey, James B," accessed May 24, 2018, https://www.sec.gov/cgi-bin/own-disp?action=getowner&CIK=0001339593; Lockheed Martin Corp., Comey James B, Form 4 (filed January 28, 2009), https://www.sec.gov/Archives/edgar/data/936468/000135159409000025/xslF345X03/edgar.xml; Lockheed Martin Corp., Comey James B, Form 4 (filed February 3, 2010), https://www.sec.gov/Archives/edgar/data/936468/000122520810003388/xslF345X03/doc4.xml.

[27]   United States Senate Committee on the Judiciary, "Chairman Charles E. Grassley, letter to Senator Blumenthal and Representative Conyers," August 10, 2017, https://www.judiciary.senate.gov/imo/media/doc/2017-08-10%20CEG%20to%20Blumenthal%20Conyers%20et%20al%20(Clinton%20Emoluments).pdf.

[28]   David Sirota and Andrew Perez, "Clinton Foundation Donors Got Weapons Deals from Hillary Clinton's State Department," *International Business Times*, May 26, 2015, http://www.ibtimes.com/clinton-foundation-donors-got-weapons-deals-hillary-clintons-state-department-1934187; Robert J. Stevens, Lockheed Martin Corporation, schedule 14A, March 12, 2010.

29   John Solomon and Alison Spann, "FBI Uncovered Russian Bribery Plot Before Obama Administration Approved Controversial Nuclear Deal with Moscow," *The Hill*, October 17, 2017, http://thehill.com/policy/national-security/355749-fbi-uncovered-russian-bribery-plot-before-obama-administration; McCarthy, "The Obama Administration's Uranium One Scandal"; Allan Smith, "Robert Mueller's 'Pit Bull' Is Coming Under Intense Scrutiny over Perceived Anti-Trump Bias," *Business Insider*, December 9, 2017, http://www.businessinsider.com/who-is-andrew-weissman-mueller-trump-clinton-russia-investigation-fbi-2017-12; Nathan Heller, "A Dark Night at the Javits Center," *The New Yorker*, November 9, 2016, https://www.newyorker.com/culture/culture-desk/a-dark-night-at-the-javits-center; Peter Nicholas, Aruna Viswanatha, and Erica Orden, "Trump's Allies Urge Harder Line As Mueller Probe Heats Up," *The Wall Street Journal*, December 8, 2017, https://www.wsj.com/articles/trumps-allies-urge-harder-line-as-mueller-probe-drags-on-1512748299.

Author's note: Andrew Weissmann, longtime Democrat described as Mueller's "pit bull," reportedly attended Hillary Clinton's official post-election party in New York. Weissmann's attendance was heavily criticized as evidence the special counsel is comprised of pro-Clinton democrats and thus "irredeemably compromised by anti-Trump partisans."

The star-studded gala-turned-funeral was also attended by Reverend Al Sharpton, Katy Perry, Bill de Blasio, Andrew Cuomo, Chuck Schumer and others. This is the event where Clinton refused to come onstage after her electoral loss instead leaving it up to campaign chairman John Podesta to issue the post-mortem. Guests were reportedly in shock and disbelief that Clinton refused to address her supporters. A reporter to *NY Mag* captured the emotions:

"I think there must be something wrong," a young man named Robbie Miller, who had voted for Bernie Sanders in the primary and then crossed over, said. "How else could she not address her own Presidential campaign?" Others seemed more dazed. "I'm catatonic," one supporter, Hedy Stempler, said. "I think I must be dreaming. I don't think I'm awake. I'm in a fog. It's a nightmare."

30   John M. Broder, "Clinton Approves Technology Transfer to China," *The New York Times*, May 11, 1999, https://www.nytimes.com/1999/05/11/world/clinton-approves-technology-transfer-to-china.html; "Fund-Raiser Charlie Trie Pleads Guilty Under Plea Agreement," All Politics, on Internet Archive, May 21, 1999, https://web.archive.org/web/20060805092557/http://www.cnn.com/ALLPOLITICS/stories/1999/05/21/trie/ (the screenshot was captured August 5, 2006); Jo Becker and Mike McIntire, "Cash Flowed to Clinton Foundation Amid Russian Uranium Deal."

31   Becker and McIntire, "Cash Flowed to Clinton Foundation Amid Russian Uranium Deal"; Stephen Braun and Eileen Sullivan, "Many Donors to Clinton Foundation Met with Her at State," Associated Press, August

24, 2016, https://apnews.com/82df550e1ec646098b434f7d5771f625; Matthew Mosk, Brian Ross, Brian Epstein, and Cho Park, "'FOBs': How Hillary's State Dept. Gave Special Attention to 'Friends of Bill' After Haiti Quake," ABC News, October 11, 2016, http://abcnews.go.com/Politics/fobs-hillarys-state-dept-gave-special-attention-friends/story?id=42615379; Grimaldi, Ballhaus, and Nicholas, "Gifts to Hillary Clinton's Family Charity Are Scrutinized in Wake of Book."

32 Barrett, "FBI in Internal Feud over Hillary Clinton Probe."

33 Braun and Sullivan, "Many Donors to Clinton Foundation Met with Her at State"; Brian Ross and Matthew Mosk, "New Docs Show Clinton Foundation Donors Sought Access to State Department," ABC News, August 23, 2016, http://abcnews.go.com/Politics/docs-show-clinton-foundation-donors-sought-access-state/story?id=41582158.

34 Solomon, "FBI Informant Gathered Years of Evidence on Russian Push for US Nuclear Fuel Deals, Including Uranium One, Memos Show."

35 John Solomon and Alison Spann, "FBI Uncovered Russian Bribery Plot Before Obama Administration Approved Controversial Nuclear Deal with Moscow," *The Hill*, October 17, 2017, http://thehill.com/policy/national-security/355749-fbi-uncovered-russian-bribery-plot-before-obama-administration.

36 Ibid.

37 "A Russian Nuclear Firm Under FBI Investigation Was Allowed to Purchase US Uranium Supply," *Circa*, October 17, 2017, https://www.circa.com/story/2017/10/17/national-security/the-fbi-uncovered-russian-nuclear-kickback-scheme-months-before-the-obama-administration-passed-uranium-one-deal-with-moscow; Olivia Beavers, "Grassley Calls for Special Counsel on Uranium One Sale," *The Hill*, October 25, 2017, http://thehill.com/homenews/senate/357136-grassley-calls-for-special-counsel-on-uranium-1.

38 U.S. Attorney's Office, District of Maryland, "Russian National and Three Others Charged in Kickback Scheme to Obtain Contracts to Transport Russian Nuclear Fuel to the U.S.," Federal Bureau of Investigation, October 31, 2014, https://www.fbi.gov/contact-us/field-offices/washingtondc/news/press-releases/russian-national-and-three-others-charged-in-kickback-scheme-to-obtain-contracts-to-transport-russian-nuclear-fuel-to-the-u.s; Federal Bureau of Investigation, "Ten Alleged Secret Agents Arrested in the United States," press release, June 28, 2010, https://www.fbi.gov/newyork/press-releases/2010/nyfo062810a.htm.

39 Solomon and Spann, "FBI Uncovered Russian Bribery Plot Before Obama Administration Approved Controversial Nuclear Deal with Moscow."

40 Richard A. Falkenrath, "The U.S.-Russian HEU Purchase Agreement: Achievements, Problems. Prospects," CSIA Discussion Paper 95-07, Kennedy School of Government, Harvard University, July 1995, https://

www.belfercenter.org/sites/default/files/legacy/files/disc_paper_95_07. pdf; United States Department of Commerce, International Trade Administration, "Memorandum from Carole Showers, Acting Deputy Assistant Secretary for Policy and Negotiations, to Paul Piqua do, Assistant Secretary for Import Administration," October 28, 2011, https://enforcement.trade.gov/frn/summary/russia/2011-28652-1. pdf; "Deputy Secretary Poneman's Remarks at the Nuclear Deterrence Summit," energy.gov, February 17, 2010, https://www.energy.gov/articles/ deputy-secretary-ponemans-remarks-nuclear-deterrence-summit.

41   Robert L. Bartley, "How Gore Lost Russia," *The Wall Street Journal*, August 21, 2000, https://www.wsj.com/articles/SB966802099717753175.

42   "Megatons to Megawatts," Centrus, accessed March 28, 2018, http:// www.centrusenergy.com/who-we-are/history/megatons-to-megawatts/; "Megatons to Megawatts – USEC Recycles 400 Tons of Weapon Grade Uranium Into Nuclear Fuel," Nuclear Street, September 10, 2010, https:// nuclearstreet.com/nuclear_power_industry_news/b/nuclear_power_news/ archive/2010/09/10/megatons-to-megawatts-usec-recycles-400-tons-of- weapon-grade-uranium-into-nuclear-fuel#.WutapC-ZO8p.

43   John Norris, "The Dog Days of Spring," in *Collision Course: NATO, Russia, and Kosovo* (Westport: Praeger Publishers, 2005), 84, https:// books.google.com/books?id=LFRq31tqR4sC&pg=PA84&dq=%22leon+- fuerth%22+%22chernomyrdin%22&hl=en&sa=X&ved=0ahUKEwjn- neyi5IraAhXL7VMKHZIvAt8Q6AEIKTAA#v=onepage&q=%22leon%20 fuerth%22%20%22chernomyrdin%22&f=false; Evan Perez, "Alleged Russian Agent Claimed Official Was His Firm's Adviser," *The Wall Street Journal*, July 2, 2010, https://www.wsj.com/articles/ SB10001424052748703517104575341633816865778?mod=WSJ_hpp_ MIDDLENexttoWhatsNewsForth.

44   Perez, "Alleged Russian Agent Claimed Official Was His Firm's Adviser."

45   World Nuclear Association, "World Uranium Mining Production," last updated July 2017, http://www.world-nuclear.org/information-library/ nuclear-fuel-cycle/mining-of-uranium/world-uranium-mining-produc- tion.aspx; Uranium One Inc., "Uranium One Completes Acquisition of UrAsiaEnergy," news release, April 20, 2007, http://old.uranium1.com/index. php/en/component/docman/doc_download/250-uranium-one-completes -acquisition-of-urasia-energy.

46   Daniel Poneman, "The Nonproliferation Implications of Regional Spent Fuel Storage," presented at the WM99 Conference, Tucson, Arizona, March 4, 1999, http://www.wmsym.org/archives/1999/p3/p3-1.pdf; John Taylor, Project Chair, *Disposing of Weapons-Grade Plutonium: A Consensus Report of the CSIS Senior Policy Panel on the Safe, Timely, and Effective Disposition of Surplus U.S. and Russian Weapons-Grade Plutonium* (Washington, D.C.: CSIS Press, 1998), https://books.google.com/books?id=ZFmX1C1ry- wEC&pg=PA1&dq=%22daniel+poneman%22+%22HEU%22+%22L

EU%22&hl=en&sa=X&ved=0ahUKEwifveyKy43aAhVqU98KHY7F-B24Q6AEIJzAA#v=onepage&q=%22daniel%20poneman%22%20%22HEU%22%20%22LEU%22&f=false; U.S. Department of State, Daily Press Briefing #113, July 12, 1996, http://www.hri.org/news/usa/std/1996/96-07-12.std.html.

47   "Nuclear," Covington, accessed May 24, 2018, https://www.cov.com/en/practices-and-industries/industries/energy/nuclear?r=%7B2541A321-50C7-4C35-A948-B08ABFFEE6E4%7D; "Daniel B. Poneman: Former Deputy Secretary of Energy," energy.gov, accessed May 24, 2018, https://www.energy.gov/contributors/daniel-b-poneman; HoganLovells.com, accessed March 28, 2018, https://www.hoganlovells.com/en/service/energy-regulatory.

48   Jeff Gerth and Don Van Natta Jr., "Threats and Responses: The Adviser; Still Very Much a Player, Scowcroft Straddles the Worlds of Business and Government," *The New York Times*, September 20, 2002, https://www.nytimes.com/2002/09/20/world/threats-responses-adviser-still-very-much-player-scowcroft-straddles-worlds.html; "Eric H. Holder, Jr.," Covington, accessed May 24, 2018, https://www.cov.com/en/professionals/h/eric-holder; U.S. Department of Justice, "Attorney General: Loretta E. Lynch," accessed May 24, 2018, https://www.justice.gov/ag/bio/attorney-general-loretta-e-lynch; Opensecrets.org, "Poneman, Daniel B," accessed May 24, 2018.

49   Kevin Bogardus and Hannah Northey, "Former Deputy Negotiated for Several Outside Jobs," *E&E News*, November 12, 2015, htttps://www.eenews.net/stories/1060027895; Department of Energy, "Memorandum from Rod O'Connor, Chief of Staff, to Daniel B. Poneman, Deputy Secretary," May 21, 2009, https://www.eenews.net/assets/2015/11/05/document_gw_02.pdf.

50   Department of Energy, "Memorandum from Susan F. Beard, Assistant General Counsel for General Law and Designated Agency Ethics Official, to Daniel B. Poneman, Deputy Secretary," March 14, 2011, https://oge.gov/Web/OGE.nsf/0/215E83AED2F7F2A485257EBC00669541/$FILE/7d7db-6620d1c4a518602117cd0e69e2f3.pdf; Office of Nuclear Energy, "Secretary Chu Announces Blue Ribbon Commission on America's Nuclear Future," energy.gov, January 29, 2010, https://www.energy.gov/ne/articles/secretary-chu-announces-blue-ribbon-commission-america-s-nuclear.

51   Department of Energy, "Memorandum from Susan F. Beard, Assistant General Counsel for General Law and Designated Agency Ethics Official, to Daniel B. Poneman, Deputy Secretary"; Office of Nuclear Energy, "Secretary Chu Announces Blue Ribbon Commission on America's Nuclear Future"; In February 2010, shortly after the commission was announced, Poneman mentioned the panel co-chaired by Scowcroft:

"As you know, we recently announced a Blue Ribbon Commission on America's Nuclear Future, under the distinguished co-chairmanship of Lee

Hamilton and Brent Scowcroft, which is bringing together leading experts to consider all options surrounding the back end of the fuel cycle, and to provide recommendations for developing a safe, long-term approach to managing the Nation's used nuclear fuel and its nuclear waste." "Deputy Secretary Poneman's Remarks at the Nuclear Deterrence Summit."

52   Ben Geman, "Hamilton, Scowcroft to Lead Nuclear Waste Panel," *The Hill*, January 29, 2010, http://thehill.com/policy/energy-environ-ment/78833-hamilton-scowcroft-to-lead-nuclear-waste-panel; "Blue Ribbon Commission Issues Final Report on Nuclear Waste," *Wise*, March 2, 2012, https://www.wiseinternational.org/nuclear-monitor/741/blue-ribbon-commission-issues-final-report-nuclear-waste.

53   Nurith Aizenman, "National Security for Sale. Government Privatization and Nuclear Terrorism," *Washington Monthly* 29, no. 12 (December 1, 1997): 17, https://www.unz.com/print/WashingtonMonthly-1997dec-00017/Contents/; Douglas Birch and Alexander Cohen, "Everything You Hate About Washington Confirmed by One Simple Job Change," *Mother Jones*, May 13, 2015, https://www.motherjones.com/politics/2015/05/daniel-poneman-united-states-enrichment-corporation/.

54   Ibid.

55   Michael Smallberg, "The Revolving Door Goes Nuclear," POGO, April 21, 2015, http://www.pogo.org/our-work/articles/2015/the-revolving-door-goes-nuclear.html?print=t.

56   Aizenman, "National Security for Sale. Government Privatization and Nuclear Terrorism."

57   Darius Dixon, "Ex-Energy Official's $1.7 Million Gig Draws Fire," *Politico*, March 16, 2015, https://www.politico.com/story/2015/03/dan-poneman-centrus-116089; Committee on Oversight and Government Reform, "Letter from Jason Chaffetz, Chairman, and Cynthia Lummis, Chairman of the Subcommittee on the Interior, to the Honorable Ernest Moniz, Secretary, U.S. Department of Energy," March 30, 2015, http://oversight.house.gov/wp-content/uploads/2015/01/2015-03-30_JEC_CML_to_Moniz-DOE_Centrus_Poneman_due_4-10.pdf.

58   "Centrus Signs $70 Million in New Nuclear Fuel Sales Contracts," *Business Wire*, September 12, 2017, https://www.businesswire.com/news/home/20170912005936/en/Centrus-Signs-70-Million-New-Nuclear-Fuel; "Centrus and Tenex Agree on Decade of Reliable Supply," Centrus, December 22, 2015, http://www.centrusenergy.com/news/centrus-and-ten-ex-agree-on-decade-of-reliable-supply/; "Centrus Signs Long-Term Supply Agreement with Orano," Centrus, May 3, 2018, http://www.centrusen-ergy.com/news/centrus-signs-long-term-supply-agreement-with-orano/.

59   U.S. Department of Justice, Exhibit A and B to Registration Statement, Under the Foreign Agents Registration Act of 1938, as amended, Hogan & Hartson (received by Dept. of Justice Criminal Division on November 21,

1991), https://www.documentcloud.org/documents/3349771-2244-Exhibit-AB-19911101-CZDCN002.html; Opensecrets.org, "Foreign Lobby Watch: Countries," accessed May 25, 2018, https://www.opensecrets.org/fara/countries?location=RUSSIA; 802 F. Supp. 469, https://www.courtlistener.com/opinion/1650009/techsnabexport-ltd-v-united-states/.

60 "New Jersey Man Sentenced for Role in Russian Uranium Bribe Scheme," Reuters, November 13, 2017, https://www.reuters.com/article/usa-crime-russia/new-jersey-man-sentenced-for-role-in-russian-uranium-bribe-scheme-idUSL1N1NK023.

61 "Russia Flexes Muscles on Ukraine Nuclear Fuel Supply," Wikileaks, accessed May 24, 2018, https://wikileaks.org/plusd/cables/09BRUSSELS1385_a.html.

62 "New Jersey Man Sentenced for Role in Russian Uranium Bribe Scheme," Reuters, November 13, 2017, https://uk.reuters.com/article/usa-crime-russia/new-jersey-man-sentenced-for-role-in-russian-uranium-bribe-scheme-idUKL1N1NK023; Solomon and Spann, "FBI Uncovered Russian Bribery Plot Before Obama Administration Approved Controversial Nuclear Deal with Moscow"; Leonid Bershidsky, "Russian Money Talks. America Was All Ears," *Bloomberg*, October 18, 2017, https://www.bloomberg.com/view/articles/2017-10-18/russian-money-talks-america-was-all-ears; Tenex, "HEU Achievement" booklet, accessed March 28, 2018, http://www.tenex.ru/wps/wcm/connect/tenex/site/resources/ca5a980045a8aa1b-89f0bb470124f4f9/HEU_Book_Final.pdf.

63 Thomas B. Cochran and Robert Standish Norris, "Russian/Soviet Nuclear Warhead Production," Natural Resources Defense Council, September 8, 1993, https://fas.org/nuke/norris/nuc_09089301a_114.pdf; Nicholas M. De Feis and Philip C. Patterson, "Using Anti-Corruption Laws to Address Overseas Security Threats," *New York Law Journal*, January 25, 2016, http://dorlaw.com/pdfs/070011637-2015-Rosatom-Article.pdf.

64 Case information and summary, U.S. v. Daren Condrey, No. 15-cr-00336, accessed March 28, 2018, http://fcpa.stanford.edu/enforcement-action.html?id=584; Solomon and Spann, "FBI Uncovered Russian Bribery Plot Before Obama Administration Approved Controversial Nuclear Deal with Moscow"; "Tenam Corp Chief on Extortion Charge," World Nuclear News, November 3, 2014, http://www.world-nuclear-news.org/C-Tenam-Corp-chief-on-extortion-charge-03111401.html; U.S. v. Daren Condrey, No. 15-cr-00336 (D. Maryland, filed June 6, 2016), http://fingfx.thomsonreuters.com/gfx/rngs/USA-CLINTON-INFORMANT/010051PX3W7/document.pdf.

65 U.S. Department of Justice, U.S. Attorney's Office: District of Maryland, "Russian National and Three Others Charged in Kickback Scheme to Obtain Contracts to Transport Russian Nuclear Fuel to the U.S.," press release, October 31, 2014, https://www.justice.gov/usao-md/pr/russian-

national-and-three-others-charged-kickback-scheme-obtain-contracts-transport.

66   Shearman & Sterling LLP, "Cases and Review Releases Relating to Bribes to Foreign Officials Under the Foreign Corrupt Practices Act of 1977," *FCPA Digest*, January 2016, https://www.shearman.com/-/media/Files/NewsInsights/Publications/2016/01/FCPA-Recent-Trends-and-Patterns.pdf.

67   U.S. Department of Justice, "Nuclear Energy Official Pleads Guilty to Money Laundering Conspiracy Involving Violations of the Foreign Corrupt Practices Act," press release, August 31, 2015, https://www.justice.gov/opa/pr/russian-nuclear-energy-official-pleads-guilty-money-laundering-conspiracy-involving; U.S. Department of Justice, "Former Russian Nuclear Energy Official Sentenced to 48 Months in Prison for Money Laundering Conspiracy Involving Foreign Corrupt Practices Act Violations," press release, December 15, 2015, https://www.justice.gov/opa/pr/former-russian-nuclear-energy-official-sentenced-48-months-prison-money-laundering-conspiracy.

68   Case information and summary, U.S. v. Daren Condrey, No. 15-cr-00336, accessed March 28, 2018, http://fcpa.stanford.edu/enforcement-action.html?id=584.

69   Solomon, "FBI Informant Gathered Years of Evidence on Russian Push for US Nuclear Fuel Deals, Including Uranium One, Memos Show"; U.S. Department of Justice, U.S. Attorney's Office: District of Maryland, "Russian National and Three Others Charged in Kickback Scheme to Obtain Contracts to Transport Russian Nuclear Fuel to the U.S."

70   U.S. Department of Justice, "Ten Russian Agents Plead Guilty and Are to Be Removed from the United States," press release, July 8, 2010, https://www.justice.gov/opa/pr/ten-russian-agents-plead-guilty-and-are-be-removed-united-states; Mary Beth Sheridan and Jerry Markon, "U.S., Russia Reach Deal on Exchanging Spies," *The Washington Post*, July 9, 2010.

71   Perez, "Alleged Russian Agent Claimed Official Was His Firm's Adviser"; John Solomon and Alison Spann, "FBI Watched, Then Acted As Russian Spy Moved Closer to Hillary Clinton," *The Hill*, October 22, 2017, http://thehill.com/policy/national-security/356630-fbi-watched-then-acted-as-russian-spy-moved-closer-to-hillary.

72   Solomon and Spann, "FBI Watched, Then Acted As Russian Spy Moved Closer to Hillary Clinton."

73   Malia Zimmerman, "Hillary Clinton Sided with Russia on Sanctions as Bill Made $500G on Moscow Speech," Fox News, July 18, 2017, http://www.foxnews.com/politics/2017/07/18/hillary-clinton-sided-with-russia-on-sanctions-as-bill-made-500g-on-moscow-speech.html; John Solomon and Alison Spann, "Bill Clinton Sought State's Permission to Meet with Russian Nuclear Official During Obama Uranium Decision," *The Hill*,

October 19, 2017, http://thehill.com/policy/national-security/356323-bill-clinton-sought-states-permission-to-meet-with-russian-nuclear.

[74] "Spies Like Us: An Unusual Spy Network is Busted by the FBI," *Economist*, July 1, 2010, https://www.economist.com/node/16486569.

[75] Eli Lake, "Obama Choked on Russia Long Before the 2016 Election," *Bloomberg*, June 27, 2017, https://www.bloomberg.com/view/articles/2017-06-27/obama-choked-on-russia-long-before-the-2016-election.

[76] Michael Isikoff and David Corn, *Russian Roulette* (New York: Hachette Book Group, 2018), 26, https://books.google.com/books?id=Tzc-3DwAAQBAJ&pg=PT41&lpg=PT41&dq=russian+roulette+david+corn+isikoff+tom+donilon&source=bl&ots=fXBRBJuJJy&sig=dRyVQdACJlMjVCAvavkpWnbT90E&hlone-armz-idAFN08246560201006 08.=en&sa=X&ved=0ahUKEwiq7Ivc64raAhVDz1MKHeEFBdcQ6A-EIMzAC#v=onepage&q=russian%20roulette%20david%20corn%20isikoff%20tom%20donilon&f=false.

[77] John D. McKinnon, "Obama Team's Finances Released," *The Wall Street Journal*, April 6, 2009, https://www.wsj.com/articles/SB123897383937190973..

[78] O'Melveny & Myers LLP, "International Trade & Investment Regulation," accessed March 28, 2018, https://www.omm.com/services/practices/regulatory-and-government-affairs/international-trade/; "FW: NRC Request – PFN Tool License," email sent on November 16, 2010, https://www.nrc.gov/docs/ML1032/ML103200239.pdf; "JSC Atomredmetzoloto Acquires Uranium One," Lexpert, October 18, 2013, http://www.lexpert.ca/article/jsc-atomredmetzoloto-acquires-uranium-one/.

[79] U.S. Department of State, "Report of the U.S. State Department Stakeholders Advisory Board (SAB) on Implementation of the OECD Guidelines for Multinational Enterprises," February 24, 2014, https://www.state.gov/e/eb/adcom/aciep/rls/225959.htm; U.S. Department of State, "Letter to Secretary Clinton Regarding the Model Bilateral Investment Treaty," October 1, 2009, https://2009-2017.state.gov/e/eb/rls/othr/2009/131096.htm.

[80] "The Podesta Emails; Part One," Wikileaks, accessed May 24, 2018, https://wikileaks.org/podesta-emails/press-release; "Jose W. Fernandez (1955-)," Office of the Historian, accessed May 24, 2018, https://history.state.gov/departmenthistory/people/fernandez-jose-w.

[81] U.S. Department of State, "Photo Gallery: April 15, 2010 Meeting of the ACIEP," accessed May 24, 2018, https://2009-2017.state.gov/e/eb/adcom/aciep/2010/pg4/index.htm; U.S. Department of State, "Photo Gallery: August 12, 2010 Meeting of the ACIEP," accessed May 24, 2018, https://2009-2017.state.gov/e/eb/adcom/aciep/2010/pg5/index.htm; U.S. Department of State, "Photo Gallery: November 18, 2010 Meeting of the ACIEP," accessed May 24, 2018, https://2009-2017.state.gov/e/eb/adcom/aciep/2010/pg6/index.htm.

82   U.S. Department of State, "Photo Gallery: August 12, 2010 Meeting of the ACIEP," accessed April 11, 2018, https://2009-2017.state.gov/e/eb/adcom/aciep/2010/pg5/index.htm; "1-Uranium One Shareholders Approve ARMZ Deal," Reuters, August 31, 2010, https://www.reuters.com/article/uraniumone-armz-idUKN3124733820100831; Becker and McIntire, "Cash Flowed to Clinton Foundation Amid Russian Uranium Deal."

83   "The Podesta Emails," Wikileaks, accessed April 11, 2018, https://wikileaks.org/podesta-emails/.

84   U.S. Department of State, "Photo Gallery: April 15, 2010 Meeting of the ACIEP"; Note: The Nuclear Regulatory Commission emails referenced above show Kassinger advising ARMZ by November 16, 2010. We can only speculate his earlier role at the time of this photo.

85   O'Melveny & Myers LLP, "Former U.S. National Security Advisor Thomas E. Donilon Returns to O'Melveny," press release, May 15, 2014, https://www.omm.com/our-firm/media-center/press-releases/former-us-national-security-advisor-thomas-e-donilon-returns/.

86   O'Melveny & Myers LLP, "International Trade & Investment Regulation," accessed March 28, 2018, https://www.omm.com/services/practices/regulatory-and-government-affairs/international-trade/.

87   "Update 2—Russia's ARMZ to Acquire Control of Uranium One," Reuters, June 8, 2010, https://www.reuters.com/article/uraniumone-armz-idAFN0824656020100608; Becker and McIntire, "Cash Flowed to Clinton Foundation Amid Russian Uranium Deal."

88   Lake, "Obama Choked on Russia Long Before the 2016 Election."

89   Byron Tau and Peter Nicholas, "State Department Lacked Top Watchdog During Hillary Clinton Tenure," *The Wall Street Journal*, March 24, 2015, https://www.wsj.com/articles/state-department-lacked-top-watchdog-during-hillary-clinton-tenure-1427239813; R. Jeffrey Smith, "Vacant State Department Inspector General Position Draws Criticism," *The Washington Post*, April 25, 2011, https://www.washingtonpost.com/politics/vacant-state-department-inspector-general-position-draws-criticism/2011/04/22/AFzrzLlE_story.html?utm_term=.50c3f152d46d.

90   Justin Elliott and Liz Day, "State Department Finally Releases List of 'Special Government Employees,'" *ProPublica*, January 30, 2014, https://www.propublica.org/article/state-department-finally-releases-list-of-special-government-employees.

91   Rachael Bade, "Hillary Named on Document Formalizing Abedin Job Change," *Politico*, September 24, 2015, https://www.politico.com/story/2015/09/clinton-abedin-state-job-approved- R214038; Louis Jacobson and John Kruzel, "What You Need to Know About Hillary Clinton, Russia, and Uranium," *Politifact*, October 24, 2017, http://www.politifact.com/truth-o-meter/article/2017/oct/24/what-you-need-know-about-hillary-clinton-and-urani/

92   Winter, Williams, and Dilanian, "Prosecutors Ask FBI Agents for Info on Uranium One Deal."

[93] Greg Gordon, "Under Pressure, Clinton Foundation's Canadian Arm Reveals 21 Donors," McClatchy DC, May 8, 2015, http://www.mcclatchydc.com/news/politics-government/election/article24784342.html; Swan, "Seven Ways the Clinton Foundation Failed to Meet Its Transparency Promises"; Rosalind S. Helderman and Tom Hamburger, "1,100 Donors to a Canadian Charity Tied to Clinton Foundation Remain Secret," *The Washington Post*, April 28, 2015, http://www.washingtonpost.com/politics/1100-donors-to-a-canadian-charity-tied-to-clinton-foundation-remain-secret/2015/04/28/c3c0f374-edbc-11e4-8666-a1d756d0218e_story.html.

[94] Matt Baker, "Moscow's American Uranium," *Politico*, October 18, 2013, https://www.politico.com/story/2013/10/moscows-american-uranium-098472.

[95] Becker and McIntire, "Cash Flowed to Clinton Foundation Amid Russian Uranium Deal."

[96] Bill Press, "Clinton Cash: No Smoking Gun," *Chicago Tribune*, April 30, 2015, http://www.chicagotribune.com/news/columnists/sns-201504301630--tms--bpresstt--m-a20150430-20150430-column.html; Jacobson and Kruzel, "What You Need to Know About Hillary Clinton, Russia, and Uranium"; Doha Madani, "MSNBC Host Skewers Claims Clinton Helped Sell Uranium to Russians," *HuffPost*, October 30, 2017, https://www.huffingtonpost.com/entry/joy-reid-clinton-uranium-one-trump_us_59f672f9e4b03cd20b827261.

[97] "This Week' Transcript: 'Clinton Cash' Author Peter Schweizer," ABC News, transcript, April 26, 2015, http://abcnews.go.com/Politics/week-transcript-clinton-cash-author-peter-schweizer/story?id=30568766.

[98] Jake Shafer, "The Stephanopoulos Mess," *Politico*, May 14 2015, https://www.politico.com/magazine/story/2015/05/the-great-stephanopoulos-mess-117971#.VVn_7DqbbBd; James B. Nelson, "Stephanopoulos' Clinton Foundation Contributions Called 'Egregious Failing,'" *Milwaukee Journal Sentinel*, May 16, 2015, http://archive.jsonline.com/blogs/news/304001221.html?ipad=y.

[99] David Martosko, "ABC Anchor George Stephanopoulos Admits His Clinton Foundation Donations Topped $75,000 and Says He Won't Moderate Republican Debates After Interrogating 'Clinton Cash' Author on the Air," *Daily Mail*, May 14, 2015, http://www.dailymail.co.uk/news/article-3081899/ABC-fire-Week-host-George-Stephanopoulos-donated-50-000-Clinton-Foundation-interrogated-Clinton-Cash-author-air.html; Evan McMurry, "Stephanopoulos Recuses Himself from 2016 Debates," *Mediaite*, May 14, 2015, https://www.mediaite.com/online/stephanopoulos-recuses-himself-from-2016-debates/.

[100] U.S. Department of the Treasury, Resource Center, "The Committee on Foreign Investment in the United States (CFIUS)," accessed March 28, 2018, https://www.treasury.gov/resource-center/international/Pages/Committee-on-Foreign-Investment-in-US.aspx.

[101] Solomon, "FBI Informant Gathered Years of Evidence on Russian Push for US Nuclear Fuel Deals, Including Uranium One, Memos Show"; Scott Shane and Charlie Savage, "In Ordinary Lives, U.S. Sees the Work of Russian Agents," *The New York Times*, June 28, 2010, https://www.nytimes.com/2010/06/29/world/europe/29spy.html?pagewanted=print&mtrref=www.nytimes.com&gwh=3AD3D50D764A749309E1B210EA2F28D3&gwt=pay.

[102] Tom Winter, Pete Williams, and Ken Dilanian, "Prosecutors Ask FBI Agents for Info on Uranium One Deal," NBC News, December 21, 2017, https://www.nbcnews.com/news/us-news/prosecutors-ask-fbi-agents-info-uranium-one-deal-n831436.

[103] Rosalind S. Helderman, Spencer S. Hsu, and Tom Hamburger, "Emails Reveal How Foundation Donors Got Access to Clinton and Her Close Aides at State Dept.," *The Washington Post*, August 22, 2016, https://www.washingtonpost.com/politics/emails-reveal-how-foundation-donors-got-access-to-clinton-and-her-close-aides-at-state-dept/2016/08/22/345b5200-6882-11e6-8225-fbb8a6fc65bc_story.html?utm_term=.865f0c6fa9b5.

[104] Brooke Singman, "'Pay-to-play' at Clinton State Department Exposed in New Emails, Watchdog Says," Fox News, September 14, 2017, http://www.foxnews.com/politics/2017/09/14/pay-to-play-at-clinton-state-department-exposed-in-new-emails-watchdog-says.html.

[105] U.S. Department of the Treasury, Resource Center, "The Committee on Foreign Investment in the United States (CFIUS)," accessed March 28, 2018, https://www.treasury.gov/resource-center/international/Pages/Committee-on-Foreign-Investment-in-US.aspx.

[106] "The New Team," *The New York Times*, January 1, 2017, https://www.nytimes.com/interactive/projects/44th_president/new_team/show/john-holdren.

[107] Opensecrets.org, "Net Worth, 2010," accessed May 24, 2018, https://www.opensecrets.org/pfds../overview.php?type=W&year=2010&filter=E.

[108] Andy Hoffman and Sinclair Stewart, "How to (Still) Get Rich in Mining," *Globe and Mail*, April 25, 2018, https://www.theglobeandmail.com/report-on-business/how-to-still-get-rich-in-mining/article685913/.

[109] We'll show that the most prominent direct investor in Uranium One is Fidelity Investments (FMR). FMR held nearly 10% interest in Uranium One. Obama's defense secretary, Robert Gates, has a long history with Fidelity, he was chairman of their independent audit committee and was heavily invested in over a dozen Fidelity funds. Additionally, Goldman Sachs is closely linked to Uranium One and advised Rosatom's ARMZ on the transaction requiring CFIUS approval as we will soon learn.

[110] Matthew Vadum, "Goldman Sachs Plugged in at Geithner's Treasury," Capital Research Center, January 29, 2009, https://capitalresearch.org/article/goldman-sachs-plugged-in-at-geithners-treasury/.

[111] "Update 2—Russia's ARMZ to Acquire Control of Uranium One"; Peter Koven, "Russian CEO Faces Hard Sell for Uranium One Control,"

Financial Post, August 9, 2010, http://www.financialpost.com/personal-finance/Russian+faces+hard+sell+Uranium+control/3378184/story.html.

[112] Jeanne Cummings, "Geithner Enlists Lobbyist as Top Aide," *Politico*, January 27, 2009, https://www.politico.com/story/2009/01/geithner-enlists-lobbyist-as-top-aide-018047; Tim Mak, "Geithner Denies He's Cozy With Banks," *Politico*, July 24, 2012, https://www.politico.com/story/2012/07/geithner-denies-hes-cozy-with-banks-078888; Andy Kroll, "The Bankers on Obama's Team," *Mother Jones*, January/February 2010, https://www.motherjones.com/politics/2009/12/henhouse-meet-fox-wall-street-washington-obama/.

[113] Laura Zuckerman, "Miners Ask Court to Lift Ban on Uranium Mining Near Grand Canyon," Reuters, November 26, 2014, https://www.reuters.com/article/us-usa-mining-grandcanyon/miners-ask-court-to-lift-ban-on-uranium-mining-near-grand-canyon-idUSKCN-0JA2DS20141126; William Perry Pendley, "Uranium too: Did the Clintons Finagle a Twofer, Including a Land-Grab?" *The Washington Examiner*, March 1, 2018, https://www.washingtonexaminer.com/uranium-too-did-the-clintons-finagle-a-twofer-including-a-land-grab.

[114] "Hanford Cleanup: The First 15 Years," Oregon Department of Energy, October 2004, https://digital.osl.state.or.us/islandora/object/osl%3A12942/datastream/OBJ/view.

[115] Drew Atkins, "The Scandals of Former Gov. Gary Locke," *Crosscut*, August 11, 2016, https://crosscut.com/2016/08/the-scandals-of-former-gov-gary-locke.

[116] Trie was a Little Rock-based restauranteur and Seng was a billionaire businessman that made his fortune in real estate while first based in Hong Kong and later in Macau. Huang and Trie were convicted in the late 1990s for their roles in campaign finance violations, while Seng was convicted on six counts of bribery, money laundering, and corruption in 2017. In the Huang case, the DNC eventually returned $1.6 million in funds. In the Trie case, Bill Clinton's defense fund and the DNC were forced to return more than $1 million in funds.

Robert Zapesochny, "Laying the Foundation for the Clinton Foundation," *American Spectator*, October 6, 2016, https://spectator.org/chinagate-and-the-clintons/.

[117] Rick Anderson, "Gary Locke's Public Service Just Scored Him a Fat Private Paycheck (Again)," *Seattle Weekly*, September 18, 2015, http://archive.seattleweekly.com/news/960796-129/gary-lockes-public-service-just-scored.

[118] Becker and McIntire, "Cash Flowed to Clinton Foundation Amid Russian Uranium Deal."

[119] "Uranium One Acquires Energy Metals," Lexpert, August 10, 2007, http://www.lexpert.ca/article/uranium-one-acquires-energy-metals/?p=%7C273&sitecode=DIR.

[120]   Energy Metals Corporation, Form 51-102F3, Material Change Report, June 8, 2007, https://www.sec.gov/Archives/edgar/data/1361605/000106299307 002200/exhibit99-2.htm.

[121]   Energy Metals Corporation, "Uranium One and Energy Metals Receive CFIUS Approval for Proposed Arrangement," *Market Wired*, July 31, 2007, http://www.marketwired.com/press-release/uranium-one-and-energy-metals-receive-cfius-approval-for-proposed-arrangement-tsx-emc-756309. htm; "Uranium One Completes Energy Metals Buy," World Nuclear News, August 13, 2007, http://www.world-nuclear-news.org/newsarticle. aspx?id=13862&LangType=2057.

[122]   Marc Berger, "Gary Locke Rejoins Davis Wright Tremaine as Senior Advisor," Davis Wright Tremaine LLP, September 18, 2015, https:// www.dwt.com/Gary-Locke-Rejoins-Davis-Wright-Tremaine-as-Senior-Advisor-09-18-2015/; "CFIUS Notice (National Security Review)," Davis Wright Tremaine LLP, accessed April 13, 2018, https://www.dwt.com/ experience/uniEntity.aspx?xpST=ExperienceDetail&experience=14349.

[123]   Mark Landler, "How Hillary Clinton Became a Hawk," *The New York Times*, April 21, 2016, https://www.nytimes.com/2016/04/24/magazine/how-hillary-clinton-became-a-hawk.html?mtrref=www.google. com&gwh=12AC699A6AB8C68A57086B0E327A54BE&gwt=pay; Daniel Halper, "Hillary: Russian Reset 'A Brilliant Stroke,'" *The Weekly Standard*, June 13, 2014, https://www.weeklystandard.com/daniel-halper/ hillary-russian-reset-a-brilliant-stroke.

[124]   Robert M. Gates, "A Better Missile Defense for a Safer Europe," *The New York Times*, September 19, 2009, https://www.nytimes.com/2009/09/20/opinion/20gates.html.

[125]   Julian E. Barnes and Megan K. Stack, "Russia's Putin Praises Obama's Missile Defense Decision," *Los Angeles Times*, September 19, 2009, http://articles.latimes.com/2009/sep/19/world/fg-missile-defense19; Eric Kleefeld, "Right-Wing Pundits React to Obama 's Missile Defense Move," Talking Points Memo, September 17, 2009, https://talkingpointsmemo. com/dc/right-wing-pundits-react-to-obama-s-missile-defense-move.

[126]   Ariel Cohen, "Obama's Rookie Blunder on Missile Defense Concessions," *The Daily Signal*, September 18, 2009, https://www.dailysignal.com/2009/09/18/ obama%E2%80%99s-rookie-blunder-on-missile-defense-concessions/.

[127]   Ross Kerber, "New U.S. Defense Secretary Leaves Behind Inquiry into Gifts at Fidelity Investments—Business—International Herald Tribune," *The New York Times*, November 7, 2006, https://www.nytimes.com/2006/12/07/business/worldbusiness/07iht-gifts.3816911.html?mtrref=www.google.com&gwh=3494A1ABB546A2F98CB41CB99AB62778&gwt=pay; Walter F. Roche Jr., "Nominee's Business Ties Raise Concerns," *Los Angeles Times*, December 2, 2006, http://articles.latimes.com/2006/dec/02/nation/na-gates2.

[128]   Julie Gordon, "Analysis: China's Nuclear Program Boosts Uranium Producers," Reuters, November 18, 2010, https://www.reuters.com/arti-

cle/us-uranium/analysis-chinas-nuclear-program-boosts-uranium-produc-ers-idUSTRE6AH5ZK20101118.

[129] FMR Corp., schedule 13-G, filed pursuant to rule 13d-1 (b) or 13d-2 (b), February 14, 2006, http://investors.centrusenergy.com/node/11091/html.

[130] U.S. Department of Justice, Alan Zametkin v. Fidelity Management & Research Company, et al., Criminal No. 1:08-cv-10960-MLW, Document 67 (filed April 8, 2010), http://securities.stanford.edu/filings-documents/1040/FUSFX_01/201048_r02c_08CV10960.pdf; U.S. Department of Justice, Alan Zametkin v. Fidelity Management & Research Company, et al., Criminal No. 1:08-cv-10960-MLW, Document 92 (filed June 17, 2011), http://securities.stanford.edu/filings-documents/1040/FUSFX_01/2011617_r01x_0810960.pdf.

[131] Opensecrets.org, "Robert Gates: Assets, 2010," accessed May 25, 2018, https://www.opensecrets.org/personal-finances/assets/Robert-Gates?cid=N99999958&year=2010.

[132] U.S. Department of Energy, Office of Policy and International Affairs, DOE O 142.5, Committee on Foreign Investment in the United States, order approved October 8, 2010, https://www.directives.doe.gov/directives-documents/100-series/0142.5-BOrder/@@images/file.

[133] Hogan Lovells, http://www.hoganlovells.com/files/upload/090206_Nuclear.pdf.

[134] Dixon, "Ex-Energy Official's $1.7 Million Gig Draws Fire."

[135] Jennifer DeWitt, "CASEnergy Coalition Advocates for Nuclear Energy," *Quad-City Times*, February 12, 2015, http://qctimes.com/business/casenergy-coalition-advocates-for-nuclear-energy/article_710d10c3-6285-5446-9052-d5aa4ae9b360.html; "Revolving Door: Career Path of Former USTR Ron Kirk," *Friends of the Earth*, accessed May 25, 2018, https://foe.org/2016-05-revolving-door-career-path-of-former-ustr-ron-kirk/; "Ambassador Ron Kirk, CASEnergy Coalition Co-Chair," CASEnergy Coalition, accessed May 25, 2018, https://web.archive.org/web/20140606140446/https://casenergy.org/our-coalition/co-chairs/ron-kirk-casenergy-coalition-co-chair/.

[136] Monica Amarelo, "FAS Honors Dr. John Holdren and Ms. Barbara Pyle," Federation of American Scientists, October 8, 2010, https://fas.org/blogs/fas/2010/10/2010fasawards/.

[137] Photograph taken on June 2, 2009, by Amarelo Family, Flickr, accessed March 28, 2018, https://www.flickr.com/photos/amarelofamily/5062632544/in/photostream/.

[138] Drew Griffin and David Fitzpatrick, "Top Clinton Department Aide Helped Clinton Foundation," CNN, August 11, 2016, https://www.cnn.com/2016/08/11/politics/hillary-clinton-cgi-cheryl-mills/index.html; Ben Brody and Nick Wadhams, "Abedin's Overlapping Jobs Renew Focus on Clinton Conflicts," *Bloomberg*, August 15, 2016, https://www.bloomberg.com/news/articles/2016-08-15/huma-abedin-s-overlapping-jobs-renew-

focus-on-clinton-conflicts; Kenneth P. Vogel, "Bill Clinton Aides Used Tax Dollars to Subsidize Foundation, Private Email Support," *Politico*, September 1, 2016, https://www.politico.com/story/2016/08/bill-clinton-used-tax-dollars-to-subsidize-foundation-private-email-support-teneo-227613.

139   Braun and Sullivan, "Many Donors to Clinton Foundation Met with Her at State."

140   Stephen Braun and Eileen Sullivan, "Ex-Bill Clinton Aide Memo Roils Wife's Campaign over Ethics," Associated Press, accessed April 13, 2018, https://elections.ap.org/content/ex-bill-clinton-aide-memo-roils-wifes-campaign-over-ethics; Braun and Sullivan, "Many Donors to Clinton Foundation Met with Her at State."

141   Helderman, Hsu, and Hamburger, "Emails Reveal How Foundation Donors Got Access to Clinton and Her Close Aides at State Dept."

142   Philip Rucker, Tom Hamburger, and Alexander Becker, "How the Clintons Went from 'Dead Broke' to Rich: Bill Earned $104.9 Million for Speeches," *The Washington Post*, June 26, 2014, https://www.washingtonpost.com/politics/how-the-clintons-went-from-dead-broke-to-rich-bill-earned-1049-million-for-speeches/2014/06/26/8fa0b372-fd3a-11e3-8176-f2c-941cf35f1_story.html?utm_term=.78b3c5e80e95.

143   David A. Fahrenthold, Tom Hamburger, and Rosalind S. Helderman, "The Inside Story of How the Clintons Built a $2 Billion Global Empire," *The Washington Post*, June 2, 2015, https://www.washingtonpost.com/politics/the-inside-story-of-how-the-clintons-built-a-2-billion-global-empire/2015/06/02/b6eab638-0957-11e5-a7ad-b430fc1d3f5c_story.html?utm_term=.5c0023293244.

144   Elana Schor, "As It Happened: Obama Nominates Hillary Clinton for Secretary of State," *The Guardian*, December 1, 2008, https://www.theguardian.com/world/deadlineusa/2008/dec/01/obama-clinton-secretary-of-state; U.S. Department of State, Case No. F-2011-03401, obtained December 3, 2013, Memorandum of Understanding, December 12, 2008, http://www.judicialwatch.org/wp-content/uploads/2014/07/Clinton-Inc-December-3-2013-production-pg-2-6.pdf.

145   Swan, "Seven Ways the Clinton Foundation Failed to Meet Its Transparency Promises."

146   "18 U.S. Code Chapter 11 – Bribery, Graft, and Conflicts of Interest," Cornell Law, accessed May 25, 2018, https://www.law.cornell.edu/uscode/text/18/part-I/chapter-11; "Beware of the Illegal Contract! Is Your Contract Void or Unenforceable Because It Is Illegal?" Brown & Charbonneau, LLP, accessed April 13, 2018, https://www.bc-llp.com/beware-illegal-contract/.

147   Craig Yeung, "How Legally Binding Is a Memorandum of Understanding?" *Smart Company*, June 25, 2012, https://www.smartcompany.com.au/startupsmart/mentor/a-potential-partner-wants-to-back-out-how-legally-binding-is-a-memorandum-of-understanding/; "Difference Between

Agreement and Memorandum of Understanding (MoU)," Key Differences, November 22, 2014, https://keydifferences.com/difference-between-agreement-and-memorandum-of-understanding-mou.html.

[148] Peter Baker and Charlie Savage, "In Clinton List, a Veil Is Lifted on Foundation," *The New York Times*, December 18, 2008, http://www.nytimes.com/2008/12/19/us/politics/w19clinton.html; "Incoming Administration: Operations," Center for Presidential Transition, May 25, 2018, http://presidentialtransition.org/timeline/operations/index.php.

[149] "Obama Names Transition Team," *U.S. News and World Report*, November 5, 2008, https://www.usnews.com/news/campaign-2008/articles/2008/11/05/obama-names-transition-team.

[150] Rosalind S. Helderman and Tom Hamburger, "1,100 Donors to a Canadian Charity Tied to Clinton Foundation Remain Secret," *The Washington Post*, April 28, 2015, https://www.washingtonpost.com/politics/1100-donors-to-a-canadian-charity-tied-to-clinton-foundation-remain-secret/2015/04/28/c3c0f374-edbc-11e4-8666-a1d756d0218e_story.html?noredirect=on&utm_term=.e779ab8962ac.

[151] Peter Koven, "Uranium One Bought by Top Russian Shareholder ARMZ for $1.3-Billion," *Financial Post*, January 14, 2013, http://business.financialpost.com/commodities/mining/uranium-one-bought-by-top-russian-shareholder-armz-for-1-3-billion.

[152] O'Melveny & Myers LLP, "International Trade & Investment Regulation," accessed May 25, 2018, https://www.omm.com/services/practices/regulatory-and-government-affairs/international-trade/#.

[153] Solomon and Spann, "FBI Watched, Then Acted As Russian Spy Moved Closer to Hillary Clinton"; Solomon and Spann, "FBI Uncovered Russian Bribery Plot Before Obama Administration Approved Controversial Nuclear Deal with Moscow."

[154] Paul Roderick Gregory, "Why Was Obama's Justice Department Silent On Criminal Activity by Russia's Nuclear Agency?" *Forbes*, October 25, 2017, https://www.forbes.com/sites/paulroderickgregory/2017/10/25/why-was-obamas-justice-department-silent-on-criminal-activity-by-russias-nuclear-agency/#4397d448be17.

[155] U.S. Department of Justice, U.S. Attorney's Office: District of Maryland, "Russian National and Three Others Charged in Kickback Scheme to Obtain Contracts to Transport Russian Nuclear Fuel to the U.S."

[156] U.S. Department of Justice, United States v. Vladimir Mikerin, Criminal No. TDC-14-0529, Document 103 (filed August 31, 2015), https://www.justice.gov/opa/file/765156/download.

[157] Jordain Carney, "Senate Votes to Confirm Rosenstein As Deputy Attorney General," *The Hill*, April 25, 2017, http://thehill.com/homenews/senate/330538-senate-votes-to-confirm-rosenstein-as-deputy-attorney-general; Rebecca R. Ruiz and Mark Landler, "Robert Mueller, Former F.B.I. Director, Is Named Special Counsel for Russia Investigation," *New York*

Times, May 17, 2017, https://www.nytimes.com/2017/05/17/us/politics/robert-mueller-special-counsel-russia-investigation.html; Mark Penn, "Rod Rosenstein Is Not Above the Law," *The Hill*, May 3, 2018, http://thehill.com/opinion/judiciary/386067-rod-rosenstein-is-not-above-the-law.

158   Matt Flegenheimer, "Andrew Weissmann, Mueller's Legal Pit Bull," *The New York Times*, October 31, 2017, https://www.nytimes.com/2017/10/31/us/politics/andrew-weissmann-mueller.html.

159   Matt Zapotosky and Karoun Demirjian, "McCabe Was Asked About Media Contacts on the Day Comey Was Fired," *The Washington Post*, March 20, 2018, https://www.washingtonpost.com/world/national-security/mccabe-was-asked-about-press-contacts-on-the-day-comey-was-fired/2018/03/20/ab5031f8-2b8d-11e8-8688-e053ba58f1e4_story.html.

160   "Election 2012, Obama to Romney: Cold War Is Over – Third Presidential Debate," posted by "*The New York Times*," October 22, 2012, https://www.youtube.com/watch?v=T1409sXBleg.

161   "Barack Obama in Open Microphone Gaffe with Dmitry Medvedev," YouTube video, posted by "*The Telegraph*," March 26, 2012, https://www.youtube.com/watch?v=MNxEDomUlXw.

162   "U.S. Gift to Russia Lost in Translation," posted by "Associated Press," March 6, 2009, https://www.youtube.com/watch?v=0GdLClHAMB0.

163   U.S. Securities and Exchange Commission, Centrus Energy Corp., Form 10-K (for the fiscal year ended December 31, 2016), http://investors.centrusenergy.com/static-files/8a252ecc-8942-42b1-9311-825436816ceb; Jim Morris and Jamie Smith Hopkins, "Ailing, Angry Nuclear-Weapons Workers Fight for Compensation," Center for Public Integrity, December 11, 2015, https://www.publicintegrity.org/2015/12/11/18936/ailing-angry-nuclear-weapons-workers-fight-compensation.

164   Gary Peach, "The Megaton Deal," *Moscow Times*, April 13, 1999, http://old.themoscowtimes.com/sitemap/free/1999/4/article/the-megaton-deal/278343.html.

165   Morris and Smith Hopkins, "Ailing, Angry Nuclear-Weapons Workers Fight for Compensation."

166   Matthew L. Wald, "Kentucky Operator to Cease Enrichment of Uranium," *The New York Times*, May 24, 2013, https://www.nytimes.com/2013/05/25/business/usec-to-shut-uranium-enrichment-plant-in-kentucky.html; "Paducah Environmental Remediation," Portsmouth/Paducah Project Office, May 25, 2018, https://www.energy.gov/pppo/paducah-site/paducah-environmental-remediation.

167   Walburn v. Lockheed Martin Corporation, No. 04-3458 (6th Cir. 2005), http://caselaw.findlaw.com/us-6th-circuit/1395786.html.

168   Morris and Hopkins, "Ailing, Angry Nuclear-Weapons Workers Fight for Compensation"; https://www.opensecrets.org/revolving/rev_summary.php?id=70344.

169   Walburn v. Lockheed Martin Corporation, No. 04-3458 (6th Cir. 2005); Morris and Hopkins, "Ailing, Angry Nuclear-Weapons Workers Fight for Compensation"; Lockheed Martin Utility Services, Inc., Memorandum for Dan Hupp from Don Butler, February 16, 1996, https://www.documentcloud.org/documents/2640371-Doc-2.html; Jim Morris and Jamie Smith Hopkins, "Report Underlines Recent Worker Hazards at Old Weapons Plants," Center for Public Integrity, January 7, 2016, https://www.publicintegrity.org/2016/01/07/19113/report-underlines-recent-worker-hazards-old-weapons-plants.

170   Morris and Hopkins, "Ailing, Angry Nuclear-Weapons Workers Fight for Compensation"; Kevin Williams, "The Cancer Cluster of Piketon, Ohio," Aljazeera America, February 25, 2016, http://america.aljazeera.com/articles/2016/2/25/the-cancer-cluster-of-piketon-ohio.html.

171   U.S. Department of Justice, "Lockheed Martin Agrees to Pay $5 Million to Settle Alleged Violations of the False Claims Act and the Resource Conservation and Recovery Act," press release, February 29, 2016, https://www.justice.gov/opa/pr/lockheed-martin-agrees-pay-5-million-settle-alleged-violations-false-claims-act-and-resource; Todd Nighswonger, "Paducah Workers Seek the Truth," EHS Today, November 30, 1999, http://www.ehstoday.com/news/ehs_imp_32526; U.S. Department of Justice, "Settlement Agreement," accessed May 29, 2018, https://www.justice.gov/usao-wdky/file/828866/download.

172   Exclusive interviews and nonpublic documents obtained by author.

173   Opensecrets.org, "Comey, James B."

174   "Top 100 for 2017," Defense News, accessed May 25, 2018, http://people.defensenews.com/top-100/; Kiran Dhillon, "What You Need to Know About the Top Federal Contractors in 3 Graphs," TIME, June 24, 2014, http://time.com/2917578/government-contractors-lockheed/.

175   John R. Schindler, "Hillary's Secret Kremlin Connection Is Quickly Unraveling," Observer, August 25, 2016, http://observer.com/2016/08/hillarys-secret-kremlin-connection-is-quickly-unraveling/.

Chapter 3: The FBI's And DOJ's Foreign Agents Problem (FARA)

1   Federal Bureau of Investigation, "Directors, Then and Now," accessed June 7, 2018, https://www.fbi.gov/history/directors; U.S. Department of Justice, organizational chart, accessed April 4, 2018, https://www.justice.gov/agencies/chart.

2   Jessica Estepa, "Trump Suggests the FBI Director Reports Directly to the President. Here's How it Really Works," USA Today, July 20, 2017, https://www.usatoday.com/story/news/politics/onpolitics/2017/07/20/fbi-director-reports-justice-department-not-president/495094001/.

3   Michael Crowley, "The Deep State Is Real," *Politico*, September/October 2017, https://www.politico.com/magazine/story/2017/09/05/deep-state-real-cia-fbi-intelligence-215537; James Bamford, "Every Move You Make," *Foreign Policy*, September 7, 2016, http://foreignpolicy.com/2016/09/07/every-move-you-make-obama-nsa-security-surveillance-spying-intelligence-snowden/.

4   American Civil Liberties Union, "NSA Spying on Americans Is Illegal," accessed April 4, 2018, https://www.aclu.org/other/nsa-spying-americans-illegal; Rand Paul, "The NSA Is Still Violating Our Rights, Despite What James Clapper Says," *The Guardian*, February 20, 2014, https://www.theguardian.com/commentisfree/2014/feb/20/nsa-violating-american-rights-rand-paul; Adam Entous and Danny Yadron, "U.S. Spy Net on Israel Snares Congress," *The Wall Street Journal*, December 29, 2015, https://www.wsj.com/articles/u-s-spy-net-on-israel-snares-congress-1451425210; Cora Currier, "Secret Rules Make it Pretty Easy for the FBI to Spy on Journalists," *Intercept*, January 31, 2017, https://theintercept.com/2017/01/31/secret-rules-make-it-pretty-easy-for-the-fbi-to-spy-on-journalists-2/; "The Nunes FBI Memo, Annotated."

5   Ken Dilanian, Julia Ainsley, and Carol E. Lee, "FBI Warned Trump in 2016 Russians Would Try to Infiltrate His Campaign," NBC News, December 19, 2017, https://www.nbcnews.com/news/us-news/fbi-warned-trump-2016-russians-would-try-infiltrate-his-campaign-n830596; Amy Chozick, "John Podesta Says Russian Spies Hacked His Emails to Sway Election," *The New York Times*, October 11, 2016, https://www.nytimes.com/2016/10/12/us/politics/hillary-clinton-emails-wikileaks.html; Jana Heigl, "A Timeline of Donald Trump's False Wiretapping Charge," *Politifact*, March 21, 2017, http://www.politifact.com/truth-o-meter/article/2017/mar/21/timeline-donald-trumps-false-wiretapping-charge/.

6   Sarah Ferguson, Jeanavive McGregor, and Justin Stevens, "Hillary Clinton Says Julian Assange Colluded with Russia to Help Donald Trump Win US Election," ABC News, October 17, 2017, http://www.abc.net.au/news/2017-10-16/hillary-clinton-says-julian-assange-helped-donald-trump-win/9047944; Gabriel Debenedetti, "Clinton Team Says Trump Is Encouraging Russian Espionage," *Politico*, July 27, 2016, https://www.politico.com/story/2016/07/clinton-team-says-trump-is-encouraging-russian-espionage-226291.

7   "The Nunes FBI Memo, Annotated"; Crowe, "Comey, Yates, McCabe, Rosenstein All Signed Off on Misleading FISA Apps."

8   "Evelyn Farkas Admits She Helped Spy on Trump for Obama," YouTube video, posted by "Very Fake News," March 28, 2017, https://www.youtube.com/watch?v=Euq0NitCFZk; Evan Perez, Shimon Prokupecz, and Pamela Brown, "Exclusive: US Government Wiretapped Former Trump Campaign Chairman," CNN, September 19, 2017, https://www.cnn.

com/2017/09/18/politics/paul-manafort-government-wiretapped-fisa-russians/index.html.

9   Byron Acohido, "Q&A: 'Guccifer' Hacks Hillary Clinton's E-mails Via Aide's Account," *USA Today*, March 19, 2013, https://www.usatoday.com/story/tech/2013/03/19/guccifer-hacker-hillary-clinton-sidney-blumenthal-george-hw-bush/2001429/.

10   Catherine Herridge and Pamela K. Browne, "Romanian Hacker Guccifer: I Breached Clinton Server, 'It Was Easy,'" Fox News, May 4, 2016, http://www.foxnews.com/politics/2016/05/04/romanian-hacker-guccifer-breached-clinton-server-it-was-easy.html.

11   Lorenzo Franceschi-Bicchierai, "We Spoke to DNC Hacke 'Guccifer 2.0,'" *Motherboard*, June 21, 2016, https://motherboard.vice.com/en_us/article/aek7ea/dnc-hacker-guccifer-20-interview.

12   Spencer Ackerman and Kevin Poulsen, "Exclusive: 'Lone DNC Hacker' Guccifer 2.0 Slipped Up and Revealed He Was a Russian Intelligence Officer," *The Daily Beast*, March 22, 2018, https://www.thedailybeast.com/exclusive-lone-dnc-hacker-guccifer-20-slipped-up-and-revealed-he-was-a-russian-intelligence-officer?via=twitter_page?ref=home.

13   "The Nunes FBI Memo, Annotated"; Jack Crowe, "Comey, Yates, McCabe, Rosenstein All Signed Off on Misleading FISA Apps"; Perez, Prokupecz, and Brown, "Exclusive: US Government Wiretapped Former Trump Campaign Chairman."

14   "Three Degrees of Separation: Breaking Down the NSA's 'Hops' Surveillance Method," *The Guardian*, October 28, 2013, https://www.theguardian.com/world/interactive/2013/oct/28/nsa-files-decoded-hops.

15   Patrick Lawrence, "A New Report Raises Big Questions About Last Year's DNC Hack," *The Nation*, August 9, 2017, https://www.thenation.com/article/a-new-report-raises-big-questions-about-last-years-dnc-hack/; Alana Goodman, "EXCLUSIVE: Cybersecurity Experts Who Were First to Conclude That Putin Hacked Presidential Election ABANDON Some of Their Claims Against Russia – and Refuse to Cooperate with Congress," *Daily Mail*, April 5, 2017, http://www.dailymail.co.uk/news/article-4376628/New-questions-claim-Russia-hacked-election.html.

16   Dmitri Alperovitch, "Bears in the Midst: Intrusion into the Democratic National Committee," CrowdStrike, June 15, 2016, https://www.crowdstrike.com/blog/bears-midst-intrusion-democratic-national-committee/; Fred Fleitz, "No, Hillary, 17 U.S. Intelligence Agencies *Did Not* Say Russia Hacked Dem E-mails," *National Review*, October 20, 2016, https://www.nationalreview.com/corner/hillary-clinton-democratic-emails-hacked-russia/.

17   Office of the Deputy Attorney General, "Appointment of Special Counsel to Investigate Russian Interference with the 2016 Presidential Election and Related Matters," Order No. 3915-2017, https://assets.documentcloud.org/documents/3726381/Robert-Mueller-Special-Counsel-Russia.pdf.

18   U.S. Department of Justice, "Special Counsel's Office," accessed April 4, 2018, https://www.justice.gov/sco; Emily Cochrane and Alicia Parlapiano, "Over 100 Charges, 19 People and 3 Companies: The Mueller Inquiry, Explained," *The New York* Times, February 23, 2018, https://www.nytimes.com/2018/02/23/us/politics/mueller-investigation-charges.html.

19   Ibid.

20   U.S. v. Paul J. Manafort, Jr. and Richard W. Gates III, Case No. 1:17-cr-00201 (assigned October 27, 2017), https://www.politico.com/f/?id=0000015f-6d73-d751-af7f-7f735cc70000.

21   Aaron Blake, "The 12-Count Manafort and Gates Indictment, Annotated," *The Washington Post*, October 30, 2017, https://www.washingtonpost.com/news/the-fix/wp/2017/10/30/the-paul-manafort-and-rick-gates-indictment-annotated/.

22   Ibid.

23   Lydia Dennett, "Manafort Indictment Demonstrates How FARA Falls Short," POGO, October 30, 2017, http://www.pogo.org/straus/issues/other-items/2017/manafort-indictment-demonstrates-how-foreign-agents-registration-act-falls-short.html.

24   Yale Law School, "Washington's Farewell Address, 1796," The Avalon Project: Documents in Law, History, and Diplomacy, accessed April 4, 2018, http://avalon.law.yale.edu/18th_century/washing.asp.

25   Joseph J. Schatz and Benjamin Oreskes, "Want to Be a 'Foreign Agent'? Serve in Congress First," *Politico*, October 2, 2016, http://www.politico.com/story/2016/10/congress-foreign-lobbying-228982.

26   U.S. Department of Justice, Office of the United States Attorneys, Criminal Resource Manual 2001–2009, "2062. Foreign Agents Registration Act Enforcement," accessed April 4, 2018, https://www.justice.gov/usam/criminal-resource-manual-2062-foreign-agents-registration-act-enforcement; Melissa Yeager, "Foreign Influence in America: A Brief Explainer on FARA," Sunlight Foundation, August 26, 2016, http://sunlightfoundation.com/2016/08/25/foreign-influence-in-america-a-brief-explainer-on-fara/.

27   Yeager, "Foreign Influence in America: A Brief Explainer on FARA"; Ben Freeman and Lydia Dennett, "Loopholes, Filing Failures, and Lax Enforcement: How the Foreign Agents Registration Act Falls Short," POGO, December 16, 2014, http://www.pogo.org/our-work/reports/2014/loopholes-filing-failures-lax-enforcement-how-the-foreign-agents-registration-act-falls-short.html.

28   U.S. Department of Justice, Office of the Inspector General, "DOJ OIG Releases Report on the DOJ's Enforcement of the Foreign Agents Registration Act," press release, picture, September 7, 2016, https://oig.justice.gov/press/2016/2016-09-07.pdf; Philip Ewing, "As Washington Gears Up to Tackle Foreign Influence, How Effective Can It Be?" NPR, February 22, 2018, https://www.npr.org/2018/02/22/587762926/as-washington-gears-up-to-tackle-foreign-influence-how-effective-can-it-be.

29 Trevor Timm, "How the FISA Amendments Act Allows for Warrantless Wiretapping, As Described by Supreme Court Justices," Eff, October 30, 2012, https://www.eff.org/deeplinks/2012/10/how-fisa-amendments-act-allows-warrantless-wiretapping-described-supreme-court; Bamford, "Every Move You Make."

30 Asha Rangappa, "What the FISA Warrants Against Paul Manafort Tell Us About Mueller's Investigation," Just Security, September 23, 2017, https://www.justsecurity.org/45255/fisa-warrants-paul-manafort-muellers-investigation/.

31 U.S. Department of Justice, "FARA Index and Act," accessed May 29, 2018, https://www.justice.gov/nsd-fara/fara-index-and-act; U.S. Department of Justice, "Office of Intelligence," accessed April 4, 2018, https://www.justice.gov/nsd/office-intelligence.

32 Federal Bureau of Investigation, "Testimony: Working Together to Protect America," March 18, 2003, https://archives.fbi.gov/archives/news/testimony/the-war-against-terrorism-working-together-to-protect-america.

33 U.S. Department of Justice, Office of the Inspector General, "Audit of the National Security Division's Enforcement and Administration of the Foreign Agents Registration Act," September 2016, https://oig.justice.gov/reports/2016/a1624.pdf.

34 Megan R. Wilson, "Companies Fretting over 'Foreign Agents' Label," *The Hill*, March 13, 2018, http://thehill.com/business-a-lobbying/378030-companies-fretting-over-foreign-agents-label; "DOJ IG Calls for More Aggressive FARA Enforcement," Baker McKenzie, October 1, 2016, https://www.bakermckenzie.com/en/insight/publications/2016/10/doj-ig-calls-for-more-aggressive-fara-enforcement.

35 "DOJ IG Calls for More Aggressive FARA Enforcement."

36 Ibid.

37 Simpson and Jacoby, "How Lobbyists Help Ex-Soviets Woo Washington"; U.S. v. Paul J. Manafort, Jr. and Richard W. Gates III, Case No. 1:17-cr-00201, https://www.justice.gov/file/1007271/download.

38 Evan Perez, Shimon Prokupecz, and Pamela Brown, "First on CNN: Virginia Gov. Terry McAuliffe Under Federal Investigation for Campaign Contributions," CNN, May 24, 2016, https://www.cnn.com/2016/05/23/politics/terry-mcauliffe-fbi-doj-federal-investigation-campaign-contributions/index.html.

39 Michael Scherer, "Virginia Gov. Terry McAuliffe Invited Chinese Donor to Hillary Clinton's Home," *TIME*, May 26, 2016, http://time.com/4348675/terry-mcauliffe-hillary-clinton-china-investigation/.

40 Baker & McKenzie, "DOJ IG Calls for More Aggressive FARA Enforcement," October 2016, http://bakerxchange.com/rv/ff002b3ff49f3affe8297a91e240a731145c4851.

41 Jill McCabe, "The President Attacked My Reputation. It's Time to Set the Record Straight," *The Washington Post*, April 2, 2018, https://www.wash-

ingtonpost.com/opinions/jill-mccabe-the-president-attacked-my-reputa-
tion-its-time-to-set-the-record-straight/2018/04/02/e6bbcf66-366b-11e8-
8fd2-49fe3c675a89_story.html?utm_term=.2d74b4088f00.

42 Schatz and Oreskes, "Want to Be a 'Foreign Agent'? Serve in Congress
First."

43 David Corn, "A Veteran Spy Has Given the FBI Information Alleging
a Russian Operation to Cultivate Donald Trump," *Mother Jones*,
October 31, 2016, https://www.motherjones.com/politics/2016/10/
veteran-spy-gave-fbi-info-alleging-russian-operation-cultivate-don-
ald-trump/; Steven Lee Myers and Andrew E. Kramer, "How Paul
Manafort Wielded Power in Ukraine Before Advising Donald Trump," *The
New York Times*, July 31, 2016, https://www.nytimes.com/2016/08/01/
us/paul-manafort-ukraine-donald-trump.html.

44 Entous, Barrett, and Helderman, "Clinton Campaign, DNC Paid for
Research That Led to Russia Dossier."

45 Jeff Nesbit, "Donald Trump's Many, Many, Many, Many Ties to Russia,"
TIME, August 15, 2016, http://time.com/4433880/donald-trump-ties-to-
russia/; Corn, "A Veteran Spy Has Given the FBI Information Alleging a
Russian Operation to Cultivate Donald Trump"; Steven Lee Myers and
Andrew E. Kramer, "How Paul Manafort Wielded Power in Ukraine
Before Advising Donald Trump," *The New York Times*, July 31, 2016,
https://www.nytimes.com/2016/08/01/us/paul-manafort-ukraine-donald-
trump.html.

46 Michael Isikoff, "U.S. Intel Officials Probe Ties Between
Trump Adviser and Kremlin," *Yahoo!*, September 23, 2016,
https://www.yahoo.com/news/u-s-intel-officials-probe-
ties-between-trump-adviser-and-kremlin-175046002.html; Chuck
Ross, "Isikoff Stunned That His Carter Page Article Was Used to Justify
Spy Warrant," *The Daily Caller*, February 2, 2018, http://dailycaller.
com/2018/02/02/isikoff-stunned-carter-page/.

47 Maggie Haberman, Alexander Burns, and Ashley Parker, "Donald Trump
Fires Corey Lewandowski, His Campaign Manager," *The New York
Times*, June 20, 2016, https://www.nytimes.com/2016/06/21/us/politics/
corey-lewandowski-donald-trump.html.

48 Glenn Thrush, "To Charm Trump, Paul Manafort Sold Himself as an
Affordable Outsider," *The New York Times*, April 8, 2017, https://www.
nytimes.com/2017/04/08/us/to-charm-trump-paul-manafort-sold-him-
self-as-an-affordable-outsider.html.

49 "Miramax Purchase Puts Colony Capital in the Hollywood Spotlight,"
The Los Angeles Times, December 6, 2010, http://latimesblogs.latimes.
com/entertainmentnewsbuzz/2010/12/miramax-purchase-puts-colo-
ny-capital-in-hollywood-spotlight.html; Ben Fritz, Cara Lombardo,
and Erich Schwartzel, "Weinstein Co. Negotiating Possible Sale," *The*

Wall Street Journal, October 16, 2017, https://www.wsj.com/articles/weinstein-co-negotiating-possible-sale-1508162396.

50　Stephanie Kirchgaessner and Lorenzo Tondo, "Close Friend of Trump Investigated Over Alleged €170m Tax Evasion," *The Guardian,* May 29, 2017, https://www.theguardian.com/world/2017/may/29/close-friend-trump-thomas-barrack-alleged-tax-evasion-italy-sardinia; Russ Choma, "Donald Trump Has a Super-PAC Problem," *Mother Jones,* June 20, 2016, https://www.motherjones.com/politics/2016/06/donald-trump-super-pac-problem/.

51　U.S. v. Paul J. Manafort, Jr. and Richard W. Gates III, Case No. 1:17-cr-00201, https://www.justice.gov/file/1007271/download.

52　Steven Lee Myers and Andrew E. Kramer, "How Paul Manafort Wielded Power in Ukraine Before Advising Donald Trump," *The New York Times,* July 31, 2016, https://www.nytimes.com/2016/08/01/us/paul-manafort-ukraine-donald-trump.html; Thomas Frank, "Podesta Lobby Group Did Not Disclose Extent of Work for Ukrainian Campaign Advised by Paul Manafort," CNN, May 9, 2017, https://www.cnn.com/2017/05/09/politics/podesta-manafort-lobbying/index.html.

53　Maggie Haberman and Jonathan Martin, "Paul Manafort Quits Donald Trump's Campaign After a Tumultuous Run," *The New York Times,* August 19, 2016, https://www.nytimes.com/2016/08/20/us/politics/paul-manafort-resigns-donald-trump.html.

54　"U.S. Presidential Election: Republican Candidate Donald Trump's Activities in Russia and Compromising Relationship with the Kremlin," August 10, 2016, https://www.documentcloud.org/documents/3259984-Trump-Intelligence-Allegations.html; Corn, "A Veteran Spy Has Given the FBI Information Alleging a Russian Operation to Cultivate Donald Trump"; Isikoff, "U.S. Intel Officials Probe Ties Between Trump Adviser and Kremlin."

55　Simpson and Jacoby, "How Lobbyists Help Ex-Soviets Woo Washington."

56　Isaac Arnsdorf, "Podesta Group Files New Disclosures in Manafort-linked Ukraine Lobbying," *Politico,* April 12, 2017, https://www.politico.com/story/2017/04/paul-manafort-lobbying-ukraine-podesta-group-237163.

57　Entous, Barrett, and Helderman, "Clinton Campaign, DNC Paid for Research That Led to Russia Dossier"; Meghan Keneally, "Timeline of Paul Manafort's Role in the Trump Campaign," ABC News, October 30, 2017, https://abcnews.go.com/Politics/timeline-paul-manaforts-role-trump-campaign/story?id=50808957.

58　Simpson and Jacoby, "How Lobbyists Help Ex-Soviets Woo Washington"; Perez, Prokupecz, and Brown, "Exclusive: US Government Wiretapped Former Trump Campaign Chairman."

59　Mark Tran, "WikiLeaks to Publish More Hillary Clinton Emails—Julian Assange," *The Guardian,* June 12, 2016, https://www.theguardian.com/media/2016/jun/12/wikileaks-to-publish-more-hillary-clinton-emails-julian-assange.

60   Ellen Nakashima, "Russian Government Hackers Penetrated DNC, Stole Opposition Research on Trump," *The Washington Post*, June 14, 2016, https://www.washingtonpost.com/world/national-security/russian-government-hackers-penetrated-dnc-stole-opposition-research-on-trump/2016/06/14/cf006cb4-316e-11e6-8ff7-7b6c1998b7a0_story.html.

61   Alperovitch, "Bears in the Midst: Intrusion into the Democratic National Committee."

62   Lily Hay Newman, "Hacker Lexicon: What Is the Attribution Problem?" *Wired*, December 24, 2016, https://www.wired.com/2016/12/hacker-lexicon-attribution-problem/.

63   Office of the Director of National Intelligence, "Background to 'Assessing Russian Activities and Intentions in Recent US Elections': The Analytic Process and Cyber Incident Attribution," January 6, 2017, https://www.dni.gov/files/documents/ICA_2017_01.pdf; Andrew C. McCarthy, "When Scandals Collide," *National Review*, October 25, 2017, https://www.nationalreview.com/corner/scandals-collide-dossier-dnc-server-perkins-coie/.

64   Andy Greenberg, "Feds' Damning Report on Russian Election Hack Won't Convince Skeptics," *Wired*, January 6, 2017, https://www.wired.com/2017/01/feds-damning-report-russian-election-hack-wont-convince-skeptics/.

65   Patrick Lawrence, "A New Report Raises Big Questions About Last Year's DNC Hack," *The Nation*, August 9, 2017, https://www.thenation.com/article/a-new-report-raises-big-questions-about-last-years-dnc-hack/.

66   Leandra Bernstein, "Questions Remain over Russian Responsibility for Passing Stolen DNC Emails to WikiLeaks," WJLA, December 15, 2016, http://wjla.com/news/nation-world/questions-remain-over-russian-responsibility-for-passing-stolen-dnc-emails-to-wikileaks; Euan McKirdy, "WikiLeaks' Assange: Russia Didn't Give Us Emails," CNN, January 4, 2017, https://www.cnn.com/2017/01/04/politics/assange-wikileaks-hannity-intv/index.html.

67   "Julian Assange on Seth Rich," YouTube video, posted by "Nieuwsuur," August 9, 2016, https://www.youtube.com/watch?v=Kp7FkLBRpKg.

68   Max Kutner, "Seth Rich Update: DNC Staffer Murdered by Serial Killer, Not in Botched Robbery, Report Claims," *Newsweek*, June 20, 2017, http://www.newsweek.com/seth-rich-murder-report-profiling-project-627634; Scott Taylor, "New Private Investigation into the Murder of DNC Staffer Seth Rich," WJLA, March 23, 2017, http://wjla.com/news/local/new-private-investigation-into-the-murder-of-dnc-staffer-seth-rich.

69   WikiLeaks, Twitter post, August 9, 2016, 10:25 a.m., https://twitter.com/wikileaks/status/763063624579551232?lang=en.

70   Philip Rucker, "Donna Brazile: I Considered Replacing Clinton with Biden as 2016 Democratic Nominee," *The Washington Post*, November 4, 2017, https://www.washingtonpost.com/politics/brazile-i-considered-re-

placing-clinton-with-biden-as-2016-democratic-nominee/2017/11/04/ f0b75418-bf4c-11e7-97d9-bdab5a0ab381_story.html?utm_term=.5655f5f49699; Max Kutner, "DNC's Donna Brazile Dedicated Her Book to 'Patriot' Seth Rich, Whose Death Made Her Fear for Her Own Life," *Newsweek*, November 6, 2017, http://www.newsweek.com/ donna-brazile-book-seth-rich-dnc-murder-conspiracy-702838.

71 Donna Brazile, *Hacks* (New York: Hachette, 2017).

72 "One-on-one with Former DNC Chair Donna Brazile," YouTube video, posted by "ABC News," November 5, 2017, https://www.youtube.com/ watch?v=AZcl9fCEvi8&feature=youtu.be&t=6m35s.

73 Ibid.

74 Kutner, "DNC's Donna Brazile Dedicated Her Book to 'Patriot' Seth Rich, Whose Death Made Her Fear for Her Own Life"; Anthony Man, "Wasserman Schultz Calls Conspiracy Theories About Seth Rich 'Vile and Disgusting,'" *Sun Sentinel*, August 4, 2017, http://www.sun-sentinel.com/ news/politics/fl-reg-seth-rich-wasserman-schultz-20170804-story.html; Max Kutner, "Donna Brazile Questioned If Seth Rich's Death Involved Russians, or His Race," *Newsweek*, November 8, 2017, http://www.newsweek.com/donna-brazile-book-seth-rich-russia-white-clinton-705424.

75 Adam Carter, "Guccifer 2.0: Game Over," g-2.space, last updated February 22, 2018, http://g-2.space/; "The Forensicator: Corrections and Clarifications," The Forensicator, accessed April 5, 2018, https://theforensicator.wordpress.com/2017/08/24/corrections-and-clarifications/; William Binney et al., "Intel Vets Challenge 'Russia Hack' Evidence," Consortium News, July 24, 2017, https://consortiumnews.com/2017/07/24/intel-vets-challenge-russia-hack-evidence/.

76 John Podesta, "John Podesta Op-ed: Something is Broken at the FBI," *Chicago Tribune*, December 16, 2016, http://www.chicagotribune.com/ news/opinion/commentary/ct-fbi-russian-hack-clinton-emails-20161216-story.html; Anthony Man, "Wasserman Schultz Disputes Homeland Security Claims About DNC Hacking," *Sun Sentinel*, June 22, 2017, http://www.sun-sentinel.com/news/politics/fl-reg-wasserman-schultz-homeland-security-wrong-20170622-story.html.

77 Katie Bo Williams, "Comey: DNC Denied FBI's Requests for Access to Hacked Servers," *The Hill*, January 10, 2017, http://thehill.com/policy/ national-security/313555-comey-fbi-did-request-access-to-hacked-dnc-servers.

78 "Podesta: 'It's on the FBI' That DNC Servers Weren't Turned Over," Fox News, video, July 2, 2017, http://insider.foxnews.com/2017/07/02/hillary-clinton-russia-podesta-dnc-hack-server-fbi; Evan Perez and Daniella Diaz, "FBI: DNC Rebuffed Request to Examine Computer Servers," CNN, January 5, 2017, https://www.cnn.com/2017/01/05/politics/fbi-russia-hacking-dnc-crowdstrike/index.html.

79 "Clintons' 'Bag Man': Middle Man Between Foundation & State Dept ID'ed," Fox News, video clip, August 24, 2016, http://insider.foxnews. com/2016/08/24/hillarys-bagman-dennis-cheng-was-middle-man-between-clinton-foundation-state-dept; "Re: Foreign registered agents," WikiLeaks, email sent on April 17, 2015, https://wikileaks.org/podesta-emails/emailid/11915; "Re: FARA," WikiLeaks, email sent on April 23, 2015, https://wikileaks.org/podesta-emails/emailid/2783; "Re: Foreign registered agents," WikiLeaks, email sent on April 17, 2015; "Re: FARA," WikiLeaks, email sent on April 23, 2015.

Relevant excerpts:

April 14, 2015 (12:57pm): Karuna Seshasai < kseshasai@hillaryclinton. com> wrote:

Wanted to follow back up on this. We're consistently flagging more FARA registrants daily. In terms of # - we're at 27 out of 370 prospective bundlers... If we were looking at these folks below on a case by case basis, I'd want to specifically raise: Tony Podesta (Iraq, Azerbaijan, Egypt), Ben Barnes (Libya), John Merrigan (UAE), Wyeth Weidman (Libya), and Mike Driver (UAE connections)

April 14, 2015 (12:57pm): Karuna Seshasai < kseshasai@hillaryclinton. com> wrote:

Following up on the call from 9:30. The policy would be to not allow any currently registered foreign agents (those who register with FARA) to contribute or raise for the campaign. If someone terminates their registration, they would be allowed to contribute or raise for the campaign. Marc, we'd especially like your perspective on adopting this policy...

On Wed, Apr 15, 2015 at 11:09 PM, Dennis Cheng <dcheng@hillaryclinton.com> wrote:

Hi all – we do need to make a decision on this ASAP as our friends who happen to be registered with FARA are already donating and raising. I do want to push back a bit (it's my job!): I feel like we are leaving a good amount of money on the table (both for primary and general, and then DNC and state parties) ... and how do we explain to people that we'll take money from a corporate lobbyist but not them; that the Foundation takes $ from foreign govts but we now won't.

On Apr 15, 2015, at 11:22 PM, Marc Elias <melias@hillaryclinton. com> wrote:

Responding to all on this. I was not on the call this morning, but I lean away from a bright line rule here...

From: Dennis Cheng <dcheng@hillaryclinton.com> Date: Thu, Apr 16, 2015 at 6:13 PM Subject: RE: Foreign registered agents

Hi all – we really need to make a final decision on this. We're getting to the point of no return...

On Apr 16, 2015, at 9:44 PM, Robby Mook <re47@hillaryclinton.com> wrote:

Marc [Elias, of Perkins Coie] made a convincing case to me this am that these sorts of restrictions don't really get you anything…that Obama actually got judged MORE harshly as a result. He convinced me. So… in a complete U-turn, I'm ok just taking the money and dealing with any attacks. Are you guys ok with that?

On Apr 17, 2015, at 1:38 AM, Jennifer Palmieri jpalmieri@hillaryclinton.com wrote: Subject: Re: Foreign registered agents

Take the money!!

[80] "Re: Foreign registered agents," WikiLeaks, email sent on April 17, 2015, https://wikileaks.org/podesta-emails/emailid/11915; "Re: FARA," WikiLeaks, email sent on April 23, 2015, https://wikileaks.org/podesta-emails/emailid/2783.

[81] Ibid.

[82] Ibid.

[83] Opensecrets.org, "Uranium One: Summary," accessed April 13, 2018, https://www.opensecrets.org/lobby/clientsum.php?id=D000065156; Richard Pollock, "Tony Podesta Lobbied for Russia's 'Uranium One' and Did Not File As a Foreign Agent," *The Daily Caller*, November 5, 2017, http://dailycaller.com/2017/11/05/tony-podesta-lobbied-for-russias-uranium-one-and-did-not-file-as-a-foreign-agent/.

[84] Opensecrets.org, "Uranium One: Summary," accessed April 13, 2018, https://www.opensecrets.org/lobby/clientsum.php?id=D000065156; Pollock, "Tony Podesta Lobbied for Russia's 'Uranium One' and Did Not File As a Foreign Agent"; "1-Uranium One Shareholders Approve ARMZ Deal," Reuters, March 7, 2013, https://www.reuters.com/article/armz-uraniumone/update-1-uranium-one-shareholders-approve-armz-deal-idUSL-4N0BZ60V20130307.

[85] "History," ARMZ Uranium Holding Co., accessed May 29, 2018, http://www.armz.ru/eng/company/history/.

[86] Adam Shaw, "Clinton Foundation Revving Back Up Despite Ethical Cloud," Fox News, May 1, 2018, http://www.foxnews.com/politics/2018/05/01/clinton-foundation-revving-back-up-despite-ethical-cloud.html; "Clinton Foundation Investigated by Justice Department," BBC News, January 5, 2018, http://www.bbc.com/news/world-us-canada-42579732; Solomon, "FBI Launches New Clinton Foundation Investigation"; H.R. Res 907, 115th Cong. (2018).

[87] Opensecrets.org, "Uranium One: Lobbyists, 2012," accessed April 4, 2018, https://www.opensecrets.org/lobby/clientlbs.php?id=D000065156&year=2012.

[88] Opensecrets.org, "Uranium One: Lobbyists, 2010," accessed May 29, 2018, https://www.opensecrets.org/lobby/clientlbs.php?id=D000065156&year=2010; Rich Lord, "Big Lobbyist Morphed into GOP Force with Bridge to Democrats," *Pittsburgh Post-Gazette*, August 17, 2015, http://www.post-gazette.com/news/nation/2015/08/17/BGR-Group-morphed-into-

GOP-force-with-bridge-to-Democrats/stories/201508170009; Opensecrets. org, "National Atomic Co Kazatomprom, Client Profile: Summary," 2007, accessed April 4, 2018.

89   Full response from BGR Group: "BGR worked for Canada-based Uranium One for a few months in late 2010 and early 2011 as our public filing indicates. As best we can recall, only one BGR employee, Stephen Rademaker, did work for the client. Rademaker left BGR for Podesta Group at the beginning of 2011 and took the client with him."

90   Simpson and Jacoby, "How Lobbyists Help Ex-Soviets Woo Washington."

91   Opensecrets.org, "Uranium One: Lobbyists, 2010," accessed May 30, 2018, https://www.opensecrets.org/lobby/clientlbs.php?id=D000065156&-year=2010id=D000065156&year=2010; Opensecrets.org, "Uranium One: Lobbyists, 2011," accessed May 30, 2018, https://www.opensecrets. org/lobby/clientlbs.php?id=D000065156&year=2011.

92   Amy Knight, "Why Mueller Named a Russian Oligarch in Court," *The Daily Beast*, April 6, 2018, https://www.thedailybeast.com/is-muellers-eye-on-some-russian-oligarchs; Joshua Hersh, "Client of Haley Barbour's Lobby Shop Linked to Iranian Nuke Efforts," *HuffPost*, on Internet Archive, March 29, 2012 (the screenshot of the site was captured April 4, 2012), https://web.archive.org/web/20120404085112/https://www. huffingtonpost.com/2012/03/29/haley-barbour-iran-nuclear-program-bgr_n_1375102.html?ncid=edlinkusaolp00000003; "Alfa-Bank Extends a Credit Facility to LLP Joint Venture Rusburmash-Kazakhstan," ARMZ Uranium Holding Co., August 27, 2008, http://www.armz.ru/eng/press/news/?id=48&p=5.

93   Schweizer, "*Clinton Cash*," 30-31; Opensecrets.org, "Government of Kazakhstan," accessed July 3, 2018, https://www.opensecrets.org/lobby/clientsum.php?id=D000046159.

94   LD-2 lobbying disclosure form for Barbour Griffith & Rogers, LLC for 2010, quarter 4, http://disclosures.house.gov/ld/pdfform.aspx-?i7d=300356117.xml.

95   Opensecrets.org, "USEC Inc: Summary," accessed June 1, 2018, https:// www.opensecrets.org/lobby/clientsum.php?id=D000058056.

96   Hersh, "Client of Haley Barbour's Lobby Shop Linked to Iranian Nuke Efforts"; U.S. Department of Justice, "FARA Index and Act."

97   Exclusive GAI content not yet public on YouTube, "Dzhakishev videos," https://youtu.be/G7CQoLQJDpk?t=7m18s; Tom Blackwell, "Former Kazakhstan Uranium Czar Blames Imprisonment on Sale of Clinton-Linked Canadian Company to Russians," *National Post*, November 2, 2017, https:// nationalpost.com/news/world/former-kazakhstan-uranium-czar-blames-imprisonment-on-sale-of-clinton-linked-canadian-company-to-russians.

98   Dzhakishev YouTube video; "Oil Prices Fall on Rising Production," Investors Hub, November 7, 2005, https://investorshub.advfn.com/boards/read_msg.aspx?message_id=8398619; Jo Becker and Don Van

Natta Jr., "After Mining Deal, Financier Donated to Clinton," *The New York Times*, January 31, 2008, https://www.nytimes.com/2008/01/31/us/politics/31donor.html.

99   "A US Consulting Firm with Ties to the Clintons Lobbied on Behalf of Russia's Nuclear Giant," *Circa*, October 19, 2017, https://www.circa.com/story/2017/10/19/nation/a-us-consulting-firm-with-ties-to-the-clintons-lobbied-on-behalf-of-russias-nuclear-giant-for-the-purchase-american-uranium; John Solomon and Alison Spann, "Clintons Understated Support from Firm Hired by Russian Nuclear Company," *The Hill*, November 28, 2017, http://thehill.com/homenews/news/362234-clintons-understated-support-from-firm-hired-by-russian-nuclear-company; Opensecrets.org, "National Atomic Co Kazatomprom: Summary," accessed June 1, 2018, https://www.opensecrets.org/lobby/clientsum.php?id=F201924&year=2007.

100   John Solomon, "Uranium One Informant Makes Clinton Allegations to Congress," *Hill*, February 7, 2018, http://thehill.com/homenews/administration/372861-uranium-one-informant-makes-clinton-allegations-in-testimony; U.S. Department of Justice, Exhibit A to Registration Statement, Pursuant to the Foreign Agents Registration Act of 1938, as amended, APCO Worldwide Inc. (received by Dept. of Justice Criminal Division on April 13, 2010), https://assets.documentcloud.org/documents/3279149/4561-Exhibit-AB-20100413-10.pdf; U.S. Department of Justice, Exhibit B to Registration Statement, Pursuant to the Foreign Agents Registration Act of 1938, as amended, APCO Worldwide Inc. (received by Dept. of Justice Criminal Division on March 31, 2011), https://www.fara.gov/docs/4561-Exhibit-AB-20110331-12.pdf.

101   Solomon, "Uranium One Informant Makes Clinton Allegations to Congress."

102   Jonathan M. Winer, "Devin Nunes Is Investigating Me. Here's the Truth," *The Washington Post*, February 8, 2018, https://www.washingtonpost.com/opinions/devin-nunes-is-investigating-me-heres-the-truth/2018/02/08/cc621170-0cf4-11e8-8b0d-891602206fb7_story.html?utm_term=.e080c8c70289; U.S. Department of Justice, Short-Form Registration Statement, Pursuant to the Foreign Agents Registration Act of 1938, as amended, Jonathan Winer (received by Dept. of Justice Criminal Division on August 14, 2009), https://www.fara.gov/docs/4561-Short-Form-20090814-20.pdf; Opensecrets.org, "Winer, Jonathan M: Employment History," accessed June 1, 2018, https://www.opensecrets.org/revolving/rev_summary.php?id=16112.

103   Jim Wolf, "U.S. Revoked Deripaska Visa – State Dep't Official," Reuters, May 11, 2007, https://www.reuters.com/article/deripaska-chrysler-usa/u-s-revoked-deripaska-visa-state-dept-official-idUSN1143738620070511.

104   Lee Smith, "Was Christopher Steele Paid by Russian Oligarch and Putin Ally Oleg Deripaska?" *Tablet*, February 12, 2018, http://www.tabletmag.

com/jewish-news-and-politics/255290/christopher-steele-putin-oleg-deripaska; Ken Silverstein, "Russian Oligarch Retains Advisory Firm Close to Hillary to Help Resolve Visa Ban," *Harper's Magazine*, June 17, 2009, https://harpers.org/blog/2009/06/russian-oligarch-retains-lobby-firm-close-to-hillary-to-help-resolve-visa-ban/; Ed Henry, "Democratic Sen. Mark Warner Texted with Russian Oligarch Lobbyist in Effort to Contact Dossier Author Christopher Steele," Fox News, February 8, 2018, http://www.foxnews.com/politics/2018/02/08/democratic-sen-mark-warner-texted-with-russian-oligarch-lobbyist-in-effort-to-contact-dossier-author-christopher-steele.html.

105 Evan Perez and Gregory L. White, "FBI Lets Barred Tycoon Visit U.S.," *The Wall Street Journal*, on Internet Archive, October 30, 2009 (the screenshot of the site was captured March 9, 2014), https://web.archive.org/web/20140309072509/http://online.wsj.com/news/articles/SB125685578903317087; Joby Warrick and Karen DeYoung, "From 'Reset' to 'Pause': The Real Story Behind Hillary Clinton's Feud with Vladimir Putin," *The Washington Post*, November 3, 2016, https://www.washingtonpost.com/world/national-security/from-reset-to-pause-the-real-story-behind-hillary-clintons-feud-with-vladimir-putin/2016/11/03/f575f9fa-a116-11e6-8832-23a007c77bb4_story.html?noredirect=on&utm_term=.25a5410a64c0.

106 Hunter Walker, "Here Are the American Executives Who Are Working on Behalf of Putin," *Business Insider*, March 5, 2014, http://www.businessinsider.com/american-executives-working-for-putin-2014-3; U.S. Department of Justice, "Supplemental Statement, Pursuant to the Foreign Agents Registration Act of 1938, as amended" (received by NSD/FARA Registration Unit on June 30, 2014), https://www.fara.gov/docs/5934-Supplemental-Statement-20140630-10.pdf.

107 Sean Davis, "Is A Former Feinstein Staffer Running Fusion GPS's Post-Election Steele Dossier Operation?" *The Federalist*, February 20, 2018, http://thefederalist.com/2018/02/20/is-a-former-feinstein-staffer-running-fusion-gpss-post-election-russia-dossier-operation/; Silverstein, "Russian Oligarch Retains Advisory Firm Close to Hillary to Help Resolve Visa Ban."

108 "Profile of Adam Waldman," Walker's Research, accessed June 1, 2018, http://www.walkersresearch.com/Profilepages/Show_Executive_Title/Executiveprofile/A/Adam__Waldman_400161083.html; "Our Work," Endeavor Group, accessed April 5, 2018, http://www.theendeavorgroup.com/work.html.

109 Harriet Ryan, "Celebrities Hire Philanthropy Consultants to Guide Their Giving," *Los Angeles Times*, November 14, 2010, http://articles.latimes.com/2010/nov/14/entertainment/la-ca-celebrity-charity-20101114; Mark Seal, "How Did Johnny Depp Find Himself in a Financial Crisis?"

Vanity Fair, August 2017, https://www.vanityfair.com/style/2017/07/johnny-depp-financial-crisis-money.

110 U.S. Department of Justice, "Supplemental Statement, Pursuant to the Foreign Agents Registration Act of 1938, as amended" (received by NSD/FARA Registration Unit on December 21, 2017), https://www.fara.gov/docs/5934-Supplemental-Statement-20171221-17.pdf; U.S. Department of Justice, "Supplemental Statement, Pursuant to the Foreign Agents Registration Act of 1938, as amended," for six-month period ending May 31, 2017, https://www.fara.gov/docs/5934-Supplemental-Statement-20170630-16.pdf; U.S. Department of Justice, "Registrations and Supplemental Statements, Pursuant to the Foreign Agents Registration Act of 1938, as amended," Endeavor Group, accessed June, 22018, https://efile.fara.gov/pls/apex/f?p=185:200:0::NO:RP,200:P200_REG_NUMBER:5934.

111 Fara.gov homepage, accessed April 5, 2018.

112 Mark R. Warner, US Senator from the Commonwealth of Virginia, "Sen. Warner on Confirmation of Jeff Sessions As Attorney General," press release, February 8, 2017, https://www.warner.senate.gov/public/index.cfm/2017/2/sen-warner-on-confirmation-of-jeff-sessions-as-attorney-general; Karoun Demirjian, Ed O'Keefe, Sari Horowitz, and Matt Zapotosky, "Attorney General Jeff Sessions Will Recuse Himself from Any Probe Related to 2016 Presidential Campaign," *Washington Post*, March 2, 2017, https://www.washingtonpost.com/powerpost/top-gop-lawmaker-calls-on-sessions-to-recuse-himself-from-russia-investigation/2017/03/02/148c07ac-ff46-11e6-8ebe-6e0dbe4f2bca_story.html?utm_term=.b96215067629; Tim Hains, "Sen. Mark Warner Grills Sessions About Potential Flynn Pardon, 'Peculiar' Timing of Comey Firing," *Real Clear Politics*, June 13, 2017, https://www.realclearpolitics.com/video/2017/06/13/sen_mark_warner_grills_sessions.html; Charlie Savage, Emmarie Huetteman, and Rebecca R. Ruiz, "Highlights from Attorney General Jeff Sessions's Senate Testimony," *The New York Times*, June 13, 2017, https://www.nytimes.com/2017/06/13/us/politics/jeff-sessions-testimony.html; "Sen. Mark Warner Speaks Against Jeff Sessions AG Nomination (2/8/17)," YouTube video, posted by "lowkell," February 8, 2017, https://www.youtube.com/watch?v=2JRpIrJIGX0.

113 Opensecrets.org, "BGR Group: Totals," accessed June 1, 2018, https://www.opensecrets.org/orgs/totals.php?id=D000021679&type=P&cycle=2010.

114 Simpson and Jacoby, "How Lobbyists Help Ex-Soviets Woo Washington."

115 Office of the Deputy Attorney General, "Rod Rosenstein's Letter Appointing Mueller to Special Counsel."

Chapter 4: The United Surveillance States of America (USSA)

1 Andrea Peterson, "How High-Powered Lobbying and PR Firms Launder Influence for Foreign Governments," POGO, January 29, 2018, http://

www.pogo.org/our-work/articles/2018/propaganda-by-proxy-lobby-ing-pr-firms-launder-influence-for-foreign-governments.html;   Julia Ainsley, Andrew W. Lehren, and Anna R. Schecter, "The Mueller Effect: FARA Filings Soar in Shadow of Manafort, Flynn Probes," NBC News, January 19, 2018, https://www.nbcnews.com/news/us-news/muel-ler-effect-fara-filings-soar-shadow-manafort-flynn-probes-n838571; Miles Parks, "A 'Toothless' Old Law Could Have New Fangs, Thanks to Robert Mueller," NPR, November 17, 2017, https://www.npr.org/2017/11/17/563737981/a-toothless-old-law-could-have-new-fangs-thanks-to-robert-mueller.

2   Charlie Savage, "N.S.A. Gets More Latitude to Share Intercepted Communications," *New York Times*, January 12, 2017, https://www.nytimes.com/2017/01/12/us/politics/nsa-gets-more-latitude-to-share-in-tercepted-communications.html?; Judge Andrew Napolitano, "Lying, Spying and Hiding by Our Government," *New Jersey Herald*, February 2, 2018, http://www.njherald.com/20180202/lying-spying-and-hid-ing-by-our-government; Brooke Singman, "Documents Suggest Possible Coordination Between CIA, FBI, Obama WH and Dem Officials Early in Trump-Russia Probe: Investigators," Fox News, March 28, 2018, http://www.foxnews.com/politics/2018/03/28/documents-suggest-pos-sible-coordination-between-cia-fbi-obama-wh-and-dem-officials-ear-ly-in-trump-russia-probe-investigators.html.

3   See Chapter 1.

4   White House visitor logs, Mary Jacoby, https://obamawhitehouse.archives.gov/briefing-room/disclosures/visitor-records.

5   Julia Glum, "Did the Obama Campaign Fund the Trump-Russia Dossier? $972,000 in 'Legal Services' Payments Scrutinized," *Newsweek*, October 30, 2017, http://www.newsweek.com/trump-dossier-obama-clinton-funded-golden-shower-tape-696402.

6   Savage, "N.S.A. Gets More Latitude to Share Intercepted Communications."

7   Ibid.

8   Ibid; Singman, "Documents Suggest Possible Coordination Between CIA, FBI, Obama WH and Dem Officials Early in Trump-Russia Probe: Investigators."

9   Michelle Ye Hee Lee, "Do Russia Probe Attorney's Donations to Democrats Threaten Their Independence?" *Washington Post*, June 28, 2017, https://www.washingtonpost.com/news/fact-checker/wp/2017/06/28/do-russia-probe-at-torneys-donations-to-democrats-threaten-their-independence/?utm_ter-m=.548af6f2a90f; "Political Contributions by Attorney," *Atlas.com*, pic-ture, accessed April 5, 2018, https://www.theatlas.com/charts/BJE0-ZivG; David Sivak, "Exclusive: Not a Single Lawyer Known to Work for Mueller Is a Republican," *Daily Caller*, February 21, 2018, http://dailycaller.com/2018/02/21/exclusive-zero-registered-republicans-mueller-lawyer/.

10 Jack Crowe, "Strzok and Page Plotted Covert Meeting with Presiding Judge in Michael Flynn Case," *National Review*, March 16, 2018, https://www.nationalreview.com/2018/03/peter-strzok-lisa-page-meeting-michael-flynn-judge/.

11 Karoun Demirjian and Devlin Barrett, "Top FBI Official Assigned to Mueller's Russia Probe Said to Have Been Removed After Sending Anti-Trump Texts," *The Washington Post*, December 2, 2017, https://www.washingtonpost.com/world/national-security/two-senior-fbi-officials-on-clinton-trump-probes-exchanged-politically-charged-texts-disparaging-trump/2017/12/02/9846421c-d707-11e7-a986-d0a9770d9a3e_story.html?noredirect=on&utm_term=.7e1814a42f35; Coleen Rowley, "No, Robert Mueller and James Comey Aren't Heroes," *HuffPost*, June 9, 2017, https://www.huffingtonpost.com/entry/conflicts-of-interest-and-ethics-robert-mueller-and_us_5936a148e4b-033940169cdc8.

12 Kevin Johnson, "Peter Strzok, FBI Agent Removed from Robert Mueller's Russia Probe, Called Trump an 'Idiot,'" *USA Today*, December 12, 2017, https://www.usatoday.com/story/news/politics/2017/12/12/peter-strzok-fbi-agent-removed-muellers-russia-probe-called-trump/946913001/.

13 Everett Rosenfeld, "New FBI Release on Clinton Email Probe Refers to 'Shadow Government,'" CNBC, October 17, 2016, https://www.cnbc.com/2016/10/17/fbi-releases-100-new-pages-on-clinton-email-probe.html; "Hillary R. Clinton: Part 04 of 06," FBI Records: The Vault, on Internet Archive (the screenshot of the site was captured February 3, 2017), http://web.archive.org/web/20170203160045/https://vault.fbi.gov/hillary-r.-clinton/hillary-r.-clinton-part-04-of-06/view.

14 Trevor Timm, "Forget Comey and McCabe. Support FBI Whistleblower Terry Albury," *Columbia Journalism Review*, April 17, 2018, https://www.cjr.org/watchdog/terry-albury.php; John Solomon and Alison Spann, "FBI Supervisor Warned Comey in 2014 that Warrantless Surveillance Program Was Ineffective," *The Hill*, March 25, 2018, http://thehill.com/policy/national-security/378730-fbi-supervisor-warned-comey-in-2014-that-warrantless-surveillance; Glenn Harlan Reynolds, "Looking for 'Solutions' to Mass Killings? Start with Punishing Failure," *USA Today*, April 9, 2018, https://www.usatoday.com/story/opinion/2018/04/09/mass-killings-failures-hold-law-enforcement-accountable-column/497285002/; Susan Zalkind, "FBI Admits It Missed Opportunities to Stop Tamerlan Tsarnaev," *Boston*, April 11, 2014, https://www.bostonmagazine.com/news/2014/04/11/fbi-admits-missed-opportunities-stop-tamerlan-tsarnaev/; Peter Hasson, "The FBI Keeps Missing Mass Shooters Before It's Too Late," *The Daily Caller*, February 15, 2018, http://dailycaller.com/2018/02/15/fbi-missing-mass-shooters-florida-nikolas-cruz-omar-mateen/; Dan Eggen, "Pre-9/11 Missteps by FBI Detailed," *The Washington Post*, June 10, 2005, http://www.washingtonpost.com/wp-dyn/content/article/2005/06/09/AR2005060902000.

html; James Kirkup, "FBI 'Missed Chance to Uncover 9/11 Plot,'" *The Telegraph*, March 28, 2012https://www.telegraph.co.uk/news/worldnews/september-11-attacks/9170297/FBI-missed-chance-to-uncover-911-plot.html; John Surico, "The Former FBI Agent Who Believes He Could've Prevented 9/11," *Vice*, September 11, 2015, https://www.vice.com/en_us/article/5gj5p3/the-man-who-thinks-he-could-have-prevented-911; Glenn Kessler, "Bill Clinton and the Missed Opportunities to Kill Osama bin Laden," *The Washington Post*, February 16, 2016, https://www.washington-post.com/news/fact-checker/wp/2016/02/16/bill-clinton-and-the-missed-opportunities-to-kill-osama-bin-laden/?utm_term=.ad8641375f66.

Several sources above highlight recent failures (which the FBI had fair warning of) include Marjory Stoneman Douglas High School shooter Nikolas Cruz, Las Vegas shooter Stephen Paddock, Pulse Night Club terrorist Omar Mateen, Boston Bombers the Tsarnaev Brothers, Charleston church shooter Dylann Roof, and Fort Hood shooter Omar Nidal.

[15] See discussion of FISA in Chapter 5.

[16] "James B. Comey," *Forbes*, on Internet Archive, accessed June 1, 2018 (the screenshot of the site was captured October 13, 2014), https://web.archive.org/web/20141013125042/http://www.forbes.com/profile/james-b-comey/; Hearing Before the Committee on the Judiciary, United States Senate, 108th Congress (2003) (confirmation hearing on the nomination of James B. Comey Jr. to be deputy attorney general, Department of Justice), https://www.fbcoverup.com/docs/library/2003-10-29-S-Hrg-108-472-James-B-Comey-Jr-Senate-Confirmation-Hearing-for-Deputy-Attorney-General-Judiciary-Committee-J-108-49-CHRG-108shrg93948-Oct-29-2003.pdf; Gerstein and Samuelsohn, "Special Counsel Robert Mueller's Finances Go Public"; Tim Marcin, "James Comey's Net Worth Ensures Fired FBI Director Won't Really Miss His Government Salary," *Newsweek*, May 9, 2017, http://www.newsweek.com/james-comey-net-worth-salary-fbi-director-trump-fired-pay-606406.

[17] Stuart Taylor Jr., "Those Job-Hopping Carter People," *The New York Times*, archives, 1981, https://www.nytimes.com/1981/05/10/business/those-job-hopping-carter-people.html.

[18] Ben Shapiro, "The Death of the DOJ and the FBI," *Real Clear Politics*, April 11, 2018, https://www.realclearpolitics.com/articles/2018/04/11/the_death_of_the_doj_and_the_fbi_136770.html.

[19] Tim Shorrock, "5 Corporations Now Dominate Our Privatized Intelligence Industry," *The Nation*, September 8, 2016, https://www.thenation.com/article/five-corporations-now-dominate-our-privatized-intelligence-industry/; Amarendra Bhushan Dhiraj, "The Top 25 Largest Defense Companies in the World, 2015," *Ceoworld Magazine*, February 17, 2016, http://ceoworld.biz/2016/02/17/the-top-25-largest-defense-companies-in-the-world-2015/.

[20] Marc Fisher and Sari Horwitz, "Mueller and Trump: Born to Wealth, Raised to Lead. Then, Sharply Different Choices," *The Washington Post*, February 23, 2018, https://www.washingtonpost.com/politics/mueller-and-trump-born-to-wealth-raised-to-lead-then-sharply-different-choices/2018/02/22/ad50b7bc-0a99-11e8-8b0d-891602206fb7_story.html; Gerstein and Samuelsohn, "Special Counsel Robert Mueller's Finances Go Public."

[21] Federal Bureau of Investigation, "Robert S. Mueller, III, September 4, 2001 – September 4, 2013," accessed June 6, 2018, https://www.fbi.gov/history/directors/robert-s-mueller-iii; "Former Director of the FBI Robert Mueller III Joins WilmerHale," WilmerHale, March 24, 2014, https://www.wilmerhale.com/pages/publicationsandnewsdetail.aspx?NewsPubID=17179871803; Glenn P. Hastedt, *Spies, Wiretaps, and Secret Operations: An Encyclopedia of American Espionage* (Santa Barbara: ABC-CLIO, 2011), https://books.google.com/books/about/Spies_Wiretaps_and_Secret_Operations.html?id=91FyAJDjAvQC; Kevin Johnson and Aamer Madhani, "Obama to Pick Comey to Replace Mueller at FBI," *USA Today*, May 29, 2013, https://www.usatoday.com/story/news/politics/2013/05/29/obama-comey-fbi/2370763/.

[22] Gerstein and Samuelsohn, "Special Counsel Robert Mueller's Finances Go Public"; Claire Cain Miller, "Tech Companies Concede to Surveillance Program," *The New York Times*, June 7, 2013, https://www.nytimes.com/2013/06/08/technology/tech-companies-bristling-concede-to-government-surveillance-efforts.html; Billy House, "Zuckerberg Says Facebook Is Cooperating with Mueller's Russia Probe," *Bloomberg*, April 10, 2018, https://www.bloomberg.com/news/articles/2018-04-10/zuckerberg-says-facebook-cooperating-with-mueller-s-russia-probe.

[23] Rick Perlstein, "More Questions for James Comey," *The Nation*, June 24, 2013, https://www.thenation.com/article/more-questions-james-comey/.

[24] "Lockheed Martin," Federal Contractor Misconduct Database, accessed April 5, 2018, https://www.contractormisconduct.org/contractors/38/lockheed-martin; "Booz Allen Hamilton," Federal Contractor Misconduct Database, accessed June 2, 2018, https://www.contractormisconduct.org/contractors/15/booz-allen-hamilton.

[25] Lockheed Martin, 2009 Annual Report, accessed June 2, 2018, https://www.lockheedmartin.com/content/dam/lockheed-martin/eo/documents/annual-reports/2009-annual-report.pdf.

[26] Ibid.

[27] U.S. Department of Justice, "Lockheed Martin Agrees to Pay $5 Million to Settle Alleged Violations of the False Claims Act and the Resource Conservation and Recovery Act," press release, February 29, 2016, https://www.justice.gov/opa/pr/lockheed-martin-agrees-pay-5-million-settle-alleged-violations-false-claims-act-and-resource.

28   Ibid. "The government's lawsuit alleged that Lockheed Martin violated RCRA [Resource Conservation and Recovery Act], the statute that establishes how hazardous wastes must be managed, by failing to identify and report hazardous waste produced and stored at the facility, and failing to properly handle and dispose of the waste. The government further alleged that this conduct resulted in false claims for payment under Lockheed Martin's contracts with the Department of Energy"; Lynn Hulsey, "Piketon Radiation Records Altered, Feds Say," *MyDaytonDailyNews.com*, May 25, 2013, https://www.mydaytondailynews.com/news/state--regional/piketon-radiation-records-altered-feds-say/akvoflisWyBpisZ9oO0PgI/; Joe Walker, "Nuclear Whistleblowers Loss of Protection Feared," *Paducah Sun*, October 4, 2003, http://www.state.nv.us/nucwaste/news2003/nn11988.htm.

29   Samuel Rubenfeld, "HSBC Names James Comey to the Board," *The Wall Street Journal*, January 30, 2013, https://blogs.wsj.com/corruption-currents/2013/01/30/hsbc-names-james-comey-to-the-board/; Tae Kim, "Ray Dalio Made $50 Billion for His Clients, Topping List of Biggest Hedge Fund Moneymakers Ever," CNBC, January 26, 2018, https://www.cnbc.com/2018/01/26/ray-dalio-made-50-billion-for-his-clients-topping-list-of-biggest-hedge-fund-money-makers-ever.html; Will Martin, "These Are the 23 Biggest Global Banks – All with More Than $1 Trillion of Assets," *Business Insider*, April 21, 2017, http://www.businessinsider.com/the-biggest-banks-in-the-world-2017-4.

30   Brett Arends, "Opinion: FBI's Comey Has a History As a Political and Corporate Fixer," *Market Watch*, November 2, 2016, https://www.marketwatch.com/story/fbis-comey-has-a-sinister-history-as-a-political-and-corporate-fixer-2016-11-02; U.S. Department of Justice, "HSBC Holdings Plc. and HSBC Bank USA N.A. Admit to Anti-Money Laundering and Sanctions Violations, Forfeit $1.256 Billion in Deferred Prosecution Agreement," press release, December 11, 2012, https://www.justice.gov/opa/pr/hsbc-holdings-plc-and-hsbc-bank-usa-na-admit-anti-money-laundering-and-sanctions-violations.

31   Matt Taibbi, "Outrageous HSBC Settlement Proves the Drug War is a Joke," *Rolling Stone,* December 13, 2012, https://www.rollingstone.com/politics/news/outrageous-hsbc-settlement-proves-the-drug-war-is-a-joke-20121213.

32   Susan Davis, "Senate Approves James Comey for FBI Director," *USA Today*, July 29, 2013, https://www.usatoday.com/story/news/politics/2013/07/29/james-comey-fbi-director-senate-vote/2596761/; Matt Taibbi, "Gangster Bankers: Too Big to Jail," *Rolling Stone*, February 14, 2013, https://www.rollingstone.com/politics/news/gangster-bankers-too-big-to-jail-20130214?print=true.

33   Christopher Woolf, "The History of Electronic Surveillance, from Abraham Lincoln's Wiretaps to Operation Shamrock," PRI, November 7, 2013, https://www.pri.org/stories/2013-11-07/history-electronic-surveil-

lance-abraham-lincolns-wiretaps-operation-shamrock; "Abraham Lincoln: Executive Order—Taking into Military Possession All Telegraph Lines in the United States," American Presidency Project, February 25, 1862, http://www.presidency.ucsb.edu/ws/?pid=69797).

[34] Woolf, "The History of Electronic Surveillance, from Abraham Lincoln's Wiretaps to Operation Shamrock"; Robert Chesney, "Historical Context for Today's Surveillance Debates: The 1945 Legal Memo on What Became Operation Shamrock," Lawfare Blog, March 29, 2017, https://www.lawfareblog.com/historical-context-todays-surveillance-debates-1945-legal-memo-what-became-operation-shamrock.

[35] United States Senate, "Senate Select Committee to Study Governmental Operations with Respect to Intelligence Activities," accessed July 3, 2018, https://www.senate.gov/artandhistory/history/common/investigations/ChurchCommittee.htm; Tim Weiner, "What Was James Comey Thinking?" *Esquire*, December 14, 2016, https://www.esquire.com/uk/culture/a12048/what-was-comey-thinking/.

[36] "J. Edgar Hoover Begins His Legacy with the FBI," History, May 10, accessed April 5, 2018, https://www.history.com/this-day-in-history/j-edgar-hoover-begins-his-legacy-with-the-fbi; Federal Bureau of Investigation, "COINTELPRO," accessed June 6, 2018, https://vault.fbi.gov/cointel-pro.

[37] "Supplementary Detailed Staff Reports on Intelligence Activities and the Rights of Americans, Book III, Final Report of the Select Comm. to Study Governmental Operations with Respect to Intelligence Activities," United States Senate. 94th Congress, Report No. 94-755, https://www.intelligence.senate.gov/sites/default/files/94755_III.pdf; "The Women's Liberation Movement and COINTELPRO," Freedomarchives.org, accessed April 5, 2018, https://www.freedomarchives.org/Documents/Curr%20C101/Cointelpro%20and%20Women's%20Liberation.pdf.

[38] Andrew Prokop, "Read the Letter the FBI Sent to MLK to Try to Convince Him to Kill Himself," *Vox*, January 15, 2018, https://www.vox.com/xpress/2014/11/12/7204453/martin-luther-king-fbi-letter; David J. Garrow, "The FBI and Martin Luther King," *Atlantic*, July/August 2002, https://www.theatlantic.com/magazine/archive/2002/07/the-fbi-and-martin-luther-king/302537/.

[39] Tim Weiner, "At a Scheme's Inception and Destruction, the F.B.I.," *New York Times*, June 14, 2012, https://www.nytimes.com/roomfordebate/2012/06/13/did-any-good-come-of-watergate/at-a-schemes-inception-and-destruction-the-fbi.

[40] "Nixon's Re-Election Employees Are Arrested for Burglary," *History*, June 17, accessed June 6, 2018, https://www.history.com/this-day-in-history/nixons-re-election-employees-are-arrested-for-burglary; Seymour M. Hersh, "Kissinger and Nixon in the White House," *The Atlantic*, May 1982, https://www.theatlantic.com/magazine/archive/1982/05/kissinger-and-nixon-in-the-white-house/308778/.

41   Bob Dreyfuss, "Seth Rich, Conspiracy Theorists, and Russiagate 'Truthers,'" *Nation*, August 25, 2017, https://www.thenation.com/article/seth-rich-conspiracy-theorists-and-russiagate-truthers/.

42   Timothy B. Lee, "In the 1970s, Congress Investigated Intelligence Abuses. Time to Do It Again?" *Washington Post*, June 27, 2013, https://www.washingtonpost.com/news/wonk/wp/2013/06/27/in-the-1970s-congress-investigated-intelligence-abuses-time-to-do-it-again/?utm_term=.36e3e00ee2a4; "Supplementary Detailed Staff Reports on Intelligence Activities and the Rights of Americans, Book III, Final Report of the Select Comm. to Study Governmental Operations with Respect to Intelligence Activities," United States Senate. 94th Congress, Report No. 94-755.

43   Kevin Poulsen, "Whistle-Blower: Feds Have a Backdoor Into Wireless Carrier – Congress Reacts," *Wired*, March 6, 2008, https://www.wired.com/2008/03/whistleblower-f/.

44   "AT&T; Whistle-Blower's Evidence," *Wired*, on Internet Archive, May 17, 2006 (the screenshot of the site was captured March 28, 2014), https://www.wired.com/2008/03/whistleblower-f/.

45   Brendan Sasso, "Report: NSA Paid Tech Companies to Comply with Surveillance," *Hill*, August 23, 2013, https://thehill.com/policy/technology/318483-report-nsa-paid-tech-giants-to-comply-with-surveillance; Robert Lenzner, "ATT, Verizon, Sprint Are Paid Cash by NSA for Your Private Communications," *Forbes*, September 23, 2013, https://www.forbes.com/sites/robertlenzner/2013/09/23/attverizonsprint-are-paid-cash-by-nsa-for-your-private-communications/#418c805543cb; Frank Konkel, "AT&T Won Secret $3.3 Billion NSA Contract Despite More Expensive Bid," Nextgov, March 21, 2018, https://www.nextgov.com/it-modernization/2018/03/t-won-secret-33-billion-nsa-contract-despite-more-expensive-bid/146853/.

46   William D. Hartung, *Prophets of War* (New York: Nation Books, 2011), 219-221; Martin Pengelly, "AT&T's 'Extraordinary, Decades-Long' Relationship with NSA – Report," *The Guardian*, August 16, 2015, http://www.theguardian.com/us-news/2015/aug/15/att-nsa-internet-surveillance-new-york-times-propublica.

47   William D. Hartung, "Is Lockheed Martin Shadowing You?" *Mother Jones*, January 12, 2011, https://www.motherjones.com/politics/2011/01/lockheed-martin-shadowing-you/.

48   Hartung, *Prophets of War*, 221.

49   R. James Woolsey, "Why We Spy on Our Allies," *The Wall Street Journal*, March 17, 2000, https://www.wsj.com/articles/SB95326824311657269.

50   William H. Jones and John F. Berry, "Lockheed Paid $38 million in Bribes Abroad," *The Washington Post*, May 27, 1977, https://www.washingtonpost.com/archive/business/1977/05/27/lockheed-paid-38-million-in-bribes-abroad/800c355c-ddc2-4145-b430-0ae24afd6648/?utm_term=.65da18dee35b; James F. Peltz, "Lockheed Agrees to Pay Record Fine:

Aerospace: Calabasas Firm Pleads Guilty in Connection with Bribing an Egyptian Politician," *The Los Angeles Times*, January 28, 1995, http://articles.latimes.com/1995-01-28/business/fi-25231_1_egyptian-politician.

51   Jeremiah Goulka, "Lockheed Martin's Herculean Efforts to Profit from Defense Spending," *The Nation*, March 11, 2013, https://www.thenation.com/article/lockheed-martins-herculean-efforts-profit-defense-spending/.

52   Jake Tapper, "Obama Administration Spied on German Media As Well As Its Government," CNN, July 4, 2015, https://www.cnn.com/2015/07/03/politics/germany-media-spying-obama-administration/index.html.

53   "The NSA's Secret Spy Hub in Berlin," *Spiegel Online*, October 27, 2013, http://www.spiegel.de/international/germany/cover-story-how-nsa-spied-on-merkel-cell-phone-from-berlin-embassy-a-930205.html.

54   James Ball, "NSA Monitored Calls of 35 World Leaders After US Official Handed Over Contacts," *The Guardian*, October 25, 2013, https://www.theguardian.com/world/2013/oct/24/nsa-surveillance-world-leaders-calls.

55   Richard Behar, "Never Heard of Acxiom? Chances Are It's Heard of You. How a Little-Known Little Rock Company – the World's Largest Processor of Consumer Data – Found Itself at the Center of a Very Big National Security Debate," CNN, February 23, 2004, http://money.cnn.com/magazines/fortune/fortune_archive/2004/02/23/362182/index.htm.

56   Ibid.

57   Ibid.

58   "Gen. Wesley Kanne Clark (Ret.)," CBS News, timeline, accessed June 8, 2018, http://www.cbsnews.com/htdocs/politics/campaign2004/04dem-timeline.pdf; Chapter 1.

59   "A Whitewater Chronology," *The Wall Street Journal*, May 28, 2003, https://www.wsj.com/articles/SB122721127833145225.

60   "Israel Angle in Foster Case," *Intelligence Online*, August, 31, 1995, https://www.intelligenceonline.com/threat-assessment/1995/08/31/israel-angle-in-foster-case,65597-ART.

61   Acxiom Data Catalogue, Acxiom, August 2017, https://marketing.acxiom.com/rs/982-LRE-196/images/Data%20Catalogue%20for%20Audience%20Creation%20and%20Analytics_UK.pdf; "The Stevens Group: Case Studies," The Stephens Group, on Internet Archive, accessed June 6, 2018 (the screenshot of the site was captured May 24, 2007), https://web.archive.org/web/20070524080130/http://stephensgroup.com/about-ourpartners/case-systematics.html; "BRIEFS; Debt Issues," *The New York Times*, archives, 1983, https://www.nytimes.com/1983/12/16/business/briefs-debt-issues.html; Christopher Knowlton, "Of Bibles, Bonds, and Billions: Those Down-Home Stephens Boys Made It Big in Little Rock. Now They Want to Bust Out and be the Investment Bankers for Middle America Too," *Fortune*, archives, February 12, 1990, http://archive.fortune.com/magazines/fortune/fortune_archive/1990/02/12/73062/index.htm.

62   The White House, President George W. Bush, photograph, October 2001, https://georgewbush-whitehouse.archives.gov/news/releases/2001/10/images/20011026-5.html.

63   William Safire, "You Are a Suspect," *The New York Times*, November 14, 2002, https://www.nytimes.com/2002/11/14/opinion/you-are-a-suspect. html; Adam Mayle and Alex Knott, "Outsourcing Big Brother," Center for Public Integrity, December 17, 2002, https://www.publicintegrity. org/2002/12/17/3164/outsourcing-big-brother; Curt Anderson, "FBI Criticized for Total Information Awareness Interest," GovTech, January 22, 2003, http://www.govtech.com/security/FBI-Criticized-for-Total-Information-Awareness.html.

64   Mayle and Knott, "Outsourcing Big Brother."

65   Department of Defense, "Letter from C. Y. Talbott, Deputy Director, to David L. Sobel, Electronic Privacy Information Center," January 23, 2004, Ref: 02-F-0753, https://www.epic.org/privacy/profiling/tia/darpaacxiom. pdf.

66   Department of Defense, "Letter from C. Y. Talbott, Deputy Director, to David L. Sobel, Electronic Privacy Information Center"; "Total Information Awareness Project Undergoes First Test," *InformationWeek*, April 10, 2003, https://www.informationweek.com/total-information-awareness-project-undergoes-first-test/d/d-id/1019277.

67   Department of Defense, "Letter from C. Y. Talbott, Deputy Director, to David L. Sobel, Electronic Privacy Information Center; Mayle and Knott, "Outsourcing Big Brother."

68   "The Surveillance-Industrial Complex: How the American Government Is Conscripting Businesses and Individuals in the Construction of a Surveillance Society, ACLU, August 2004, https://www.aclu.org/files/FilesPDFs/surveillance_report.pdf.

69   DARPA, "Information Awareness Office," on Internet Archive (the screenshot of the site was captured August 2, 2002), http://web.archive.org/web/20020802012150/http://www.darpa.mil/iao/.

70   Mayle and Knott, "Outsourcing Big Brother."

71   Ibid; Matt Kessler, "The Logo That Took Down a DARPA Surveillance Project," *The Atlantic*, December 22, 2015, https://www.theatlantic. com/technology/archive/2015/12/darpa-logos-information-awareness-of-fice/421635/; Chris Hayes, "Before PRISM There Was Total Information Awareness," MSNBC, July 2, 2013, http://www.msnbc.com/all-in/prism-there-was-total-information-awar; Siobhan Gorman, "NSA's Domestic Spying Grows As Agency Sweeps Up Data," *The Wall Street Journal*, March 10, 2008, https://www.wsj.com/articles/SB120511973377523845.

72   Noah Shachtman, "The Bastard Children of Total Information Awareness," *Wired*, February 1, 2004, https://www.wired.com/2004/02/the-bastard-children-of-total-information-awareness/; American Civil Liberties Union, "Booz Allen Not An Independent Check on SWIFT Surveillance:

A Memo by the American Civil Liberties Union and Privacy International for the Article 29 Working Party of the European Commission," September 14, 2006, https://www.aclu.org/files/pdfs/safefree/boozal-len20060914.pdf; Gorman, "NSA's Domestic Spying Grows As Agency Sweeps Up Data"; Ben White and R. Jeffrey Smith, "Clark, the Four-Star Businessman," *The Washington Post*, January 29, 2004, http://www.washingtonpost.com/wp-dyn/articles/A58300-2004Jan28.html; Department of Homeland Security, "Fact Sheet: CAPPS II at a Glance," press release, February 13, 2004.

[73] Marc Ambinder, "What's the Counterintelligence Field Activity Doing in Budget Documents?" *The Atlantic*, May 24, 2010, https://www.theatlantic.com/politics/archive/2010/05/whats-the-counterintelligence-field-activity-doing-in-budget-documents/57177/; Hartung, *Prophets of War*, 220-221.

[74] As quoted in Hartung, *Prophets of War*, 220.

[75] See section on Comey's and Mueller's conflicts near the end of Chapter 4.

[76] Barton Gellman and Laura Poitras, U.S., British Intelligence Mining Data from Nine U.S. Internet Companies in Broad Secret Program," *The Washington Post*, June 7, 2013, https://www.washingtonpost.com/investigations/us-intelligence-mining-data-from-nine-us-internet-companies-in-broad-secret-program/2013/06/06/3a0c0da8-cebf-11e2-8845-d970ccb04497_story.html; Glenn Greenwald, Ewen MacAskill, and Laura Poitras, "Edward Snowden: The Whistleblower Behind the NSA Surveillance Revelations," *The Guardian*, June 11, 2013, http://www.theguardian.com/world/2013/jun/09/edward-snowden-nsa-whistleblower-surveillance.

[77] Duncan Campbell, "Global Spy System ECHELON Confirmed at Last—by Leaked Snowden Files," *The Register*, August 3, 2015, https://www.theregister.co.uk/2015/08/03/gchq_duncan_campbell/?page=5; Barton Gellman, Julie Tate, and Ashkan Soltani, "In NSA-Intercepted Data, Those Not Targeted Far Outnumber the Foreigners Who Are," *The Washington Post*, July 5, 2014, https://www.washingtonpost.com/world/national-security/in-nsa-intercepted-data-those-not-targeted-far-outnumber-the-foreigners-who-are/2014/07/05/8139adf8-045a-11e4-8572-4b1b969b6322_story.html.

[78] Gellman, Tate, and Soltani, "In NSA-Intercepted Data, Those Not Targeted Far Outnumber the Foreigners Who Are."

[79] Glenn Greenwald, "XKeyscore: NSA Tool Collects 'Nearly Everything a User Does on the Internet,'" *The Guardian*, July 31, 2013, https://www.theguardian.com/world/2013/jul/31/nsa-top-secret-program-online-data.

[80] Morgan Marquis-Boire, Glenn Greenwald, and Micah Lee, "XKEYSCORE: NSA's Google for the World's Private Communications," *The Intercept*, July 1, 2015, https://theintercept.com/2015/07/01/nsas-google-worlds-private-communications/.

81   Daniel Fromson, "Weekend Reading: The N.S.A.'s Chief, Seasteading, Reputation Scrubbing," *The New Yorker*, June 22, 2013, https://www.newyorker.com/books/page-turner/weekend-reading-the-n-s-a-s-chief-seasteading-reputation-scrubbing; Laura Hautala and Alfred Ng, "WikiLeaks: Here's How the CIA Hacks Your Phones, TVs and PCs," CNET, March 8, 2017, https://www.cnet.com/news/wikileaks-cia-hacking-tools-phones-apple-samsung-microsoft-google/.

82   Peter Finn and Sari Horowitz, "U.S. Charges Snowden with Espionage," *The Washington Post*, June 21, 2013, https://www.washington-post.com/world/national-security/us-charges-snowden-with-espionage/2013/06/21/507497d8-dab1-11e2-a016-92547bf094cc_story.html.

83   Gellman, Tate, and Soltani, "In NSA-Intercepted Data, Those Not Targeted Far Outnumber the Foreigners Who Are."

84   "Barack Obama's Response to Bush's Final State of the Union," YouTube video, posted by "BarackObamadotcom," January 28, 2008, https://www.youtube.com/watch?v=cmNCALGHOC4.

85   Hearing Before the Committee on the Judiciary, United States Senate, 108th Congress (2003) (confirmation hearing on the nomination of James B. Comey Jr. to be deputy attorney general, Department of Justice).

86   Ibid.

87   "James Comey Fast Facts"; Hartung, *Prophets of War*, 219; Alexandra Stevenson and Matthew Goldstein, "Bridgewater Associates, World's Biggest Hedge Fund, Shakes Up Leadership," *The New York Times*, March 1, 2017, https://www.nytimes.com/2017/03/01/business/dealbook/ray-dalio-bridgewater-hedge-fund.html.

88   Garrett M. Graff, "Forged Under Fire—Bob Mueller and Jim Comey's Unusual Friendship," *The Washingtonian*, May 30, 2013, https://www.washingtonian.com/2013/05/30/forged-under-firebob-mueller-and-jim-comeys-unusual-friendship/; Dan Eggen and Paul Kane, "Gonzales Hospital Episode Detailed," *The Washington Post*, May 16, 2007, http://www.washingtonpost.com/wp-dyn/content/article/2007/05/15/AR2007051500864.html.

89   Graff, "Forged Under Fire—Bob Mueller and Jim Comey's Unusual Friendship."

90   Tim Weiner, "What Was James Comey Thinking?" *Esquire*, December 14, 2016, https://www.esquire.com/uk/culture/a12048/what-was-comey-thinking/.

91   Benjamin Wittes, "James Comey's Damning Testimony," Brookings, May 17, 2007, https://www.brookings.edu/opinions/james-comeys-damning-testimony/.

92   Ryan Lizza, "State of Deception," *The New Yorker*, December 16, 2013, https://www.newyorker.com/magazine/2013/12/16/state-of-deception.

93   Daniel Klaidman, "Is James Comey too Self-Righteous to Save Us from Terror?" *Newsweek*, June 5, 2013, http://www.newsweek.com/2013/06/05/james-comey-too-self-righteous-save-us-terror-237482.html.

94   Derek Hawkins, "Twice Robert Mueller Threatened to Resign from the FBI. Twice He Decided Not to," *The Washington Post*, May 18, 2017, https://www.washingtonpost.com/news/morning-mix/wp/2017/05/18/twice-robert-mueller-threatened-to-resign-from-the-fbi-twice-he-decided-not-to/ Graff, "Forged Under Fire—Bob Mueller and Jim Comey's Unusual Friendship."

95   Chris Edelson, "Opinion: Clinton Emails Give FBI's Comey a Second Chance to Influence a Presidential Election," *Market Watch*, October 30, 2016, https://www.marketwatch.com/story/clinton-emails-give-fbis-comey-a-second-chance-to-influence-a-presidential-election-2016-10-30.

96   Luis Sanchez, "FBI Chief Refuses to Deny Reports He Threatened to Resign Amid Pressure," *The Hill*, March 20, 2018, http://thehill.com/homenews/administration/379425-wray-refuses-to-deny-reports-he-threatened-to-resign-over-pressure-to; Garrett M. Graff, "What Christopher Wray Learned from the Last Two FBI Directors," *Wired*, June 7, 2017, https://www.wired.com/2017/06/christopher-wray-fbi-director/.

97   Graff, "Forged Under Fire—Bob Mueller and Jim Comey's Unusual Friendship"; Colleen Shalby, "Comey, Mueller and the Showdown at John Ashcroft's Hospital Bed," *The Los Angeles Times*, May 17, 2017, http://www.latimes.com/politics/la-na-pol-mueller-comey-ashcroft-domestic-surveillance-20170517-story.html.

98   "James Comey Testifies Before Senate Judiciary," YouTube video, posted by "frajam," May 15, 2007, https://www.youtube.com/watch?v=fm-m1W-H8L-4; "Senate Hearing on U.S. Attorney Firings," *The Washington Post*, transcript, May 15, 2007, http://www.washingtonpost.com/wp-dyn/content/article/2007/05/15/AR2007051501043.html.

99   Wittes, "James Comey's Damning Testimony"; Bethany McLean, "The True Story of the Comey Letter Debacle," *Vanity Fair*, February 21, 2017, https://www.vanityfair.com/news/2017/02/james-comey-fbi-director-letter.

100   Eggen and Kane, "Gonzales Hospital Episode Detailed"; Ruth Marcus, "A Tale of Two Comeys," *The Washington Post*, June 12, 2017, https://www.washingtonpost.com/opinions/a-tale-of-two-comeys/2017/06/12/4ffa9d8e-4fb5-11e7-b064-828ba60fbb98_story.html?utm_term=.8114ffdeb7dc.

101   James Risen and Michael S. Schmidt, "2004 Shutdown Shaped Reputation of Pick for F.B.I.," *The New York Times*, June 21, 2013, https://www.nytimes.com/2013/06/22/us/politics/obama-says-comey-will-strike-balance-on-security-and-privacy-at-fbi.html; Ruth Marcus, "A Tale of Two Comeys," *The Washington Post*, June 12, 2017, https://www.washingtonpost.com/opinions/a-tale-of-two-comeys/2017/06/12/4ffa9d8e-4fb5-11e7-b064-828ba60fbb98_story.html.

102   U.S. Department of Justice, U.S. Attorney's Office: Southern District of New York, "Deputy U.S. Attorney Richard Zabel Delivers Cybersecurity Keynote at Thomson Reuters Forum: 'Defending Corporations and Individuals in Government Investigations,'" press release, December 11, 2014, https://www.justice.gov/usao-sdny/speech/deputy-us-attorney-richard-zabel-delivers-cybersecurity-keynote-thomson-reuters.

103   Joseph Cox, "How Private Contractors Are Profiting from Government Surveillance," *Vice*, February 11, 2014, https://www.vice.com/sv/article/dp9gkv/NSA-private-companies-profit-from-surveillance; Shorrock, "5 Corporations Now Dominate Our Privatized Intelligence Industry."

104   Senate Select Committee on Intelligence, "Questionnaire for Completion by Presidential Nominees," accessed June 6, 2018, https://fas.org/irp/congress/2010_hr/072010clapper-quest.pdf.

105   Associated Press, "Obama Nominates Clapper to Head Spy Agencies," NBC News, June 5, 2010, http://www.nbcnews.com/id/37526849/ns/politics; "Clapper: I Worry About the Assault on Truth," YouTube video, posted by "CNN," August 1, 2017, https://www.youtube.com/watch?v=HbXdY6yCusk; Ken Dilanian and Corky Siemazko, "Director of National Intelligence James Clapper Resigns," NBC News, November 17, 2016, https://www.nbcnews.com/news/us-news/director-national-intelligence-james-clapper-resigns-n685301; Jonathan Turley, "Clapper's Actions Sure Do Look Like Political Manipulations," *The Hill*, April 28, 2018, http://thehill.com/opinion/white-house/385351-clappers-actions-sure-look-like-political-manipulations.

106   Jonathan Turley, "James Clapper's Perjury, and Why DC Made Men Don't Get Charged for Lying to Congress," *USA Today*, January 19, 2018, https://www.usatoday.com/story/opinion/2018/01/19/james-clappers-perjury-dc-made-men-dont-get-charged-lying-congress-jonathan-turley-column/1045991001/; Sean Davis, "Declassified Congressional Report: James Clapper Lied About Dossier Leaks to CNN," *The Federalist*, April 27, 2018, http://thefederalist.com/2018/04/27/house-intel-report-james-clapper-lied-dossier-leaks-cnn/.

107   Turley, "James Clapper's Perjury, and Why DC Made Men Don't Get Charged for Lying to Congress"; Brian Fung, "Darrell Issa: James Clapper Lied to Congress About NSA and Should be Fired," *The Washington Post*, January 27, 2014, https://www.washingtonpost.com/news/the-switch/wp/2014/01/27/darrell-issa-james-clapper-lied-to-congress-about-nsa-and-should-be-fired/.

108   James Comey, financial disclosure, 2013, https://www.fbcoverup.com/docs/library/2013-06-19-Comey-James-B-OGE-Form-278-New-Entrant-Financial-Disclosure-Year-2012-submitted-06-19-2013-Office-of-Government-Ethics-Jun-19-2013.pdf. Note: sourced information only from Comey's OGE Form 278.

[109] "Revolving Door," accessed on April 13, 2018, https://www.opensecrets. org/revolving/; U.S. Office of Government Ethics, public financial disclosure reports, https://extapps2.oge.gov/201/Presiden.nsf/PAS%20Index? OpenView.

[110] Dan Alexander, "How the Clintons Have Made $230 Million Since Leaving the White House," *Forbes*, October 13, 2015, https://www.forbes. com/sites/danalexander/2015/10/13/how-the-clintons-made-more-than-230-million-after-leaving-the-white-house/#44732d4b2ae3.

[111] Caroline Howe, "EXCLUSIVE: How Besieged FBI Director James Comey Lived Like a King in One of America's Wealthiest Towns (Home to Martha Stewart, Paul Newman and Harvey Weinstein) but Now Can't Unload His $3 Million Estate," *Daily Mail*, November 8, 2016, http:// www.dailymail.co.uk/news/article-3914350/Besieged-FBI-director-James-Comey-lived-like-king-one-America-s-wealthiest-towns-home-Martha-Stewart-Paul-Newman-Harvey-Weinstein-t-unload-3-million-estate.html; Author's note: The Office of Governmental Ethics lists at least 12 types of assets that individuals are not required to disclose. Therefore, Comey's real estate assets considered "residence" (which could include vacation homes) is not reported; United States Office of Government Ethics, "Public Financial Disclosure Guide: Part 6: General Guidance," accessed June 13, 2018, https://www.oge.gov/Web/278eGuide.nsf/Resources/ Part+6:+General+guidance.

[112] U.S. Securities and Exchange Commission, "Comey, James B"; Lockheed Martin Corp., Comey James B, Form 4 (filed February 4, 2010).

[113] "Lockheed Martin Corp.," Market Watch, accessed June 8, 2018, https:// www.marketwatch.com/investing/stock/lmt; Author's note: Comey's 40,400 options shares at $74.89 per share = $3,025,556; If 40,400 shares exercised/sold on February 15, 2018 ($361.00/share) that would amount to $14,584,400—Net gain would be $11,558,844.

[114] See Chapter 2 endnote 29 for an additional breakdown of 2009 stock options potential; U.S. Securities and Exchange Commission, "Comey, James B."

[115] Anne Marie Squeo, "Deputy Attorney General Comey to Take Post at Lockheed Martin," *The Wall Street Journal*, August 4, 2005, https://www. wsj.com/articles/SB112311824367904610; Robert J. Stevens, Lockheed Martin Corporation, schedule 14A, March 12, 2010.

[116] Federal Bureau of Investigation, "FBI Announces Award of Sentinel Contract," press release, March 16, 2006, https://archives.fbi.gov/archives/ news/pressrel/press-releases/fbi-announces-award-of-sentinel-contract; Michael Cooney, "FBI Hits Back at Criticism of $450 Million Sentinel Computer Overhaul," *Computer World UK*, October 25, 2010, https:// www.computerworlduk.com/security/fbi-hits-back-at-criticism-of-450-million-sentinel-computer-overhaul-3245700/.

117   U.S. Department of Justice, Office of the Inspector General, "Audit of the Status of the Federal Bureau of Investigation's Sentinel Program," September 2014, https://oig.justice.gov/reports/2014/a1431.pdf.

118   Federal Bureau of Investigation, "FBI Announces Contract Award for Next Generation Identification System," press release, February 12, 2008, https://archives.fbi.gov/archives/news/pressrel/press-releases/fbi-announces-contract-award-for-next-generation-identification-system; "Lockheed Wins FBI Contract Potentially Worth $1 Billion," Reuters, February 12, 2008, https://www.reuters.com/article/us-lockheed-fbi/lockheed-wins-fbi-contract-potentially-worth-1-billion-idUSN1228318120080212; Hubler, "Lockheed Team Rolls Out Next Gen ID System for FBI"; Jason Miller, "IBM Protests Lockheed's FBI Win," *Washington Technology*, February 29, 2008, https://washingtontechnology.com/articles/2008/02/29/ibm-protests-lockheeds-fbi-win.aspx; John W. Whitehead, "Smile, the Government Is Watching: Next Generation Identification," The Rutherford Institute, September 17, 2012, https://www.rutherford.org/publications_resources/john_whiteheads_commentary/smile_the_government_is_watching_next_generation_identification.

119   "Mueller, Robert," employment history, accessed April 6, 2018, https://www.opensecrets.org/revolving/rev_summary.php?id=80227.

120   Fisher and Horwitz, "Mueller and Trump: Born to Wealth, Raised to Lead. Then, Sharply Different Choices."

121   James Rowley, "Washington Today: Former Justice Official Returns to War on Crime," Associated Press, August 23, 1996, https://www.nexis.com/docview/getDocForCuiReq?lni=3SJ4-J190-0006-H3V3&csi=280434&oc=00240&perma=true.

122   "Mueller Nominated FBI Director," CNN, July 5, 2001, http://www.cnn.com/2001/LAW/07/05/fbi.director/; Howard Mintz, "U.S. Attorney Quits Amid Criticism, Resigns a Year After Losing Judgeship Bid," *San Jose Mercury News*, July 24, 1998, https://www.nexis.com/docview/getDocForCuiReq?lni=471D-TJB0-01K4-D4CT&csi=280434&oc=00240&perma=true; Harriet Chiang, "U.S. Attorney Yamaguchi Announces Resignation," SFGATE, July 24, 1998, https://www.sfgate.com/news/article/U-S-Attorney-Yamaguchi-Announces-Resignation-3000301.php.

123   Confirmation hearing on the nomination of Robert S. Mueller, III to be director of the Federal Bureau of Investigation, hearing before the Subcommittee on the Judiciary, United States Senate, 110th Congress (2001), S. Hrg. 107-514, https://www.congress.gov/107/chrg/shrg80335/CHRG-107shrg80335.htm; Jackie Calmes, "Obama Seeks to Extend Mueller's Term as F.B.I. Director," *The New York Times*, May 12, 2011, https://thecaucus.blogs.nytimes.com/2011/05/12/obama-seeks-extension-of-muellers-term-as-fbi-director/?mtrref=thecaucus.blogs.nytimes.com&gwh=974BD8F0A9A40B47344A5FA2377946C1&gwt=pay.

[124] Olivia B. Waxman, "FBI Directors Are Appointed for 10-Year Terms. Here's Why," *TIME*, May 10, 2017, http://time.com/4774610/james-comey-fbi-term-limit/: "Privacy and Consumer Protection," WilmerHale, accessed April 4, 2018, https://www.wilmerhale.com/cybersecurity-privacy-and-communications/privacy/; "Jason C. Chipman," WilmerHale, accessed April 4, 2018, https://www.wilmerhale.com/Jason_Chipman/; "Former US Deputy Attorney General Joins HSBC Board," HSBC, January 30, 2013, https://www.hsbc.com/news-and-insight/media-resources/media-releases/2013/former-us-deputy-attorney-general-joins-hsbc-board; Matea Gold and Rosalind S. Helderman, "Justice Dept. to Review Possible Ethics Conflicts Involving Mueller's Former Law Firm," *The Washington Post*, May 18, 2017, https://www.washingtonpost.com/politics/justice-department-will-review-possible-ethics-conflicts-involving-muellers-former-law-firm/2017/05/18/fff63f00-3bfa-11e7-a058-ddb-b23c75d82_story.html; Celia Ampel, "Bank of America to Pay $3.4M Whistleblower Settlement Over Foreclosure Practices," *Daily Business Review*, January 29, 2018, https://www.law.com/dailybusinessreview/sites/dailybusinessreview/2018/01/29/bank-of-america-to-pay-3-4m-whistleblower-settlement-over-foreclosure-practices/.

[125] Sam Reisman, "Mueller Made $3.4M at WilmerHale Before Russia Probe," Law360, August 9, 2017, https://www.law360.com/articles/952601/mueller-made-3-4m-at-wilmerhale-before-russia-probe; Booz Allen Hamilton, "Booz Allen Confirms Illegal Attack on Information Technology System," press release, July 12, 2011, http://investors.boozallen.com/releasedetail.cfm?releaseid=745676.

[126] Johnson and Madhani, "Obama to Pick Comey to Replace Mueller at FBI"; David Ingram, "FBI Says U.S. Will Hold Snowden Responsible for NSA Leaks," Reuters, June 13, 2013, https://www.reuters.com/article/us-usa-security/fbi-says-u-s-will-hold-snowden-responsible-for-nsa-leaks-idUSBRE95910O20130613.

[127] Robert S. Mueller, financial disclosure, 2016, https://www.politico.com/f/?id=0000015d-c404-d494-a77f-e6163c3a0001; Mary Clarke Jalonick, Barbara Ortutay, and David Hamilton, "Hardly 'Friends': Zuckerberg Fends Off Senators on Privacy," Associated Press, April 11, 2018, https://apnews.com/75f8ec6489b340d9a1ce723502fe0ad2; Glenn Greenwald and Ewen MacAskill, "NSA Prism Program Taps in to User Data of Apple, Google, and Others," *The Guardian*, June 7, 2013, http://www.theguardian.com/world/2013/jun/06/us-tech-giants-nsa-data; Cathaleen Chen, "The Future of Retail Is… Surveillance?" *TheStreet*, January 17, 2018, https://www.thestreet.com/story/14451446/1/the-future-of-retail-nrf2018.html.

[128] Gerstein and Samuelsohn, "Special Counsel Robert Mueller's Finances Go Public"; Robert S. Mueller, financial disclosure, 2016; Nuclear Energy Institute, "Nuclear Fuel Supply Forum: Participant List," July 31, 2012,

https://resources.nei.org/conferences/NFSF/Parts%20List.pdf; Nuclear Energy Institute, "Ex Officio to Executive Committee," May 29, 2018, https://www.nei.org/CorporateSite/media/filefolder/Membership/board-list.pdf.

129 Gerstein and Samuelsohn, "Special Counsel Robert Mueller's Finances Go Public"; Robert S. Mueller, financial disclosure, 2016.

130 Matthew Rosenberg, "At Booz Allen, a Vast U.S. Spy Operation, Run for Private Profit," *The New York Times*, October 6, 2016, https://www.nytimes.com/2016/10/07/us/booz-allen-hamilton-nsa.html.

131 Scott Shane, Matt Apuzzo, and Jo Becker, "Trove of Stolen Data is Said to Include Top-Secret U.S. Hacking Tools," *The New York Times*, October 19, 2016, https://www.nytimes.com/2016/10/20/us/harold-martin-nsa.html.

132 Booz Allen Hamilton, "Booz Allen Hamilton Announces External Review," press release, October 27, 2016, http://files.shareholder.com/downloads/AMDA-1HZQ6C/6123097083x0x914267/CC18388D-7956-4AD0-A5B6-6933F09503E6/BAH_News_2016_10_27_Financial.pdf; Christian Davenport, "Booz Allen Hires Former FBI Director to Conduct Security Review," *The Washington Post*, October 27, 2016, https://www.washingtonpost.com/business/economy/booz-allen-hires-for-mer-fbi-director-to-conduct-security-review/2016/10/27/15d8ee0c-9c92-11e6-b3c9-f662adaa0048_story.html.

133 Jaikumar Vijayan, "Booz Allen Fires Snowden, Leaker of NSA Spy Docs," *Computerworld*, June 11, 2013, https://www.computerworld.com/article/2497685/data-privacy/booz-allen-fires-snowden--leaker-of-nsa-spy-docs.html; "NSA Spying," Electronic Frontier Foundation, accessed June 13, 2018, https://www.eff.org/nsa-spying; Duncan Campbell, "GCHQ and Me: My Life Unmasking British Eavesdroppers," *The Intercept*, August 3, 2015, https://theintercept.com/2015/08/03/life-unmasking-british-eaves-droppers/; Glenn Greenwald, "Obama's New FBI Chief Approved Bush's NSA Warrantless Wiretapping Scheme," *The Guardian*, May 30, 2013, https://www.theguardian.com/commentisfree/2013/may/30/james-com-ey-fbi-bush-nsa; Michael J. Sniffen, "Despite FBI Abuses, Mueller Defends Patriot Act," *The New York Sun*, March 28, 2007, https://www.nysun.com/national/despite-fbi-abuses-mueller-defends-patriot-act/51296/; "Snowden Leaks Caused US 'Significant Harm'—Mueller," BBC News, June 14, 2013, http://www.bbc.com/news/world-us-canada-22884566.

134 Harvey Silverglate, "How Robert Mueller Tried to Entrap Me," WGBH, October 17, 2017, https://news.wgbh.org/2017/10/17/sil-verglate-how-robert-mueller-tried-entrap-me; Jennifer Smith, "How Mueller Tried to Entrap Me: Lawyer Who Went to Princeton with Special Prosecutor Describes His 'Shady' Tactics and Eagerness to Convict As He Warns Russia Probe Should Be Taken 'With a Grain of Salt,'" *Daily Mail*, October 21, 2017, http://www.dailymail.co.uk/news/article-5003775/Boston-lawyer-tells-Mueller-tried-entrap-him.html.

135   Silverglate, "How Robert Mueller Tried to Entrap Me"; Lynn Parramore, "Maybe Jeffrey MacDonald Was Innocent After All," *Salon*, November 30, 2012, https://www.salon.com/2012/11/30/maybe_jeffrey_macdonald_was_innocent_after_all/; Andrew Anthony, "The Fort Bragg Murders: Is Jeffrey MacDonald Innocent?" *The Guardian*, April 13, 2013, https://www.theguardian.com/film/2013/apr/14/jeffrey-macdonald-murder-errol-morris; Amelia McDonell-Parry, "5 Convicted Murderers Who Might Actually Be Innocent," *Rolling Stone*, January 10, 2018, https://www.rollingstone.com/culture/pictures/5-convicted-murderers-who-might-actually-be-innocent-w508604/jeffrey-macdonald-w508611.

136   William Safire, "Essay; B.C.C.I.: Justice Delayed," *The New York Times*, archives, 1991, https://www.nytimes.com/1991/07/25/opinion/essay-bcci-justice-delayed.html.

137   Howard Schneider, "Clandestination: Arkansas," *The Washington Post*, July 21, 1994, https://www.washingtonpost.com/archive/lifestyle/1994/07/21/clandestination-arkansas/e2c39f46-602b-4f4c-91fd-1ce94c743d69/?utm_term=.b8517acf204f; Maureen Orth, "The Face of Scandal," *Vanity Fair*, August 14, 2008, https://www.vanityfair.com/news/2001/06/rich200106; Stephen Pizzo, "Family Value$," *Mother Jones*, September 1, 1992, https://www.motherjones.com/politics/1992/09/family-value/.

138   Steve Lohr, "Agent Tells of Failures on B.C.C.I.," *The New York Times*, November 22, 1991, https://www.nytimes.com/1991/11/22/business/agent-tells-of-failures-on-bcci.html; "BCCI and Law Enforcement: The Justice Department," Federation of American Scientists, accessed June 13, 2018, https://fas.org/irp/congress/1992_rpt/bcci/08just.htm.

139   Jessica Reaves, "Pardongate Play-by-Play," *TIME*, February 27, 2001, http://content.time.com/time/nation/article/0,8599,100795,00.html.

140   Evan Perez, "Why Comey Stood Alone: Inside the FBI's Announcement," CNN, July 6, 2016, https://www.cnn.com/2016/07/05/politics/james-comey-fbi-hillary-clinton-decision/index.html.

141   Ronald Brownstein and Geraldine Baum, "The Lobbyist Behind Rich's Pardon," *The Los Angeles Times*, February 1, 2001, http://articles.latimes.com/2001/feb/10/news/mn-23711; "An Indefensible Pardon," *The New York Times*, January 24, 2001, https://www.nytimes.com/2001/01/24/opinion/an-indefensible-pardon.html.

142   Carl M. Cannon, "Comey, Mueller Bungled Big Anthrax Case Together," *Orange County Register*, May 21, 2017, https://www.ocregister.com/2017/05/21/comey-mueller-bungled-big-anthrax-case-together/.

143   David Freed, "The Wrong Man," *The Atlantic*, May 2010, https://www.theatlantic.com/magazine/archive/2010/05/the-wrong-man/308019/; "FBI Used Aggressive Tactics in 'Anthrax Killer' Investigation," Fox News, August 5, 2008, http://www.foxnews.com/story/2008/08/05/fbi-used-aggressive-tactics-in-anthrax-killer-investigation.html; "Anthrax 'Person of

Interest' Sues Ashcroft, FBI," CNN, August 27, 2003, http://www.cnn.com/2003/LAW/08/26/lawsuit.hatfill/.

144 Kevin Cullen, "One Lingering Question for FBI Director Robert Mueller," *The Boston Globe*, n.d., http://archive.boston.com/news/local/massachusetts/articles/2011/07/24/a_lingering_question_for_the_fbis_director/?page=1; Robert Barnes and Paul Lewis, "FBI Must Pay $102 Million in Mob Case," *The Washington Post*, July 27, 2007, http://www.washingtonpost.com/wp-dyn/content/article/2007/07/27/AR2007072700282.html; Patrick Radden Keefe, "Assets and Liabilities," *The New Yorker*, September 21, 2015, https://www.newyorker.com/magazine/2015/09/21/assets-and-liabilities.

145 Howie Carr, "Not So Honorable: Docs Show Mueller's FBI Denied Justice to Four Innocent Men," *The Daily Caller*, June 5, 2018, http://dailycaller.com/2018/06/05/mueller-fbi-wrongful-conviction-case/; U.S. Department of Justice, Federal Bureau of Investigation, "Letter from Charles S. Prouty, Special Agent In Charge, by Frank M. Davis, Chief Division Counsel, to Nicole K. Cheries," May 9, 2002, http://dailycaller.com/wp-content/uploads/2018/06/Mueller-directs-resp-to-Greco-posthumous-pardon.pdf; Barnes and Lewis, "FBI Must Pay $102 Million in Mob Case"; Cullen, "One Lingering Question for FBI Director Robert Mueller."

146 Michael S. Schmidt, "Former Bush Official Said to Be Obama Pick to Lead F.B.I.," *The New York Times*, May 29, 2013, https://www.nytimes.com/2013/05/30/us/politics/obama-to-pick-james-b-comey-to-lead-fbi.html.

147 Michael Maiello, "We Owe Martha Stewart an Apology," *The Daily Beast*, May 22, 2015, https://www.thedailybeast.com/we-owe-martha-stewart-an-apology.

148 Brian Ross, Rhonda Schwartz, and Joseph Rhee, "FBI, SEC, Federal Reserve 'Failed to Connect the Dots' to Wall Street," ABC News, October 6, 2008, https://abcnews.go.com/Blotter/story?id=5962615&page=1; Marian Wang, "Why No Financial Crisis Prosecutions? Ex-Justice Official Says It's Just too Hard," *ProPublica*, December 6, 2011, https://www.propublica.org/article/why-no-financial-crisis-prosecutions-official-says-its-just-too-hard.

149 Jesse Eisinger, "Why Only One Top Banker Went to Jail for the Financial Crisis," *The New York Times*, April 30, 2014, https://www.nytimes.com/2014/05/04/magazine/only-one-top-banker-jail-financial-crisis.html.

150 David Dayen, "Eric Holder's Longtime Excuse for ot Prosecuting Banks Just Crashed and Burned," *The Intercept*, July 12, 2016, https://theintercept.com/2016/07/12/eric-holders-longtime-excuse-for-not-prosecuting-banks-just-crashed-and-burned/; Lee Fang, "Eric Holder Returns As Hero to Law Firm That Lobbies for Big Banks," *The Intercept*, July 6, 2015, https://theintercept.com/2015/07/06/eric-holder-returns-law-firm-lobbies-big-banks/.

151 Solomon and Spann, "FBI Uncovered Russian Bribery Plot Before Obama Administration Approved Controversial Nuclear Deal with Moscow."

152 "Alerting GOR of Delivery of Seized HEU During September 21 FBI Director's Trip to Moscow," Wikileaks, August 17, 2009, https://wikileaks.org/plusd/cables/09STATE85588_a.html.

153 Joshua Philipp, "As FBI Chief, Special Counsel Robert Mueller Watched and Allowed Clinton Deals with Russia," *The Epoch Times*, October 23, 2017, https://www.theepochtimes.com/as-fbi-chief-special-counsel-robert-mueller-watched-and-allowed-clinton-deals-with-russia_2339883.html; Simon Shuster, "Inside the Uranium Underworld: Dark Secrets, Dirty Bombs," *TIME*, April 10, 2017, http://time.com/4728293/uranium-underworld-dark-secrets-dirty-bombs/.

154 Chris York, "Wikileaks Says Robert Mueller Gave Russia Nuclear Material—But That's Not the Whole Story," *HuffPost*, July 30, 2017, https://www.huffingtonpost.co.uk/entry/wikileaks-russia_uk_597df631e4b02a4ebb75ffec.

155 "FBI Director Nomination Hearing," C-SPAN, video clip, July 9, 2013, https://www.c-span.org/video/?313811-1/cmte-hears-fbi-director-nominee-james-comey&start=2910.

Chapter 5: Foreign Intelligence and Surveillance Abuse

1 "The Black Chamber," NSA.gov, May 3, 2016, https://www.nsa.gov/about/cryptologic-heritage/center-cryptologic-history/pearl-harbor-review/black-chamber.shtml; "Electronic Surveillance," Cornell Law, accessed June 13, 2018, https://www.law.cornell.edu/wex/electronic_surveillance.

2 "FBI Founded," *History*, July 26, accessed June 14, 2018, https://www.history.com/this-day-in-history/fbi-founded; "ACLU History: Wiretapping: A New Kind of 'Search and Seizure,'" American Civil Liberties Union, accessed June 14, 2018, https://www.aclu.org/other/aclu-history-wiretapping-new-kind-search-and-seizure.

3 Rowley, "No, Robert Mueller and James Comey Aren't Heroes."

4 Andrew C. McCarthy, "House Memo Details Use of Steele Dossier to Spy on Trump Campaign Adviser," *National Review*, February 2, 2018, https://www.nationalreview.com/2018/02/republican-house-releases-fisa-memo-confirms-steele-dossier-suspicions/; Sharyl Attkisson, "Justice Dept. and FBI Personnel Changes Amid Probes," Sharyl Attkisson's website, February 11, 2018, https://sharylattkisson.com/2018/02/11/justice-dept-and-fbi-personnel-changes-amid-probes/; Sharyl Attkisson, "Investigating the Investigators at DOJ and FBI," Sharyl Attkisson's website, December 25, 2017, https://sharylattkisson.com/2017/12/25/investigating-the-investigators-at-doj-and-fbi/.

The names are:
FBI: James Comey, director (fired)

FBI: Andrew McCabe, deputy director (fired)
FBI: James Rybicki, chief of staff (resigned*)(fired?)
FBI: James Baker, general counsel (resigned)
FBI: Mike Kortan, assistant director for public affairs (resigned)
FBI: Peter Strzok, counterintelligence expert (demoted; escorted from building on June 14,2018)
FBI: Lisa Page, attorney (demoted; resigned)
FBI: Josh Campbell, special assistant to James Comey (resigned)
FBI: James Turgal, executive assistant director (resigned)
FBI: Greg Bower, assistant director for office of congressional affairs (resigned)
FBI: Michael Steinbach, executive assistant director for national security branch (resigned)
FBI: John Giacalone, executive assistant director of national security branch (resigned)
DOJ: Sally Yates, deputy attorney general (fired)
DOJ: Bruce Ohr, associate deputy attorney general (twice demoted)
DOJ: David Laufman, counterintelligence chief (resigned)
DOJ: Rachel Brand, deputy attorney general (resigned)
DOJ: Trisha Beth Anderson (resigned)
DOJ: John P. Carlin, assistant attorney general, National Security Division (resigned)
DOJ: Peter Kadzik, assistant attorney general, congressional liaison (resigned)
DOJ: Mary McCord, acting assistant attorney general, National Security Division (resigned)
DOJ: Matthew Axelrod, principal assistant to deputy attorney general (resigned*)
DOJ: Preet Bharara, U.S. attorney, SDNY (fired)
DOJ: Sharon McGowan, civil rights division (resigned)
DOJ: Diana Flynn, litigation director for LGBTQ civil rights (resigned)
DOJ: Vanita Gupta, civil rights division (resigned)
DOJ: Joel McElvain, assistant branch director of the civil division (resigned)
*Forced out

5 Colleen Shalby, "The Last President to Fire an FBI Director? Bill Clinton," *The Los Angeles Times*, May 9, 2017, http://www.latimes.com/politics/washington/la-na-essential-washington-updates-last-fbi-director-to-get-fired-before-1494368709-htmlstory.html.

6 Nicolas Fandos, "Despite Mueller's Push, House Republicans Declare No Evidence of Collusion," *The New York Times*, March 12, 2018, https://www.nytimes.com/2018/03/12/us/politics/house-intelligence-trump-russia.html.

7 Ed Rogers, "The Media is Ignoring Ties Between the Clinton Campaign and Russians," *The Washington Post*, February 13, 2018, https://www.

washingtonpost.com/blogs/post-partisan/wp/2018/02/13/the-media-is-ignoring-ties-between-the-clinton-campaign-and-russians/?utm_term=.d6b963e686ae.

[8] United States Senate, Select Committee on Presidential Campaign Activities (The Watergate Committee), February 7, 1973, https://www.senate.gov/artandhistory/history/common/investigations/Watergate.htm; Senate congressional record (1973), https://www.senate.gov/artandhistory/history/common/investigations/pdf/Watergate_ResolutionDebate1973.pdf.

[9] An Act to Authorize Electronic Surveillance to Obtain Foreign Intelligence Information, S. 1566, 95th Congress (1977), https://www.congress.gov/bill/95th-congress/senate-bill/1566/actions.

[10] Ted Gottfried, *Homeland Security Versus Constitutional Rights* (Twenty-First Century Books: Minneapolis, 2003).

[11] Bamford, "Every Move You Make."

[12] Ibid.

[13] Tim Weiner, "What Was James Comey Thinking?" *Esquire*, December 13, 2016, https://www.esquire.com/news-politics/a51446/what-was-comey-thinking/.

[14] Ibid; Hearings before the Select Committee to Study Governmental Operations with Respect to Intelligence, 94th Congress (1975: vol. 2), https://www.intelligence.senate.gov/sites/default/files/94intelligence_activities_II.pdf.

[15] John M. Crewdson, "Documents Show Nixon Approved Partly 'Illegal' '70 Security Plan: Laird Takes Ehrlichman White House Job," *The New York Times*, June 7, 1973, https://www.nytimes.com/1973/06/07/archives/documents-show-nixon-approved-par-tlyillegal-70-security-plan-laird.html.

[16] Weiner, "What Was James Comey Thinking?"

[17] Federal Bureau of Investigation, "Watergate (Summary), Part 1 of 2," File No. 139-4089, July 23, 1974, https://vault.fbi.gov/watergate/watergate-summary-part-01-of-02; Joseph Finder, "Call the Plumbers," *The New York Times*, archives, November 16, 1997, https://archive.nytimes.com/www.nytimes.com/books/97/11/16/reviews/971116.16findert.html?mcubz=0.

NYT Excerpt:

"Arguably the scandal began in 1971 with the publication of the Pentagon Papers, a classified 7,000-page Defense Department document on the origins and conduct of the Vietnam War that had been obtained by The New York Times. Nixon saw the publication as evidence of a great liberal Democratic Establishment plot against him. And his inability to do anything about it triggered a towering rage.

"We're up against an enemy, a conspiracy," he thunders to Haldeman and Henry Kissinger on July 1, 1971, in a newly published transcript. "They're using any means. We are going to use any means. Is that clear?'" This included dispatching a secret White House team, "the Plumbers," to dig up dirt on Daniel Ellsberg, the former Kissinger aide who said he was the one who had leaked the Pentagon Papers to the press."

Author's note: The fact Nixon suffered damaging (and possibly illegal) leaks, such as the infamous "Pentagon papers," does not mean that the Plumbers were a justified retaliation. However, it does mitigate the Watergate scandal to a degree insofar as the Plumbers were a defensive operation rather than an offensive one. Compare Nixon's Watergate operation with Obama's so-called "spy-gate" operation of Trump (who had nothing to do with any leaks) and it's easy to see why some find Watergate less offensive.

[18]   William M. Welch, "Hillary Clinton Recalls Role As Watergate Lawyer: 'It Was Unbelievable,'" Associated Press, May 25, 1992, https://www. apnews.com/9aac7305f7f7a407204cec2f5afb3a43; George Lardner Jr., "Chappaquiddick," *Washington Post*, November 11, 1979, https://www. washingtonpost.com/archive/politics/1979/11/11/chappaquiddick/ ca82c55f-9187-415b-88a1-be621ceb57c2/; Walter Karp, "The Hour of the Founders," *American Heritage* 35, no. 4 (June/July 1984), https://www. americanheritage.com/content/i-hour-founders.

[19]   Julian Zelizer, "Russiagate: What Kind of Scandal?" CNN, February 20, 2017, https://www.cnn.com/2017/02/19/opinions/russiagate-scandal-zelizer-opinion/index.html.

[20]   Weiner, "What Was James Comey Thinking?"

[21]   Seymour M. Hersh, "Kissinger and Nixon in the White House," *The Atlantic*, May 1982, https://www.theatlantic.com/magazine/archive/1982/05/kissinger-and-nixon-in-the-white-house/308778/; Matthew M. Aid and William Burr, "Secret Cold War Documents Reveal NSA Spied on Senators," *Foreign Policy*, September 25, 2013, https://foreignpolicy.com/2013/09/25/ secret-cold-war-documents-reveal-nsa-spied-on-senators/.

[22]   Laura K. Donohue, "NSA Surveillance May Be Legal – But It's Unconstitutional," *The Washington Post*, June 21, 2013, https://www.washingtonpost.com/opinions/nsa-surveillance-may-be-legal--but-its-unconstitutional/2013/06/21/b9ddec20-d44d-11e2-a73e-826d299ff459_story. html.

[23]   "Electronic Surveillance"; "Fourth Amendment," Cornell Law, accessed June 13, 2018, https://www.law.cornell.edu/constitution/fourth_amendment.

[24]   "Writs of Assistance 1761–72," Amendment IV, University of Chicago, accessed April 4, 2018, http://press-pubs.uchicago.edu/founders/documents/amendIVs2.html; James M. Farrell, "The Child Independence Is Born: James Otis and Writs of Assistance," in *Rhetoric, Independence and Nationhood* (Michigan State University Press: Michigan, 2014), https://scholars.unh.edu/cgi/viewcontent.cgi?referer=https://www.google. com/&httpsredir=1&article=1004&context=comm_facpub.

[25]   Michael Mink, "James Otis' Fiery Rhetoric Sparked America's Revolutionary Fervor," *Investor's Business Daily*, July 3, 2017,

https://www.investors.com/news/management/leaders-and-success/james-otis-fiery-rhetoric-sparked-americas-revolutionary-fervor/.

[26] U.S. Constitution's Fourth and Fifth Amendments.

[27] "14th Amendment," Cornell Law, accessed April 4, 2018, https://www.law.cornell.edu/constitution/amendmentxiv; "Incorporation Doctrine," Cornell Law, accessed June 14, 2018, https://www.law.cornell.edu/wex/incorporation_doctrine.

[28] "Fruit of the Poisonous Tree," Cornell Law, accessed April 4, 2018, https://www.law.cornell.edu/wex/fruit_of_the_poisonous_tree.

[29] "Probable Cause: Definition," Cornell Law, accessed April 4, 2018, https://www.law.cornell.edu/wex/probable_cause; U.S. Constitution's Fourth Amendment.

[30] "Why the FISA Amendments Act Is Unconstitutional," American Civil Liberties Union, accessed April 4, 2018, https://www.aclu.org/sites/default/files/images/nsaspying/asset_upload_file578_35950.pdf.

[31] Federal Bureau of Investigation, "Testimony: Global Threats to the U.S. and the FBI's Response," February 16, 2005, https://archives.fbi.gov/archives/news/testimony/global-threats-to-the-u.s.-and-the-fbis-response-1; Justice Information Sharing, "The Foreign Intelligence Surveillance Act of 1978," 50 U.S.C. §§ 1801-11, 1821-29, 1841-46, 1861-62, 1871, accessed April 6, 2018, https://it.ojp.gov/PrivacyLiberty/authorities/statutes/1286.

[32] Mark Hosenball, "NSA Collected Americans' Phone Records Despite Law Change: Report," Reuters, May 2, 2017, https://www.reuters.com/article/us-usa-security-surveillance/nsa-collected-americans-phone-records-de-spite-law-change-report-idUSKBN17Y2LS.

[33] It is important to point out, Barsoomian actively worked against the interests of transparency by opposing disclosure in FOIA suits that sought to reveal various pervasive government abuses thereby protecting surveillance state interests. And if that's the case, she worked against the American people. Given Rod Rosenstein's pattern of stonewalling, he and his wife seem to be well suited for one another.

Electronic Privacy Information Center v. Department of Justice, et al., Civil Action No. 00-1849 JR, https://epic.org/privacy/carnivore/schedule_motion.pdf; "FBI Ditches Carnivore Surveillance System," Fox News, January 18, 2005, http://www.foxnews.com/story/2005/01/18/fbi-ditch-es-carnivore-surveillance-system.html; Gregory Smith v. U.S. Department of Justice, No. 00-5211, 251 F.3d 1047 (D.C. Cir. 2001), https://openjurist.org/251/f3d/1047/gregory-smith-v-u-s-department-of-justice; Judicial Watch, Inc. v. F.B.I., No. Civ.A.01-0248 (2002), https://www.leagle.com/decision/2002219190fsupp2d291217.

[34] "FAQ: What You Need to Know About the NSA's Surveillance Programs," *ProPublica*, August 5, 2013, https://www.propublica.org/article/nsa-da-ta-collection-faq; Jenna McLaughlin, "NSA's Epic Fail: Spy Agency Pays Lawyers That Sue It," *The Intercept*, August 5, 2015, https://theintercept.

com/2015/08/05/ironic-way-privacy-groups-get-bankrolled-nsa/; "Court Rejects Domestic Spying Appeal," *USA Today*, February 19, 2008, http://usatoday30.usatoday.com/news/washington/2008-02-19-domestic-spying_N.htm.

35   Ashley Gorski, "Court Chooses to Ignore Overwhelming Evidence of NSA's Mass Internet Spying," American Civil Liberties Union, October 24, 2015, https://www.aclu.org/blog/national-security/privacy-and-surveillance/court-chooses-ignore-overwhelming-evidence-nsas-mass; American Civil Liberties Union and American Civil Liberties Union Foundation v. United States Department of Justice, No. 13 CIV 7347, United States District Court, Southern District of New York, October 17, 2013, https://www.aclu.org/sites/default/files/assets/faa_notice_foia_complaint_-_stamped.pdf.

36   Erika Eichelberger "FISA Court Has Rejected .03 Percent of All Government Surveillance Requests," *Mother Jones*, June 10, 2013, https://www.motherjones.com/crime-justice/2013/06/fisa-court-nsa-spying-opinion-reject-request/.

37   David Ruiz, "EFF and 23 Civil Liberties Organizations Demand Transparency on NSA Domestic Phone Record Surveillance," Electronic Frontier Foundation, June 1, 2018, https://www.eff.org/deeplinks/2018/05/eff-and-x-civil-liberties-organizations-demand-transparency-nsa-domestic-phone.

38   "Rule 41. Search and Seizure," Cornell Law, accessed June 14, 2018, https://www.law.cornell.edu/rules/frcrmp/rule_41; "Katz v. United States," 389 U.S. 347 (1967), Cornell Law, https://www.law.cornell.edu/supremecourt/text/389/347.

39   Glenn Greenwald, "Fisa Court Oversight: A Look Inside a Secret and Empty Process," *The Guardian*, June 18, 2013, https://www.theguardian.com/commentisfree/2013/jun/19/fisa-court-oversight-process-secrecy; Ezra Klein, "Did You Know John Roberts Is Also Chief Justice of the NSA's Surveillance State?" *The Washington Post*, July 5, 2013, https://www.washingtonpost.com/news/wonk/wp/2013/07/05/did-you-know-john-roberts-is-also-chief-justice-of-the-nsas-surveillance-state/.

40   Conor Clarke, "Is the Foreign Intelligence Surveillance Court Really a Rubber Stamp?" *Stanford Law Review*, February 2014, https://www.stanfordlawreview.org/online/is-the-foreign-intelligence-surveillance-court-really-a-rubber-stamp/; Courtney Minick, "On FISA and Access to the Law," *Justia*, January 10, 2013, https://lawblog.justia.com/2013/01/10/on-fisa-and-access-to-the-law/.

41   Evan Perez, "Secret Court's Oversight Gets Scrutiny," *The Wall Street Journal*, June 9, 2013, https://www.wsj.com/articles/SB10001424127887324904004578535670310514616.

42   "FISA Court Appears to Be Rubber Stamp for Government Requests," NPR, transcript, June 13, 2013, https://www.npr.org/2013/06/13/191226106/

fisa-court-appears-to-be-rubberstamp-for-government-requests; Clarke, "Is the Foreign Intelligence Surveillance Court Really a Rubber Stamp?"
[43] Administrative Office of the United States Courts, "Letter from James C. Duff, Director, to the Honorable Bob Goodlatte, Chairman, Committee on the Judiciary, United States House of Representatives," April 20, 2017, https://www.documentcloud.org/documents/3674719-FISA-Court-Annual-Report-2017.html.

[44] Justice Information Sharing, "The Foreign Intelligence Surveillance Act of 1978," 50 U.S.C. § 1801-11, 1821-29, 1841-46, 1861-62, 1871.

[45] Ibid; Robyn Greene, "How the Government Can Read Your Email," *Politico,* June 22, 2017, https://www.politico.com/agenda/story/2017/06/22/section-702-surveillance-program-national-security-000463.

[46] "NSA Spying: Word Games" Electronic Frontier Foundation, accessed June 14, 2018, https://www.eff.org/nsa-spying/wordgames.

[47] "The Nunes FBI Memo, Annotated."

[48] Ibid.

[49] Matt Apuzzo, Adam Goldman, and Nicholas Fandos, "Code Name Crossfire Hurricane: The Secret Origins of the Trump Investigation," *The New York Times,* May 16, 2018, https://www.nytimes.com/2018/05/16/us/politics/crossfire-hurricane-trump-russia-fbi-mueller-investigation.html; Lee Smith, "How the Code Name 'Crossfire Hurricane' Undermines the FBI's Russia Story," *The Federalist,* May 25, 2018, http://thefederalist.com/2018/05/25/code-name-crossfire-hurricane-evidence-fbis-russia-cover-story/.

[50] Chuck Ross, "Exclusive: A London Meeting Before the Election Aroused George Papadopoulos's Suspicions," *The Daily Caller,* March 26, 2018, http://dailycaller.com/2018/03/25/george-papadopoulos-london-emails; Glenn Greenwald, "The FBI Informant Who Monitored the Trump Campaign, Stefan Halper, Oversaw a CIA Spying Operation in the 1980 Presidential Election," *The Intercept,* May 19, 2018, https://theintercept.com/2018/05/19/the-fbi-informant-who-monitored-the-trump-campaign-stefan-halper-oversaw-a-cia-spying-operation-in-the-1980-presidential-election/; Information accessed via Pacer database, June 20, 2018.

[51] Stef W. Kight, "Go Deeper: Digging into Trump's Latest "Spygate" Tweet," *Axios,* June 6, 2018, https://www.axios.com/trump-tweets-spygate-strzok-page-gateway-pundit-conspiracy-5fa36da4-d07a-454b-8aba-4e30fe5fc651.html; Tom Hamburger, Robert Costa, and Ellen Nakashima, "Cambridge University Perch Gave FBI Source Access to Top Intelligence Figures – and a Cover As He Reached Out to Trump Associates," *The Washington Post,* June 5, 2018, https://www.washingtonpost.com/politics/cambridge-university-perch-gave-fbi-source-access-to-top-intelligence-figures--and-a-cover-as-he-reached-out-to-trump-associates/2018/06/05/c6764dc2-641e-11e8-99d2-0d678ec08c2f_story.html; Tom Hamburger and Rosalind S. Helderman, "Hero or Hired Gun? How a British Former Spy Became a Flash Point in the Russia Investigation," *The Washington*

Post, February 6, 2018, https://www.washingtonpost.com/politics/hero-or-hired-gun-how-a-british-former-spy-became-a-flash-point-in-the-russia-investigation/2018/02/06/94ea5158-0795-11e8-8777-2a059f168dd2_story.html.

52 Flegenheimer, "Fusion GPS Founder Hauled from the Shadows for the Russia Election Investigation" ; Jeff Carlson, "Sir Richard Dearlove & UK Intelligence Ties," *Markets Work*, May 20, 2018, https://themarketswork.com/2018/05/20/sir-richard-dearlove-uk-intelligence-ties/; Luke Harding and Alice Ross, "Sir Andrew Wood, Former UK-Moscow Ambassador, Consulted on Trump Dossier," *The Guardian*, January 13, 2017, https://www.theguardian.com/us-news/2017/jan/13/trump-dossier-uk-ambassador-moscow-john-mccain-andrew-wood.

53 John Solomon and Alison Spann, "Australian Diplomat Whose Tip Prompted FBI's Russia-Probe Has Tie to Clinton," *The Hill*, March 5, 2018, http://thehill.com/376858-australian-diplomat-whose-tip-prompted-fbis-russia-probe-has-tie-to-clintons.

54 "Clinton Best Option for US-UK 'Special Relationship' – Ex-White House Official," Sputnik, March 11, 2016, https://sputniknews.com/politics/201611031047032702-clinton-us-uk-cooperation/.

55 Clarice Feldman, "The Office of Net Assessment Paid Stefan Halper... Why?" *American Thinker*, May 15, 2018, https://www.americanthinker.com/blog/2018/05/the_office_of_national_assessment_paid_stefan_halper__why.html; John Solomon, "London 'Bridges' Falling Down: Curious Origins of FBI's Trump-Russia Probe," *The Hill*, June 1, 2018, http://thehill.com/opinion/white-house/390228-london-bridges-falling-down-curious-origins-of-fbis-trump-russia-probe; Jonathan Turley, "FBI Source in Russia Probe Raises Alarms Over Political Surveillance," *The Hill*, May 22, 2018, http://thehill.com/opinion/judiciary/388785-FBI-source-in-Russia-probe-raises-alarms-over-political-surveillance.

56 Hamburger, Costa, and Nakashima, "Cambridge University Perch Gave FBI Source Access to Top Intelligence Figures – and a Cover As He Reached Out to Trump Associates"; Solomon, "London 'Bridges' Falling Down: Curious Origins of FBI's Trump-Russia Probe"; Stef W. Kight, "Go Deeper: Digging into Trump's Latest "Spygate" Tweet," *Axios*, June 6, 2018, https://www.axios.com/trump-tweets-spygate-strzok-page-gateway-pundit-conspiracy-5fa36da4-d07a-454b-8aba-4e30fe5fc651.html; Hamburger and Helderman, "Hero or Hired Gun? How a British Former Spy Became a Flash Point in the Russia Investigation"; Debra Heine, "Strzok-Page Texts Refer to 'Oconus Lures' (Spies) in December of 2015," PJ Media, June 6, 2018, https://pjmedia.com/trending/strzok-page-texts-refer-to-oconus-lures-spies-in-december-of-2015.

57 "The Nunes FBI Memo, Annotated"; Paul Sperry, "What Really Happened Between the FBI and Carter Page," *Real Clear Politics*, June 10, 2018,

https://www.realclearinvestigations.com/articles/2018/06/07/carter_page_russian_spy__or_fbi_honor_scout.html.

58 United States Senate, "Senate Select Committee to Study Governmental Operations with Respect to Intelligence Activities (The Church Committee)," January 27, 1975, https://www.cop.senate.gov/artandhistory/history/common/investigations/ChurchCommittee.htm.

59 "Ex-Snoop Confirms Echelon Network," CBS News, February 24, 2000, https://www.cbsnews.com/news/ex-snoop-confirms-echelon-network/; Hartung, *Prophets of War,* 221; Campbell, "GCHQ and Me: My Life Unmasking British Eavesdroppers."

60 Ibid; Richard Norton-Taylor, "Menwith Hill Eavesdropping Base Undergoes Massive Expansion," *The Guardian*, March 1, 2012, https://www.theguardian.com/world/2012/mar/01/menwith-hill-eavesdropping-base-expansion; United States Computer Emergency Readiness Team, "Alert (TA18-074A): Russian Government Cyber Activity Targeting Energy and Other Critical Infrastructure Sectors," press release, March 16, 2018, https://www.us-cert.gov/ncas/alerts/TA18-074A; Dan Goodin, "It's Official: US Election Systems Designated As Critical," Ars Technica, January 6, 2017, https://arstechnica.com/tech-policy/2017/01/us-election-systems-officially-designated-as-critical-infrastructure/.

61 David Horsey, "Dianne Feinstein Outraged that CIA Spied on Her Senate Staff," *The Los Angeles Times*, March 13, 2014, http://articles.latimes.com/2014/mar/13/nation/la-na-tt-feinstein-cia-20140313; Conor Friedersdorf, "A Brief History of the CIA's Unpunished Spying on the Senate," *The Atlantic*, December 23, 2014, https://www.theatlantic.com/politics/archive/2014/12/a-brief-history-of-the-cias-unpunished-spying-on-the-senate/384003/.

62 Spencer Ackerman, "CIA Admits to Spying on Senate Staffers," *The Guardian*, July 31, 2014, https://www.theguardian.com/world/2014/jul/31/cia-admits-spying-senate-staffers; Tal Kopan, "Graham 'Glad' NSA Tracking Phones," *Politico*, June 6, 2013, https://www.politico.com/story/2013/06/lindsey-graham-nsa-tracking-phones-092330; Mike Masnick, "Senator Feinstein Finally Finds Surveillance to Get Angry About : When It Happened to Her Staffers," *TechDirt*, March 11, 2014, https://www.techdirt.com/articles/20140311/07212926527/senator-feinstein-finally-finds-surveillance-to-get-angry-about-when-it-happened-to-her-staffers.shtml; Dianne Feinstein, "Continue NSA Call-Records Program," *USA Today*, October 20, 2013, https://www.usatoday.com/story/opinion/2013/10/20/nsa-call-records-program-sen-dianne-feinstein-editorials-debates/3112715/; Tim Mak and Burgess Everett, "Feinstein: NSA 'Protecting America,'" *Politico*, June 6, 2013, https://www.politico.com/story/2013/06/dianne-feinstein-on-nsa-its-called-protecting-america-092340; FISA Amendments Reauthorization Act of 2017, Pub. L.

No. 115-118, 115th Cong. (2018), https://www.govtrack.us/congress/votes/115-2018/s12.

63 John Shiffman and Kristina Cooke, "Exclusive: U.S. Directs Agents to Cover Up Program Used to Investigate Americans," Reuters, August 5, 2013, https://www.reuters.com/article/us-dea-sod/exclusive-u-s-directs-agents-to-cover-up-program-used-to-investigate-americans-idUS-BRE97409R20130805.

64 Ibid.

65 Ibid.

66 Kevin Johnson, "Justice Department ReviewingDEA's Shielding of Sources," USA Today, August 5, 2013,https://www.usatoday.com/story/news/nation/2013/08/05/justice-dea-special-operations-shield/2620439/.

67 U.S. Department of Justice, Office of the Inspector General, "Drug Enforcement Administration," accessed April 4, 2018, https://oig.justice.gov/ongoing/dea.htm; Brad Heath, Twitter post, March 19, 2018, 9:17 a.m., https://twitter.com/bradheath/status/975768288889393158.

68 Andrea Peterson, "Snowden: NSA Employees Share Intercepted Sexts," The Washington Post, July 17, 2014, https://www.washingtonpost.com/news/the-switch/wp/2014/07/17/snowden-nsa-employees-share-intercepted-sexts/.

69 Ibid.

70 Solomon and Spann, "FBI Supervisor Warned Comey in 2014 That Warrantless Surveillance Program Was Ineffective."

71 Ibid. John Solomon, "Watch: Full Interview with Retired Supervisor Bassem Youssef," The Hill, March 16, 2018, http://thehill.com/video/national-security/378877-watch-the-full-interview-with-fbi-informant-bassem-youssef.

72 Charlie Savage, "U.S. Subpoenas Times Reporter Over Book on C.I.A.," The New York Times, https://www.nytimes.com/2010/04/29/us/29justice.html?scp=1&sq=Risen&st=cse; James Risen, "The Biggest Secret," The Intercept, January 3, 2018, https://theintercept.com/2018/01/03/my-life-as-a-new-york-times-reporter-in-the-shadow-of-the-war-on-terror/.

73 Howard Kurtz, "After Reporter's Subpoena, Critics Call Obama's Leak-Plugging Efforts Bush-like," The Washington Post, April 30, 2010, http://www.washingtonpost.com/wp-dyn/content/article/2010/04/29/AR2010042904656.html; Matt Zapotosky, "Former CIA Officer Jeffrey Sterling Convicted in Leak Case," The Washington Post, January 26, 2015, https://www.washingtonpost.com/local/crime/jurors-tell-judge-they-cant-agree-in-cia-leak-trial-of-jeffrey-sterling/2015/01/26/db819f78-a57c-11e4-a7c2-03d37af98440_story.html.

74 "Gov't Obtains Wide AP Phone Records in Probe," Associated Press, May 13, 2013, https://www.ap.org/ap-in-the-news/2013/govt-obtains-wide-ap-phone-records-in-probe.

75 Ibid.

76   FBI affidavit in support of application for search warrant. James Rosen - Fox News - Steven Jin-Woo Kim, No. 10-291-M-01, United States District Court, May 20, 2013, https://www.scribd.com/document/142623236/FBI-Affidavit-Rosen-Fox-News-Stephen-Jin-Woo-Kim; Ann E. Marimow, "A Rare Peek into a Justice Department Leak Probe," *The Washington Post*, May 19, 2013, https://www.washingtonpost.com/local/a-rare-peek-into-a-justice-department-leak-probe/2013/05/19/0bc473de-be5e-11e2-97d4-a479289a31f9_story.html?noredirect=on&utm_term=.df1bcbbaf875.

77   David Martosko, "Justice Department Also Seized the Phone Records of Fox News Reporter's Parents, Documents Reveal, *Daily Mail*, May 22, 2013, http://www.dailymail.co.uk/news/article-2328855/James-Rosen-Justice-Department-seized-phone-records-Fox-News-reporters-parents.html; "'Mr. and Mrs. Rosen!?' Megyn Kelly Says DOJ Probe of Fox News 'Is Lunacy,'" Fox News, video clip, May 22, 2013, http://insider.foxnews.com/2013/05/22/mr-and-mrs-rosen-megyn-kelly-says-doj-probe-fox-news-lunacy.

78   Sharyl Attkisson, "Obama-era Surveillance Timeline," Sharyl Attkisson's website, December 5, 2017, https://sharylattkisson.com/2017/12/05/obama-era-surveillance-timeline/.

79   Sharyl Attkisson, "CBS News Confirms Sharyl Attkiss-on's Computer Hacked," CBS News, August 7, 2013, http://www.cbsnews.com/news/cbs-news-confirms-sharyl-attkissons-computer-hacked/.

80   Phillip Swarts, "Washington Times Settles Case with Homeland over Improper Seizure of Reporter's Notes," *The Washington Times*, September 29, 2014, https://www.washingtontimes.com/news/2014/sep/29/homeland-security-settles-lawsuit-with-washington-/; Rob Bluey, "Government Agrees to Settlement for Raiding Reporter's Home, Seizing Confidential Files," *The Daily Signal*, October 2, 2014, https://www.dailysignal.com/2014/10/02/government-agrees-settlement-raiding-reporters-home-seizing-confidential-files/.

81   Anita Kumar, "Obama Administration Targets Reporters in Crackdown on Leaks," McClatchy DC, May 24, 2013, http://www.mcclatchydc.com/news/politics-government/white-house/article24749407.html.

82   "Re: Following Up," Wikileaks, email sent on May 4, 2009, https://wikileaks.org/podesta-emails/emailid/20133.

83   Josh Gerstein, "Holder Sees 'Resolution' in Risen Case," *Politico*, October 29, 2014, http://www.politico.com/blogs/under-the-radar/2014/10/holder-sees-resolution-in-risen-case-197829.html; Emily Bazelon and Eric Posner, "Secrets and Scoops, Part 2," *Slate*, July 22, 2013, http://www.slate.com/articles/news_and_politics/jurisprudence/2013/07/should_james_risen_have_to_testify_against_jeffrey_sterling_in_the_government.html; "Unfinished Business on Press Freedom," *The New York Times*, October 29, 2014, https://www.nytimes.com/2014/10/30/opinion/attorney-general-eric-holder-and-rules-on-journalists.html.

84   Glenn Greenwald, "Committee to Protect Journalists Issues Scathing Report on Obama Administration," *The Guardian*, October 10, 2013, https://www.theguardian.com/commentisfree/2013/oct/10/cpi-report-press-freedoms-obama.

85   Jon Greenberg, "CNN's Tapper: Obama Has Used Espionage Act More Than All Previous Administrations," *Politifact*, January 10, 2014, http://www.politifact.com/punditfact/statements/2014/jan/10/jake-tapper/cnns-tapper-obama-has-used-espionage-act-more-all-/.

86   Eugene Robinson, "Snowden's NSA Leaks Show We Need a Debate," *The Washington Post*, June 10, 2013, https://www.washingtonpost.com/opinions/eugene-robinson-snowdens-nsa-leaks-show-we-need-a-debate/2013/06/10/002911b6-d203-11e2-8cbe-1bcbee06f8f8_story.html?utm_term=.09645680f30e; James Vincent, "Nude Photos of Strangers Are a 'Fringe Benefit' for NSA Employees, Says Snowden," *The Independent*, July 18, 2014, https://www.independent.co.uk/life-style/gadgets-and-tech/nude-photos-of-strangers-are-a-fringe-benefit-for-nsa-employees-says-snowden-9614097.html.

87   Andrea Peterson, "Snowden: NSA Employees Share Intercepted Sexts," *The Washington Post*, July 17, 2014, https://www.washingtonpost.com/news/the-switch/wp/2014/07/17/snowden-nsa-employees-share-intercepted-sexts/?utm_term=.74cbe3dac6d7; Solomon and Spann, "FBI Supervisor Warned Comey in 2014 That Warrantless Surveillance Program Was Ineffective."

88   U.S. Department of Justice, Federal Bureau of Investigation, "FBI National Press Office," press release, December 18, 1996, https://fas.org/irp/offdocs/pitts_nr.htm.

89   Ibid; Neil A. Lewis, "Ex-F.B.I. Supervisor Pleads Guilty to Espionage," *The New York Times*, March 1, 1997, https://www.nytimes.com/1997/03/01/us/ex-fbi-supervisor-pleads-guilty-to-espionage.html.

90   Rebecca Roberts, "Robert Hanssen: A Brief History," NPR, February 4, 2007, https://www.npr.org/templates/story/story.php?storyId=7152496; USA v. Robert Philip Hanssen, Affidavit in Support of Criminal Complaint, Arrest Warrant and Search Warrants, accessed June 20, 2018, https://fas.org/irp/ops/ci/hanssen_affidavit.html; John Pike, "Measurement and Signature Intelligence (MASINT)," Federation of American Scientists, May 8, 2000, https://fas.org/irp/program/masint.htm; Michael Ellison, "FBI Agent 'Sent Spies to Their Death' for Cash and Diamonds," *The Guardian*, February 20, 2001, https://www.theguardian.com/world/2001/feb/21/michaelellison.

91   Elizabeth Nix, "Robert Hanssen: American Traitor," *History*, May 10, 2017, https://www.history.com/news/robert-hanssen-american-traitor.

92   Office of the Inspector General, "A Review of the FBI's Performance in Deterring, Detecting, and Investigating the Espionage Activities of Robert Philip Hanssen," August 14, 2003, https://oig.justice.gov/special/0308/

index.htm; Mary-Jayne McKay, "To Catch a Spy," CBS News, January 30, 2003, https://www.cbsnews.com/news/to-catch-a-spy-30-01-2003/.

93   "Hung Jury in Trial of FBI Agent," *Chicago Tribune*, November 8, 1985, http://articles.chicagotribune.com/1985-11-08/news/8503170312_1_secret-fbi-documents-gold-and-cash-svetlana-ogorodnikova;   Judith Cummings, "The F.B.I.'s Most Unwanted Spy Case," *The New York Times*, February 10, 1985, https://www.nytimes.com/1985/02/10/magazine/the-fbi-s-most-unwanted-spy-case.html.

94   James Risen, "Gaps in C.I.A.'s Ames Case May Be Filled by F.B.I.'s Own Spy Case," *The New York Times*, February 21, 2001, https://www.nytimes.com/2001/02/21/us/gaps-in-cia-s-ames-case-may-be-filled-by-fbi-s-own-spy-case.html; Joseph Finder, "The Spy Who Sold Out," *The New York Times*, archives, July 2, 1995, https://www.nytimes.com/1995/07/02/books/the-spy-who-sold-out.html.

95   United States Attorney's Office, Eastern District of New York, "Former FBI Agent Sentenced to Six Years of Imprisonment for Racketeering and Securities Fraud," press release, October 2, 2006, https://www.justice.gov/archive/usao/nye/pr/2006/2006Oct02.html.

96   Alison Frankel, "For FBI Leakers, Insider Trading Case Is Chilling Tale of Consequences," Reuters, March 6, 2017, https://www.reuters.com/article/us-otc-leak/for-fbi-leakers-insider-trading-case-is-chilling-tale-of-consequences-idUSKBN16D2Q8; Document 65-1, 1:16-cr-00338-PKC (filed January 4, 2017), http://static.reuters.com/resources/media/editorial/20170306/usvwalters--govtletteronleaks.pdf; "Investment Chat Board Lawsuits," *Silicon Investor*, December 15, 2004, http://www.silicon-investor.com/readmsgs.aspx?subjectid=28509&msgnum=6884&batch-size=10&batchtype=Next; Hamburg v. Clinton, 1:98-cv-01459-TPJ (filed June 11, 1998).

97   Frankel, "For FBI Leakers, Insider Trading Case Is Chilling Tale of Consequences."

98   The Foreign Intelligence Surveillance Act of 1978, 50 U.S.C. §§ 1801-11, 1821-29, 1841-46, 1861-62, 1871.

99   Cory Bennett, "How the Government May Have Spied on Trump's Team," *Politico,* March 23, 2017, https://www.politico.com/story/2017/03/trump-team-surveillance-obama-236410.

100   Tim Shorrock, "Obama's Crackdown on Whistle-blowers," *The Nation*, March 26, 2013, https://www.thenation.com/article/obamas-crack-down-whistleblowers/; Michael B. Kelley, "Latest Glenn Greenwald Scoop Vindicates One of the Original NSA Whistleblowers," *Business Insider*, June 27, 2013, http://www.businessinsider.com/nsa-whis-tleblower-william-binney-was-right-2013-6; "Mindblowing Corruption at FBI – NSA Whistleblower Reveals," YouTube video, posted by "The Jimmy Dore Show," February 20, 2018, https://www.youtube.com/watch?v=bGYSuULFzt0.

101   Glenn Greenwald, "Rand Paul Is Right: NSA Routinely Monitors Americans' Communications Without Warrants," Intercept, March 13, 2017, https://theintercept.com/2017/03/13/rand-paul-is-right-nsa-rou-tinely-monitors-americans-communications-without-warrants/; Sara Carter, "Who's Spying on Who?" Sarah A. Carter's website, December 14, 2017, https://web.archive.org/web/20180106175433/https://saraacarter.com/2017/12/14/whos-spying-on-who-fbis-use-of-nsa-surveillance-pro-gram-needs-to-be-investigated-say-whistleblowers/; Spencer Ackerman, "NSA Warned to Rein in Surveillance As Agency Reveals Even Greater Scope," *The Guardian*, July 17, 2013, https://www.theguardian.com/world/2013/jul/17/nsa-surveillance-house-hearing.

102   Shorrock, "Obama's Crackdown on Whistleblowers."

103   Michael B. Kelley, "Former Stasi Officer: The NSA Domestic Surveillance Program Would Have Been 'A Dream Come True' for East Germany," *Business Insider*, June 28, 2013, http://www.businessinsider.com/sta-si-talks-about-nsa-surveillance-state-2013-6; Michael Sontheimer and Andy Müller-Maguhn, "Interview with Ex-Stasi Agent: 'The Scope of NSA Surveillance Surprised Me,'" *Spiegel Online*, June 18, 2014, http://www.spiegel.de/international/germany/interview-with-former-stasi-agent-about-the-nsa-a-975010.html.

Conclusion

1   United States Senate Committee on the Judiciary, "Letter from Lindsey O. Graham, Chairman of the Subcommittee on Crime and Terrorism, to the Honorable Dianne Feinstein, Ranking Member, Committee on the Judiciary," February 8, 2018, https://www.judiciary.senate.gov/imo/media/doc/2018-02-08%20CEG%20LG%20to%20Rice%20(Russia%20Investigation%20Email).pdf.

2   Ibid.

3   Ibid.

4   Singman, "Grassley Says Comey Leaked Classified Information to Professor Pal, Demands Answers."

5   Aaron Blake, "Why Trump Should be Very Afraid of James Comey's Memos," *The Washington Post*, May 17, 2017, https://www.washingtonpost.com/news/the-fix/wp/2017/05/16/president-trump-should-be-very-afraid-of-james-comeys-memos/?utm_term=.f153e1da6492.

6   Brooke Singman, "Reps. Green and Sherman Announce Plan to File Articles of Impeachment," Fox News, June 7, 2017, http://www.foxnews.com/politics/2017/06/07/reps-green-and-sherman-announce-plan-to-file-articles-impeachment.html.

7   U.S. Department of Justice, Office of the Inspector General, "A Review of Various Actions by the Federal Bureau of Investigation and Department of

Justice in Advance of the 2016 Election," June 2018, https://www.justice.gov/file/1071991/download.

8   Matt Zapotosky, Karoun Demirjian, and Devlin Barrett, "Justice Department Watchdog Says Probes Ongoing into Disclosure of Comey Memos, FBI Leaks," *Chicago Tribune*, June 18, 2018, http://www.chicagotribune.com/news/nationworld/ct-michael-horowitz-christopher-wray-congress-20180618-story.html; Justin Caruso, "Comey Under Investigation for Handling of Classified Information," *The Daily Caller*, June 18, 2018, http://dailycaller.com/2018/06/18/comey-under-investigation/; Kenneth P. Bergquist, "Eight Laws Hillary Clinton Could Be Indicted for Breaking," *The Daily Caller*, September 21, 2015, http://dailycaller.com/2015/09/21/eight-laws-hillary-clinton-could-be-indicted-for-breaking/.

9   James Comey, *A Higher Loyalty: Truth, Lies, and Leadership* (London: Macmillan, 2018).

10   Ibid, 204.

11   Sam Stein, "Chuck Schumer Says He's Lost Confidence in James Comey," *HuffPost*, March 11, 2016, https://www.huffingtonpost.com/entry/chuck-schumer-james-comey_us_581a6527e4b0c43e6c1de4a2.

12   Jim Geraghty, "James Comey's Inadvertent Admission," *National Review*, April 13, 2018, https://www.nationalreview.com/the-morning-jolt/james-comeys-inadvertent-admission/.

13   Tom McCarthy and Martin Pengelly, "Comey Book Likens Trump to a Mafia Boss 'Untethered to Truth,'" *The Guardian*, April 13, 2018, http://www.theguardian.com/us-news/2018/apr/12/james-comey-book-trump-unethical-untethered-to-truth-a-higher-loyalty.

14   Aaron Blake, "The Curiously Republican Leaders of the Supposed 'Deep State' Conspiracy Against Trump," *The Washington Post*, January 29, 2018, https://www.washingtonpost.com/news/the-fix/wp/2018/01/29/the-men-allegedly-leading-the-deep-state-conspiracy-against-trump-are-surprisingly-republican/.

15   Tom Fitton, Twitter post, February 12, 2018, 1:01 P.M., https://twitter.com/tomfitton/status/963156231480373250?lang=en.

16   "Delayed, Denied, Dismissed: Failures on the FOIA Front," *ProPublica*, July 21, 2016, https://www.propublica.org/article/delayed-denied-dismissed-failures-on-the-foia-front.

17   Ibid.

18   Jack Moore, "Here's Paul Manafort's Perp Walk into the FBI," *GQ*, October 30, 2017, https://www.gq.com/story/paul-manafort-perp-walk; Ainsley, Lehren, and Schecter, "The Mueller Effect: FARA Filings Soar in Shadow of Manafort, Flynn Probes."

ABOUT THE AUTHOR

Seamus Bruner is the Associate Director of Research at the Government Accountability Institute (GAI). Seamus has worked with GAI since 2013 providing research and support for numerous *New York Times* bestsellers and *60 Minutes* exposés.

Visit SeamusBruner.com to learn more, provide whistleblower tips, and access primary source documents.

Made in the USA
Lexington, KY
06 March 2019